SELECTED PROSE

SELECTED PROSE

Louis Simpson

PARAGON HOUSE • New York

First edition, 1989

Published in the United States by

Paragon House
90 Fifth Avenue
New York, NY 10011

Copyright © 1989 by Paragon House

Library of Congress Cataloging-in-Publication Data

Simpson, Louis Aston Marantz, 1923–
   [Prose works. Selections]
   Selected prose / by Louis Simpson.
     p.   cm.
   ISBN 1-55778-048-X
   1. Simpson, Louis Aston Marantz, 1923–
—Authorship. 2. Poetry.
   I. Title.
   PS3537.I75A6   1989
818'.5408—dc19   88-28598
                                          CIP

Manufactured in the United States of America

This book is for my father,
Aston Hedley Laselve Simpson

Contents

Foreword   ix

1. THE OTHER JAMAICANS   1

    Prologue   *3*
    The Other Jamaicans   *5*

2. ON LINE   63

    Letters 1943–45   *69*
    On Line   *117*
    Jimmy   *149*

3. VIEWS FROM A WINDOW   153

    Dogface Poetics   *157*
    "Baudelaire, three injections!"   *159*
    Furnished Rooms   *164*
    Literary Life   *184*
    Grigoryev and I   *192*

4. LIVES AND WORKS   199

   W. B. Yeats   *201*
   The Santa Claus of Loneliness   *205*
   Apollinaire! The Perfect Romantic   *211*
   Cloud's Processional   *227*
   The Author of Prufrock   *235*
   Words and Their Intervals   *250*
   The Split Lives of W. H. Auden   *271*
   The Color of Saying   *276*
   Honoring Whitman   *321*
   Disorder and Escape in the Fiction of V. S. Naipaul   *326*

5. ON THE ART OF POETRY   333

   Walt Whitman at Bear Mountain   *335*
   The Terms of Life Itself: Writing "Quiet Desperation"   *339*
   "Chocolates"   *347*
   Rhythm   *352*
   To Make Words Disappear   *354*
   Rolling Up   *356*
   Images   *362*
   English Poetry 1900–1950: An Assessment   *366*

6. MOTIONS OF THE WINDS   371

   The Poet's Theme   *373*
   "The Man Freed from the Order of Time": Poetic Theory in
      Wordsworth and Proust   *420*

7. ENTRIES   437

   1962–1980   *439*
   Late Entries   *492*
   Afterword   *514*

Foreword

I have selected passages from my writing—autobiography, fiction, literary criticism, poems, letters, and a journal—to make this book about life and literature.

It begins as a narrative of my early life in Jamaica, my experiences as a soldier in the Second World War and as a young man engaged in writing. The narrative is followed by studies of the lives and works of poets. There are essays on the art of poetry, and the book concludes with extracts from a literary journal.

My background is described in "The Other Jamaicans," but I shall set the facts down plainly here. I was born in Jamaica when the island was a British colony. My father was a lawyer, an active professional man with a wide circle of friends and acquaintances. My mother's background could not have been more different. She grew up in a village in southern Russia and as a young girl emigrated with her family to New York.

She worked in the garment district, then became an actress in silent movies. In 1915 she travelled to Jamaica with a troupe of bathing beauties to make a movie. There she met my father. She had a falling out with the director—he wanted his beauties to pose in the nude as statues—and sailed back to New York. My father went there to court her. They were married and he brought her to Jamaica. They set up house at Cross Roads in the suburbs of Kingston.

The class to which my father belonged looked to England as the Mother Country. My brother Herbert and I were sent to a boarding school modeled on English public—that is, private—schools. We were taught to think and behave like Englishmen. We were in the minority—most Jamaicans knew a very different way of life, that of their African ancestors.

Our family was not typical of its class. Though our mother played golf and every afternoon tea was served on the veranda, the stories she told were of Russia: the cold, the rats, the cossacks. And she missed her family in New York. Sometimes she would go to visit them and be absent for weeks.

There was a divorce and she went to live in Toronto. My brother and I continued to live with our father and, when he married again, a stepmother. From time to time our mother came to the island to see us.

The section opens with two letters—the first written when I was a small boy at Munro College. This was a hundred miles west of Kingston, on a mountain overlooking the sea. I would be at Munro, with time out for vacations, until I was seventeen.

1

THE OTHER JAMAICANS

Prologue

To Rosalind Marantz[1]

Munro Collage

Dear Mommie,

How are you? I like school very much, and I have made friends with a boy named Mac.pherson. I am second in my class, but I hope to go up in to a higher form soon. Thier has been a lot of rain lately, but I hope that we will not have any more as badly as before. Two football matches have been played up here lately, the first match was going on well for us but at the last half they came down on us with fresh men and beat us up badly, the score was three nill. The second match we were much quicker than the other men and as they were out of practise we beat them five to four. We realy owed a lot to our goaly who was very good, his name is Depens. I hope to recieve my watch soon, as you said in your letter that you had sent it on some time ago. I miss Buster, but I hope to find him well when I go back. Daddy writes a lot to me. I still have your pictures. I would like a fountain pen as mine is bad. I am sorry to hear you are not well but I hope you will be

---

[1] My mother. In 1930, following the breakup of her marriage, she left Jamaica and went to live in Toronto. She sold cosmetics, her business taking her to the U.S., then to Central and South America.

The letter is undated. It would appear to have been written in my first term at Munro, the Christmas term of 1932.

better soon. I put away my little train before I left home so I hope to find it allright when I go back. The holidays are very long in coming but I am not anxious to go home.

With Love
from Louis.

To Rosalind Marantz

Munro College,
Malvern,
18/5/39.

Dear Moms,

Daddy died on the way to Panama yesterday (Wednesday).

They are bringing back his body to Kingston for the funeral. I am going down to the funeral tomorrow with Mr Fraser, who has been kind enough to offer me a seat in his car.

Of course I don't know what plans will be made for Herbert and myself now. Whatever happens, I know that I will finish my course at school and then go to England to study for the bar. Daddy told me that he had made provision for me against any such occurence.

Herbert is another affair entirely. It would be best for him to stay in Kingston and study law until he can take it up as a profession. He, and Douglas Fletcher (whose admirable qualities you know), will be partners in business, taking over Daddy's office. Whatever happens Herbert must become independent: he has all the facilities for doing so. The rest will follow.

As my course of study for the bar only requires 3 years, I will be independent when I am about 21.

Please remember, Mother—we must stand first on our own feet, before we can do anything else. I am referring especially to Herbert. If he works hard, he will have an excellent opening in the business that Daddy left behind. Douglas Fletcher has been in charge of the business during Daddy's illness, and he has done excellently.

Thanks a lot for the pocket-money you sent me . . . I received, at different times:—

$1.00 (cash)
10/—from Kingston (sent by Miss Brandon)
$5.00 (postal order)

Yrs with love
Louis

The Other Jamaicans

I

I watched Jabez cooking his midday meal. He placed a pan over some stones and piled twigs and sticks underneath. He was making dumplings.

Jabez was the garden boy. His people came from Africa. My father said that they didn't like people to watch them eating. When my father came by, Jabez would cover his mouth with his hand. But he didn't mind if it was my brother or myself, and when he finished eating he would tell me a story.

One day Annancy and Brother Tiger went to the river to bathe.

"Annancy said to Tiger, 'Bro'er Tiger, so you are a big man, if you go in a river with your fat you a go drownded, so you fe take out your fat so lef' it here.' "

So Tiger left his fat on the river bank and went into the water. While he was bathing Annancy ate up Tiger's fat. After eating it he was afraid of Tiger and ran away.

Reprinted from Louis Simpson, *North of Jamaica*. New York: Harper and Row, 1972.

He went to Little Monkey Town and he taught the monkeys to sing, "Yesterday this time me a nyam Tiger fat"—meaning, "Yesterday this time I ate Tiger's fat." The monkeys loved the song so much that they sang it over and over. Then they gave a ball, and there everyone was singing the song.

When Annancy got back to the river he found Tiger looking for his fat. Tiger said, "Bro'er Annancy, I can't find me fat at all." Then Annancy told him about the song the monkeys were singing. So Tiger and Annancy went to the ball. They hid in the bush and heard the monkeys singing, "Yesterday this time me a nyam Tiger fat."

Then Tiger asked the monkeys for his fat. They said they didn't know anything about it—"Tis Mister Annancy larn us the song." Then Tiger wanted to fight the monkeys, but they sent to Big Monkey Town for some soldiers, and the soldiers came and flogged Brother Tiger and Annancy.

"So Bro'er Tiger have fe take bush an' Annancy run up a house-top."

From that time Tiger lives in the wood and Annancy in the house-top.

My father's people came from Scotland long ago. Aunt Annie sang:

> Maxwelton Braes are bonny
> Where early fa's the dew,
> And 'twas there that Annie Laurie
> Gie me her answer true.

She was an old lady in a black dress and high-buttoned shoes. She came driving up to the gate in a black buggy. Once she took a mango out of her handbag. The mango was soft and squashy. She told me to give it to the horse. I held out the mango and the horse turned his head quickly and snapped it out of my hand with his long yellow teeth. When he was eating the mango, yellow foam came down from his jaws.

My father's name was Aston Simpson and he was a lawyer. Every morning he went down town to the office.

One morning he said we were going to start doing exercises. It would help us to keep fit and grow strong. My father, my mother, my brother Herbert and I stood in front of the Victrola in our pajamas. My father put a record on the Victrola, "The Stars and Stripes Forever—march—Sousa." Above the band a man's voice shouted in time to the music, "Feet apart! Hands on hips, place! Now, bend forward—up! To the left—up! To the right—up!"

Then we got dressed and had breakfast. Father was dressed in a white suit. When he went to work he wore a Panama hat and carried a leather bag. He drove a red Essex. I could hear the engine starting, then going down the driveway. It turned into the lane and then I could no longer hear it.

After breakfast my mother sat at the piano, practising. She made a humming sound in her throat and sang, "Do-re-me-fa-so-la-di!" She sang songs from *Samson* and *Lucia di Lammermoor.* Her voice was loud, and there was something about it that frightened me. When she sang she had a faraway look on her face. I pressed my hands to my ears.

Once she saw me doing this, and asked if I didn't like her singing. I didn't know what to say. She went away with a hurt look on her face.

But I liked the Victrola. She would put on a record and I would wind it up. The handle was hard to turn. "Gems from Pagliacci"—it began with bells and voices. "Floradora." I could hardly make out the words; they came with a faint scratching from a great distance, across the sea.

I looked at the pictures in the *Victor Book of the Opera.* There were photographs of fat men and women with odd names—Galli-Curci, Melba, Scotti, Schumann–Heinck, Caruso. They wore jewelry and tights. They brandished swords, rode in boats pulled by swans, leaned out from balconies. One man was lying flat on his back, with lighted candles at his head and feet. On another page I came upon the same scene, but with a different man lying on his back. How could this be? Wasn't the story true?

In the twilight, when fireflies were glimmering, my father came home from the office. I could hear his car turning on the gravel into the driveway. Sometimes when he came up the stairs on to the veranda he would be carrying a rolled-up newspaper. This was the

Daily Mirror, all the way from England. There were funnycuts in it, about a dog named Pip, a penguin named Squeak, and a rabbit named Wilfred. There were also a Russian dog named Popsky and his master, Witoffsky. Popsky and Witoffsky made bombs. When the policeman came in his helmet they ran away.

Once when my father came home he was carrying a round leather case. He opened it and took out a tube of brass. He said it was a telescope. He pulled at one end of the tube and it got longer. There was a circle of glass at each end. He placed the telescope on a stand on the veranda, and when it got dark we took turns looking through the eyepiece.

I looked at the moon; it was bright as a shilling. There were shadows on the face of the moon. A sea breeze rustled the vines that grew on the veranda, and a lizard hopped on to the railing. It cocked its head sideways, looking at us, and puffed out the wattle under its throat in a threatening manner. There were millions of glittering stars. He said that if I looked I would see the constellations.

At bedtime Mother would read us stories. She read a story called "The Happy Prince." Or else she would tell stories about Russia when she was a child. Russia was covered with snow and the wind was freezing cold. Wolves howled in the distance. People rode in sleighs with jingling bells. In Russia there were cossacks. . . .

"What are cossacks?"

"People who ride horses. There were also gypsies and moujiks."

"What's a moujik."

"A Russian. One of the people."

It was so cold in Russia that people froze to death and were found the next day with ice on their faces. Once on her way to school she was almost frozen. Her hands and feet were numb, and she was shivering all day.

Also, in Russia there was a terrible sickness called typhus. She was sick with typhus and almost died. But for a woman who lived next door and took care of her, she would have died. Her older sister Lisa was sick too, and her mother was taking care of Lisa. So nobody paid her any attention, except the woman who lived next door. When she was well again they brought her a mirror, and when she looked into it she hardly knew herself. They had cut off her hair. And they had burned all her clothes, and burned her doll—she had never had a real doll of her own, only a stick which she dressed in rags, and they had burned it. Then they told her that her sister Lisa had died.

They sent her away to Odessa on the Black Sea, for her health, to stay with relatives. Odessa was a big town—not like Lutsk, where her family lived. On the last day in Odessa she wanted to buy a present to take back to the family. She had saved all her money. She saw a basket of plums in a window.

"What are plums?"

"Fruit."

"Like bananas?"

She laughed. "Oh no. Much better than bananas. Small and round, with red inside. Sweet and delicious."

She bought the plums. No one in Lutsk had ever been able to buy them. They would be pleased.

But the train took days to go from Odessa to Lutsk. The weather was warm and the plums started to spoil. She didn't know what to do. What would you have done?

I'd heard the story before, so I said, "Eat them."

"Yes, I ate them, so they wouldn't be wasted. When one of the plums got soft, I ate it. So I ate them one by one, and soon the basket was half empty. And every time I ate one of the plums I would cry, because I didn't want to eat them, you know, I wanted to give them to my mother and my sisters. The people on the train were astonished—a child who would eat a plum and cry!"

When she got off the train at Lutsk the basket was empty.

When she had kissed me good night and tucked me in, I lay awake, with the moon shining through the window. The same moon shone in Russia, on the plains covered with snow and the people dressed in furs, riding in sleighs, with jingling bells. In the distance a wolf was howling. It was the same moon shining here. The moon came all the way from Russia, to shine here in the tropics, on the sea and the mountains.

II

Mummy would be proud of me when she came back. Did I know where Mummy was? Yes, that was right, in America.

America was a place with tall buildings called skyscrapers. Did I know what Americans did that was important to us?

Yes, they made movies. But also they ate sugar and bananas. Jamaica sent lots of bananas in ships to New York and the people who lived there bought them and ate them. And with the money they paid for bananas and oranges and grapefruit we were able to buy the things we needed—such as motorcars and iceboxes. For everything had a purpose.

The cat came into the room, with a lizard in its mouth. It was a green tree lizard; its mouth was gaping.

"Shoo!" Miss Haughton shouted. She stamped her foot and the cat ran across the room, purposefully, carrying the lizard. It went out the door.

Once Mummy saw a cat with a mouse and she screamed. There were bubbles at the corners of her mouth. And once when I was talking to her, facing her, I saw a mouse run along the wall. She saw where I was looking, and she didn't turn her head, but she became still and said, "What is it? What is it?" Then the mouse vanished, and I was too frightened to tell her. So I said nothing.

In Lutsk when she was a child there were swarms of rats. They carried the typhus that made people die. And they crawled over the faces of people in the night. Rats lived in the attics of houses.

What's an attic?

The dark part of the house between the ceiling and the roof. The rats lived there, and if a child went in they would swarm over him, biting off his fingers. They would eat him all up.

I was frightened of the rats. She talked about them often, how they would bite children and eat them.

It was to get away from the rats that she and her family went to America. They lived in New York, and she went to work. She was only a young girl, but she had to work hard, in a loft with a lot of other young girls.

What's a loft? Like an attic?

No, she laughed. It seemed to please her that I remembered about the attic and the rats. In the loft the girls sat working at sewing-machines, making dresses and pieces of clothing. It was hot and crowded. Her arms ached from guiding the pieces of cloth into the machine, and at the end of the day she was glad to get home, walking through the streets of New York. In the winter going home it was dark, and snowflakes came whirling down between the lights, the lights of New York City.

She lived with her mother and two sisters, Ruth and Annette, and a brother named Joe, and two nieces named Molly and Dorothy whom her mother also took care of. Molly's and Dorothy's mother had been Lisa.

The one who died in the typhus epidemic?

That's right. And her mother, my grandmother, was taking care of them all. But Mummy had to work in the loft, with the sewing-machines, all day long.

And then one day a man came.

Oh yes, tell about it!

A man came into the loft, and the foreman—the man who walked up and down the rows of machines, watching so that the girls didn't stop working—told them that the strange man was going to speak to them, and to stop the machines. Then the strange man said that he was from a motion picture company, and they were looking for girls to try out for parts. So the next day she went to the address that he gave.

What did it look like?

It was a swimming pool, that was where they were making the screen tests. The test was to jump into the pool and pretend to be drowning. And I went up to the side of the pool and looked down. I couldn't swim at all.

Then I jumped.

I was really drowning, but they thought I was a wonderful actress. And so I was hired and became one of the motion picture company, one of Annette Kellerman's Bathing Beauties. Then one day the company traveled to Jamaica to make a movie, and I met your father. And so we were married.

And lived happily ever after.

On Saturdays Nanny took me to the movie matinee at Cross Roads. This was at the Movie Theatre, which was indoors. I saw Rin-Tin-Tin, and Laurel and Hardy, and Louise Fazenda. On Saturday nights my father would take us to the Gaiety Theatre. It was open and you could see the sky. But we stopped going there because the English soldiers and the black people got into fights. The soldiers fought with their belt buckles.

The Palace was the best of all. It was an open-air theatre like the

Gaiety. We sat upstairs in the balcony. First there were advertisements for Issa's Store, and Delaware Punch, and Four Aces. There would be a cartoon, Felix the Cat, or Mickey Mouse. And then—

Rio Rita
The Cat and the Canary
Evergreen—with Jessie Matthews

It's the loveliest theeng
To be evergreen,
It's the loveliest theeng, I know . . .

"But you're not doing your letters!" said Miss Haughton. "You've only copied three letters in all this time."

The letters of the alphabet marched down the left side of the page. I was supposed to dip the point of the pen in the ink and copy each letter ten times, all the way across the page.

"Don't you want to learn, so that you'll know how to write when Mummy comes back?"

"If your Mother loved you," said Aunt Ethel, "she'd be here with her children. Not in New York City."

My bottom lip trembled. A weight seemed to be dragging down the corners, and my eyes were filling with tears. I turned my head aside. I wasn't going to let her see me cry. But it didn't help . . .

"What are you crying about?" said Aunt Ethel. She enjoyed these heart-to-heart talks.

Aunt Ethel was my father's sister, and had come to stay and take care of us while Mummy was away in America. She wore glasses and smelled of eau-de-cologne. On Sundays she took us to church.

Onward Christian so-o-o-old-iers
Marching as to-o war,
With the cross of Je-sus,
Go-ing on before!

Aunt Ethel saw that I washed behind my ears. "Let's look at the potato patch," she'd say. She saw to it that my nails were clean and that there were no spots on the suit I put on in the afternoon when we had tea.

My brother Herbert said that Aunt Ethel was an "old maid."

"What's that?"

"Nobody ever wanted to marry her."

Herbert played a trick on Aunt Ethel. He put a dead frog in her bed, and that night when father came home he called for me. I went into the study. My father was sitting down and Herbert was standing in front of him.

My father said to me, "Did you put a frog in your aunt's bed?"

I was so frightened I hardly knew how to answer. But I shook my head. No.

"Liar!" my father shouted at Herbert. Then, to the air over his head, "The boy is not only mischievous, he's also a liar."

To Herbert, "Well, I'll see to it that you don't play any more dirty tricks. And tell the truth."

He left the study and shouted for the servants. They came in, the maid, then the cook, wiping her hands on her apron. Their eyes were wide and they looked frightened. Aunt Ethel didn't come—she was in her bedroom, crying because she had been insulted.

When my father came back into the room he was carrying the leather strap on which he sharpened his razor.

"Take down your trousers," he said to Herbert.

Herbert took down his trousers. I could see his bottom. Then my father seized him and in a moment he was sitting down, with Herbert lying face down across his lap. He lifted the strap and brought it down. There was a crack, and a red welt across Herbert's bottom. He shouted "No!" and kicked out his legs.

My father brought down the strap again and again. Herbert yelled and wept.

Cook said, "Lawks, Massa Aston, that sufficient!" But my father continued to flog Herbert.

At last he let him go. Herbert ran out of the room.

"Let that be a lesson to you too," my father said. "Not to tell lies."

When I went into the nursery Herbert was hiding under the bed. He came out and grabbed me by the arm. He was eleven years old, five years older than I, and much stronger.

He bent my arm behind my back. I uttered a cry.

"What's this?" said my father. He appeared in the doorway. "Are you bullying your brother? Do you want me to give you another flogging?"

He went away. Herbert glared at me. Then he put his hands to his cheeks and pulled them down. The flesh was drawn away from the bones and I could see the outlines of a skull. The Phantom of the Opera.

III

"Why don't you say anything," Mother said, "aren't you glad to see me?" She smelled of perfume. She hugged us to her and tears ran down her face. She was laughing and crying at the same time.

She let us watch while she unpacked her trunks. She had beautiful dresses and jewelry. Then she took out a box wrapped in paper. And another. They were presents for us. Mine was a train that you wound up and it ran on a track.

And books. *Black Beauty. Penrod and Sam. Tarzan and the Jewels of Opar.*

That night at the dinner table everyone was talking, and my father didn't seem to mind. Aunt Ethel smiled and made a remark now and then too, but I could tell she wasn't really pleased. Now she would have to go away. She wouldn't be keeping an eye on us and she wouldn't be taking us to church on Sunday.

"Good riddance," Herbert said.

The house had been getting quieter and quieter, especially in the evening when my father was home. But now it was noisy again. Mother played the piano and sang:

> Pale hands I loved
> Beside the Shalimar . . .

"We ought to give a party," she said.

My father said, "For what reason? I can't just ask people to come to a party."

"Why not? I'll tell them it's my birthday."

He laughed. He didn't seem to mind if she told a lie.

Everyone talked about the party for days. It was to be a "lawn tennis party." The garden boy was put to work, rolling the tennis court and clipping hedges. The maid polished the silver, and some new records for the gramophone came from a store on King Street. Mother wouldn't let us play them, we could only look at the names. "Valencia," "Nola." We couldn't play them because they were for dancing, and we might scratch or break them.

"There ought to be something for the children too," Mother said. "They could have a fancy-dress party. And play games, like Pin the Tail on the Donkey."

Herbert and I were to be pirates. We would have red bandanas around our heads and scarfs round our waists, and we would each have a sword. Mother painted a moustache on my face, with pointed ends. Like Henry Morgan the Buccaneer. Yo ho ho and a bottle of rum.

"Well, that does it," my father said. "The Manleys aren't coming."

"Why? What does he say?"

"That Mrs. Manley isn't feeling well. But that's not true. The fact is, he knows he isn't welcome in this house."

Mother said, "They came to dinner."

"Yes, with other colored people—to use your very own words. And Norman Manley is the most brilliant barrister on the island. A Rhodes Scholar."

Mother was silent.

"I'm colored myself," he said, "or haven't you heard about it?"

Still she didn't say anything.

He said, "I can't arrange my life according to your likes and dislikes. The people I work with are a damn sight better than the people from the Liguanea Club you think are so wonderful. I have to work with Norman Manley. Moreover, his wife is a white woman. She's English. That ought to please you." His voice took on the sarcasm my brother and I knew so well, and he imitated our mother's way of speaking: "I love the way the English pronounce their words."

That night in the bedroom Herbert and I discussed this conversation.

"You're colored," Herbert said.

"I'm not." I didn't know what "colored" meant, but I didn't like the way he said it. I held up my hand in the moonlight. It looked yellow.

"You are," said Herbert.

"Well, then," I said, with a feeling of triumph I hardly ever had in these arguments, "you're colored too."

Herbert jumped out of bed. I heard him coming, and pushed as hard as I could against the wall. But he hit me on the arm.

"That'll teach you to be rude and impertinent."

On the day of the party the lane was filled with cars. All kinds of people came—my mother's friends from the Liguanea Club and my father's friends, solicitors, barristers, and clerks. The men wore blazers and white flannels, and the women wore white skirts. They were carrying tennis rackets. On the lawn they leaped about, striking at the balls, and the garden boy, who served for every purpose and had been dressed in white for the occasion, ran up and down in the hedge looking for lost balls.

Behind the baseline, card tables had been set up with glass pitchers of ice and lemonade and decanters of whisky that glowed amber in the sunlight. There were open tins of Players cigarettes; on the label there was a picture of a bearded sailor and a "dreadnought." The people who were not playing sat in deck chairs and now and then one of them would call out, "Well played!" My father leaped about with the rest. He came off the court wiping sweat from his brow.

"Jolly well played, Aston," said one of the young men. He was a clerk in my father's office. He was fat and brown, and spoke with a Jamaican accent. I had seen him when I was taken to the office, coming in to stand in front of my father's desk, holding a paper in his hand. "Well, give it here," said my father, irritably. "You'd damn well better have it right this time." But now he was calling my father "Aston," and my father smiled and didn't seem to mind.

The children were having their fancy-dress party. We played Pin the Tail on the Donkey. It was my turn and I was blindfolded. I went toward the tree where the donkey had been pinned, but I couldn't find it.

"Never mind," Mother said. "You can have a prize too."

This gave me a funny feeling. I had tried very hard to stick on the tail, and if I was going to get a prize anyway, it seemed that my trying so hard didn't count.

Then there were prizes for costumes. Mother gave the first prize to Herbert and myself for our pirate costumes. The other children looked sulky. Then she gave them prizes too. So all the children were happy.

When it grew dark and the swallows dipping over the court began to be mistaken for tennis balls, everyone went inside. Mother put a record on the Victrola, and the young people danced.

> Valencia,
> In my dreams it always seems
> I hear you calling me . . .

The fat brown clerk from my father's office stood at the side of the drawing room smiling at everyone. I was standing beside him, watching the dancers.

"Oh, jolly well danced," he said loudly. My father came by. "This isn't the tennis court, Henriques," he said. The clerk was silent and I felt sorry for him.

Then everyone went home. I stood in the lane watching them driving away. The English people from the Liguanea Club got into their Baby Austins and waved goodbye. The clerk had a motorcycle, which he started with a roar. Then they were all gone.

The next day the lawn was littered with cigarette butts, tinfoil and empty packets. There were glasses under the hedge. The garden boy was cleaning the lawn. He picked up all the cigarette butts and put them in a can. He smoked them for weeks, taking a butt out of the can after he had eaten lunch.

"Players are best," he said, with the air of a connoisseur. "But Four Aces are also very good."

From time to time as he went about his duties in the yard he would stop and make striking motions with an imaginary tennis racket. Then he'd say, "Jolly well played." And sometimes, "Oh, hard luck!"

Then he'd shake his head, and go back to pushing the lawn mower.

IV

Arithmetic: Eight times eight are sixty-four.

History: Jamaica was first inhabited by Arawak Indians. The

name Jamaica comes from an Arawak word meaning "isle of wood and water."

The island was discovered by Columbus (1494) and colonized by the Spaniards, who introduced slavery. In 1655 Jamaica was captured by the British. Today, with its crops of sugarcane, citrus fruits, and bananas, the island is one of the brightest jewels in the crown of Empire.

Eight times nine are seventy-two.

After lunch we played in the school yard. There was a tamarind tree. Pods fell from the boughs and lay scattered on the ground. If you opened them there were seeds inside covered with sticky brown stuff—sweet, but it set your teeth on edge.

After school the chauffeur came to pick me up and take me home. But one day, instead of the chauffeur, it was Aunt Ethel.

She said, "You're to stay with Uncle Percy and Aunt Agnes."

"Can't I go home?"

"Not tonight. Maybe tomorrow."

We traveled in a tram car to the South Camp Road. When we got there Aunt Agnes showed me to a room where my cousin Nigel slept. She said I would share the bed with Nigel.

"But I want to go home."

"You have to stay with us for a while. Your Mummy and Daddy are very busy and they said you are to stay with us."

There were Aunt Agnes and Aunt Ethel, and cousins Gwen and Dora. They sat on the veranda fanning themselves.

"Where is the boy?" said Aunt Ethel.

"I left him in the bedroom to rest," said Aunt Agnes.

But I wasn't in the bedroom, I was on the other side of the door.

"I knew no good would come of that marriage."

"What is to become of the children?"

Later my cousin Nigel came home—he whose bed I was to share. Nigel was older than my brother Herbert. He went to Jamaica College, where he was good at games. He was also a brilliant student. "Come on," he said, "I'll teach you how to play marbles." He had a can full of glass marbles, shining, with whorls of color. Some of the marbles were white and twice as big as the others. He took me out to the yard and drew a circle in the dust. He put twelve marbles in the circle. Eight twelves are ninety-six. He held a marble between his thumb and forefinger, then flicked his thumb. The marble shot against the marbles in the circle and four rolled out. Four from twelve leaves eight.

I tried, but I couldn't do it. My marble missed the circle entirely. I burst into tears.

"You shouldn't cry over a game," Nigel said. "Only girls cry." Then he said, "Come on then, let's do something else."

"I don't want to do anything. I want to go home."

"Would you like to see the turkeys?"

I nodded, and he led me round the house to the back yard. There were turkeys, ducks, and chickens walking up and down.

"Here," he said, "here's a turkey feather. See, if you let it go it flies like an aeroplane."

It was true. The feather drifted slowly to the ground. Each of us held a feather and let it go. They collided and whirled down, falling more quickly.

"Look at this," he said. He was holding out a winged seed. "Doesn't it look like an aeroplane propeller?"

It was true. It did.

I walked toward my Camel. I climbed into the cockpit, and the mechanic stood by the propeller.

"Contact!"

The engine burst into life with a roar. There was a smell of castor oil. The plane trembled, pressing against the chocks. The rest of the squadron was warming up. I pulled the goggles down over my eyes, raised my gloved hand and let it fall. My plane rolled forward, bumping, gathered speed, and the ground fell away beneath.

The squadron flew east, into the clouds streaked with rays of the rising sun. The dawn patrol. We passed over a village and the people waved. We were flying over trenches and barbed wire; then No Man's Land. I could see the shell holes. The poor bloody infantry!

Below me, close to the ground, I saw a Hun two-seater sneaking back to the German lines. A sitting duck—but I had more important business in hand.

Young Charteris was lagging. I throttled back and flew alongside his plane, motioning with my hand—"Keep up!" Why did they send us these youngsters? Yesterday we'd lost two. They had probably had only twenty hours' flying time between them.

I fired a burst to clear the guns . . .

"Coo-e-e-e!" That was Aunt Ethel calling from the house. Nigel went ahead and I followed.

We sat at a long table. Everyone became silent, and Uncle Percy, sitting at the head of the table, closed his eyes and said, "For these and all his mercies may the Lord's name be praised." Uncle Percy worked at the Institute of Agriculture. Nigel's older brother Dennis was also present. He was articled to my father and worked in his law office. Everyone was busy eating. The food was different from the kind we had at home. There were big dishes filled with sticky white rice, and pieces of boiled breadfruit, and a dish full of yellow yam, mashed up. It all tasted alike. There were no green vegetables. The meat was odd-looking—flat and white with holes in it.

"What is it?" I asked.

"That's tripe," said Aunt Agnes. The meat had a strong smell like when you went to the toilet. I pushed my plate away.

"Don't be rude," said Aunt Ethel.

"Waste not, want not," said Cousin Dora, who was sitting on the other side of the table. Then she giggled. She was fat and silly.

Cousin Gwen, who was sitting next to me, pushed my plate back in place, and whispered, "Be a good boy. Show them how well you can behave."

I picked up my fork and tasted the tripe again. It wasn't so bad, if you didn't think about going to the toilet. I ate a spoonful of rice. I was hungry.

After dinner I followed Dennis. He went into a bedroom and stood in front of a mirror brushing his hair and humming.

I said, "What happened to my father?"

He was startled. "What do you mean what happened?"

"They won't let me go home, and they talk about my mother and father."

I was once more on the verge of tears.

Dennis hummed. It was a tune of the year called "La Cucaracha." I had heard that he liked to go dancing at the Silver Slipper. Aunt Ethel said that Dennis thought he was a "lady's man," and my father said that he was the "black sheep of the family."

He finished brushing his hair and looked at himself in the mirror. He met my eye and winked. Then he whistled a tune called "Green Eyes."

"The ladies," he said, "the ladies."

I bit my lip to keep back the tears. How could he be so stupid! Why wouldn't he tell me?

He put a straw hat on his head and tilted it at a becoming angle. He took a pack of cigarettes from the bureau and put it in his side pocket. He raised his left foot and polished the toe of his shoe with his handkerchief. Then his right shoe. He put the handkerchief back in his breast pocket.

"Ask me no questions," he said, "and I'll tell you no lies."

He winked again and went away, humming "La Cucaracha."

My brother Herbert was now at a boarding school in Mandeville so I had no one to confide in. Nigel was always busy, kicking a football, hitting a tennis ball against the door of the garage. By the thumping of the tennis ball you could tell when he was home. Also he collected postage stamps and tram tickets—green tickets in one packet, white in another. He had a shoe box full of tickets, each packet neatly tied with a rubber band.

In the evenings Nigel had to do lots of homework. I watched as he covered pages with adding, subtracting, multiplying, dividing. And this was only a beginning. He worked with a compass and a ruler, making circles and triangles and rectangles with letters of the alphabet at the corners and numbers along the sides. He was also learning algebra. $5ab \times 3a^2b^3 = 15a^3b^4$. When I was as old as Nigel, even the letters of the alphabet would have turned into sums.

He was learning Latin. There were parallel columns of Latin nouns and verbs to be learned by heart, and no sooner had he memorized one set of columns than he had to memorize another. Also he had to study English, which consisted of learning poems by heart. He handed me the book and told me to follow the lines on the page and to stop him if he made a mistake. He closed his eyes and said very quickly:

> Lars Porsena of Clusium
> By the Nine Gods he swore
> That the great house of Tarquin
> Should suffer wrong no more.
> By the Nine Gods he swore it,
> And named a trysting day,

> And bade his messengers ride forth,
> East and west and south and north,
> To summon his array.

In this way he had learned hundreds of lines which he could recite without stopping and without making a mistake. He was the best at English in his class.

This would prove useful later on, for Nigel was going to be a lawyer, like my father. His older brother Dennis was already articled, but it was Nigel who had the brains and worked hard, while Dennis stayed out late at night. One night Dennis didn't come home until very late, and when he did he was wearing a paper hat and blowing a paper trumpet. He said "Yippee!" three times, then he went to bed. The next morning, which was Sunday, everyone spoke in hushed tones; Aunt Ethel said that Dennis was going to bring his father to an early grave.

On Saturday mornings we went swimming. Aunt Agnes, Aunt Ethel and Cousin Dora didn't like the water, but Uncle Percy, Nigel and I, and cousin Gwen—who was a sport though she was a girl—set off in the car. It was an old Ford and it rattled. We drove through Kingston and then the streets began to thin out. We were getting close to the beach. We saw coconut trees and huts roofed with sheets of zinc and palm leaves. Then the bathhouse and the sea breaking in long lines of white surf.

We swam in an enclosure. Wooden posts painted with tar had been driven into the floor of the harbor, making four sides, and wire mesh was attached to the posts. This was to keep out sharks and barracudas. The wind was strong, and waves came rolling in to break on the sand. We frolicked in the waves, splashing each other. We dived down to the bottom. It was dark and muddy on the bottom. There was seaweed and also sea eggs with prickles. If you got a prickle in your foot it would have to be taken out with a needle.

The coconut trees tossed in the wind and the coconuts thudded together. Across the harbor we could make out the blue line of the Palisadoes, stretching toward Port Royal. Gulls were beating against the wind. Now and then one would swoop down and make a splash and rise with a fish in its beak. On some rotting posts close to the shore perched a group of pelicans, each solitary on its post, its beak tucked in its chest. From time to time one of the pelicans would extend bat-like wings and fly creakily away.

When we came back from swimming we were tired and happy.

Sunday was a day of rest. Uncle Percy, Aunt Agnes, Aunt Ethel and my cousins Gwen and Dora sat in rocking chairs on the veranda, fanning themselves and looking across the South Camp Road at the hills in the distance. You could hear the tramline starting to hum. Then you heard the tram coming a long way off. It made a grinding sound on the rails. Then it stopped. The bell clanged and the tram started again. The sound got louder. The tram went by; you could see people sitting on the benches with a railing along the side. The better-dressed people were on the front benches. Then the sound of the tram grew fainter and died away.

A john crow flew over, very high, gliding in lazy circles.

On Sunday I had to sit still. I wasn't allowed to play games like tiddly winks and snakes-and-ladders or run around in the yard. I could read a book if it wasn't too exciting.

At the midday meal on Sunday, grace was twice as long as usual. We ate for a long time, and after lunch everyone went off to take a nap. I had to lie down and not make any noise. I had some halves of walnut shells under my pillow. I pushed them along the sheet. *England expects every man to do his duty.* I had a handful of small brass cartridges Nigel had given me. He was on the rifle team at school. *Up Guards and at 'em!*

In the afternoon again we sat on the veranda, and in the evening we went to church. I stood beside Cousin Gwen, looking into the black hymn book.

> How sweet the name of Je-sus sounds
> In a believer's ear.

On the way home from church my aunts and cousins discussed the service and the minister's sermon. Aunt Ethel had almost married a minister, Reverend Jones. When his name was mentioned she pursed her mouth and shook her head. She had refused to marry Reverend Jones in order to help her sister Agnes to raise her family. It was a sacrifice. We must sacrifice our own selfish desires so that we may do the will of our Lord.

V

Then I was home with my father again, and Herbert was home from boarding school. I watched him unpacking his trunk. Everything smelled moldy and his khaki school clothes were stained with "red dirt." His school, he said, was on a mountain that was all composed of that bleeding substance. He showed me a slingshot, and a wooden gig with a sharp metal point, and a piece of flint.

As soon as Aunt Ethel—once more in charge of the household and supervising this unpacking—was out of earshot, I asked where Mother was. Had she gone to America again?

"She's right here in Kingston," Herbert said in a whisper, "staying at the Manor House Hotel, at Constant Springs."

"How do you know?"

"She wrote me a letter at school."

But why wasn't she living with us? Herbert did not know the answer. Nor was Aunt Ethel any more enlightening. She said, "Oh, go away. Don't bother me! There are things you children shouldn't know."

With a certain delicacy I sensed that as my father had not told us, he must not want to. There were reticences, dumb depths, that must not be stirred. It would be shameful on my part to ask him where my mother was. Every morning he went to work as usual, and the household went about its business, the housemaid on her knees smearing the floor with beeswax and thumping it with a brush of coconut fibre. She washed down the veranda with a mop. I stared into the bucket in which "civil" orange halves were floating. It was as though my mother had never existed. I went into her bedroom and looked in a closet. There were still a few dresses on hangers, smelling of perfume, hatboxes, and beads on the floor.

I tried reading "The Happy Prince," the story she had liked reading aloud at bedtime. And the books she brought from America. There was a set of books called *Journeys Through Bookland*. Book I was for the nursery, Book II for children learning to read, and so on, increasing in difficulty. The books were illustrated with drawings in line and color. I opened one of the middle volumes and came upon a picture that made me jump—of a skeleton sitting bolt upright, a thing of bones and ribs, wearing a suit of armor. The eyes of the skull were hollow, the jaws were open, and one fleshless hand was raised in the air.

> Speak! speak! thou fearful guest!
> Who, with thy hollow breast
> Still in rude armor drest,
>   Comest to daunt me!
> Wrapt not in Eastern balms,
> But with thy fleshless palms
> Stretched, as if asking alms,
>   Why dost thou haunt me?

This must be poetry, for the lines on the page were short, each began with a capital letter, the ends of lines sounded alike, and the words were not the words that people used, so that I could hardly tell what they meant.

Then, starting from the page, a line that mystified me . . . Speaking of the "maiden" in the story, the skeleton said, "She was a mother." Hadn't she always been a mother? Could it happen suddenly? If she hadn't always been a mother, what had she been?

The next line said: "Death closed her mild blue eyes." She was a mother and then she died.

I read through to the end. The Viking fell on his spear and his soul, "Bursting these prison bars," fled into the sky. The story ended with a frightening shout: "*Skoal!* to the Northland! *Skoal!*"

The volume exerted a dreadful fascination. Whenever I was in my father's study, where the books were kept, I knew that this book was there, with the picture of the skeleton, the maiden of whom it was said that "Death closed her mild blue eyes," and the word "*Skoal!*" that sounded like "skull."

Our father was not a religious man, and though he let Aunt Ethel take us to church, he himself spent his Sundays in the "carpenter's shop" where he hammered, sawed, and filed. He liked using his hands, filing pieces of brass and iron to one purpose and another. A leaky faucet could keep him happy for hours. If only life could be banged and twisted so that it ran properly!

My toy train kept flying off the track. He stuck a wad of putty on to the engine. This slowed it down so that it did not fly off the track. I could no longer imagine that the thing with a lump of putty on its side was a locomotive engine, but he looked on with a satisfied expression. He didn't care what things looked like as long as they worked.

On this principle he set about making a model steamboat. Finally it was five feet long, standing on the trestle. It had a round boiler in the middle from which a steam gauge protruded. Steam jetted out, the propeller whirled, and the trestle shook. He took this machine down to the Yacht Club on a Sunday and sent it plowing through the waves in a circle. It was watertight, unsinkable, and unconvincing. In contrast, there was a model frigate belonging to one of the members—it had billowing sails and little guns that slid in and out; when it passed over the waves you could imagine the seamen on board and hear the boatswain's whistle. You could almost see Horatio Nelson on the quarterdeck.

He put the steamboat on the trestle again, in order to carry out some further improvements.

I said, "Why don't you get a real boat?"

He stopped work, chisel in hand, and looked at me seriously. I had never before said anything that made such an impression. Within the month he had bought a real boat—a motorboat with an outboard engine, and it lay bobbing offshore at the Yacht Club. But though the boat was real, it managed nevertheless not to look like a boat. Whereas all the other boats anchored offshore had a bow, my father's boat had a blunt end, as though it had been cut short for the sake of economy.

He entered it in a few races. But though he was willing to race, he was somewhat cautious, or else the shape of the boat was wrong, for he always came in last. I grew embarrassed watching him.

In one race the contestants were to come in to shore, pick up a passenger, and go out again. He told me to stand on the dock and to jump into the boat when he gave the signal. I watched the boats cruising slowly up and down. Then my father's boat turned toward the dock. It was several feet away and moving. I jumped for it and fell in the bottom, nearly breaking my neck.

"You were supposed to wait till I stopped!" he said. He had only been making a practice run.

It was like him to be making a practice run. No one else had felt the need to. He wanted to make sure.

My brother and I grew bored with Sundays at the Yacht Club. It was as dull as church, put-putting around Kingston Harbor in his motorboat. The only good thing was that it didn't go on too long.

But he had a better idea. Some of the members had bought cabin cruisers. The rage now was all for cabin cruisers. But instead of buying a cabin cruiser or having one made along the usual lines, my father decided to build one to his own design. He managed to get hold of a lifeboat somewhere. He got an engine somewhere else. He built a cabin in the middle of the boat, square up and down. When, after some months, the cruiser slid down the runway and floated, it looked like something between sea and land, a kind of water-going tram. Needless to say, it ran with relentless efficiency, at a slow rate. He would spend hours going out to Port Royal in the morning and coming back.

The garden boy was now serving as an able seaman. But my father ran the engine himself. Also, he did not trust anyone else with the wheel, and there was nothing for the rest of us to do but sit on the benches along the sides, like schoolbenches, and watch the shorelines sliding by. If I kept my eyes fixed on the roof of a house I could see that we were actually moving.

Sometimes a school of porpoises broke the surface. Once or twice we saw the fin of a shark.

When we got to Port Royal the waves from the open sea made the boat roll to and fro. He steered closer to shore. There were pelicans on the posts, and we could see the streets of Port Royal—tumbledown shacks where there had once been a town. The old town had been sunk in an earthquake and tidal wave—it was lying under the waves, deep down, with all the treasure that the pirates had taken from the Spaniards. We looked down into the murky water but couldn't see anything—not a gleam of pirate gold.

I saw a cigar-shaped shadow on the bottom, and, moving my gaze upward, made out the shape of a barracuda, hanging motionless between the shadow and the surface, with its eye fixed steadily upon mine.

We steered close to Fort Charles, where Nelson as a young naval officer had paced up and down, gazing out to sea, yearning to be off to the Nile and Trafalgar. We looked at the lighthouse, then turned back, making the tedious journey over the harbor to the Yacht Club. The sun at noon beat down and the hills beyond Kingston shimmered in the heat. The wake we left behind us was straight as a ruler. I listened for the chords of music that were playing under the monotonous engine sound.

When there was a ship in the harbor—a tanker or one of the white Grace Line steamers—we would go around it. Once there was a big ocean liner, the *Empress of Britain*. Sometimes—and this made me forget the dreary expeditions—there would be a British or American warship with its turrets, great guns and seaplane hoisted on the catapult. Once, as in a dream, I saw the battle cruiser *Rodney*.

If we went in the other direction, to the east end of the harbor, there would be a seaplane, one of the Pan-American clippers, resting on the water like a white bird. It had flown all the way from America, flying across the sea. This was as hard to believe as stories about dragons.

VI

From going so often to the sea my father had the idea of living near it. One day I went with him—Herbert was not with me, as he was away at school—to look at a house he was thinking of buying. This was near Bournemouth. We walked through the front door and found no one there. Planks and wood shavings were scattered about. There were holes in the floor and empty cans of paint. Everything was being done at once and nothing was finished.

We were standing in a space that he said was to be the dining room, when my mother appeared. She stood in the doorway without moving, then she took a step into the room and raised her hand and pointed it at my father. Her hand was holding a revolver. Seconds passed while my heart beat wildly. Then my father moved—he walked across the floor toward her, saying, "Now, Rosalind!" He put his hand on the barrel of the gun and started to take it away. She let it go. Then she uttered a scream and fell to the floor. She lay on her back, rigid, the cords of her neck standing out. Her face was white and bubbles of froth appeared at the corners of her mouth.

After a while he lifted her up and carried her to the car. He placed her on the seat between us, and we drove back to town. She was moaning, her eyes turned back in her head so that only the whites showed. When we came to Cross Roads he told me to get out and walk the short distance home. Then the car drove away.

VII

The day came that I was to go to boarding school with my brother. A big yellow Buick touring car turned into the driveway. The driver strapped our suitcases on to the luggage carrier. We got into the car. It was filled with boys of all sizes. One of them said to my brother, "What's his name?"

"Simpson Two," said my brother.

We drove to Halfway Tree, where there was a tower with four clock faces. Then we turned west on a road where, from time to time, a huddle of shacks and shops appeared, to be snatched away behind. The car drove faster and faster. We were on the Spanish Town road, straight and flat between fields of sugarcane. On the left a train was traveling, belching smoke. There were white, hump-backed cattle and stacks of logwood in the fields. We drove through a narrow street of shacks pressing close together. There was the smell of a Chinaman's shop, kerosene oil and salt fish. Black children, clothed to the waist and naked beneath, stared from the side of the road.

My companions shouted the school song: "Hillcastle! Hillcastle!"

We were climbing into green hills. Mandeville, a little town of white houses and rose gardens, where English people lived. . . .

Then we were descending by hairpin turns in clouds of dust. Then climbing again, into more hills. My companions were smoking. One of them got sick and vomited inside the car, on the floor. The driver stopped and tried to clean it out. Then we started again and kept going up, around hairpin turns. There were john crows flying below us. The air became noticeably cooler.

A long wall of stones lay ahead. We passed through the gate, and there was a driveway lined with willows. This curved to the right, to a chapel and a sprawling two-story building with a red roof. This was Hillcastle, where I would stay for eight years—an eternity, with vacations at Christmas, Easter, and in the summer.

New boys reported to the matron, who assigned them to a dormitory. I was in C Dormitory. It contained twenty beds, each with its own chamber pot made of tin with white enamel. At each end of the room there was a washstand with pitchers and basins. The roof was supported by square wooden beams.

The dormitory filled up with boys. They greeted each other with shouts. They had all done wonderful things in the holidays. The new boys sat on their beds, a race apart, trying not to be seen.

"Stand up," said a big boy. "What's your name?"

"Simpson Two."

"What form are you in?"

"I don't know."

He pushed me in the chest. I staggered back and fell over another boy who had placed himself on all fours behind me.

When I got to my feet, two other big boys came up, with a small boy between them.

"He says he's a Canadian," they explained to the boy who had pushed me.

He turned to me. "Can you lick a Canadian?"

I didn't know what he meant, but then someone shouted, "Simpson Two is going to fight the Canadian," and more boys came up and formed a circle. They pushed me in the back and I bumped into the Canadian. He had a pleasant, friendly face, round and freckled, with short, blond hair. He hit me in the eye.

I punched him in the chest. Then we were rolling on the floor. In a while I managed to get an arm around his neck, and squeezed. We were both exhausted. We lay there smelling each other.

Then the circle of boys went away, and when I looked up a man was standing there. It was one of the masters. I scrambled to my feet. He looked at us silently, then went away.

A big bell rang, and everyone ran downstairs. It was supper time and we gathered outside the dining room, "under the arches." The main building was supported by an old-fashioned archway. Bats were flying about, making a squeaking noise.

A handbell rang, and we went into the dining room. I was in Coke House, so I sat at a long table with the other Coke House boys. I would be eating with them as long as I was at Hillcastle. At the end of the table sat our housemaster, Mister Powell.

Mister Dickson the headmaster appeared at dinner on the first night of term and other important occasions. He was a fat man with a yellow moustache and glasses. He rapped his spoon on the table. Everyone stood up, and one of the long benches fell over. This often happened, I would discover later, and whenever it did the master who was about to say grace would keep us standing in silence, to show his disapproval.

This evening the headmaster himself said grace. "For what we are about to receive may the Lord make us truly thankful."

Then we sat down, and Mister Powell chatted to the boys around him as he helped meat from a bowl into the plates beside him. Tonight it was corned beef and cabbage. The plates were passed down the table, and we helped ourselves to rice and mashed potatoes from the bowls set in the middle. Mister Powell laughed a lot, showing his teeth, and talked about what he had done during the holidays.

In the years to come I would discover that everyone always said they had had a wonderful time during the holidays. The luckiest boys were those who lived in town, Kingston, Montego Bay, or Port Antonio, and the most unfortunate were those who lived in the country and never got to go to movies. There were even a few boys whose homes were not far from the school. What they did during the holidays we could not imagine, and they were too ashamed to speak of it.

On this first night, as there was no homework—but they weren't home, so they called it Prep—the boys walked up and down on the barbecue with their friends in twos and threes. The new boys walked up and down too, pretending they had friends. The barbecue was a square paved with concrete around which the buildings were situated. At the far, southern side the barbecue ended at a wall. Standing by the wall, looking down, you saw the hill sloping to the football fields, then the mountain fell away again, a greater distance, till it came to a wide plain. To the right, at the periphery, was a town named Black River. The river itself was said to be full of alligators. It went winding through the marshes, and a cape like a lizard projected into the sea. In front the horizon was unbroken sea and clouds, now rayed with the light of the setting sun. At nightfall lights began to shine from Black River, but most of the people who lived down there on the plain had no lights and lived in darkness.

The bell rang, and everyone went to chapel. On the first night the masters and boys sang loudly, and Mister Wiehen at the organ pulled out the stops so that the walls seemed to shake, though they were made of stone.

> He who would valiant be
> 'Gainst all disaster,
> Let him in constancy
>   Follow the master.
> There's no discouragement
> Shall make him once relent
> His first avowed intent
>   To be a pilgrim.

They trooped out of chapel to the dormitories. In a few minutes they were in bed and it was "lights out."

I lay in bed on this, my first night at school, feeling the rough sheets and listening to the noises the boys made as they settled to sleep. There was whispering and the flicker of a candle. Then "Hush!" and the candle went out. Someone stood in the doorway— one of the masters. They would give you a licking if they caught you out of bed or talking. Or else they would give you five hundred lines. He went away and the boys listened to his steps retreating. Outside the wind was blowing in gusts so that the roof creaked on the beams. The night was colder than at home and I was glad of my blanket. We never had to use a blanket at home. A light came through windows from the moon scudding through clouds. They said that if you had to get up at night and go to the toilet, which was in another building some distance away, you would meet the Rolling Calf. The Rolling Calf had eyes as big as plates, shining like automobile headlights, and it came rolling toward you, roaring as it came.

But then you were asleep.

VIII

First Bell was at six. You didn't have to get up—there were a few boys, however, who went running to the showers, across the barbecue, in bare feet and naked except for a towel. These were the sportsmaster's pets, the runners and players of football and cricket. There were also a few early risers who had to do lines: they had to write maybe a thousand times, in clear handwriting on lined sheets of foolscap, "I shall not disturb the class by talking." There were one or two boys who got up early to snatch a few blessed minutes when the world had not yet burst in, shouting and interfering. They pasted stamps in an album, or turned the pages of a book. *Chums*, the red annual with stories about English boarding schools, the Foreign Legion, fighting on the Western Front, racing car drivers and explorers . . .

At Second Bell everyone had to get up. The first ones at the washstands got plenty of water. Those who rose last found only an inch in the pitcher, not enough water to clean the accumulated scum out of the basin. Then everyone out! to the dining room, for a cup of hot cocoa and a slice of bread with margarine. This was real margarine, not one of your substitutes for butter. It was white and rancid, straight from the locomotive shed, and it had one advantage—it killed the weevils in the slice of bread, and if it failed to kill them, bogged them down so that they could not be seen moving.

There was an hour of morning Prep, then chapel—a piece of Scripture, a psalm, a hymn, and two prayers. Then breakfast, and after breakfast, classes.

Form Two, in which I began, was the lowest. The forms were numbered up to Six, where the prefects were. Every number was divided into a lower form and an upper, B and A, so that the years were a series of downs and ups, a year of obscurity to be followed by a year of light. It seemed that the rooms for the lower forms were cramped and uncomfortable, your desk pushed in a corner, and it was then that the miserable things happened. It was in IIIB that I always seemed to be greasing the football players' boots and shining their shoes—and it was when I was in IIIB that I looked through the Sixth Form window.

"Come here, boy," said Weller. He was big, about six feet tall. "What you looking in the Sixth Form window for?"

The Sixth Form boys lined up in two rows facing each other. Weller put me at the far end, looking down the rows. Some of the boys seemed sheepish—they didn't enjoy these occasions as much as Weller did. I was given a push forward, and after that I didn't have to walk or run—I was propelled by one kick after another so that I went flying to the door. The last kick was the worst, from Weller with the point of his shoe. I picked myself off the concrete and limped away.

In IIIA, on the other hand, I found a friend—Peter Lopez. Peter was my trains and boxing friend. Pacing the barbecue from the main building to the wall and back again, we talked about these matters. Peter liked *The Flying Scotsman* while I liked *The Royal Scot*. We talked the great fights again—Corbett-Fitzimmons, Dempsey versus Tunney. I was for Dempsey and thought he had been cheated by the "fourteen count."

I also had a friend named Beverly Dodd, who stuttered. Beverly was my reading friend—we read novels and passed them to each other. *Bulldog Drummond. The Scarlet Pimpernel. The Thirty-Nine Steps.*

But IVB, again, was a time of darkness. It was during this year that the bell tolled in the middle of the day and the school assembled in the hall in the main building. What was happening? No one knew.

The headmaster, Mister Dickson, entered. He had a cane under his arm. He stood on the platform facing us. He was fat and had a drooping, yellow moustache; his eyes were sunk in fat and concealed by the glint of his spectacles. He read a list of names—"Forsyth, Mair I, Cargyll." I saw these boys go up to the platform, snatched from our very midst. Then the headmaster called for four of the prefects to come up. He told them to move a table to the middle of the platform. He told Mair I to lie face down on the table, and told the prefects to hold him by his arms and legs. Then he stepped forward and brought the cane down with all his strength on the boy's back. He brought it down six times, and each time the body on the table stiffened. Then he said "Get up!" and Mair I got to his feet and walked off the platform. He was moving with difficulty, but he had not uttered a sound.

The same for Forsyth and Cargyll.

We watched this execution in silence. Every cut of the stick seemed to bite into our flesh. When the headmaster had finished beating the three boys, he announced that they had been swimming in the water tank. This was one of the worst, almost unheard-of, offences. It was nearly as bad as being caught smoking, or going out-of-bounds, over the school wall, for which there was an even greater punishment—being expelled. If you were expelled your life would be ruined.

Yet, underneath this regime we developed a life of our own. Then, everybody had his speciality, a game he could play or thing he could make, and some had a moment of glory. I too had mine and it came unexpectedly.

We ate our meals at long tables, sitting in two rows with a master at the head of the table. We were allowed to ask for "seconds" by passing our empty plates up to the master, who would serve meat from the dish in front of him. As I've said, we were badly fed; we had plenty of fresh fruit, oranges and mangoes, but the rest was yam and rice, meat that was sometimes rotten, bread with weevils in it. But we had to eat, and sometimes we asked for seconds.

One evening I passed up my plate for a second helping of pork— gobbets of fat swimming in gravy. You were supposed just to pass your plate without saying anything, but I said "Meat please!" The boy sitting next to me, as he passed my plate, also said "Meat please!" I hadn't thought he would—I'd meant it only as a joke between the two of us. Or had I? As my plate made its way to the end of the table so did the whisper, increasing in sarcasm. I would have done anything to call back the plate, but it went tilting on its way, increasing in velocity as though it had a will of its own and had been waiting for this release, saying "Meat please!" Heads turned toward me, then the master stared down the table. It was obvious that I was guilty—I was the one who had no plate in front of him. "There are some small boys . . ." the master began, in a cracked voice. I did not hear what he said—I was stunned. But I knew that it was loud and the whole school was listening.

Afterwards I was slapped on the back and congratulated—not least by the boys who, by passing on the words, had got me into that fix. I hadn't really intended, except for the fraction of a moment, to rebel; but perhaps this is the way rebellions start. You throw your-self forward on an impulse, then find you must abide the conse-quences.

As we couldn't fight back, we learned how to cheat. One day we were taking an exam in hygiene and the master left the room for an hour. Immediately all the desks flew open and we copied the answers out of the textbook. This was incredibly naïve, and the next day the frightful rumor flew round that the master was going to call us in to explain our answers. I sat down and memorized the relevant pages. When it was my turn to go in and see the master I was able to recite the text word for word. He let me go without making any comment. He too must have been remarkably naïve, for he might simply have asked me a question that would have required a word-for-word knowledge of some other part of the text. To this day I can remember the words of one answer, concerning the ability of an English family in reduced circumstances, living in the Midlands, to support itself "by ringing the changes on pease and beans."

Much of our education was of this kind. It was assumed that we would be living in England and no attempt was made to translate what we learned into Jamaican. So we learned how to keep warm in Birmingham in the winter, and where coal was mined, and how English children went to look at the Changing of the Guard. We were being fitted for a life that we would never have and being made to understand that the life we did have was inferior.

And of course there was no place in the classroom for "bad English"—that is, Jamaican words and expressions. The most important weapon of a ruling class is language, which controls everything. The native language must be suppressed so that the natives cannot communicate with one another directly but only through their masters.

Am I making too much of the life of schoolboys? Hillcastle was an epitome of Jamaica; it was there we developed a colonial mentality.

As Jamaicans did not govern themselves they felt inferior in other respects. "Among the legacies of a colonial culture is the habit of thinking of creative sources as somehow remote from itself." This was true of the Jamaicans.

They were only a remote branch of England. They were not self-sufficient, and had created no important works. The history of

Jamaica was the history of the Europeans who had ruled it, and there were no native heroes who might be mentioned in the same breath with Nelson. Jamaicans might become lawyers and doctors, but this would be only a kind of playacting, for the centers of law and medicine were thousands of miles away. The very trees and hills of Jamaica were only a kind of papiermâché—the famous landscapes were in England. No Jamaican bird could sing like Keats's nightingale, and Jamaican flowers were not as beautiful as Wordsworth's daffodils.

But when I was promoted to Form IVA the time was again filled with light. It was then that I wrote an essay on the coronation of George VI that won a prize and was printed in *The Daily Gleaner*, the newspaper published in Kingston. Years later I came across a letter that my father wrote to my mother on this occasion. She was living in Toronto, Canada, working for a firm that sold cosmetics. He had taken the trouble to write: "See what the boy has done."

I had copied a circumstantial account of the coronation from an article in the *Gleaner*, selecting the more colorful episodes—as perhaps the writer in the *Gleaner* had taken his account from a London newspaper. I began by comparing London to a beehive. I showed the procession of men and horses. I added touches of my own, quoting Gray:

> Girt with many a Baron bold
> Sublime their starry fronts they rear;
> And gorgeous Dames, and Statesmen old
> In bearded majesty, appear.

I also quoted Shakespeare, who had said discouraging things about the burden of wearing a crown, and rebuked him for not sufficiently respecting the royal family, our king, our queen and their children. Shakespeare, I thought, could stand it; he could afford to be dispraised, and at this point finding fault with him gave a fillip to my essay, which was threatening to be just a description. An argument between Shakespeare and myself should hold the reader in suspense.

First prize. Five pounds. L. A. M. Simpson. Age 14.

With this, the first money I had earned, and the most I had ever held in my hand—five pounds, a fortune!—I bought a bicycle. This was during the holidays, and my stepmother watched me learning to ride.

"You're a clever boy," she said. "Your father's very proud of you. If only your brother would work harder and not make his father angry."

IX

For my father had married again. I received the announcement one night at school. Around me boys were bending over their books, in the room that shone like a lighted box. They were doing sums, but I was trying to penetrate a mystery of human behavior.

"She's attractive," my father wrote, "and I'm sure you'll love her. She has red hair, like Clara Bow."

I was surprised, and had a peculiar feeling, like shame. It made me feel embarrassed to see my father thinking about a woman. I had never heard him speak of the relations between men and women, yet now it seemed that he had been strongly attracted. By red hair.

Clara Bow was a motion picture actress. No doubt he'd been trying to think of some way to recommend his new wife to his children. Then he hit upon the solution: he knew that we liked movies. His wife had red hair, like Clara Bow in the movies. Therefore we would love our stepmother. That it might be in poor taste to recommend, in terms of physical attractiveness, the woman he had chosen to replace our mother, did not enter our father's head. Such sensitivity as he possessed—and it had never been much—had been exhausted in the law courts.

When he was a young man, in his bachelor days, he had let himself dream. There were books of adventure in his study, worm-eaten, tunneled through and through, and a powder fell out when you opened them—tales of voyages up the Orinoco and African explorations. They were illustrated with pictures of wild animals—jaguar, buffalo, crocodile—and pictures of savages and bearded men with rifles.

In his office, framed on a wall, were some lines of poetry showing that he'd once meditated on the theme of love.

> The night has a thousand eyes,
>   And the day but one;
> Yet the light of the bright world dies
>   With the dying sun.

> The mind has a thousand eyes,
>   And the heart but one;
> Yet the light of a whole life dies
>   When love is done.

This poem mystified me every time I saw it. It hinted at a side of my father I had never seen—sad and, had I known the word, sentimental. It haunts me to this day—I want to say to him: Don't you see what bad poetry it is? What eyes can the brain have? Or the heart? And in any case, if the brain has a thousand eyes, whatever this means, why shouldn't the heart have a thousand, too?

But he looks at me in a puzzled manner. He doesn't know what I'm talking about. It's not supposed to make sense, it's only a poem, that he hung up long ago. That was when he was a bachelor, before he married.

The only thing you can depend on is intelligence and hard work. All this thinking about love is nonsense—making a lot of trouble for people.

He had made a new life for himself, rearranging everything after the confusion of the divorce. He had married again and bought a new house. He devoted himself entirely to his work and stayed home with his wife. He no longer went into society or invited friends to his home.

He was worried about Herbert, however. Herbert, having left school, was now at the office, studying law. But he wasn't passing his exams—this was what my stepmother meant. Herbert sat staring at the pages of law, but he was day-dreaming. His only enthusiasm was for Physical Culture—he subscribed to Bernarr Macfadden's magazine, and studied photographs of men with bulging biceps and triceps and ridged stomach muscles, in statuesque poses. He exercised morning and night. He was becoming more and more muscular. The mornings long ago when he had stood in front of the Victrola, with his mother and father, doing exercises to the sound of music, were having this result. Then he had been happy, when to touch his toes twelve times in succession had brought an approving smile to his father's countenance.

Also, Herbert boxed—and his father, no doubt hoping that if he encouraged Herbert in this foolishness, out of gratitude he would become a brilliant lawyer, went so far as to hire a prize-fighter, an old welterweight named McVey, who came every week and gave us boxing lessons. I say "us" because for some reason it was assumed that I wanted to box too. I could if I had to, but I preferred swimming.

And my bicycle . . . I took long rides in the afternoon, through the lanes of Kingston, and sometimes as far as the Manor House Hotel at Constant Springs. This was where we stayed on the occasions when our mother came back to the island. She visited sometimes for a few weeks in the summer, and my brother and I would stay with her.

The hotel was a rambling structure with long verandas, surrounded with green lawns and beds of flowers. We were close to the hills. They shone like crystal in the dewy atmosphere. There were tennis courts and a golf course. At times it seemed that my mother, Herbert and I were the only guests—except for an English couple who kept to themselves, only saying "Good morning" in the polite, dismissive English way as they took their place at the breakfast table. And an American businessman, reading his home-town paper. I could not make sense of American newswriting—it seemed like a foreign language.

Then our mother would go back to Canada, and we went back to our father's house. This was at Bournemouth—a new house, right on the harbor, with its own beach. His boat lay tied securely to the dock.

X

Aunt Ethel said, "Aston married her for her legs."

But this did not have the effect my aunt intended, to paint an erotic picture. Separating my stepmother's legs from the rest of her body made me think of a museum where the parts of ancient statues are kept in glass cases—here an arm, there a leg. I thought of my father not as driven by passion, but by curiosity. Perhaps he had wished to possess my stepmother's legs, but this was a failing for which one could not help having a certain admiration—as one would for a man so curious about statues that he took them out of the museum and carried them home to study them at his leisure.

It seemed, indeed, that my father had been taken out of the usual course of his life by a feeling he could not entirely control. With a touching eagerness to have us cooperate, he said to my brother and myself that we would have to find a name for our stepmother—we couldn't call her mother, or Elizabeth, as he did. We ought to call her by some sort of nickname, the kind of name that would be thought up by stepchildren for a stepmother of whom they had grown fond. Bitsy! That was it. We were to call her Bitsy from now on.

It must have struck our stepmother as odd to be called by a name she had never heard before, but no doubt our father explained to her that my brother and myself had grown so fond of her that we were impelled suddenly to call her Bitsy. He liked to have a clear understanding all around.

Nevertheless, I became fond of Bitsy on my own account. In the first year of marriage she was making an effort to be nice to her stepchildren. I was grateful to her for being kind, but I was more grateful to her for being a woman. It had been a long time since I had been included in the atmosphere a man and woman living together generate round them. There was an exciting warmth in the house—opposite to the drab piety in the house of Uncle Percy and my aunts. And compared to boarding school it was pure magic.

I brooded over the Montgomery Ward catalogue with Bitsy. Which glider should she get for the veranda? The one with green and white stripes, or the one that came apart in sections? And would it be here in time for Christmas? Together we studied the pictures of red barns, silos, and tractors with huge tires. There was a boy in boots trudging over the landscape and pulling a little wagon behind him. What a strange place America was!

Then she turned to the women's foundation garments. Stout women, middle-sized women, slender women. And women's underwear—there were beautiful girls with blonde, brunette and red hair, all lined up for inspection and practically naked. Others were in pajamas. I was blushing furiously.

"Isn't that a pretty one?" Bitsy said, pointing to a picture. Soon after this I found a reason to excuse myself and left. I was shocked. I had not imagined women pointing out such things to a member of the opposite sex.

At the end of the year Bitsy gave birth, and if the atmosphere of the house had been feminine, now it was maternal. There were diapers on lines and a smell of warm mash, baby powder and urine. One day, I came upon Bitsy in, of all places, my father's study, with a breast exposed. The baby was clamped on to it by the mouth. Bitsy did not seem disturbed by my presence, nor did she make an attempt to cover herself. I backed rapidly out of the room. Another shock.

When the baby was old enough to be taken outside, I accompanied Bitsy as she wheeled the carriage down to the beach. We sat for an hour and watched the waves breaking. The trailing smoke of a ship passed across the sky, on the other side of the Palisadoes. My father's boat lay anchored at bow and stern and roped to the dock fore and aft, so that nothing short of a hurricane could tear it loose; the hull gave off a cheerful, slapping sound.

It was almost as though I had a family of my own.

XI

H. J. Andrews had been hired from Scotland to teach us English. He was round-shouldered and peered through glasses with thick lenses. He would open the book and ask us to read aloud in turn.

> I know you all, and will awhile uphold
> The unyoked humour of your idleness.
> Yet herein will I imitate the sun,
> Who doth permit the base contagious clouds
> To smother up his beauty from the world,
> That when he please again to be himself,
> Being wanted he may be more wond'red at,
> By breaking through the foul and ugly mists

Of vapours that did seem to strangle him.
If all the year were playing holidays,
To sport would be as tedious as to work;
But when they seldom come, they wished for come,
And nothing pleaseth but rare accidents:
So, when this loose behaviour I throw off,
And pay the debt I never promised,
By how much better than my word I am,
By so much shall I falsify men's hopes,
And like bright metal on a sullen ground,
My reformation, glitt'ring o'er my fault,
Shall show more goodly, and attract more eyes,
Than that which hath no foil to set it off.
I'll so offend, to make offence a skill,
Redeeming time when men think least I will.

He spoke of the character of the prince. Hal was a brave soldier and, in spite of appearances, a dutiful son. He would be the hero of Agincourt and an efficient king. As this speech proved, he was level-headed, foresighted, calculating. You might call him a hypocrite.

We shall find a similar character in *Antony and Cleopatra*—Augustus, whom Shakespeare opposes to Mark Antony. Augustus, also, is calculating and efficient, and he defeats Antony, as Prince Hal defeats Harry Hotspur. But the question arises: what do these calculating people win? And isn't there something about the character of an Antony or Hotspur or Falstaff that makes us prefer them to the hero with all his victories?

This is not to say that Shakespeare wishes to show the prince in a bad light. To the contrary, he is presenting the model of what a king has to be. But, at the same time, because he is a poet he cannot falsify life—just as people who have no poetry in them never manage to see life as it is.

Let us consider the character of Falstaff, this wine-bibber, this tub of lard, this coward . . . well, is Falstaff a coward? Mair II?

Yes, sir, he won't fight.

And a good thing too! If Falstaff had tried to tackle Hotspur he would have been carved up in fat little pieces. And notice, on Gadshill, Falstaff *does* fight—for a while, before he takes to his heels. Is that the action of a coward?

But sir, he's always bragging. And he's a liar.

Is he? Do you suppose for a moment that Falstaff expects to be believed? Don't you see what he's doing? "I am not only witty in myself, but the cause that wit is in other men." The lies Falstaff tells are not meant to be believed—they are meant to be found out. See how the others egg him on, to tell bigger and bigger lies, and see how he obliges them. Do you imagine that Falstaff isn't aware that you can't see colors in the dark, and that he has upped the number of men in buckram from one line to another? No, obviously it's for the purpose of making people laugh, to make them come alive. Prince Hal seems alive only when he is with Falstaff.

So I was shown for the first time that literature is a reflection of life rather than a bundle of clichés. Shakespeare was creating characters out of life, not cardboard figures of virtue and vice.

Then we read *Macbeth* and *The Tempest,* and by this time it was all over with me—I would be attached to poetry for the rest of my life. The ground I walked on seemed no more solid than the imaginary green fields of England and the moors of Scotland. I could believe with Prospero that the great globe itself was a dream. In which case, the poets who dreamed so well made better worlds, for they did not fade.

I began sending my pocket money to England for books. *Vanity Fair* was said to be a great novel; moreover, it had a description of the battle of Waterloo. Ever since early childhood, when I saw a movie about it, I had been fascinated with Waterloo. I would have been on the French side, in the cavalry that Ney launched again and again at the British squares—it was more romantic. So I sent a postal money order to London for *Vanity Fair.* It took two months for the book to arrive. I read it in a corner of a classroom while around me boys were shooting wads of paper at each other with rubber bands. I took my book out under the willows, with clouds streaming over. This was the first "classic" I read on my own account and not as a school assignment. I read every word and finished with a sense of triumph.

Then I read Dickens, and novels by Austen, Hardy, and Conrad. I was reading not because I had to, but because it was a pleasure, and as I read I became filled with a desire to write. I wanted to tell stories and write poems of my own. Perhaps to be admired—but more important, because there were things I had seen and felt that I wanted other people to see and feel.

I had a talent for writing essays. These were set every week, and I would cheerfully have written on any subject.

I tried my hand at a story. *The Daily Gleaner,* where I had been awarded a prize for my coronation essay, was now holding a short-story competition. I wrote a story about a poor country boy who went to Kingston and was involved in an earthquake. (I had an uncle who had lost a leg in an earthquake and was nicknamed "Corkfoot." Besides, I had seen an earthquake in the movie *San Francisco.*) In my story one of the earthquake victims, as he lay dying, gave the hero a wallet full of money. The country boy returned to his village; but he found his old mother dying, and the last words of the story were, "Too late! Too late!"

This, too, won a prize and was published in *The Gleaner.*

In bed at night, in the row of sleeping boys, I would lie listening to the wind that roared across the commons, making the roof creak like a ship. I was envisioning cities, battles, and beautiful women, and my adventures were always taking place across the sea—in England or France.

XII

During the holidays I went swimming at Bournemouth, right down the street from our house. On weekdays I had the pool pretty much to myself and lay for hours reading and looking at the white caps driving across the harbor. But on Saturdays and Sundays the pool filled up with people; you could hear them shouting a long way off.

One Saturday when I came out of the locker room I found myself face to face with gray eyes, a fine nose, long bright hair. This vision also had a body, slenderly curving. She passed me with a steady gaze, looking into my eyes, and when she had gone by, in the rear of her bathing suit there was a moth hole as big as a threepence.

She played in the pool, throwing the ball to her young brother. I found a way to speak to him, and learned his name and that of his sister. I became friends with him, and urged him to come swimming often and bring his sister with him.

When I plucked up courage to speak to her she must have known by my awkwardness how I felt. Though she came to Bournemouth several times I remained just as tongue-tied. But at night in my thoughts before sleep it was another matter. There I spoke and acted well and she looked at me with admiration.

I persuaded her brother to come to a movie with me and bring her along. This was at the Carib Theatre, the new movie house at Cross Roads in comparison with which everything else of the kind paled into insignificance. I waited outside, and at last they got off a tram. She was wearing her school uniform and a crucifix on a chain down her neck.

They were playing *The Firefly*. I thought that the girl sitting beside me was like the woman in the picture. We were living in Spain and listening to wonderful music.

I was always thinking about her. I had great plans. I would do . . . what? Nothing in particular, and everything. I was drawn out of my body and seemed to walk on air. Knowing that she lived on a certain street made it a dangerous place, and when I came near on my bicycle my pulse beat faster and my legs were weak. Suppose she came out and we met! But she never did, and I saw her only when she came to the pool.

She is a figure painted by Botticelli, against a seascape with clouds and palms. The bathing suit that grips her slenderness is old and worn, and has moth holes in it, one to the side and one behind, so that her skin shines through. Her hair is long and comes down her back. Her eyes are gray and gentle. She has a soft voice, speaking the Jamaican way—in a kind of sing-song, mistaking the vowels and accents.

When I went back to school I dreamed of her and talked of her continually to my friend Peter. At this time it seemed I could do nothing wrong, either at work or play.

> The isle is full of noises,
> Sounds and sweet airs that give delight and hurt not.

I applied myself to my books and went in for sports with a light heart. On the rifle range the bull sat on my front sight without wavering. I practiced on the bar and rings in the gymnasium, and was the best boxer in my weight.

The external world was changing as though in sympathy with my feelings. The mad old headmaster fell sick, and the boys, who were not sentimental, strummed their ukeleles, singing "I'll be glad when you're dead, you rascal you!" He did die, and a new headmaster came from Canada. He set about improving the school. He cut down the flogging and bullying, though not entirely, and gave the bigger boys a taste of freedom. We were allowed to stay up an extra hour after lights-out, and athletics were no longer compulsory.

So when other boys were playing cricket I would lie under the willows, gorging on poetry and novels. Wind sighed in the leaves, and shadows of branches and clouds flitted over the page.

> On Wenlock Edge the wood's in trouble;
> His forest fleece the Wrekin heaves;
> The gale, it plies the saplings double,
> And thick on Severn snow the leaves.

Or I would be reading *The Dynasts.*

> By degrees the fog lifts, and the Plain is disclosed. From this elevation, gazing north, the expanse looks like the palm of a monstrous right hand, a little hollowed, some half-dozen miles across, wherein the ball of the thumb is roughly represented by heights to the east, on which the French centre has gathered . . .

There were also poems by T. S. Eliot. I could not make sense of them, yet I was haunted by the images and the music of the lines.

> I will show you something different from either
> Your shadow at morning striding behind you
> Or your shadow at evening rising to meet you;
> I will show you fear in a handful of dust.

The new headmaster introduced us to such esoteric material as the writings of Aldous Huxley. We had discussions of Huxley's *Ends and Means,* during which we considered what he meant by non-attachment. They were like the discussions that prefects had with their headmaster at the better English schools. Sometimes the headmaster would tell jokes from *Punch,* and we laughed at these in a sophisticated way. I do not wish to be ungrateful to Mr. Gordon, but I have wondered whether these man-to-man talks, when the man is thirty and the boy is sixteen, are not more damaging in the long run than the brutality of the old system. Under the old regime we had known what masters were and what we were—there was no confusion of our attitudes. They were the enemy, and we had a code of our own, our own friends and beliefs. But under Mr. Gordon's enlightened regime we were being absorbed into the Establishment. We were learning the attitudes of the English ruling class. We were learning that we were superior and that many things were ridiculous. German seriousness was ridiculous; French frivolity was ridiculous; Americans with their devotion to the dollar were ridiculous. The only people who were not ridiculous were those who had gone to a British public school and were going to Oxford or Cambridge.

We were learning English manners. But there was a catch— Jamaicans were not Englishmen and never could be, even the few who would go to English universities. I was beginning to see the paradox, the fundamental contradiction that made it impossible for the Empire to continue. The English were always educating people beyond their place in the class system. Then the young men came up against class barriers and were frustrated. So they became rebels, educated ones, and set about driving out the English. At a later time a similar situation would come about in England itself. Young Englishmen from lower-class families were educated beyond their class at the redbrick universities. Then they came up against class barriers and were "angry young men," fulminating against the system.

XIII

Everyone was singing "Stormy Weather." Gales knocked down the banana trees, drove flat swathes through the sugarcane, and tore the roofs off houses and sent them flying. At last came a hurricane and a flood that poured down the gullies, carrying away the shacks that people had built on the gully beds. A number of drowned bodies, with the carcasses of mules, pigs and chickens, were floating on the sea. The sharks had a feast. For weeks the sea kept rejecting these gifts, casting them back, shark-bitten and the worse for wear, onto the beach.

Herbert and I baited a hook with a lump of pork and caught a shark. We hauled it on to the beach and stood, taking care not to get close to its teeth, pumping bullets into its head from a rifle. The bullets merely disappeared, and at last when the shark expired it was of suffocation.

A cadaver with naked feet, in a white shirt and trousers, floated down to our fence where it was caught, and when the water subsided the dead man lay in the mud. Long after the body had been removed, on nights when I would be walking home from the tram, with the movie I had been to running through my head, as I approached our house I would see the hollow filled with lamplight in the shape of a man lying close to the gate.

A light was on in my father's study. Working late on his cases. . . . And a light in the bedroom I shared with my brother. He too would be working.

Herbert had again failed his law exams. What obstinacy! Every morning my father set out for the office with Herbert. They left in silence. What could they have had to say to each other on those rides? Herbert had failed his exams again and again. Was he trying to make a laughingstock of his father? How could the most famous defense counsel on the island have a son who could not pass exams?

For Aston Simpson was famous—everyone knew about his cases. Crown *vs.* Lowy, for example. The case had been reported in England, even in the American newspapers. Mrs. Lowy had gone to bed one night with her husband and waked the next morning to find that he had been shot through the head. The finger of suspicion pointed to the widow, and my father as defense counsel, together with Manley as barrister, undertook to defend her.

Manley's wife was artistic, and they asked her to make a model of the dead man's head in plaster of paris. Through this they made a hole with a brass curtain rod. When the head was brought into court and exhibited to the jury they were astonished. My father passed the curtain rod through the hole, demonstrating the direction of the bullet, and argued that it must have been fired by someone standing outside the bedroom. A burglar, presumably. The jury returned a verdict of Not Guilty. The plaster of paris head was standing in a closet at home. If you opened the door—Bang!—there was the head with a hole through it.

Yet his son could not pass exams!

Anyone could pass if he put his mind to it. Young Nigel, whom my father had taken into his office, was already preparing his finals, and Nigel was the same age as Herbert. Nigel would be a lawyer when his own son was still trying to pass an exam.

When he was a young man he did not have a father with a profession he could inherit. He came down from the country when he was a boy in order to study law, and that was what he had done. No one would have helped him if he had failed, given him food and a roof over his head. Nevertheless, he had made his way, without asking for help from anyone, and today the name Aston Simpson was known throughout the island.

Herbert was obstinate, that was his trouble. It was worse than obstinacy—it was sullenness and ingratitude. He had set himself against his father.

What was that junk Herbert was always reading? Physical Culture! Physical Culture indeed! Was he hoping to earn a living by Physical Culture?

He knew what was at the root of the trouble, and it was no use Herbert's trying to deny it—he resented his stepmother. Well, there'd be a stop to that!

Thus, the ride from the house at Bournemouth to the office on Duke Street. When my father got there he wrote a letter to Herbert's mother, putting the case plainly so that any fool could see it.

> Dear Rosalind,
>
> I must ask you again not to put foolish ideas in Herbert's head. He has failed his exams, and he says that you have written to him saying that he may be able to study medicine, and go to McGill in Canada. This is out of the question. Herbert has no ability in that direction, and must persist in the study of law. If he puts aside the foolishness of Physical Culture and boxing and attends to his books, he will pass his exams. In any case he will stay in Jamaica. Your children would not be able to live in Canada or the United States. Let me remind you that they are Jamaican, *with all that this implies!*
>
> I do not know what is wrong with your sons. They are always reading and have no interest in practical things. They have no interest in the motorboat or the cars. I shall not be here forever to

pay for their food and keep a roof over their heads. In any case, I have other obligations.

I am not worried about Louis, however. He will do well—as I told you in my last letter, he came first in the Senior Cambridge and is now working for his Higher Schools Certificate. He will be the first boy at Hillcastle to take this examination in literature rather than science. Of course, he will never be able to argue a case in court, because of his teeth. It was a pity you sent him the skates.

(My father had come to believe—at least, he persisted in declaring—I had broken my teeth while roller-skating. This was not true—I broke them roughhousing with Herbert. He was on all fours and I was on his back; he reared up and I was pitched on to my face, smashing my teeth. Throughout my boyhood I had to wear a gold cap to protect the remnant of a top front tooth. The gold was conspicuous, and I tried to talk without opening my mouth so that no one would notice it.)

But though Louis will not be able to address a jury, I have no doubt that he will make his way as a solicitor.

To return to Herbert—I must ask you not to encourage him in these foolish ideas—about going to Canada and studying medicine. And let me advise you again *not* to fill his head with ideas of a more personal, resentful nature. You are at liberty to think that you have been treated unfairly, but it is foolish to make Herbert think so. I will not tolerate rudeness from Herbert, to *anyone*. He has to live in this house and be on good terms with *everyone* in it.

I am glad to hear that your health has improved and that you are now employed by the firm of Helena Rubinstein. This seems more sensible than your traveling from place to place. "A rolling stone gathers no moss."

I hope that the next time I write to you I shall have better news of Herbert. All that he needs is to get down to work and not have his head filled with *foolish ideas*.

As ever,
Aston

Thus, my father. And therefore Herbert was up late at night, studying Estovers and Emblements, and Contracts and Incorporeal

Hereditaments—trying to come to terms with Pledge, Chattel, Mortgage, and Lien—to tell a Malfeasance from a Misfeasance, and a Non-Feasance from either, and to make his peace with Torts.

The situation, hinted at in my father's letter, was that Herbert and his stepmother were no longer on speaking terms, and therefore his father was furious with him.

How had this come about? At the beginning, as I have said, Bitsy had been eager to be nice to her stepchildren. But then she saw that it did not matter—she could please herself. Aston would not find fault with her—at least not on behalf of the children by his first wife. So Bitsy no longer made the effort.

She had a child of her own and was pregnant with another. The children of her husband's first marriage were a nuisance, if not a definite obstacle. She had to think of the future and look out for her children and herself.

On one or two occasions Bitsy was snappish. Herbert, on his side, immediately retired into silence. In a short time they were no longer speaking to each other. Then Bitsy had reason to complain of Herbert to his father, over some matter of household management, and Herbert was given a talking-to. From this time forward he regarded his stepmother as a traitor—not to be trusted. She and his father were in league against him. On their side, they believed that Herbert resented the woman who had taken his mother's place. Herbert's attitude—this was the root of the trouble. They treated him as though he were resentful, and so, of course, he was.

On one occasion Herbert wrote a long letter to his stepmother, asking her if their misunderstandings couldn't be patched up; immediately she showed the letter to his father, and he burst in upon us, where we were reading in our bedroom, and launched into a tirade against Herbert, as though he were a criminal in the dock, accusing him of being envious of his little half-sister. Herbert was astonished; he was reduced to silence and an obstinacy that endured for the rest of our lives in that house.

If I seem, in this account, not to have the affection for my father that I should have, there is reason for it. In time he became less like the man we had known when we were small. His humor disappeared, his sarcasms became more frequent, and he was, almost as a policy, unjust to my brother. When Herbert failed his examinations his father treated him with what I can only describe as hatred. On the other hand, I must have been a source of some satisfaction to my father, for I shone at school and, being of a more pliant nature than Herbert, I did not come in for the harsh words to which he was subjected. At times, I was even privileged to have confidential talks with Bitsy. Nevertheless, Herbert was my brother and I was fond of him; we lived together and I suffered from the outbreaks of anger that were directed against him and the coldness in the days that followed.

In recent years my brother has reminded me of the atmosphere in that house, where he and I were treated like boarders. Our father would go for a walk in the evening with his wife and new child, excluding us, and we were made to feel that it was not our home, but that we were there on sufferance. Our father's behavior was a demonstration of Rochefoucauld's maxim, that we never forgive those whom we have injured. He had injured our mother, and we were a living reproach. To sum up, this man, who was regarded as one of the best lawyers in Jamaica, was unjust to his own children and behaved in a way a peasant would have been ashamed of. Indeed, there were peasants in Jamaica who were uneducated and had their children out of wedlock, yet treated them with far greater affection than was known in our family.

As I write this account of my father and stepmother, I am aware that there is something "underbred" about it. This is not a dramatic story—there was only bad feeling, day after day. There was in fact something lower-class about these people—and I am using the word deliberately. I have known poor people who are generous—they are the upper class in my opinion—but I would say that my father and his second wife, with all their money, were lower-class, for they had low emotions. They treated themselves well and other people badly.

It is the kind of story you read about in Chekhov, and I think of Chekhov's letter to his brother, where he speaks of their bad upbringing, of "that flesh raised on the rod," the brutalized, inconsiderate life of people who are emotionally or culturally—in the deep sense of the word—illiterate. It is necessary to refine oneself, to lift oneself by one's bootstraps out of the muck of insensitivity. The secret of living well is to treat other people decently, that's all. It was a secret my father never learned, and all my life I have been trying to learn it.

XIV

When I came into the house my father was not in his study. The light came from his bedroom. As I went past the door he said, "Louis?" I knocked and went in.

He was sitting up in bed, with books and papers around him. Bitsy had moved the typewriter into the bedroom, and was taking dictation. On a table by the bed there were bottles of medicine, a glass, and a spoon. He had been ill of late—the doctor had come several times—but he did not let this keep him from going to the office.

"I want to talk to you," he said. Whereupon Bitsy went out of the room.

Against the sheets he looked darker than usual, and somewhat smaller. He peered at me over his glasses. I could not imagine what he wanted to talk about. I was going back to Hillcastle the next day—perhaps he wanted to talk about my schooling.

"Did Bitsy give you your pocket money?"

I said that she had.

"Well, then, everything seems to be in order."

He paused for a while, then said, "I don't want you to worry. Whatever happens, you'll be well taken care of."

What did he mean? Worry about what? I was embarrassed, as I always was by any attempt on his part to talk of personal matters.

"Well, then," he said. "When are you leaving?"

"At nine."

He nodded, and I took it to be goodnight. I left and went to my own room.

"It was a good movie," I said to Herbert. He looked up in silence, then returned to what he was doing. He was studying a book called *How to Win Friends and Influence People,* underlining sentences and writing comments in the margin in a large round hand. Besides his interest in Physical Culture, he was fond of books on self-improvement.

In a little while I heard my father's voice giving dictation. Then a clatter of typewriting. He used to work late into the night, preparing his cases for the next day.

XV

One morning, halfway through the term, I was sent for by the headmaster. When I entered he rose to his feet and came around the desk. He said, "I am sorry, I have to tell you that your father has died."

I did not say a word. He said he had known I would take it like a man.

I saw many streets and houses. I was in a thousand rooms; I walked about, and sat, and lay down, and when I looked again I was no longer there. I heard a thousand voices. Some spoke only a word, and others seemed to go on speaking. I had a vision of my life, and there was an unreality about it. I would have to go out and take part in a world that was busy to no purpose. For I could only pretend to be interested.

There had been someone with me up to this point, but from now on I would be alone.

The coffin had been placed on the veranda. It was of some shining metal. Inside it my father lay on his back, dressed in a dark suit. I had never seen him in a dark suit.

Fifty yards away palm trees swayed in the breeze. Whitecaps were coming to shore, and the motorboat faced the chop of the waves. I could not believe that I was not in a dream. The coffin would be rolled away, and my father would come down to breakfast, dressed in a white suit as usual. I would hear his car driving away, and in a while I would go swimming, taking a book with me, and lie at the edge of the pool. For these were the summer holidays and there was all the time in the world.

We came out of the graveyard, my stepmother being supported by some male relative who had appeared for the occasion. Now that I think of it, Bitsy never seemed to have any relations. We did not know where she came from; she had entered our lives as though she had lighted from another planet. We had known nothing about her family or her past.

As I was going out of the gate a man whom I had seen in my father's office fell in step beside me. His name was Henriques—he was rather boring. Whenever I went to Duke Street he would smile and scrape, eager to please the son of his employer. He would make a joke of the kind that, he thought, would appeal to a schoolboy. He was too familiar.

He said, "I wish to offer my condolences. There are many people who say that Aston Simpson was a hard man. Notwithstanding, I feel that I can state that he was an outstanding member of the legal profession."

He continued in this vein for some moments. His face was soft and wrinkled, as though thousands of small cares had made their way across the surface, day by day, of his smiling affability. Now that his employer was dead he was free to speak, to make a frank estimate of Aston Simpson's qualities. Fearlessly he spoke his mind—and as he spoke he seemed to be aware that, at this time and place, what he had said was rude, that it showed his lack of breeding. And so he persisted, in order to find one sentence, after all, that would justify his bad manners. But the more he spoke the more foolish he sounded. Though my father was not there to hear him, he was still too familiar. He sounded impertinent. He became vindictive. Positively he was hissing. He spoke about an injustice, some matter of a brief that my father had accused him of drawing up wrongly.

"It was not nice to say that in front of the others. Moreover, in all matters of that sort, it was understood that Dennis was to be responsible, not myself. Aston Simpson was very rude on this occasion."

Alfred Henriques was still speaking when I turned away suddenly and went to the car where my brother was waiting. For some reason it had been understood, in making the funeral arrangements, that it would be necessary for my brother and myself to go to the graveyard in one car, and our stepmother in another.

We gathered to hear the reading of the will. It was clear and to the point. Herbert was to get a thousand pounds, my father's guns, and the *Encyclopaedia Britannica*. I was given five hundred pounds more—presumably because I was younger and had further to go—and a share in the guns and the *Encyclopaedia*. Aunt Ethel had a hundred pounds. Everything else went to his dear wife, Elizabeth. The house, the law firm, everything. Bitsy was now a rich woman.

My brother and I, said the lawyer, would have to find other accommodations. This was our father's intention. He certainly hadn't intended for Bitsy to support us. Nor was she responsible for my schooling—I would have to pay the fees myself.

When the lawyer had gone, and Aunt Ethel had gone too, saying, "Aston must have taken leave of his senses. To leave everything to that woman!"—my brother told me that we would have to leave the very next day. On this point he was certain—he could not wait to be out of sight of his stepmother.

I did not share Herbert's feelings. I was fond of Bitsy—and I didn't know what Aunt Ethel meant. Fifteen hundred pounds struck me as a fortune. But everyone seemed to be agreed that I had to leave. And Bitsy seemed to think so too. At least, she made no objection.

My brother and I would find a room somewhere. As the furniture as well as the house had been left to Bitsy, the beds in which we had slept since we were children also belonged to her and would have to stay.

So I said goodbye to my half-sister, Bitsy's child, and walked out of the house, carrying my clothes in a suitcase and my books in a box. I would have to come back later to get my bicycle. That was mine, Bitsy admitted—I had paid for it with money I had earned myself. But I would have to fetch it soon. She didn't want it lying around. The same went for the guns and the *Britannica*.

XVI

Jamaicans were struggling for Independence. At night in the streets a crowd would gather and throw stones at the English soldiers. The soldiers fired at the people, and they ran away, leaving two or three lying by the gutters. The next night they were back, to throw more stones.

At the same time a group of Jamaican writers were putting out a newspaper called *Public Opinion* in which they rallied the people to the cause of Independence. Together with news and editorials there were poems and short stories—written from a Leftist or at least a modern viewpoint.

I came to know these people—among them "Dossie" Carberry and a black poet named Campbell who wrote poems about night, flowers, love—and a young man named Smith who wrote sophisticated prose in which from time to time he used mathematic equations instead of sentences. Smith spoke of authors I had never heard of. In Britain, W. H. Auden and his friends. In America, William Saroyan and Thomas Wolfe. He mentioned a banned book called *Ulysses*—the way he talked about it, *Ulysses* was some sort of black magic.

I tried to read the writers Smith recommended and—with the exception of Wolfe and Saroyan—they struck me as too hard to understand. I admired them all the more. If I could only write like that! Though I couldn't, I tried to write something of my own that would be sophisticated and shocking—that would make people take notice. As I had nothing to say and no story to tell, I wrote confessions: I wrote about the girl I was in love with, in a sort of stream of consciousness—confessing how I felt about her and what I would like to do if I had the opportunity. I titled this "In Love and Puberty," and sent it to *Public Opinion,* thrilled and alarmed by my own daring. The story was published. Aunt Ethel read it and handed it back to me with a sniff. Evidently she thought it disgusting. I had succeeded! *Epater le bourgeois.* I too was now a member of the *avant-garde.* There would be no turning back.

When the English troops were called out and there was shooting in the streets, as I bicycled to meet my friends on *Public Opinion* I felt that I was being involved in a drama of revolution. No one took Jamaica seriously—it was just a place where they grew bananas. But now it had a revolution. It was making history. You could get killed if you weren't careful.

This thought made me happy; I stayed up late at night, writing poems and stories. It was like being in love . . . and, besides, I *was* in love. At night when I went back to the house where I shared a rented room with my brother, I was ecstatic. I could hardly keep from dancing. The smell of hibiscus and night jasmine, the stars, the shadows of the Blue Mountains looming by moonlight . . . I couldn't sleep for thinking of the philosophy of Marx—as explained by Smith—and some poems by D. H. Lawrence I had read, and Saroyan's *Daring Young Man on the Flying Trapeze.* All this was mixed up with Gloria's eyes and her figure in a bathing suit.

I was filled with impatience to be going about my life, starting my life's work, whatever it might be—I didn't much care. Looking back, I suppose that I intended to be a writer, but I am not at all sure. I think it would be truer to say that a writer was one of the things I intended to be, but that the thought of devoting myself to a profession had not yet become a reality with all its appalling implications. Young men think, when they think about their lives, that they haven't yet begun in earnest. They will get around to writing a masterpiece now and then, when they feel like it and have the time. They will write great novels and poems. But most of the time they will be having romantic adventures. They will run away with beautiful women. They will make speeches in Congress or Parliament. They will be sent to Siberia, and suffer hunger and cold. They will write with a splinter dipped in dye which they have obtained by boiling their shirt. All this without losing their good looks.

But being just a writer? God forbid! Working at it? A dismal prospect. The proper attitude for young men to have in regard to writing was expressed once and for all in the preface to Byron's first book, *Hours of Idleness,* where it says that he "handles his pen with the negligent ease of a gentleman."

But when would I be starting these adventures? In spite of my successes in the *Gleaner* and *Public Opinion,* and the fact that I had an audience—for there must have been others like my aunt who had been alarmed—in spite of being noticed by the world, I was still going to school. I was studying for an exam which, if I did well enough, would send me to Oxford.

I had already passed this exam. Moreover, I had taken it a year earlier than usual. This had put the noses of my enemies out of joint. For I had enemies at school, and they were in science. When the results of exams came in, and my name was at the top of the list, having got there through literature, history and French, instead of by means of physics and chemistry, these people were visibly disconcerted. They looked at me askance as though I must have cheated; they slinked away and whispered in corners. It had always been the science people who won scholarships to England. Now I had spoiled their plans. And what was I going to make of the success I had, in this surprising, somehow underhanded manner, wrenched out of their grasp? Not much, they wagered. Only poems and stories. They lurked and bided their time. They wished I would fall and break my neck.

Yes, Virginia, there are Two Cultures. But I have never felt sorry that I did not like physics and chemistry. Throughout my boyhood I was compelled to study them—I can't imagine what school it was that C. P. Snow attended, where the readers of poetry, it seems, were not compelled to study chemistry and physics. The moment I could close those infernal books I did so, and have never looked back.

It is said of the poet Gray that long after he left Eton he would have dreams in which he was still there—confined and subject to their rules. I too have dreamed that I am still at school. I am sitting in the classroom at night. It is like a lighted box, casting light outward on the barbecue. Other lighted boxes are visible in the dark. These boxes are fed electricity by a dynamo, throbbing on the far side of the barbecue, with now and then a change of sound and an uneasy flickering.

Islands of the night . . . and of the day. For by daylight it is no better. The sun shines every day and time is passing.

The sadness of the tropics is the thought of life vanishing without a mark. You are cut off from the world, and nothing you do will ever be noticed. The indifference of nature is felt more acutely in these out-of-the-way places. "Two things," says Grigoryev, "cry out continually in creation—the sea and man's soul." On an island, the sea is greater than the soul.

Once this was brought home to me when I was with my father. It was Christmas morning; we were in the motorboat, cruising near the Kingston docks. At one spot a crowd of people were getting into excursion launches. We saw one setting out, packed to the gunwales. My gaze wandered away—to the sky, the peninsula enclosing the harbor, a tanker making its way between the buoys. When I looked at the shore again, the boat of Christmas trippers had vanished. As I gazed, not realizing anything in particular, a moaning sound came from the docks. My father swung the boat in that direction. When we came to the place where the launch had been, only a hat or two floated on the water. The vessel had capsized, carrying forty souls to the bottom with scarcely a splash, and the shining sky was as clear as ever.

I dream that I am still at Hillcastle. Then someone enters, bringing the mail which arrives every night, and he hands me a letter. It tells me that I am to leave for America.

What rushing to pack my suitcase and say goodbye! But then things start to go wrong. I can't find something . . . that I must take with me. I seem to be moving more slowly, and my suitcase hasn't been packed. And the ship is leaving. It has already left. I have missed the connection—and am doomed to stay here forever, pacing the barbecue, from the main building to the wall—looking down at Alligator Pond and Black River and the empty sea stretching to the horizon.

But this did not happen. When my mother wrote to me I did, indeed, pack in a hurry. Would I like to come to New York for the summer? Indeed, I would. I would have gone anywhere—for all ways led in the same direction, toward my life.

Did I know that I would never be back? I don't think I knew, but unconsciously this may have been what I intended. In any case, a sea voyage and a summer in New York was enough. I did not need to think further than that.

The next day I waited by the road for the mail van. Every afternoon, just before dusk, it climbed the road to Hillcastle, having come through some forsaken country places. It stopped for a few minutes to drop a mail bag and take on another. Then it went around the road lined with willows and out the gate. It would go down the mountain to Balaclava, where it connected with the train. And the train would take me, huffing and clanking, with a smell of coal, by way of the cane fields, and the fields with stacks of logwood, and the slums, to Kingston. From there I would sail for New York.

I put my suitcase on the van and climbed on the front seat beside the driver. The van drove toward the gate. Two boys I knew were sitting on the wall, kicking their heels. They were startled to see me passing. One of them shouted "Where are you going?"

I shouted, "To America!"

2

ON LINE

My mother was renting an apartment in Manhattan, at 21 West 53rd Street where the Museum of Modern Art now stands. She was often absent on business, selling cosmetics, and the apartment was occupied by her sister Ruth and her niece Dorothy. They made up a bed for me on the couch.

On Friday I took the subway to my grandmother's apartment in Brooklyn. It was then I came to understand that we were Jews. It was a new idea; I had been brought up as a Christian and had no liking for the people I saw walking on Kingston Avenue: men in black overcoats and bowler hats, conversing in a strange tongue.

My grandmother showed me snapshots of our relatives in Russia. She had visited them only a few years before. They wore ill-fitting clothes and looked hopefully at the camera as though it might be able to help them.

I went to the World's Fair with my uncle Joe, to the theater with my aunts, and concerts at Lewisohn Stadium. But more than anything else I walked . . . all over Manhattan, absorbing sights and sounds. For soon I would be returning to Jamaica. I had to go back to school and take the Higher Schools examination a third time, in the hope of winning a scholarship and going to Oxford. And what if I didn't win one? They always went to some science or engineering student. And Britain was at war—I might be trapped in Jamaica for the duration, perhaps the rest of my life.

I was with my mother on a bus that passed Columbia University when she asked if I'd like to go there rather than back to Jamaica. She didn't have to ask twice. I applied to the College and was accepted, and when the Fall term began I had a room in John Jay Hall. I arranged my books on the shelf: the copy of *Pride and Prejudice* I had brought from Jamaica, A. C. Bradley's *Oxford Lectures on Poetry,* and a copy of Whitman's poems. I had a typewriter and radio, and was perfectly happy.

All students at Columbia had to take a course called Humanities, another called Contemporary Civilization and, to my dismay, a

65

course in science. In Humanities you discussed great books: works of history, philosophy, drama, epic poetry, and fiction, ranging from Homer to Kafka. In Contemporary Civilization you read excerpts from political science and sociology, and *The Making of the Modern Mind* by John Herman Randall, a book written in prose so clotted as to be indigestible.

For Humanities I drew Lionel Trilling. I took a course in English literature with Raymond Weaver who, it was said, had discovered "Billy Budd" and other tales by Herman Melville. Then I took a course with Mark Van Doren in the poetry of Thomas Hardy and W. B. Yeats.

Mark had no "teaching method"—we read poetry and exchanged ideas . . . that was all. Yet how much this was, with a mind like Mark's to act as guide and fill in the silences!

The university had a literary magazine, *The Columbia Review.* I submitted a poem, "Jamaica," and it was accepted.

> Far from your crumpled mountains, plains that vultures ponder,
> White gulches, wounded to pythons from gunshot of thunder:
> >   What should I sing in a city of stone,
> >   Drawing the bow across skull, across bone?

The stanzas and rhymes were an imitation of W. H. Auden—at that time Auden had a wide influence. I gave free rein to my fancy: the speaker's ancestors were a pirate and a "black and gold-hearted girl." She betrayed him to his enemies . . . "Still she cherished in womb the chromosomes for whiteness." The course in science had not been a total loss after all.

In one place I speak of "plump bourgeois banana's yellow skin" . . . a bow here to Marxist jargon. The poem concludes with a description of the island that shows how glad I was to get out of it:

> Life is a winter liner, here history passes
> Like tourists on top-decks, seeing the shore through sunglasses:
> >   And death, a delightful life-long disease,
> >   Sighs in sideways languor of twisted trees.

Here are other imitations of Auden: his seeing in some sad landscape the psychology of the people who live there; his personification of history; his up-to-date imagery: ocean liners, tourists, and sunglasses. The poem imitates the leftish attitudes of Auden, Stephen Spender, and their friends—young men who have gone to the best schools and universities.

A short story I published in *The Columbia Review,* "Abashev: The Doctor's Hands," shows that I have been reading Russian authors.

Every year Columbia published an anthology of students' poetry edited by Van Doren. I submitted some poems and they were accepted. These too were imitations . . . of T. S. Eliot:

> Late hours
> Are lonely. There are few things so alone
> As empty streets with one illumined window
> Hinting at people dancing to and fro . . .

and A. E. Housman:

> If Hell is not, nor fire
> I pray that they will be
> For that official liar
> Who took your life from me.

I took a swipe at a much-anthologized poem by Spender. "I think continually," I wrote, "of those who were never great."

In the summer of '42 I worked as a busboy at a resort in New Jersey. The guests were shipping clerks and bank tellers and stenographers from Newark. Besides waiting on table and washing up, the busboys and girls had to do chores, but in the intervals I would find an hour of solitude and row out on the lake. The water and sky were part of the nature I had known since a child—America wasn't all city streets and crowds. I shipped oars, let the boat drift, and read a book of poetry.

> Who, if I cried, would hear me among the angelic
> orders? And even if one of them suddenly
> pressed me against his heart, I should fade in the strength of his
> stronger existence. For Beauty's nothing
> but beginning of Terror we're still just able to bear . . .

I could not grasp the full meaning of Rilke's words, but they thrilled me like a clarion call to a higher existence.

America was at war, and with other of my classmates I waited to be drafted. In the meantime I studied and wrote—I was writing a novel. Twice a week I tutored two children and took them for a walk on Riverside Drive. It was so that I met the girl I have called Mona in a novel. She was pretty and flirtatious, and I fell in love. I brought her up to Columbia to show her how I lived. Then a friend informed me that she was meeting others. This made me miserable and I resolved never to see her again.

I entered the army in January 1943 and was assigned to a tank regiment in Texas for basic training.

Letters 1943–45

I have not revised these letters written during the war. If I corrected the spelling and punctuation I might be tempted to improve them in other ways. As they stand they are an authentic record.

From Mark Van Doren

393 Bleecker Street
New York   1/28/43

Dear Louis:

Let me call you that, since Mr. won't do now, and Pvt. is awkward.

In Texas! Well! And worried because life isn't hard! Don't worry, it will be hard enough. I've never heard that tanks are toys, and I'm confident that war at best is nothing to wish more of than one already has. Or less. Take what there is, Besonian, and be glad.

Columbia will miss you. As a matter of fact it will have to do without me this spring, since I am retiring to write a book about liberal education. The subject is important, but I'd rather be in a tank, and don't doubt that I mean it.

I've heard nothing from Holt about your book. This is probably a good sign, but I won't insist that it is, for luck. Don't you want me to try it elsewhere if they turn it down? I'll be glad to. But meanwhile I'll find out what Ted Hoffman knows about your wishes in the matter. And in any case the ms. will be taken good care of.

Please write as often as you please—and never if that pleases you. No obligation, surely. But I shall always be happy to hear from you.

Sincerely,
Mark Van Doren

To Mrs. Lawrence Cohn[1]

United States Army
[Camp Bowie, Texas]

Dear Mollie,

I feel a pig for enjoying your birthday candy so much & getting the cute card, & not replying yet. Alright, I'm a———, but you can wait till I get my furlough & then tell me off personally. That's a bargain for me, 'cos I won't be having a furlough till Xmas, it looks like. It's a military you know, but I'll be busy this summer somewheres, & Old N.Y. will be a ghost town, for I won't be there. Gosh my English is awful. The punctuation keys are missing in my pen, so please excuse, as our friends the Japs say.

This week I'm officers' orderly, & make their bunks, sweep floors, etc., pick up their litter, and look at their letters. Some private lives! And if you've ever seen an officer bawl out a G.I. soldier for flicking the ash from his cigar, you'll understand how indignant I am at picking up the piles of chewing gum, tobacco, & photos of Ann Sheridan which litter their lairs. Anyway, I get off at 2:00 p.m. & lie around nattily dressed till the boys come in from the tanks.

It's barely possible that us fellows with officers' I.Q.'s will get a chance to be officers, but I doubt it. Deep in this wilderness, where the only animal is a chow-hound, & the natives make their living by selling hot-dogs & cokes to soldiers from Brooklyn— deep, that is, in the heart of Texas, there seem to be no officers' schools, & no roads going there. But I think I'll get a chance at it—later on. Really tho', I don't mind being a "man in the ranks," tho I would like to throw cigarettes on the floor, & bawl out hard- working privates, like the looeys do.

Bob Hope gave a broadcast from here last night. About 12,000 fellows were in the audience, and as this is really a "tank

---

[1] Mollie and her sister, Dorothy Miller, were my mother's nieces and my cousins.

destroyers' " camp Bob kept making remarks about how the tanks are obsolete, & how the T.D.'s (destroyers) are tops; I'd like to see him up at Fort Knox, which is the tank center—I bet he tells them the tanks are O.K. If he got in front of one of these rolling houses with a few cannon & machine guns, not to mention the tracks, he'd talk a lot nicer about us, I'm sure. I'm now a truck driver, & hope to handle a tank soon; the trouble with tanks is not driving them, which is easy, but seeing that you don't wind up a street or a few people in the bogies.

Lately, on week-ends, I've been hitch-hiking a few hundred miles around Texas. It reminds me of Jersey, except for the statues of Lee, and the Mexican families, and the drawl which all Southern girls cultivate from having seen *Gone With the Wind;* and the sombreros & Harlem shirts the fellows where.(!) wear Of course I haven't met any snakes yet, but I expect to meet them next bivouac. I'm told, however, that some are friendly and only bite you, the others bite you and aren't friendly.

Write soon,

Love,
Louis

To Rosalind Marantz

United States Army

Dear Mom,

Thanks for writing so often—I really appreciate it.

Last week was a busy one. We went on an overnight march, in our tanks; we ate & slept out in the open. Isn't it funny—I never slept on the ground under an open sky till I came into the army. Of course it was cold, but we're all well dressed, and we must be getting tougher, for nobody I know got a cold, or ill. When we came back we cleaned up the tanks: they were chock full of dust. (You should see us after driving—we're all masked, in dirt!)

My basic training will be over in about 6 weeks' time—then I'll be able to get a 2-week furlough, I think.

I'm getting a job on the camp newspaper—this will be something special, outside of the routine training. I didn't want to take it at first, but some of the boys spoke up for me. Maybe I should have been more pushing—but I thought it might mean a "soft" job, white-collar work. And I don't want that. However, on thinking it over, I see it may mean advancement—& anyway, if they want a fellow for it, why not me? . . .

My Barnard friend hasn't written. We made a kind of agreement not to write. I hate dragging out things, to no purpose. Dots writes me short letters quite often, & Mollie too.

I'm glad you write so often. Sometimes I can't, & you'll understand.

I do hope we'll be able to travel north together.

Love,
Louis

To Dorothy Miller and Ruth Manners[2]

United States Army
[Fort Hood, Texas]

Dear Dots & Ruth,

I haven't written since we moved. We're now about 135 miles further south, & if they keep moving us we'll soon be in Mexico City, I hope. this camp is "Tank Destroyers," except for us, who're the only tank outfit. We're supposed to train with & against the "Destroyers"—so we're completely surrounded by hostile troops with calculating eyes & big guns.

Mother's written me a couple nice letters. She likes the climate immensely. It's really surprising how much the weather matters when you're travelling, or camping. It's not just conversation— but, if you're doing 3-hr. sentry duty you feel every degree on the thermometer.

Last night we marched 6 miles (marched, not drove) with full field equipment. When we were all bundled up, with about five straps going every which way, we looked like polar bears. Then we trampled gayly thru the woods. We sang everything from Dixie to Rule Brittania en route, that is, for the first five miles—then we just grunted & puffed. We landed up in a little hollow, pitched our tents, ate chow (with my influence I pulled strings, broke thru the red tape, & got a second helping of pie). Then we sang again around campfires—very bad from a military point of view, but lots of fun. We went to bed, which means an army blanket on pine needles. At 12:00 p.m. somebody ran down the hollow, pulling out tent ropes—we nearly got the———! but he ran too fast. Then we set our guards, & the jiu-jitsu sergeant tried to "jump" the guards & tie 'em up. We beat off that attack. The place was in bedlam. Then the captain came round & said: "If

---

[2] Ruth Manners was my mother's younger sister.

you———guys (or rather, "If you *gentlemen*") don't keep quiet now, we'll go for a 10 mile hike starting now"—dead silence. At 3:30 a.m. I went on guard & looked at the Texas sky. Went back to bed: had breakfast, etc. Then, just as we were moving out, gas was let loose from every direction. If you think your little nephew is lazy, you should see his speed when putting on a gas-mask. The other day I got a lungful of phosgene, & ever since then I've been fast, but *fast!* We got back to camp, checked equipment, & relaxed. This is Saturday evening, & my first chance to write since last Thursday, so here I am doing it.

Moving from one camp to another means packing tanks on a train, cleaning equipment etc. And I had guard duty one night. Boy, have I been busy!

Today we got another "shot" (inoculation). Honestly, I have more needle stuff in my veins than blood.

By the way, Dots, are you still giving out with the blood? And, of course, I want to be kept up to date on Ruth's progress avec les beaux yeux—is she back in circulation? And Grandma—is she kicking? I won't ask about Freddie & Lee & Bob—those kids are more than healthy & they should be in the marines.

Momma writes & asks me if I need any money. You should see how much cash I carry. There's nothing to spend our pay on, except ice-cream & cigarettes & we actually clink when we walk. I'd send some to you, to boost the home-front, but I'll be darned if I know how to.

Tonite there's a double feature at the movies—it's either "Frankenstein Returns Once More" or "Two-Gun Hogan," or something like that. I think I'll go. You should see my G.I. (Government Issue) haircut. It's about ¼ inch high, & 2 inches across.

I read that a radio star got slugged & robbed on 53rd St.—take care;—or maybe it was a Marantz job.

Write when you can, of course.

Love,
Louis

To Dorothy Miller and Ruth Manners

United States Army

Dear Girls,

I haven't written for a while, but I was in a place where a pen would've been a lot of extra weight anyway. We marched out a week ago and pitched tents on a commando course 11 mls. out of camp. Well, 11 mls. doesn't sound much, but it's another world entirely. Just like Bataan.

This course is the toughest in the U.S. Army. Not my imagination, but a matter of fact. When I tell you that several men have been killed training there, & that they've been hundreds of casualties in the short 6 months of its existence, you'll begin to see what we were in for. Maybe you've seen it in the newsreels. Some photographers from *Life* were up there to look at us take it, & a few generals, & some amused ladies. We weren't very amused though.

I won't give you a blow-by-blow description, but I'll try to give you an account of one day's training. There were seven days in all, without a break.

Up at 5:30 & ran out to the course. Took the obstacle course: this means we raced over a 10 ft. wall, up a hill, over a 15 ft. wall, under barbed wire with small bombs being thrown at & around us, climbed a 15 ft. rope, jumped a ditch, & climbed a 45° hill called "puke hill."

First class at 8:30 a.m. We ran between classes, in fact we were not allowed to walk anywhere. First class was, let's say, street fighting. We advanced down a village, supposed to be Nazi, firing as we went at silhouette targets. As all guns were loaded, & no "safeties" were used, we stood a good chance of being blown to——! There were also booby traps—dynamite that got you if you were careless.

Next class: judo, or dirty fighting. There we learned how to knife, break necks, etc.

Ran back to lunch—a mile. Had ½ an hour off, ran back to course.

1:00 p.m. went thru infiltration course. This is 50 yards of mud, strung with barbed wire. At one end are two machine guns. The whole course is heavily mined. To prepare us for actual battle, we were put thru this stretch—which I won't lie about—it was pretty tough.

You see, we lined up. Then the signal was given & a bomb exploded. We fell on our faces & the machine guns opened up, firing at us, eight inches over our heads. If we raised up a little too high, ——! At the same time, dynamite charges were exploded around us. All over the course there are crosses which mark the spot where some poor sucker put up his head, or a hand. We crawled thru this course as fast as we could, because the last guy in would have to do it again. When we tumbled into the trench at the end, a grenade was thrown at us, & we got out quick. We ate mud & liked it.

We did that particular course twice last week. The week before us, 13 men were hit on it. We were luckier.

I wouldn't be telling you all this if I didn't see the other fellows writing *their* folks about it, & I guess you can take it too.

Let's see—our last class of this day was woods fighting. Here again we stood a good chance of being shot from behind by some dope. No safeties on triggers.

Beside these classes, we had night fighting with pistols, ambushes, bomb-throwing, battle-firing.

I can tell you one thing: I'm a lot more hardened than I was 8 days ago. I have 16 scars on two hands, & lost 7 pounds. Also, I don't care any longer about grenades going off a foot away, or 30 caliber bullets over my head. That's the idea of commando training you see—to get rid of the kids. I was in there with the best of them, all the time, & I'm not a kid anymore, anyway.

To finish the week we had a double-time 5-mile hike, & my company won.

The idea of this training is to get us ready for battle, & if I ever had doubts that my outfit's going over, they've disappeared now. Of course I wouldn't tell Mother or Grandma this, but I had to get it off my chest, so I told you.

I just got a letter from Pops, & things seem to be looking up at home. I hear Ruth's taking that rest, & I'm glad, 'cos she needs it alright.

Mollie's candy box reached me, & it certainly went down well. It created, as the French or somebody says, a sensation. Candy here is eaten on a communist basis.

The tracer from Schrafts arrived, & I ate it too. Thanks much.

If you want to send me a carton of *Luckies* on my birthday I won't love you anymore, but I'll love you just as much.

Louis

P.S. even if you don't send them, anyway.

P.S.S. We just got helmets, & really look like soldiers. My basic's almost over, but I don't know if & when we get furloughs.

To Rosalind Marantz

United States Army

Dear Moms,

I lie on my bunk at about 9:00 p.m. & write. I hope I finish this before lights out. I wrote Herbert, or rather Dickie Ashenheim, as writing Herbert doesn't get results. I put in as strong & plain language as I could, how important the transfer of funds is. Hope it isn't too late.

I was very glad to hear you speak over such a long way. What I was trying to tell you when the censor cut in was really non-military, as it's in the newspapers: I'd just returned from a week of "commando" training. It was a tough but educating time. We climbed walls, dodged grenades & bullets, learned street-fighting & close combat, etc. After that, we went into spring training, which means days of firing on the range. The weather isn't cold anymore: no more frigid reveilles when you hate putting your feet on the floor.

At the end of spring training we should get furloughs. First furloughs will be given from May onward: tho', of course, I may not get a break till July. The furlough should be 15 days, maximum, which means about 5 days travelling, & 10 in New York.

I'm well as ever, & happy—plenty friends. You mustn't worry about me getting hurt, as you were over the phone—the army's safe enough, & a deal healthier than civilian life.

I got so much candy from Mollie & Nettie & Bob, & so many cards from the girls, together with cigarettes, that my birthday was very lush indeed, & my barracks bag bulges like a super Xmas Stocking. It's nice to think that, at 20, I've travelled so much & seen so much. Munro, Kingston, New York, & Jersey, & across to Texas, with plenty more to come—& I've had such variety:—Caribbean beaches, Columbia & Riverside Drive, 53rd St., the Army. I'm getting experience enough for another, real book, when I get back.

I got my permit today as a light truck & car driver. I'll soon be driving a tank, 32 tons, as well as most fellows in the outfit.

I just got your last letter in which you tell about buying me a lighter—silver too! you certainly treat me better than I deserve. That's not just what I would like—it's better than that, it's what I need. Matches are scarce, & a lighter will be very useful: I don't need a watch, & it would be broken in short time.

I almost forgot to tell you about the silver medal from Columbia. It's something good, I guess, but I just don't feel its importance so much. Not till after the war, anyway.

I think, like you, that planning for after-the-war is comforting, & it's as important as the war itself. I like to hear you talk of a home in N.Y., and all that goes with it. I have no ideas how long it'll take to get there, but we must plan always.

I guess you're right about going to N.Y. to help Ruth & Grandma. The family's the best thing we know, better than a steady job.

I'll write again, probably as soon as tomorrow.

> Love from,
> Louis

To Mrs. Lawrence Cohn

United States Army

Dear Mollie,

I disremember if I wrote you when I was at the U.S.O. in town, for I start a lot of letters & tear them up again—Coco-Cola & ice-cream gets all over them, eating between the lines as it were. But in tents, under the spreading cactus tree, with only snakes & sergeants to disturb me, I manage to write something.

I wrote Dots & thanked her—I thought I'd done it before. Maybe, the more I get like a soldier, the more I forget other things—I don't chew tobacco yet, however—tho' I *have* tried rolling my own.

We've been pretty busy. No sooner had we gotten set for the duration in barracks, with regular working days & weekends off, when we could go to Waco & serenade the cowgirls, than Headquarters decided to break up our enjoyable & super-civilian life.

"Enuff of this goldbricking," sed the C.O. "Enuff of these 6 cups of coffee per meal, and following of W.A.A.C.'s. Enuff of lying in bed till 12 in the morning, and breakfast in slippers. Too many men are gaining weight at the Govt's. expense. We must go to war."

So they moved us out, overnite really. We scrapped our silk kimonos, buried our cocktail shakers, packed up our pin-up girls in our portable sex sets, and, with nostalgic sighs, put on our leggings. Night marches, rocks for pillows, Texas mud, the unstable innards of a tank—these are now our lot. There's a stern austerity about our present life. On our marches we slopped thru so much water that we could be overseas without knowing it—the conditions are about the same.

Our Colonel, a gent with a gimlet eye & a tongue like a time-bomb, says we're a very advanced & on-the-ball bunch—we mite go into action sooner than usual. I hope so, 'cos I've got too much of Texas in mah blood.

P.S. I may get to officer's school soon. I sed "may."

Your report on "Junior Miss" Lee was fascinating. People do grow up à la Hollywood, after all. I suppose Freddie knows more Army slang than I do. I met a kid, about 8 yrs. old, who told me more about the Tank Corps than I ever knew. The younger generation (don't smile) will be all Mickey Rooneys, I expect. Such vitality is a little bit frightening.

I chased a lieutenant the other day—very exciting. I was riding my M.4 in 5th gear thru a big field, and this guy was taking a siesta under a bush, under the excuse of camouflage practice. When he saw 32 tons of Chrysler Corp. with me at the controls, coming at him, he ran for about 2 miles. He was a "Tank Destroyer," so the chase was rather gratifying. Our tank threw a track, so we spent last week with sledgehammers under it. I must be getting tough, 'cos the sledge bounced off me once, & I was too astonished to lie down. We certainly learn a lot, from how to tell a chigger bite from a tick, down to how K.P. can pay, in the way of stolen apples.

Love,
Louis

To Mrs. Lawrence Cohn

United States Army
[June 14, 1943]

Dear Mollie,

I hope *Esq.* & *The New Yorker* think as highly of my brain-children someday as you do now, so I'll be able to support myself at my own expense, instead of the government's.

You've lost the patter of little feet—today I'm recovering from the trample of hob-nailed boots, meaning the Colonel and his bar-boys, who inspected us yesterday. It's not enuff for them that we're a crack combat outfit—we must also make like window dummies. As the Colonel said, flicking a speck of dust from my collar with a horse-whip—"Suh, the Ahmy, and espeshully the Tank Cur, is attired, not merely dressed." (Fiction, of course. The Colonel wouldn't come within spitting distance of me personally. He raises an eyebrow, the Captain sneers, the second lieutenant glowers, the top-sergeant curses, and my platoon sergeant gives me K.P. These things have to go thru the proper channels.)

We did get complimented, tho'. My work in the tank earned the comment "this tank is in good condition" (posterity please quote) from the Major. And the Colonel said we were smart; that it would be unhealthy for any enemy outfit that met up with us right now, and that by September we'd be ready for combat. Farewell Texas. From now on, may all my snakes be pink ones.

On Friday we had a combat problem on which I was gunner, so I had a sweaty but swell time. The people who think up these courses must also do those children's puzzles which go from the town A to the seaside B, "how can Babs & Maisie get there without

1. breaking their necks over a 10 ft. hurdle
2. being sidetracked by a garrulous veteran of the Civil War
3. getting entangled with a python
4. getting into the White Slave market—?"

You see, not only did these lost geniuses dig ditches for our blind & awkward tanks, but they also swung silhouettes (Japs to us) from trees right under our bleedin' noses, planted anti-tank guns where we couldn't see them, mortars behind small pebbles, and infantry in ant-holes. I blew up 2 out of 4 targets with the 75 m.m., and got a few Japs with the machine gun—but I understand we were blown to blazes by a non-extant infantryman with an imaginary bazooka. So this letter comes to you via Ouija board.

I took new life again, however, on Saturday evening, and sped from the woods townward, clutching a week-end pass in my grubby paws. I should have stood in bed. We were standing in one place for 2 hrs., holding each other's thumbs up, while the landscape & sky were getting all set for a Hitchcock murder picture, Grade B. At 2 in the morning we got back to camp. Today we tried again. This time we got as far as Kileen, which is a thriving community for a couple thousand pale wives from New Jersey, all set to divorce their soldier husbands, about one thousand shoe-shine boys, all future Rockefellers, one brindle cow, and a Texan who just sits in the gutter and spits. When we got back this evening our lieutenant was sitting there with a smile, and sed: "You men just got back in time to do the day-room."

It is now seven, and I'm writing this from the cover of a friendly cactus plant, where even lieutenants fear to tread.

Love,
Louis

To Rosalind Marantz

Co. D A.S.T.U.
Louisiana State Univ.
Baton Rouge, LA.

Dear Mom,

I've gotten "adjusted" again to a new kind of life: maybe I'll have to get adjusted all over again in a few months to some other kind, but for the present this is alright. The actual school term hasn't begun, but till it does we are taking 3 class periods a day, to refresh us in the things we forgot when we quit high school. Where the wind blows, I follow.

I hope you get to Cuba or Mexico for the winter. I know how the cold treats you. But my greatest wish would be realised if we could only be together in New York for a short time. That is, after all, our home—and however happy we are to see each other in Waco, or any place anywhere, it isn't like being among people & streets we know. I feel like a stranger in the South; so do all the other boys. And their way of thinking is so different from ours.

I'm glad they've started sending you the allotments. You get more than $20.00 don't you? The govt. adds something, doesn't it? I'm sorry I had to send you the dunning telegram for $10.00, but I haven't been paid for over 2 months, and the situation was getting impossible—in spite of the $50.00 you had sent me. Changing places takes some money.

I shall certainly suggest to Herbie that he take the Ja.' Govts.' offer of medicine, and try to branch out into a new field. But will he even read my letter? I mean, will the words, written on paper, make enough impression in flesh & blood so he'll jump up & say: "Yes, I'll *see* about that . . ."?

I wonder.

I have some good friends here, who came with me from the Tank Corps. We have a lot of fun together: when you've been working in the field—and even in the kitchen—with fellows for 7 months, you have a close bond with them—I guess common experience counts even more than common ideas. And I'm making more friends among the men I've met since I came here.

Dots wrote me a nice letter. We were always good pals.

Don't send me any books, etc., Mom—not even my adored typewriter. I'm still in the Army, and every extra pound is an extra pain in the neck. Our equipment must be displayed in a certain way. We are marched to & from classes. We are checked for absence continually, even at night. Of course these trivialities are nothing, after the last months.

How does Grandma feel? I'm sure Ruthie will tackle her job as she did before, and make a go of it.

Write soon.

Love,
Louis

To Mrs. Lawrence Cohn

[Oct. '43]

Dear Mollie,

This comes to you snatched out of the teeth of time, which is a poetic sort of lie, because time is what I've got plenty of if nothing else, but the phrase is fine, and might adorn a book: ' "In Time's Teeth," a war novel;—in this epic of the Louisiana bayous . . .' but there I go, all schizophrenzic again. No, the fact is, as I lay dreaming under a mossy oak, waiting for an acorn to drop inter me mouth, and as the clouds went drifting by, and Grandpappy drifted by on his way to the Esquire outhouse—why, I sed to meself, this is a good time to rite them thar furriners up Nawth. So I plucked a feather out of the nearest available coed, and put pen to paper.

How are you-all? I guess Woodmere is in there pitching, with knitted socks, preserved turnips, and bottled applesauce for the service. Have any more saboteurs turned up on the Coney Island boardwalk? I always imagined you standing off a Nazi pilot with firm courage, like Mrs. Miniver, if you remember. I shall pray for any Nazi pilot who falls into your garden, what with Freddie so zealous, etc.

It looks like I won't get a chance at K.P. for a couple months yet, as I passed my mid-term exams. How such a mistake could have occurred I don't know, unless they're trying to keep me out of the line outfits, where I do most harm. Meanwhile, life goes on, in the good old Southern way of life, all magnolias and lynchings.

Every other day we go thru two hours of exercise, and if there's a job vacant in New York for rubber men and contortionists, you just tell them to hold it for me. What exact point of the Atlantic Charter is furthered by having me put the sole of my left foot under my right ear, I have yet to discover.

Is it true Broadway is lit up again? I may be home Xmas, if the hitch-hiking is good, and I hope to see it lit up like a Christmas tree.

Till then, as they say,
   auf wied . . .?
      auf weinest . . .
         au reveille

well, anyway, g'bye,
Louis
Avec amour

To Dorothy Miller

[Oct. 23, 1943]

Dear Dots,

This here missile comes to you from my post-exam brain, which is not in any too good shape. The tests weren't hard, but my studying wasn't too hard either, so they kind of cancelled each other. I may have made a B average. Anyway, I'm sure I passed. The Colonel promised us a week's furlough at Xmas, if we passed, so I guess my shining face will turn up on the doormat of the 53rd St. ménage, when snow & John Paul Jones are sifting thru the winter air. Sing ho for life! Banzai.

Talking to you all on long distance was a thrill, even tho it sounded something like this:
   Me: "Hello"
   Mom: "Hello"
   Both of us together: "Hello, how are you, take care of yourself, goodbye."
   Dots: "Hello"
   Me: "Hello"
   Dots: "This is Joey . . ."
   etc. . . .
There isn't much to report. I'm experimenting with a moustache; just for the sheer helluvit, and for a two-bits bet. Me and a few friends we jest sit around all day waiting for our moustaches to grow. I'm coming second, by a hair, but there are clear signs I'll get in the lead once I really get started. The odds are pretty even.

The Govt. still has an idea that we should go to bed & get out again early, and that we should work for a living, so I let Washington have its way, and listen to what my sergeant suggests. My former fighting outfit is on manoeuvers, and I hear they're going thru every kind of experience. If I go back to the line, I intend to get in the infantry. It's more pleasant to walk to a mess than to be jolted to it & then dumped in it, before even having a chance to see what you're getting into. Vague, but I hope you understand.

I'm writing Grandma, Mollie & everybody, soon as I can, which is this weekend.

Love,
Louis

To Mr. and Mrs. Lawrence Cohn

Co. A, 289 Inf.,
APO 451,
Fort Leonard Wood, Mo.

Dear Mollie & Larry,

I am in fatigue uniform with leggings, rifle belt, bayonet & rifle (first time I had one all my own) and feeling rakish as old ————, in a machine-gun squad in a rifle company in the mud in Missouri. We are going on manoeuvers soon and then somewhere else, on account of we all are advanced troops & the backbone of the nation. The tank corps has no more claim on me. I took the air corps test & was alright in the head and body, but I couldn't line up two cigarettes with pulley ropes at twenty feet, so they said I could not land a plane, and they would try to win the war in the air without me. Right away, however, an opportunity was found for me in the infantry. It is a nice place here, and I hope the Japanese have many camps like this. Alternating rain & snow, without turning a tap. If you think I am bitching to use a regulation army term, you are right, but I am really enjoying myself, and you get used to mud in no time. I take good care of my rifle. If you find a long hunting knife, send it to me, and I shall have it chained to my jaws so I can look like a Marine. My appetite has come back, and I sleep nights without having test papers and trignometric devils dancing on the next floor. The authorities are dissolving ASTP, so hah hah I was only one jump ahead of doom, and can talk down the small voice of conscience.

Thanks for the Xmas card, which was my first link with the old world. I have been thru so many states now I feel like a pioneer. Write soon, I hope.

Love,
Louis.

To Mrs. Lawrence Cohn

Dear Mollie,

Thanks muchly for the socks. We've been bivouacking in the snow, and our feet get coldest quickest, so my dogs extend their warm thanks too. In the process of getting ready for manoeuvers we've been taking long hikes with full packs, digging foxholes thru old Mother Rock, chasing an invisible enemy & being chased. You know the song about the Bear who went over the mountain & saw another mountain: well, that's the general idea, or rather, the General's idea.

I'm a machine-gunner, which means that whereas the riflemen only dig a foxhole, I dig a U-shaped deluxe gun emplacement, which is good for building up the back & arms. I also have a nice long knife & a carbine. They feed us too, to keep our appetite keen. After manoeuvers we should be something to see. Anyway, we breathe air, instead of that high octane gas which the tankers thrive on.

Mother's automatic watch is doing well, But I wish it wouldn't wake me up in the middle of the night to tell me the time. That's being a bit too independent.

I'm learning how to sew, & following the fundamentals you told me on furlough.

Love,
Louis

To Mrs. Lawrence Cohn

U.S. Army
[Feb. 18, 1944]

Dear Mollie,

For the last 4 days we dug holes & froze in them—so if my letters have been on the sorry side you know why. But today— well, let me make a short story long. Last nite we dug in as usual with our guns facing the red flags which, up to now, are our only enemy, and prepared to freeze. Would you believe it—it started to rain, even tho it was too cold for it. By Ripley, strictly. All of a sudden an order came that the situation was not tactical, & we could light fires & pitch tents. Well, I'm sure the only reason was that they didn't want us to get our equipment too wet, because that's bad for equipment.

Shouts of joy! We made fires, pitched tents in an old railroad bed, hit the hay.

Comes 3 A.M. Whoosh! A storm, including hail etc. hits us. I must have been drugged by the G.I. coffee, cos I slept right thru it. When I woke up at 6 however there was a river running thru my tent. Well, we rolled our blankets, made our packs, set out for the chow truck. There was a 20 ft creek in our railroad bed by now, and the first sergeant ses: "Cross over by these logs, boys! It only comes up to your ankles!" Well, his ankles must grow out of his neck, because my machine gun section gurgled & sank like a stone. If you've ever seen it in the movies it's funny. We got to chow with a strong breast-stroke, and ate heartily of dehydrated eggs & coffee dregs. But we finally got dried out, dug in again, and heard that the problem was called off till 3 (p.m.) tomorrow. The Colonel must have got his feet wet.

So the sun came out & we've got fires, and the P.X. truck sold us chocolates & smokes, & we washed down to our necks, cleaned our guns, & I got a letter from mother & a new *Time* magazine which ses our boys overseas are cold & wet—and I hope I go overseas so's I'll get some credit for being wet too.

Thanks for the Valentine Freddie, good for morale.

Love,
Louis

To Mrs. Lawrence Cohn

Mar. 9, 1944

Dear Mollie,

Thanks for the candy. Believe me, it was eaten, in the full sense of the term.

I'm on my way overseas—unless not being a citizen throws a last-minute wrench in the works. We get fed well, & can buy beer & baccy & go to the movies. We also wash.

I may be able to see youall before I go. If not, you can start the V-mail rolling.

Does Freddie read the comic books? I mean "Daredevil" & other such things. I hope not. There's a babe in my latest copy of "Daredevil" who lures men into her boudoir & stabs them to death. Very upsetting for my generation. I fear the effects upon the young of such printed matter.

Write old address, will you.

Love,
Louis

To Ruth Manners and Dorothy Miller

Pvt. Louis Simpson 32697552
Co. P. INF.
APO 15178, New York, N.Y.
Apr. 9, '44

Dear Ruth and Dots,

I'm in North Ireland, which is a lot better than a lot of other places. Cultivating a brogue, which together with my Southern drawl should be quite horrible. I've just finished eating a whole fried chicken, and once more broke my front tooth, but the chicken was good all the same. We really live well here, a great deal better than the natives—but so long as they can get some gum they're happy. They desire gum like some people yearn after likker. And their kids are born cussin.

You're allowed to send me a five pound package every month, *if I ask you to send it,* and you'll have to show my letter of request at the post office. So here I am requesting some candy. Write V-Mail only, as it's fastest. I can send you 50 pound packages, so if you find a German machine gun on your door-step, you'll know why.

Love,
Louis

To Mrs. Lawrence Cohn

Pvt. Louis Simpson 32697552
Co. G., 327 Glider Inf.
APO 472 c/o PM, New York, N.Y.
Apr. 27, 1944

Dear Mollie,

By now I've seen half the world from the soldier's viewpoint, and can tell you all about ships' holds, rats, docks, railroad sidings, coffee & doughnuts, cakes and ale, and the Irish brogue, the English accent, and, in fact everything which the civilian traveller pays little attention to. There may be ancient ruins and ghosts which invite study, but when a cold wind blows through them & down your neck, and there's an historic smell of generations of horse————one longs for the cafeteria smells of 6th Ave. Of course, certain things are the same over here; they have the same weird idea of time, and drag us out of bed at 6, if not earlier: the unsung heroes of this war, my two feet, are still struggling to keep their God-given curves, and I get hungry three times a day.

By some accident I've landed in a good camp, where they really feed us: we draw luxuries such as candy & cigarettes on a ration basis. But of course outside camp everything is rationed but good. By the way, I'm in England now.

I can't tell you what branch of the service I'm in, but I *can* give you my address. Maybe you'll guess the branch. My mail should arrive someday, so write like a good girl, will you.

Love,
Louis

To Mrs. Lawrence Cohn

Pvt. Louis Simpson 32697552
Co. G., 327 Glider Inf.
APO 472 c/o PM New York, N.Y.
May 9, 1944

Dear Mollie,

Here I am again spreading joy and light. But I must confess, if there weren't four———count them, four———beautiful blisters on my hooves, I'd probably be in town imbibing a little light . . . beer, and some Joyce—which is the name of a nice number from Churchill's garden—her only trouble is she walks like she has a lot of pent-up energy from working in a factory, while I walk like I've been walking all day. Irony of life, huh? Sometimes I wish I were in a soft outfit like the Rangers.

I'm so glad you're at the Red Cross and getting whistled at. I wish I could see the younger generation again just for a while; I can imagine Bob on a dance-floor, but Freddie eludes the imagination—I mean, I can see him singing Shoo Shoo Baby with one hand and thinking up Bob Hope cracks with the other. Lee must be quite a kid. Does she still collect stamps? I can get a lot of British Empire stuff for her, if she wants them.

Charlie Macarthy is on the radio with Ginny Simms and Veronica Lake, which makes my evening pretty good and I—typical gag: Waiter:–"You pay for everything here except the roof—that's on the house . . ." silly, but such fun. And here comes Mortimer Snerd! Oh yes, as I was saying I can almost forget the blisters. The program is a transcript recorded for the Armed Services. We get treated well, don't we?

Love,
Louis

To Mrs. Lawrence Cohn

> Pvt. Louis Simpson 32697552
> Co. G., 327 Glider Inf.
> APO 472, c/o PM New York, N.Y.
> May 21, 1944

Dear Cuzzin,

Don't you think I'd like to be back there writing a book? Of course you do, and I do. And I have material and it's coming at me so fast I'll probably spend the rest of me life trying to remember it. The [me] is Cockney. Local color and all that. It ud be a bloody proper shime if we didn't knock old Jerry off this year. I ope to send Gerhardt some Krauts for Christmas, in the coldest camp in Illinois.

We had a barn dance tonight, but I wasn't there. I took my girl to a pub instead, where she lapped up a vile mixture of beer and lemonade. Her last Yank is doing five years in the guardhouse for burglary. You know I'm actually starting to feel American. Some day the authorities may decide I'm a solid enough character to get my papers.

Yes, I do enjoy hearing about your maid trouble. I don't mean that, that way—because I expected her to become a sort of Southern Mammy—but such details do mean a lot, for the Army is becoming serious. I took it on only as a summer job, you know.

> Love.

To Mrs. Lawrence Cohn

> Pvt. Louis Simpson 32697552
> Co. G., 327 Glider Inf.
> APO 472, c/o PM New York, N.Y.
> May 27, 1944

Dear Molly,

This mail business is funny. I'm just now getting batches of your & Mom's mail, which read something like this: "When are you coming home on furlough?" or "Tomorrow you will be twenty-one." Eerie.

I'm lying on a blanket in the sunshine. Somebody opened a box of K rations and there was a can of Sunshine, 1 Day, m.f.d. Los Angeles, Calif.—wonderful what U.S. ingenuity will accomplish.

Your candy hasn't come yet. But I can wait.

How is Freddie growing on your cooking? Lee? Bobbie? I'm afraid I'm a disappointment to the Younger Gen:—no stripes, no

Love, no nuttin. Anyway, I lead an interesting life. Wish I could tell you about it.

Love,
Louis

To Dorothy Miller and Ruth Manners

Pvt. Louis Simpson 32697552
Co. G., 327 Glider Inf.
APO 472, c/o PM, New York, N.Y.

Dear Dots and Ruth,

This is from somewhere in France. I've been in combat, and I guess you can get the general idea from your papers. I'm very well, and feeling fine. I'll tell you the details later, and if it isn't the most exciting story you've ever heard, I'll eat a K ration—another one. My French has proved priceless—I scrounge up wine and vittles for my outfit, and introduce them aux demoiselles.

A batch of yours & Mom's mail came this evening—
I can't talk, and I'll split so I better stop.

Love,
Louis

To Mrs. Lawrence Cohn

Pvt. Louis Simpson 32697552
Co. G., 327 Glider Inf.
APO 472, c/o PM. New York, N.Y.
24 June, 1944

Dear Molly,

This is from somewhere in France, and I can only tell you I've been shot and bombed *at,* and I have an under shirt with a hole in it, also a zinc-lined stomach from K rations. I had a German rifle as a souvenir, but it was too heavy to carry—so you'll have to be content with the shirt, and the scar what goes inside it.

We're in no danger apart from getting killed. The cognac was also a menace, but all the bottles have gone down the drain now. My French came in useful for questioning prisoners and getting eggs, so you can tell Lee to study, because who knows she may be a WAC in the next war.

Love,
Louis

To Mrs. Lawrence Cohn

Pfc. Louis Simpson 32697552
Co. G., 327 Glider Inf.
APO 472, c/o PM, New York, N.Y.
July 3, 1944

Dear Molly,

I guess you'll get this after a heavy date with the U.S.O., but anyway listen to another bull session. I'm still in this wet hole. The local wine is off limits, and the local female talent looks best under a cow, I mean for comparison. The fighting, while we had it, was hottern hell, but the Air Corps and the Marines are winning the war, so we don't worry. The Germans take everything with them as they go, and the French hand us the bill. A simple plan for post-war Europe. Me, I plan to stay alive, so I can lie on a beach someday eating too much ice-cream and grunting whenever somebody stumbles over my lazy carcass. I also want to finish at Columbia, even though I probably won't graduate till the class of '54. You know, a few courses such as "Peace, it's wonderful" or "Work is hell." But everytime the 8th Ave. subway starts up I'll jump out of bed and grab for my shovel. And never say B-R-R-R-T!* behind me. I made a dirty crack about the Air Corps on p.I.—well, they certainly cleaned out Jerry above us. Only one bombing, and a Spit. pilot knocked down 2 Me 109's in 10 secs. flat over us. More fun in my next issue of Foxhole Frolics.

Love,
Louis

*Reader's note: This is the sound Jerry the Joker makes with his machine pistol.

To Rosalind Marantz

Pfc. Louis Simpson 32697552
Co. G., 327 Glider Inf.
APO 472, c/o P.M., New York, N.Y.

Dear Mom,

Of all people I want to write to you most, and yet, because of the mail service to S.A., I find it very difficult to get a steady correspondence going. I wrote you before France, during the invasion, and after my return safely to England—yet your letters don't indicate that you've received any such information. So I'm going to send all my letters to you by way of Ruth, and I hope the extra delay will be better so far as getting in touch, anyway.

I am back in camp training, for even though we did well in battle it's necessary always to review and re-equip, so that next time we can do better. The fighting was hot and terrible, but the Germans are showing clear signs of cracking up, and we can hope for an end soon. I can't say that I'll be back soon, or that I am not in danger, but remember that the job we're doing is more necessary than our own lives, and you needn't fear for me.

I had a full-length photograph taken in London at an expensive studio, and they are sending it on to you via A.S. Cullen. It was taken a week after I came back from France, and if I look well in it, that's because I had about $50.00 in my pocket and a whole week of leave in London ahead of me. Even the blitz by the robot bombs couldn't spoil my time. I went to shows, had a lot of dates, and went rowing on the Serpentine in Hyde Park. I know the West End pretty well, from Marble Arch to Piccadilly Circus.

There aren't any good plays in London, and very little music. I think the best of everything has moved [missing]

To Mrs. Lawrence Cohn

> Pfc. Louis Simpson
> Co. G., 327 Glider Inf.
> APO 472, c/o PM, New York, N.Y.

Dear Molly,

I'm lazing around after a 7-day furlough to London which was exciting and expensive. Exciting because of the [censored] for one thing—[censored] (silence)—[censored]!!! And London, esp. the West End, is like New York, with the added attraction that nobody knows you, and anyway Americans are expected to do the craziest available thing, which they do. It was all rather smashing.

Of course I saw Buckingham Palace and the Abbey and Big Ben, but only in passing, so to speak, from one pub to another. Many a sunny (yes, even in England) hour did I dally away rowing in Hyde Park—somebody took a picture of me being rowed by a nymph, me looking like an Eastern Potentate. Women do more for men here. A lot of G.I.'s are getting a lot of ideas from the Old World.

We (glider troops) now get paratroop pay. I'm due for the Purple ♡ also. And more rumors of other pay raises. Who'd be a civilian.

> Love,
> Louis

P.S. You should see our new boots.

To Dorothy Miller and Ruth Manners

July 24, 1944

Dear Dots and Ruth,

Did you get the French Invasion money? Sorry I told you about the close bullet. You know, I'm getting the Purple Heart, altho I only lost a little skin. But the best news is our raise in pay as airborne troops. I of course didn't tell Mom anything about the fighting. But you know I had to tell somebody, and when I come home in '50, the memory may be too dim.

I just got back from a 7 day furlough in London—the reward for France.

Well honey, I had the time of my life and that I'm still single is quite a miracle. I sowed some very wild oats, but it happens in the best of families and as ours is the best, it just had to happen. But before I lost consciousness and cash, I had a photograph taken— a big one—which I'll send you, so you can please send it on to Mom. You see it is very important as it marks an epoch in my crazy career.

I met some wonderful girls, one specially whom I took boating in Hyde Park and to a show. But I stood her up the next night and she stood me up the night after. Does it sound silly? It was.

I got the socks, Ruthie, they're wonderful, and the second pipe and candy, also *Time* mag. so I love you still. I'm paying for allotments to Mother, but she doesn't tell me if she gets the money.

London is a wonderful city. Just like N.Y. Of course I saw a lot of buzz bombs, and they really are hell, even if you don't worry about them. The English are a very great race however and take things in their stride without the dramatization Americans love. Any girl will show you a picture of her family and mention as tho it were funny, that they were blitzed and that brother John was killed in Africa last year. Sometimes this apparent coldness makes me shiver. I prefer our over-emphasis on the value of life.

Oh, I wish I were home, dears, and I think it may not be too long. Be good and write, will you?

Love,
Louis

To Mrs. Lawrence Cohn

Pfc. Louis Simpson 32697552
Co. G., 327 Glider Inf.
APO 472, c/o PM, New York, N.Y.

Aug. 28

Dear Cuzzin,

I am healthy in body & presumably mind, and am putting in a few hours of work per day as a gesture of gratitude to my draft board. I am terribly broke this week, but will be rich next. Meanwhile I sponge off my friends, so that I can slip away to the livid days and bilious nights of London. Apart from hearing that we will not return to civilian life on Z Day & 1, but will linger on to be rationed home on some obscure points scheme, I'm content. I also suffer from an Anglo-American contretemps with a nice English girl (wolf-cub she calls me), but I think I shall recover. Youth, you know, will out. I also suffer from a shortage of mail, but I guess you're so busy avoiding Navy characters with beards in the U.S.O. that tempus is very fugit. I hope the Navy's hand is so alcoholic it cuts its jugular vein when shaving, but let that pass.

Your son & daughter make me feel old. Ask Lee, (I got a letter from her) what she means by a "short snorter," and also send me a simple guide-book to American language. I dread my return in one way. Think of me sitting in class at dear Alma Mater surrounded by cheerful 18-year olds & being re-educated. There are only two sentences necessary to an Army man:

"Yes sir."

or, "Aw, go ———. .———. .———!"

How is Rockaway this summer? We had a nice summer here the week-end before last.

Love,
Louis

To Rosalind Marantz

Pfc. Louis Simpson 32697552
Co. G., 327 Glider Inf.
APO 472, c/o P.M. New York, N.Y.
Sept. 16

Dear Mom,

This is just to tell you I'm well and thinking of you. I get your letters, and I hope you get mine. I wish I could celebrate Xmas with you too, but you shouldn't even hope for it—count on Xmas 1946, but not before. In the meanwhile I [censored] and saving money too, which I couldn't do a few years ago. The world has certainly improved.

I would take notes if I were a methodical person, but any value

I get out of this war will be stored up in my bloodstream, not a matter of dates, but of attitude. Besides, I do not enjoy what I see, and the chief importance of these scenes is that I shall recall them against my will. I'll drown my memories in beer (larf).

Herbert wrote me a kind but rather remote letter. He is waiting to pass his law before going anywhere else. I wish he knew how precious every second of life is. The trouble with the tropics is no winter, and no war.

The girls write. So did Grandma & Pops. They had a bang-up wedding in D.C.

Love,
Louis

To Rosalind Marantz

Pfc. Louis Simpson 32697552
Co. G., 327 Glider Inf.
APO 472, c/o P.M. New York, N.Y.
Sept. 29

Dear Mom,

This comes to you from, of all places, Holland. I'm well and generally alright. I got your two letters together yesterday, & one from Mollie. They write pretty often from N.Y.—Well, in answer to your questions, all I can tell you about a glider is that it's what the gentleman you mentioned said it was—yes, that's how we go places. *Time* magazine comes too, and is all my reading material. Thanks for keeping an eye on my investments, etc. I'm glad they had a fine time at Eugene's wedding. It's a little hard to understand why some people should be blown to bits while others have it easy, but I guess that's the way it goes.

Love,
Louis

To Ruth Manners

Pfc. Louis Simpson 32697552
Co. G., 327 Glider Inf.
APO 472, c/o P.M. New York, N.Y.
Sept. 29

Dear Ruth,

I am in Holland. I'm well and doing alright. If I can get my hands on a pair of wooden shoes I'll send them to you. In the meanwhile will you please get your hands on a few pairs of warm socks size 10 and send them to me. Also—very important—a pair of leather gloves with a fur lining—not too bulky, but warm. Also candy—peanut brittle, chocolates if possible (plenty)—& a new pipe & tobacco pouch.

Sounds greedy, but you know.

Love to everybody, and above all, write.

Love,
Louis

To Mrs. Lawrence Cohn

Pfc. Louis Simpson 32697552
Co. G., 327 Glider Inf.
APO 472, c/o P.M. New York, N.Y.
Sept. 30

Dear Mollie,

Holland is a fat country and if I could speak double-talk I'd probably get fat too, but I guess I'll have to get back to France. I wish somebody had warned me in school that I'd one day be a wanderer across the face of Europe, not to mention Asia, and I'd have concentrated on languages. You can hold me up to the young ones as a horrible example of what will happen to *them* if they don't know their irregular verbs. Somebody else will get the schnapps, the souvenirs, the frauleins.

Today I had a shower and lost my nice warm crust, also the barnyard smell which Elisabeth Arden will never capture in a bottle, and takes nights of sleeping with chickens, cows and pigs to cultivate.

All this sounds fairly dull, but the true story, which would raise your scalp, is censorable. I shall tell you if & when.

Love,
Louis

To Rosalind Marantz

Pvt. Louis Simpson 32697552
Co. G., 327 Glider Inf.
APO 472, c/o P.M. New York, N.Y.
Oct. 18, '44

Dear Mom,

This is to let you know I'm alright, except for an abscessed tooth which I'm having treated right now.

I wish I could get in touch with that portrait studio in London—either they take an extraordinary time to deliver, or they specialise in swindling servicemen. If I see England again, I shall go there and find out. Anyway I'll have another portrait taken and sent on to you via New York.

The girls write pretty often, but you're my best correspondent. Mail is really our only reminder of normal life, and means everything. Give a soldier a letter, a plate of hot chow, a clean pair of socks and a dry blanket, and he thinks he's in heaven.

Holland is a beautiful country—rich, up to date, cultivated. At the clinic where I am being treated there was a small floor show, and three of the girls who sang looked just like American High School girls. They got a big hand. The people are friendly, and seem to have every good quality. The French were poor and inferior in comparison.

I shall write Herbert & try to bridge the gap. Please really try to get him to the States. I hope you go to N.Y. yourself for a while, to see the family.

Love,
Louis

To Mrs. Lawrence Cohn

Pvt. Louis Simpson 32697552
Co. G., 327 Glider Inf.
APO 472, c/o P.M. New York, N.Y.
Oct. 19, '44

Dear Mollie,

This edition comes from a little hospital where I'm having an abscess treated before returning to duty.

Well, as I say to all my friends, Xmas is coming. The Army has an excellent Xmas package service. Get it?

I have been busted to private again for mislaying a radio in the shock of war, but I have every hope that, owing to his industry, courage, character & long years of service, the year 1945 shall once more see Louis Simpson a p.f.c. But when the Germans have about fifty 88 m.m. guns firing at you, not to mention hand grenades and machine guns—well, it doesn't really matter about stripes. Then, to use the immortal words of General Grant:

"Dig, brother, dig like ———!"

The only souvenir I have is a Belgian pistol, a neat 32., which I mean to bring back to old Morningside Drive and open business with. Lugers are scarce in my line of work: some rifleman always frisks Fritz first, while I am busy running messages such as: "Cap'n, Lieutenant Scheitzelburg reports three panzer divisions moving up on his lead squad. What does he do now?" In short, I miss the laurels, if not the lead.

Love,
Louis

To Rosalind Marantz

Pfc. Louis Simpson 32697552
Co. G, 327 Glider Inf.
APO 472, c/o P.M. New York, N.Y.
Oct. 29

Dear Mom,

I'm still in [censored] and still well; I had an abscess, but had it treated and a tooth (one of the broken ones) pulled. I haven't had any mail from you lately, but I expect it all at once.

This country is very modern, and the schools, hospitals, etc. are as good as anything in the U.S. Of course, I've spent most of my time in the mud, but, the war forgotten, this is a swell country. Yet I haven't seen any place this side of the Atlantic I want to stay, you know what I mean. I tried to get a [censored] doll, or some [censored] for you, but after these years there's only junk in the stores. You can't imagine how bare of luxuries their lives are—a cake of soap or a pack of cigarettes is worth much more than money to them. Prices are sky-high too. Keep writing, I will when I can.

Love,
Louis

To Mrs. Lawrence Cohn

Pfc. Louis Simpson 32697552
Co. G, 327 Glider Inf.
APO 472, c/o P.M. N.Y., N.Y.
2 Nov. '44

Dear Molly,

Some of the boys went to Brussels & you should hear the stories they tell. 26 plus flavors of ice-cream, cognac, feather beds, beaucoup de belles femmes, kudos, kisses etc. When they pulled out a cigarette three waiters lit it, etc. Allowing for the over-heated soul of the dogface fresh from his dugout, one must admit that it sounds swell, and if I can, I shall.

The other night we had a good old-fashioned Halloween, fireworks and all. I do hope however that I'm not around for New Year's. We had a movie the other day and just as Harry James hit a high note the celluloid burned up, so we don't know how it ended. That's what makes war rugged. But when things get tough I read Lil Abner and think of *his* troubles, come Sadie Hawkins. Not to mention Burma's.

You see what two years of college has done for me. Oh yes, and two years as the life of the army latrine. Tell Freddie to move over.

I shall send you quelquechose for Christmas maybe.

Love,
Louis

To Rosalind Marantz

Pfc. Louis Simpson 32697552
Co. G, 327 Glider Inf.
APO 472, c/o P.M. New York, N.Y.
17 Nov. 44

Dear Mom,

I'm well and satisfied esp. when I get mail from home. Haven't had much lately, owing to the snafu around here, but Dot & Ruth say there's plenty en route, so I have something to look forward to.

Don't worry about me. I have been, as you put it, "in extreme danger," but that time is past, and I think it will be easier now. Of course, living conditions are hard, mud everywhere, but bearable. You know, I'd write you longer letters, but these single V-Mail sheets get thru quicker. I hope you can manage the travelling without hurting yourself. Cuba should be pleasant.

What worries me is the thought that, after the war, I won't be able to make enough to keep us, not if I want to finish college. And even if I finish, my kind of work is precarious. But then, it's the only work I like, and I know I can get to the top—granted a little time.—About Herbert. I hate to say it, but if he doesn't write, I wouldn't like you to risk another mess in Jamaica.

Love,
Louis

To Rosalind Marantz

7 Dec. '44
[Rheims]
France

Dear Mom,

The company's mail-clerk has gone to Paris for two days, and I've taken over—so I have a little time this morning to write you.

I got a pair of leather gloves with fur from Mollie, rather, I should say—from you, via Molly. They're very good and I'll do my best not to lose them. I have a surprise for you too, a small French gift, but I doubt if you'll get it until long after Xmas. I wanted to get something for everybody, but the exchange is so unfavorable that I just couldn't. So I sent you a present, and Grandma, and Ruth and Dot—but that's all.

On Saturday I'm going to Paris. These passes are hard to get, so I'm lucky. You don't know how glad I am that I can speak French—it makes all the difference. Instead of being surrounded by a blank wall of silence, I can strike up a conversation on the wine, or the "Boches," or "les Americains." They are voluble when they discover "on parle francais," and speak so fast I think they have been stuffed with opinions which they could not express before. I asked one old workman the other night if he knew an open café, and before I could escape I had to listen to his views on the merchants "who sold only to the Boches," and collaborators in general. I gave him some cigarettes, for which he shook my hand near off, and he said he had not had a drink in four months. I have found a washerwoman in a village near camp who does my laundry. Of course I supply the soap.

The amazing thing however is the abundance of jewels, expensive clothes and luxuries in the stores. It proves what I read, that the Germans meant to keep France in the state of a mistress, that is, to allow her everything her heart desired except liberty and honor . . . and bread.

The boys are rather disappointed that life is not as gay and licentious as the stories tell of France—but when one remembers that the people are religious and that a French peasant is reputedly the most shrewd bargainer, it is easy to understand why—I think the French women are much more decent, and more attractively dressed, than the English.

I sent Herbert a card for Christmas. Did you hear from him?

I hope you carry out your wish of going to New York in January.

I can't see the reason for your driving yourself—of course it is better to be busy, but not so busy you can't see the family.

Last, I got your picture, the one taken beside the plane. You look beautiful, and one of the fellows asked me "who the movie-star was." So you see . . .

Love,
Louis

To Ruth Manners and Dorothy Miller

Dec. 14, 1944

Dear Femmes,

This is the Parisian Story, so lean back and breathe deep. o.k. Dot, put that novel down.

Well, they allow a certain small number of combat troops to go to Paris every other day. I was lucky on the draw and got in the second bunch. So I polished up my p-trooper boots, brushed up my good conduct medal, put 4000 francs in my socks, and two cartons of cigarettes in my bedroll, and—on a cold French morning the convoy pulled out. Not toward Germany this time, but to Paris, fabulous Paris.

We rolled over miles of wide open farming country, freezing of course, and looking at the old wrecks of tanks, trucks etc. along the banks, which had happened to get in the way of General Patton.

Well, at last we crossed a couple of bridges and even tho it was snowing we saw we were there. We stopped in front of a hotel, about the best in Paris, and they took us in and gave us ration cards for meals—you can't eat outside the Red Cross—and we went up to our room. Millionaires used to live there once. We had hot showers and beds, real beds with mattresses.

Well, we ate downstairs and went over to a manicurist, where we had our hands held. Then, mes cheries, we stepped out into the Rue de Main Drag. The first thing that struck our eye were—guess—well you're right. They were, they are, beautiful. All shapes and sizes and all beautiful. And they dress to beat anything I ever saw, and that includes N.Y.C. They don't have the materials—I mean dress materials, but they roll their own, but good.

To top it all, they think Americans are something straight from heaven, and they give the snazzy airborne uniform a definitely venez-ici look.

That being Sunday, I couldn't buy any presents—that's why the bunch I sent you are so ordinary. But they have them, furs, jewelry, silk thingamejigs, perfume—everything, in profusion. Of course when the dollar drops into the franc it sinks, so I couldn't have bought much anyhow. A silk bandana, like the one I sent Mom, costs 1,760 francs—that's 35 bucks.

All thru the town there are hotels for troops, where they have dancing, the best orchestras, floor shows—free. I never saw the Folies—that was at Montmartre, as you know Ruth, and I did all my serious savagery in Pigalle. I only saw the Colonne de la Vendome from a distance: I didn't see Notre Dame, or the Eiffel Tower. There were bus tours for us, and shopping tours conducted by bi-lingual French girls, but I took off for a cafe with four other airbornes.

Cognac is 20 francs a shot, like whiskey back home, and it goes down very smoothly with beer. You get a high glow, but you don't get violent. We imbibed our way downtown, my French getting more venaculer at every stop, and finally we got to this place Pigalle by the Metro . . . that's their subway you know.

Pigalle is a sort of little Coney Island, and if you ask the orchestra to play your favorite polka, they do. Only afterwards do they blackjack you and roll you. And of course the midinettes, Toulouse-Lautrec.

In that way 24 hours went, leaving us and then 24 which went too.[3] But even though it was Monday the shops were closed, to save electricity. So I wandered around a sort of artist's hangout where they paint and sell their stuff on the sidewalks. I was going to buy a bright painting of the F.F.I. slaughtering Germans on the barricades, to send to you, but it was too big to pack back. Besides I thought the day was young. It wasn't.

Well, two of us wound up in a sort of night-club, and there, at another table were two pipperoos—something like Danielle Darrieux, and her kid sister. Well, says Gordon, you speak French what are you waiting for, anyhow? I ses let's have a couple more and you come too. So we crossed that dance floor, and all those people watched us. It was like when the Germans get the range on you and shrapnel snarls at you, or a bullet sort of burns your cheek. Anyway we made it, no litter cases.

"Veuillez boire avec nous?"

[3] The V-mail letter was lost; this is a typed copy. I think "leaving us and then 24" should read "leaving us another 24."

"Si."

And we sat down, and everything I said went double. They laughed like anything at everything, and told us how they lived at Deauville on the sea and were fashion designers, and made their own clothes, and we gave them chocolate. That caused a sensation. We walked them to their train and said goodbye.

Then we wound up in Pigalle again.

On Tuesday morning when we were rounded up to get on the trucks it seemed that all Paris was walking by. It was torture. The fellows kept making a last dash for a quick one, and a character gave a sidewalk imitation of a French banker at the Opera, with a concertina tophat, cigar and cane—and his G.I. uniform.

How they ever got that bunch back to camp, beats me, but they did.

And to think there are soldiers who are actually stationed in Paris!

Well, to return to realities . . . I'm back in regular training, with nothing but my memories, movies, chow and hope, to sustain me. It's muddy here.

I'm sending you a hundred bucks in this letter, for my career. That makes $150 I've snatched out of the paws of Paris and I hope it all gets to you alright.

Your packages haven't come yet.

The gloves Mollie sent, did come. They are good, and I mean to write her about them. So did your letter with the needed addresses. Columbia also sent me some addresses of old '44 classmates. One's in France too. The non-graduates of '44, la la.

I am eligible for a 30-day furlough for the states, but they draw only 8 for the regiment out of a hat every month—so no soap.

Mom sent me a swell photo of herself getting on or off a plane. The boys think she's something. If I can get one taken in a nearby town, I'll send it to you.

I get my laundry done by a French family in town, and instead of ventilating the shirts and crumpling the pants as the G.I. laundry does, they turn out a press-job for just a few francs.

I hope the ship hasn't sunk with my Xmas packages. If it has, I shall begin to dislike the Germans.

The day after tomorrow I'm on wood-chopping detail: "Pfc. Simpson will report to Capt.———with axe, canteen, first aid packet." My aching back.

I turned in my pistol to the supply-room.

And that's all for now.

You can now wake up Dot. Ruthie, I think you're smoking too much.

Goodnight.
Love,
Louis

P.S.—A day later—the Xmas packages are coming thru—one from Grandma with eats.

To Mrs. Lawrence Cohn[4]

Merry Xmas 1944

Dear Mollie,

Frighten the kids with this, come Xmas.

Hope to be bouncing something older on my knee.

Love,
Louis

P.S. Chimes to you-all.

To Rosalind Marantz[5]

[Rheims, France
Dec. '44]

Dear Mom,

I hope you have a happy Christmas, wherever you are.

I wish I could be with you.

But next time, perhaps.

Love,
Louis

To Rosalind Marantz

March 9th [1945]

Dear Mom,

I'm writing this with the wonderful present that just came from you. The Venus pen. My job now surely needs a pen as I have to handle the company's mail and money orders, and I was waiting eagerly for it. The box came in perfect shape because it was well packed—so many of the fellows get packages broken and spoiled just because somebody wouldn't take the extra trouble.

The socks of course are fine, and warm, and you know what that

[4] This was written on the back of a picture postcard that showed an American soldier holding a little French boy on one knee, a little French girl on the other.
[5] This was written on the back of a picture postcard. It showed a soldier climbing the Eiffel Tower and waving a sprig of holly.

means to me after my recent illness. The fruit cake looks and smells super; I'm saving it for a Sunday blow-out, together with the sardines. We don't get enough fruit here, so the figs were a good thought. In fact, it was the best package I've had this year, and really brought me a whiff of Xmas, even in March. It reminds me of when I was a kid at Munro and you used to send me mysterious packages, which, to me and the other kids, seemed to come from the end of the world. Well, we're still kids, insofar as little things mean a great deal. I haven't got any expensive ideas yet.

As I told you, I'm handling a lot of money nowadays, and I have to keep many details in mind—it's the first time I've had a job like that, and it's different from the rather easy, though exhausting, routine of drill and combat training. Of course this kind of work is done within a rifle company, so I still go into combat; you mustn't hope for any "soft" spot for me. There won't be any soft spots for Americans for a long time.

I have been awarded the Bronze Star; did I tell you? The girls write regularly. I sent home $80 to Ruth two days ago, toward my postwar plans. I may be able to save a tidy sum at this rate. I make about $120 per month including flying pay—which is rather uncertain—plus my allotment. There's nothing to buy either, except when, once in a blue moon, we get a Paris or London pass.

I'm very glad to hear about your stay in New York and I hope you'll be able to tell me more about what you did—special things like shows, or just ordinary things like walking in Central Park— for it's a long time since we did them together, and to hear you tell of them would make me almost feel that I'd been there too. I can imagine how it was at Grandma's. I'm glad she liked the brooch. I haven't got any letters from the rest of the girls yet saying they got my presents. I hope you liked yours. The French girl said it would suit you, when I was hanging over the counter trying to make up my mind.

The light—which is a hank of rope stuck in a gasoline bottle, is throwing soot all over the tent, so I guess I'd better put it out. Write soon and tell me if you were able to stop in Kingston and see Herbert, and how you are feeling, and if the work is more pleasant than last time. Dot says you looked fine when you came to N.Y. Have you got a picture? I'll try to have one made in a small town nearby.

Love,
Louis

To Mrs. Lawrence Cohn

13th Mar. '45
France

Dear Molly,

Thanks much for the all-purpose package, and the socks. I use everything you sent, and where I'm at we can't buy anything in the P.X. but candy and cigarettes (yes, cigarettes, remember? the little pre-war gadgets people bought); I was going to send you some cigarettes for Xmas, but I read that all the girls are smoking pipes now, and chewing tobacco, and I couldn't find any plug-cut. I'm sorry to hear you had an annoying woman around the Red Cross insulting the sailors. I can't say too much for the Navy, but I dislike bad women even more. My "poor cold feet" are still poor on cold mornings, so I stay in my sleeping-bag till some of the other boys get up & fix the stove, then I dash out to reveille and stagger back to bed. If there are flapjacks for breakfast I might get up, otherwise I sleep thru to 8 a.m., when I have to rise but be darned if I'll shine.

I'm making so much money now that, if I didn't have a boy in the service, namely me, I wouldn't mind the war at all. I never had so much pocket-money before, or so many people around with their hands in my pocket. Vive la France. In case you don't know, I am in the 101st Airborne Division—the secret is out, the dark curtain of censorship has risen, by permission. I stand before you unmasked.

I had a nice front tooth put in at Paris, but I lost it around here, I think at a girl's house—I was going with her for a while, but we parted—of course I dramatically drank all her papa's cognac before I left, exclaiming in French (sly dog) "Tomorrow who knows" and other excerpts from high-school French such as "My Aunt's pen is in the garden, but where is the cat." Thus, with Act 5 flourishes of despair I got thru a great deal of liquid, but such is the malignancy of fate that I lost my tooth in the ending scene, and was in no condition to find it—cognac is like that. Anyway, I have in mind a striking epilogue to my amour. As the door slams behind me and I stagger down the street singing "Boola boola," the young 'lady' shrugs her shoulders and says "Zese Americans! Quels saluds!"

And she throws herself into a chair.

Right on my lost tooth, which bites her! Au derriére.

You see the irony, the almost Shakespearian climax . . . contact Moss Hart please, if not Jimmy Savo.

Give Freddie a pat for me, and tell Lee she writes nice letters, and I'm going to write Bobby myself soon.

Love,
Louis

T/5 Louis Simpson 32697552

To Rosalind Marantz

T/5 Louis Simpson 32697552
Co. G., 327 Glider Inf.
APO 472, c/o P.M. New York, N.Y.

Dear Mom,

Just got your letter from Curacao, and agree that the Dutch are very nice people, except that the way I saw them I thought they weren't exactly overjoyed to see us. You see, these people think we're Santa Claus, which we aren't, merely good boys trying to do a job we never relished.

Today is officially a Victory day, because the Germans have signed certain pieces of paper, but of course with Germans that means nothing, and there's a big mess in front of us. Routine with us is the same. We are a little bit cynical about Santa Claus. Not like 1918 when everybody kissed the mademoiselles, got drunk, and went home, and talked about the Argonne. I tell you, Mom, these people are so corrupt, beaten up, and foxy, that the very sunshine in Europe seems like a good bottle of old wine that's been left to get sour. Lord how we long for a clear American day, with decent people walking the streets, and smiling because they mean it, not because they've been told to, or because they want "shockolade" or "zigarretten." The women are the worst. They know we are not allowed to talk to them, and they try their best to get us in trouble. Really, the only way to treat them is coldly, as if they don't even exist.

The girls are swell with the mail. I keep sending Ruth slugs of my monthly pay, which must be a small headache, but she never kicks about doing chores like that. She's the practical one. Dot's letters are good morale-builders, because we understand each other so well, and she's really able to say the darnedst things in the cutest way. Even Nettie and Bobbie and Freddie and Lee have written me. You know those kids frighten me. I was never that smart or chipper, or had such a bright outlook on things. Bobbie has some sort of idea about joining the Marines, but if I have anything to say about it, he won't. The U.S. has enough men now to finish this filthy war, and I don't see why anymore clean kids should get into it. War is something we have to do, not something we should want to do, and if it's necessary, it's certainly not good. The first thing I'm going to do when I get home is take a bath.

Then I'm going to buy a record-changer, and play Gershwin till I'm good and sick of it. And then I'll go to a musical. And then I'll see the city. Write often.

Love,
Louis

To Elise Cohn[6]

Germany
13 May '45

Dear Lee, (& Whoever else is looking over your shoulder)

This is Sunday and I've been framed into taking Charge of Quarters, while all the smart boys are out riding or mountain-climbing . . . the war being over . . . so I'm writing this while I can get close to a typewriter. It's a German typewriter, so don't be at all surprised by the queer things it does.

You want to know what a T/5 is. Well, every now and then the Army finds itself confronted by a queer animal, which can read two-syllable words, which has an almost intelligent look on its face when you pat it on the head, and yet which goes to sleep during drill, and only wakes up when a shell goes off right under its tail. Well, they call it a technician, pay it more, and leave it alone with its bones. I am one.

I've been in this beautiful country for a while now, and have found out a couple things. First, nobody here was a Nazi, they are all good people who like to yodel, and all the wicked Storm-troopers are in the next town . . . when you get to the next town, they tell you there are no bad people there either . . . they are all in the town you just left. And why did we bomb them, and kill all those women and children. Güten mörgen!

You ask me if I've learned French. Why Lee, I'm almost an Apache. The last time I saw Paris I used to climb over the hospital wall and toddle down the metro to Montmartre, and when the M.P.'s came up to me and said, gently (stroking their clubs)

---

[6] Daughter of Mr. and Mrs. Lawrence Cohn. Elise had a younger brother, Alfred, referred to in these letters as Freddie.

"Soldier, let me see your pass!" . . . I'd answer, "Je suis le frère de cette mademoiselle-ci. Je viens du Midi pour vendre les pomme de terre."—Translate that, kid.

If I have la bonne chance I'll have me a furlough to the Riviera, where the sands are white, the Mediterranean is blue, and the Army lets you do anything for a week, but anything, from surf-riding to art.

The way it looks, I'll be spending some time in the Army of Occupation. I won't get a chance to see the Pacific theater . . . I hope. Romantic as it may be to sit around a café saying "Remember Bill the time them Heinies had us surrounded before breakfast, and remember the churchyard at Veighel when they near blew us out our holes, or the time at Carentan when they were waiting for us on the canal-bank . . ." romantic as all this sounds, I don't know any sane people who ever want to smell it again.

The roads are clogged with Frenchmen, Poles, Italians, every nationality under the sun, trying to walk home. The German Army is also getting home. Me and three other boys went up into the hills recently in a captured German car, and we found a German civilian who said he knew where we could get some pistols—pistols are the best souvenir, you see . . . So we followed him right into a nest of 42 men and 6 officers, all sitting around looking like the war hadn't caught up with them. I told the officers, with my international gestures, that we were part of a huge patrol which right at that moment was coming up behind them, that we had a tank at the foot of the hill—our friend down there was racing the car engine like a tank battalion—and would they please give me their guns. The officers gave me six pistols, and the other boys collected Lugers off the enlisted men. Then we backed down the hill, them watching the backs of our heads very closely, and then we jumped in the car, slid it off the road into a ravine, skidded about two hundred yards, it felt like, and ditched it. Then we grabbed another car, the German major's I hope, and got away. I sweated away five pounds on that trip I think.

See, I'm not so bad when I get started with this letter business. I don't get started often enough though I guess.

Freddie sent me some pictures culled from his tour of the Natural History Museum, and at first I thought I noticed a striking resemblance to certain soldiers I know, but Freddie had labelled them Diplodocus, etc., so I must be mistaken. I think this Army is making me a cynical man.

If you see Cousin Dorothy, please ask her not to drop bomb-shells casually. I mean like saying, "I suppose you know Herbert got married."—Herbert is my brother. No, I didn't know.

Everybody asks me to ask for things, so while I feel in this mood, I'm going to put the bite on your Mom. Please, Mollie, send me candy. There, you asked for it. Hey, though, seriously, please send me swimming trunks, sun-glasses, and a box of cigars. Before winter sets in. I mean it. You can sort of spread the shock around the whole Marantz tribe. And I'm serious about the cigars too. The ones I took of that Heinie prisoner are giving out. But can you get cigars over there? We can't.

Write again soon, Lee. Your letters are very nice.

Love,
Louis

P!S! We've just been given permission to tell where we are. We're in Berchtesgaden, Bavaria, the roost of the old bustard himself. The Tyrol, you know, part of the Alps.

To Mrs. Lawrence Cohn

8 June 45

Dear Mollie,

Got your nice letter, and am answering while I digest the little dinner we got.

Am glad Herbert Cohn was in on the surrender. I doubt if he told them off, however, because we don't tell German officers where to get off. They are treated very well.

I'm having a wonderful time. In a few weeks the water will be warm. Some of the fellows are getting 2-day passes to France.

In answer to your questions:

1) I'm not getting a 30-day furlough to the States;
2) Don't expect to be in the States for a couple years yet;
3) I gave my home-town address as 21 W., but my decorations aren't important;
4) I have 72 points. I may go to the Pacific, but the chances are about 50-50. On the one hand, I have already seen a lot of combat. But on the other, I am in the younger age group, and have no responsibilities, so I stand pretty high on the priority list.

Love,
Louis

To Mrs. Lawrence Cohn

Berchtesgaden
[June 12, 1945]

Dear Mollie,

This is a rush note, thanking you for sending the swim-suit and sun-glasses so quickly. The packages were postmarked June 1 and got here today, June 12, which is good time.

Your selection was good too, but it's a pity you couldn't send the furlough, in a nice shade of red paint, which would go so well with them.

Love,
Louis

To Mrs. Lawrence Cohn

26 June 45

Dear Mollie,

Thanx for the film. I don't know if it'll fit my camera, which isn't here yet, but if it doesn't I'll borrow somebody else's. The country here is made for taking pictures, witness the photography shops everywhere. A tourist center too of course.

I have a desk job now, in case you hadn't heard, and am left strictly alone. So I contrive to be at the lake at Konigsee on hot afternoons. The water is cold, but anyway I get a good tan, and some amusement watching the guys and girls swimming together and sedulously looking in opposite directions.

Chow is better sometimes, and sometimes it's much worse.

Our general, Taylor, fresh from a trip to Washington D.C., told us today that it seems we shall be here till January. Then we'll all have 30 day furloughs overseas, I mean in the Old Country, and proceed in a westerly direction. We may put in some training in the States first. If this applies to men with critical scores, such as I will have by then (85 points are worn with a white beard this season), I haven't been told.

Yesterday we stood in the sun for four hours waiting for his Limey Excellence, Gen. Alexander, to accord us the honor of a few words. The Heinies stood around laffing their square heads off as the boys passed out cold from heat. At last he came, saluted, and stepped into a boat silently, which wafted him gently around the lake. The regiment would have cheered loudly if that boat had sunk like a rock, but no such luck. We went home. This was Sunday.

Tonight we have a movie, if the machine works.

Love,
Louis

To Mrs. Lawrence Cohn

30 June 45

Dear Mollie,

This is a thank you for the film, the writing paper & envelopes, the chocolate powder, the candy, which last came with Mom's cigars intact. Sending them first class was a bright idea, and if you need a reference of any kind from the Armed Forces in your hectic life at the U.S.O., you know where you can get it.

I am busier than usual breaking in a new man to my job, so that if ever I have to leave this lovely Army and return to civilian life, I shall not be essential. Also, it frees me for a possible furlough, which I have been sweating out for a year . . . not to the States, of course, but to some place in Europe.

There is a strong rumor that the critical discharge score will be lowered to 78 or 80. This will be fine for me, as, everything added up, I have 77. Just enough to stay in.

This valley of the Alps has lovely sunshine for three days, and thoroughly detestable rain for six. On good afternoons I goof off to the lake, lie around, jump in the water and out again, smoke cigarettes in chains and look at the peaks thru smoke rings. The other evening we had a sort of U.S.O. show by a Bavarian group, and the fact that Americans went wild over Lili Marlene sung in German, indicates that one can't hate in the abstract for too long a time. I wish the Japs would realise this.

Boredom is really acute. We get a good movie now and then. One about Chopin and his disastrous affair with Mme. George Sand (the boys really hated Merle Oberon in that one, because they've been hearing a lot about manpower shortage lately, and think they're the answer to a maiden's prayer, and they sure hated her superior ways): then there was "Brewster's Millions" about the guy that had to spend a million in a month, and the guys that've been to Paris thought that wouldn't be so hard to do . . . I want to see "Double Indemnity," and I enjoyed "Murder My Sweet" which you recommended. That about winds up my social life, though I forgot to mention there was a dance the other day, and I got so close to the floor I could see the tops of the heads of the four French-Polish what-have-you girls who were staggering around the middle.

I have a big map of S. America, and am following Mother's beachhead closely. I think the Argentines better surrender before they're completely submerged beneath the sheer weight of Rubinstein's mud-packs.

The people are hurting here. The kids form a chow line at our garbage can, and take what's left from our mess-kits. That of course is more than the Jews at Dachau got, but still the kids are innocent, and it makes us sorry for them anyhow.

Love,
Louis

To Dorothy Miller and Ruth Manners

St. Johann, Austria
July 17, 1945

Dear Dot, Dear Ruth,

First did you get my request to send 200 smackers to Herbie as a wedding present? If you didn't I repeat.

My reaction to Mom's reactions to their marriage is this: I thought it was swell for them, and couldn't understand her prejudices. She's toned down somewhat, but still says Herbert needs someone to "give him a push." Well, if anybody *I* marry tries to pull a first sergeant on me, I think (with due respect) I'll give her a push too, into the nearest lake.

Peggy wrote me a nice letter, and it seems they have decided to go to England (God help them) where Herbert will study for the bar (the English bar, you know, is not one of those things with brass railings, which it might be better for him to study), while she ekes out a living working for the Shell Oil Co. and perhaps with her relations. Mom doesn't like this idea, and frankly I think it stinks. I know more about England than any of them, and it's a fine place to be from. As for making a living there—better he should stay in bed. But I guess advice is one thing people won't take.

I am now a character (don't make any remarks such as "What does he mean by now") . . . anyway, I am managing editor of the regt. newspaper. We started work today in a pretty Austrian town on one of the gutters to the Danube. We have German presses, a good staff, a real organization with Sports Editor, News Editor, even Editorial Editor—which sounds funny. We have a jeep, travelling facilities, cameras, the Colonel's blessings, and plenty paper. How I got this don't ask. I believe I am one of the lucky people. However much I try to look like a soldier, however deep I get into mud and laziness, my good fairy, in the guise of an Army Clerk, taps me on the derriere with a magic wand, saying: "Rise Yardbird, thou wert meant for better things!" So here I am, proving that the typewriter is mightier than the sword. One catch—I threw my furlough for this job. But life unquote is like that. This should be a permanent assignment, until the first issue is off the press at least. I'll send you one.

Was glad to hear the cannon came alright. Has Larry seen them, and can he find time to fix up the .22 for Bob?

Yes my bank balance is growing. I'm sending you 300 bucks soon, and don't ask how I got it. If you would only make one of those nose-dives we do, you'd think we earned it. A regular infantryman from the Rainbow went with us on the last flights, and when he crawled out on Mother Nature again, he said, "You guys can have the extra pay. Me I wanna go home."

I was awarded the Cluster to the Bronze Star. For going without girls, I think, I can't imagine any other reason.

Love,
Louis

To Dorothy Miller

St. Johann,
Austria
26/7/45

Dear Dot,

My daily typewriter hammering is over—ending with a passionate article on France & asking my comrades not to smash up that country again when they return—which they shall, about two weeks from now . . .

Glad to hear you got the doo-dads—but don't let any of your friends assemble those German rifles. I'd hate to start a crime wave.

The regt's band is putting out with Shoo-Shoo-Baby in the middle of town, and the Austrians stand around with their teutonic mouths wide open. Sech noise—ach, dese Amerikaner!

The colonel liked our first issue, so my job seems assured. And if Japan gives up, I shall come back to college, and if I had ham I'd have ham & eggs if I had eggs.

I find the evenings dull. There's a swell swimming pool & occasionally I leave the newspaper office to interview somebody, my swim-suit under my arm. But in the evenings I smoke my pipe & figure whether I shall plunge into learning when I return, lining my room with cork (as Proust did) to muffle the outer world—or marry some understanding person & devote my other talents.

The Belgian Govt. has awarded us a decoration for Bastogne—a colored rope worn over the shoulder. We may also get a cluster to the Presidential Citation, for Holland. And did I tell you I got the Bronze Star again?

All very glamorous, it says here in small print.

I don't know I like the idea of Ruthie's going to Mexico. I think she has a good thing now, and more secure. Also, there is no place like home. Unquote.

Darkness descends. Tomorrow I rise at 6:30 & hurry over to a *good* breakfast—meals have improved, believe it or not. Maybe because I'm not with the rifle company any more.

Write, honeychile, write.

Love,
Louis

To Mrs. Lawrence Cohn

Sens, France
26/8/45

Dear Molly,

To say that I feel a louse w'd be putting it mildly. I probably am. I don't write home, I don't acknowledge things, I get all wrapped up in my work & only emerge once a week, to rush down to Paris & haunt the haunts. In short, I am pretty normal again & may be able to re-convert to civ. life without trouble.

Last night as usual was our deadline for going to press, and I stayed up till 5 a.m. We had to hold the press at the last minute to remake the front page as the division boxing results came in. We have a great deal of trouble getting the French printers to lino-type the paper without errors.

We too think that V-J was swell news, but nobody is in any hurry to get us out of the army, and I believe there's a large class of brass & politicians that'd like to see us "healthy young men" guarding the outposts of empire or something—the army makes men of us, you know. I only hope the families of servicemen have enough pull to knock out any such bright Nazi idea.

Tomorrow is our slack day & I'm going to be in Paris with nothing to do but have a good time. I'm taking my camera & two rolls of film. I hope to pick up some etchings too, & some books. We have gotten enough film to run our "Skyrider" cameras 3 months, & enough paper too—all by beating against brass knockers in Paris. The other regimental papers in the div. couldn't even get a printer, & folded.

I am now a 3-striper, but the extra money will go down the drain I fear. This isn't like Berchtesgaden. Prices in Paris are terrific, and I feel too young to be careful. I want to have some expensive memories for my old age, as I sit in the easy chair smoking a havana & sipping claret—God! Where do I get those ideas of grandeur?

I read your little stories of the kids with great interest. "Bob the Beanstalk, Freddie the Imp, Lee the Languid"—or do I get the wrong idea? I look forward to seeing them so much, but I wish you'd start explaining to them right now that I am not what you would call the backbone of the Army—that life is full of optical illusions—and that Hollywood & the stork are not to be trusted.

Write soon.

Love,
Louis

P.S. Please send me a Purple Heart ribbon & a cluster for the Bronze Star. Can't buy 'em here, & am supposed to wear 'em.

To Mrs. Lawrence Cohn

Sens,
France
24 Sept. 45

Dear Mollie,

Cheers & all the bloody best, as they say in England, but why send me a Purple Heart & cluster without writing? Agreed I am a rat & all that, but that was the emptiest envelope of my career. Thanx for the jewelry anyhoo.

I am about to begin the Long Voyage Home, having 84 points. I may catch a truck out this week-end, or 10 days later—anyhow, I shall be redeployed soon. Our outfit has been way behind on this; every other outfit is sending home 60 pointers.

The General just got relieved because the records were all

fouled up, and the morale has fallen, and consequently the VD rate has gone up—so we're moving home faster now. The dear Brass just doesn't want to let the enlisted men go—they'll have to go back to running elevators then.

I hope we leave before snow falls. There is no central heating in this room. French plumbing is also something for the birds. Of course it's better than last year, but one should look forward to that Post War World. (advt.)

Love,
Louis

On Line

We were in England, in the last stage of training. The rifle companies marched under moist skies in which cloud cumuli massed. Above the clouds, fleets of planes droned at a great height, drawing behind them vapor trails like ostrich feathers. Our rifle platoon ran, crawled, and assumed firing positions under green trees. We rested in the shade of gardens. At night—and the night of that time was profoundly dark, like a mental condition—we drank the beer of Britain, tepid "half-and-half," and gnawed on fish and chips. On our way back to camp, in the lightless streets of Reading, we sang the barrel-organ songs of the year and haunting "Lili Marlene":

> Underneath the lantern by the barrack gate
> Darling I remember the way you used to wait;
> 'Twas there that you whispered tenderly
> That you loved me
> You'd always be
> My Lili of the lamplight,
> My own Lili Marlene.

The bloody Heinies! When they weren't killing you, they were making you cry.

Reprinted from Louis Simpson, *Riverside Drive*. New York: Atheneum, 1962.

117

* * *

We have been removed in the usual trucks—snug as a sardine, pack at your feet, rifle between your knees—from Reading to the marshaling area, a camp of tents. Rumor: "Tomorrow." "Tomorrow what, you dumb bastard?" "The invasion." "Invasion my ass!" (On the eve of Agincourt, I once learned, men spoke otherwise. Still, if you want rhetoric, there's Churchill.)

Why do I feel so short-winded and out of condition? Because there's nothing to do now but wait and eat. Meanwhile one's imagination goes racing. If it is to be by air, in the gliders, I see the canvas box—it's really nothing more than that—bursting open in mid-sky and emitting rows of dummies which as they hurtle earthward reveal themselves, with flailing arms and open mouths, to be myself and my companions. Or else the glider comes to earth crashing against a tree, a pointed stake, a house. And if it is to be by sea? I fancy, with my imagination corrupted by so many movies (indeed, so pervasive are movies, magazines, and all the other inventions, that it is difficult to know if one has an imagination at all—whether one has conceived anything by oneself, or experienced anything, or is merely repeating someone else's fantasies), I fancy a beach littered with bodies, and a sea wall that erupts sparks of fire and black explosions, while I stagger about in the sand, groping with my hands for a purchase. I'm stifling, and my feet slither in the same place. I'm bound here by the weight of my equipment.

And really, it's getting to be a joke, our equipment. Somewhere in the depths of London or Washington, wherever the bemedaled commanders bark out their orders, it has been decided to prepare us against all possible contingencies. If we have our nightmares, it seems, so do they—on a larger scale. Suppose the Germans use gas? It's not enough to have our gas mask, like an extra lung, strapped to our chest—and not enough that our combat fatigues have been stiffened with some kind of chemical—but we must also have a flat package which, when you shake it open, becomes a transparent bag; this we are to draw over ourselves, encasing our bodies. God knows how you are to handle a gun inside it. But then, maybe the Germans will also be encased in bags, and the two armies will lie prone while the gas settles on them. Also, we are given an extra set of K-rations to pack into our pockets. And socks. Yes, we already have an extra pair of socks, but just in case—so we get another pair of socks. And in our pack, also, we have an extra pair of boots. Fully equipped with helmet, pack, rifle—and in some cases men also carry a rocket launcher or a machine gun or ammunition boxes—with pack straps and belt, from which hang a canteen, grenades, a bayonet, and entrenching tool, with a dagger strapped to one leg and two bandoleers of bullets crisscrossed from our shoulders and pockets filled with boxes of rations—with all this, it is as much as we can do to stand upright. Our faces are nearly invisible under the rims of the helmets. We look all pockets, pockets, and baggy pants. The only visible human parts are two hands. And these golems, invented by generals of supply, are to run and leap over obstacles.

In the tent, on my canvas cot, I read another detective story. So much interest in the death of one person! Is there really a world where, if someone dies violently, everyone immediately drops all other matters and labors to discover the cause of his death? How quaint! Around me, the letter writers are at it again, heads bowed over their pens and sheets of paper. The silent chorus of our theater.

Once more to my book. In the hothouse the hero finds a clue and jumps to a conclusion—he's always jumping to conclusions. But the detective will correct any errors he makes.

Far overhead, pressing continuously against our eardrums, the drone of bombers. . . .

If I had my life to live over, what would I do?

As on a screen appears the figure of a girl, naked, with young breasts and *mons Veneris,* smiling with a mixture of shyness and licentiousness.

The stories of my companions in this line aren't all imagination. This would probably have been the best, after all. I've never met a man who regretted making love.

No. I feel an abhorrence, an instinctive shrinking from the thought that it would have been possible to live in any other way, for one hour, than the way I have actually lived. For to wish this would be to want to be someone else—that is, to wish that I did not exist.

And when you think of the future, of all the others who are to replace you—and so many will be wiser and more useful than you are—you tremble and cling to your own part. Your life!

Why, then, are you willing to risk it? For you did not have to arrange matters so that you would be in this place, in a rifle company.

At Agincourt the king, casting about for words to encourage his soldiers, found this supreme reason: You'll have something to talk about afterward.

As history grew near and large, my mind was censoring the details. The troops were loaded in convoys, went down to the Channel ports, entered ships, and crossed the Channel. Of all this I remember nothing. I begin once more to see things when we are off the coast of Normandy. A shore line appears ahead; it thickens; houses are visible here and there. Trees, too, and hedgerows. It looks dreadfully clear. To right and left of our LST other ships are standing to. A battleship fires at the shore. Surely, so unhurried is that firing, it can't be serious! Columns of smoke are rising from behind the brow of land which cuts off our view abruptly. On the other side of the slope, what? Two or three pursuit planes roll over in the sky, dart down, and vanish on the other side of the horizon. The rattle of their guns comes back to us. They fly up again.

We are a hundred yards from shore. Closer. The ramp lowers. We plod heavily forward and down into the water. It is shallow, only up to our hips. I put my feet down carefully; it would be a disaster to fall under this load.

And now in two files, at combat interval, we are walking up the slope. No one is shooting at us. So much for my vision of a slippery landing! As we march, we begin to look around us. There are green fields sparkling in the cool, dewy air of June; there are hedgerows and apple trees. There is even a road for our convenience.

From somewhere in front comes a rattle of machine guns. But it seems far away. Over our heads pass fluttering ghosts. Shells from the battleships. It all seems quite impersonal. When we have marched for an hour, the column telescopes. "Fall out!" I lie against the bank of the road, propped on my pack, my helmet dragging my head back. I fumble in my breast pocket, pull out a cigarette, light it, and inhale.

Rumor: "They're Japs up ahead!" "What do you mean, Japs?" "Jap snipers."

Japs? Why not. All I see is the lane and the half-dozen men in front and behind me. In every direction thickset hedges, tall as a man, block the view. No more than a hod-carrying Egyptian slave do I see the pyramids of which my bricks will be part. What do I know of Montgomery's master plan or Bradley's tactics? Orders arrive suddenly and must be suddenly obeyed; they are counter-manded, and again we obey. I have grown accustomed to the incon-sequence of everything.

"Fall in!" Again we advance, marching in two files. The bursts of fire are beginning to seem closer. We are silent, bowed under the weight of our equipment and our fantasies. Then, against the bank on the left, appears a heap of dusty, gray-green clothing, from which are thrust two boot soles. At the other end, a blond head with open eyes and an open mouth revealing sharp teeth. The complex-ion is yellow. Around the heap are littered a helmet—the coal-scuttle helmet of the German—a rifle. . . . In a brief moment I pass. Here's another. This one is also on its back, boot soles thrust out. The jacket is tightened with a black belt from which hangs a gray cylinder, the gas mask. Under it and around, a scattering of papers. Another. Half turned on its side, as though sleeping against the bank. Beside it there is a machine gun, with tripod and stock, something like our Browning automatic rifle, but it looks stamped out of tin. This corpse also is blond and yellow-complexioned; he, too, is gray with dust.

In passing these sights, we devour them with our eyes. No visible wounds. The eyes left open—naked eyeballs, unshielded from the dust, and not feeling it! They must have been surprised. Imagine the moment. I'd want to shout: This isn't fair! Let's start again, as of five minutes ago. This can't be final. Jaws clenched in protest. No, surely. . . . *Kaput!* A fly crawls on your teeth. Dust on naked eyes.

If we kill them, they'll kill us back.

This is very obvious. But I hadn't really understood it before. I seem to have known many things without understanding them. It is one thing to know, another to exist.

That night we dug foxholes in the apple orchards. The hedgerows on every side boxed us in, dividing one squad from another. The darkness was thick. To our rear, batteries of seventy-fives pounded away, and the shells went whispering over. To our front the sky flickered and rumbled; now and then a spattering of rain swept the fields. From time to time a plane would go over. I was awakened by a strange droning overhead—an enemy plane. It seemed to go back and forth very slowly. There was a whistling fall, an explosion, and the ground trembled. Not a word from my companions—but I imagined they, too, were wide awake, listening. A few minutes later a machine gun went off in the next field. I threw off my blanket, scrambled upright, and pushed my rifle out in front of me, pointing at the hedgerow in front. But nothing happened. The branches of an apple tree stirred gently and the grass, when I put out my hand, was wet with dew. I propped my rifle in a corner of the hole and settled down again, my head in my helmet for a pillow, my shelter-half under me, blanket wrapped around.

But before I could fall asleep, the helmet and shoulders of the guard loomed over me. "You're on," he said. I extricated myself from the cocoon, found my M-1, and took his place under a tree. The leaves dripped moisture and the cool air smelled like cider. In the next hedgerow a farmer's cow was clumsily foraging. From time to time a great shell rumbled overhead—the battleship, still pounding the inland crossroads and villages. And intermittently a single shot or machine gun staccato . . .

Before daybreak the company breakfasted on the K-ration—a can of cold egg and fortified biscuits—and set off again down the road. In the fields the corpses of cows lay with their legs in the air, as straight as toy animals. Those were our night alarms.

The sky was blue; it was a perfect June day.

Now we are approaching a canal. Or rather, two channels of water divided by a lane of green trees. We march into this lane. The path we follow is lost in the trees; on my left there are gleams from the canal.

A gun fires. At once, by its sound, it reveals itself as that of the enemy. I throw myself down on the earth. A machine gun. "Burp!" The purr of the bullets is wicked. There must be several guns. Short, smooth bursts. The air is filled with whining. In front of my eyes the trunk of a tree gashes white. Twigs fall to the earth. The lane is being shaved. I press my face into the ground, and every muscle is contracted.

Then, a whistling overhead, and an explosion that jars me from the ground. Another. Again.

A voice shrieks, *"Mamma mia!"*

Other explosions. Bits of metal whir through the trees and clang against the branches. The shells are walking up and down the lane.

The purring of the machine guns continues. "Burp, burp"—a scythe moving a few inches above the ground. We're unable to move, pinned down, while the shells, falling out of the air with whistles, stride up and down the length of the canal.

"Medic, medic!" Another cry.

I find myself, with the entrenching tool I have somehow removed from its carrier without raising my body, scraping a hole out of the earth. The only other man I can see, ten feet away, is doing the same.

"Bell!"

The squad sergeant, who has crawled up somehow, is motioning to me. I slide my entrenching tool back into its carrier and wriggle toward him.

"Go back and tell the first sergeant we need the mortars up here."

I proceed, wriggling. Then on hands and knees. Here the whining bullets seem less near; I go on in a running crouch. I pass men face down, digging and burrowing into the earth. I am slightly astonished to find so many other men—my solitude, in the last minutes, has seemed complete.

At last I find headquarters section and the first sergeant. He is a taciturn, large-boned man who virtually runs the company. He repeats the message to the captain, a small man who is always calm. But his calmness is not reassuring; it is sinister. He has a calculating look in his eyes, like a dentist.

The mortar crew are ordered forward and disappear among the trees, crouching and ducking with their green pipe. A lot of good that will do!

Some minutes later, as I crawl back to my digging, I see the mortar men tinkering with their apparatus. The tube is set upright. One of them fiddles with the adjustment. Another drops a shell into the mouth of the tube and ducks down, pulling his hand away. "Kerplunk!" It seems an insane ritual that cannot possibly have any practical effect.

Nevertheless, as it turns out, our mortars manage to bring their shells to bear on the German machine guns—enough, at any rate, to spoil their shaving the napes of our necks and our buttocks. Also, the captain, by means of the company radio, is able to appeal to a battery of seventy-fives somewhere to our rear. They range in on the enemy mortars—those whistling shells that fall out of the air straight down on top of us are mortars, it seems. In an hour the crisis is over. We rise to our feet and file up the lane.

Here and there we see the results. The medics are busy lifting a man onto a stretcher. With his eyes closed, gray-faced—helmet, rifle, and shovel left on the ground. I know him—a rifleman in the second platoon. And here, lying on his face in absolute stillness, is another.

Muscles begin to unclench. We have had enough experience to last a lifetime.

I can measure the importance of that first fire fight by the depth to which, by some cog or lever in my mind, it was thrust down into forgetfulness. Like most of the war, it vanished completely. But one night in Paris, a few years afterward, I dreamed the episode again, from the beginning. Once more we approached the canal with its green banks and lane of trees. Again we passed between the trees, and all at once the firing began. From this dream I woke with extravagant gladness; it seemed that the fog was lifting.

Afternoon. The outskirts of Carentan.

We are lying under an embankment, spread out side by side like infantry of 1917 about to go over the parapet of a trench. The embankment is being shaved by machine gun fire. If the order comes and we must rise above the earth, we will be cut in half.

The order does not come.

Under a hedge, another dead German—a big, yellow-haired fellow, his face crusted with black blood. He is dressed in spotted, leopard-like camouflage, and his boots are daintily pointed. His helmet, also, is different. Near his hand lies the burp gun, the famous Schmeisser. A parachutist—one of the elite regiment who have been sniping at us from trees, machine-gunning us from foxholes under the hedgerows.

Around this corpse hangs a smell not simply of death, but of what we have come to recognize as Germany—a compound of sausage and cheese, mildewed cloth, and ideas. Some ideas stink. Every German hole—and they cut very neat holes in the ground—exudes the smell of their philosophy.

A month on line, and then we were shipped back to England. This was one of the advantages of being an airborne division; we wouldn't be used as cannon fodder. Our part was to lead invasions. Saying so, we congratulated ourselves; in the pubs of Reading and down in Piccadilly—where we managed to get, with or without leave—we told each other what fine fellows we were. We were tested, first-rate fellows, veterans of great battles, cunning in the ways of war. "Burp, burp!" we said, imitating the Kraut machine guns. Or "Whee-pow!" in appreciation of their famous all-purpose artillery piece, the 88. "Do you remember . . ." we urged each other. As we reminisced, we selected those aspects of carnage that would most flatter our endurance. Sure, we'd been scared spitless. By describing our fear of death we seemed to make death somehow not real, but a kind of illusion. For it had been only an illusion, after all; here we were, safe and sound, drinking our beer. So, in this fashion, truth turns into history.

With what bravery we polished our paratrooper boots! And strutted in them! And spoke our contempt of all other troops. The cooks caught it, and after the cooks, the supply people, and the other divisions who had never left England at all! We were showing off like crazy. But where was the Becky to our Tom Sawyer?

"Oi there, Yank, 'ow'd you loike to 'ave a good time?"

Becky, it seemed, was an English tart, with a mouth as red as an open sore. She had the chipper courage that the reporters in their radio broadcasts commended. It was plain she would never be beaten by any concatenation of foreigners. She would lie down on the landing beaches, in the streets, and in the hills. She had nothing to offer but blood, sweat and tears. Someday, when the lights went on again all over the world, from the door of the pub which she'd bought out of her wages, she would hear a bluebird singing over the white cliffs of Dover.

"Come ahn, Yank! Ahnly two quid!"

Henry James, had he heard the obscenities issuing from an air-raid shelter, might have revised in some degree his comparison of American coarseness and English refinement. But, then, Henry only knew duchesses. In the minds of some of my friends, as with the men of '76, was implanted the suspicion that a society that had produced the Cockney whine, English houses, and English cooking might be, in some respects, defective. They would never again be able to take the visiting Englishman quite seriously; and the voice of the would-be duchess that prevails in cultured American society would remind them inevitably of the other side of culture. The decline of old England was accelerated when they allowed other people into their homes. It was not for nothing that an Englishman's home had always been his castle. The foreigner, who had only seen the Englishman abroad, now had a chance to see the fish-and-chips grubbiness, the incredibly ugly, unimaginative, chilling life of the sahib at home. And the English, as we walked their streets, seemed to know they had made a mistake. A necessary mistake, perhaps—but no less calamitous for that. Things would never again be quite the same.

"It's a cold night, ducky. 'Ow about a quick one?"

Many of the English were brave, and many more of them lacked imagination. The combination had destroyed the *Luftwaffe* and could handle the buzz bombs that were now falling out of the London sky. As I sat in a rowboat, rowing a Cockney stenographer around the pond, admiring her knees which peeped out of the short skirt of the period, one of these contraptions puttered across heaven like an old bus; the pulsing ceased; moments passed; then a ponderous crash flattened some place where we happened on the statistical chance not to be. The city, which had been holding its breath, exhaled and resumed its monotonous life, the heartbeat of the internal combustion engine. I continued to explain myself to the stenographer—not so much myself, as America, for the whole of which, it seemed, every American was responsible. I had made bad Hollywood movies and tinny Ford cars. I had stayed out of the war, laying away millions of dollars, and after the war I would say I'd won it. I was always swanking about Texas or Brooklyn, my birthplace, and I ate with my fork in the wrong hand.

Later I would have conversations with a Frenchman, who told me that I knew nothing about "style"; a Belgian, who accused me of ruining his business; and a German, who complained of the war I waged from the air against women and children. In comparison, the English were tolerant. Besides, they had character. They accepted responsibility for their failures, as they had once taken the profit of their victories. They were the only honest people in Europe.

I had forgotten the reality of the Norman hedgerows. Other men were smelling the rotten apples. The tanks hammered at Caen. Then Patton's armor broke through the hedgerows, raced to the Seine, and Paris had been recaptured.

But there is an extra sense which warns you that your luck is running out; that it is your turn to support the sheet, sagging with misery, of the sky. The weight is always the same; now it is supported by some people, now by others. Rumor, always mistaken about times and places, was right at last: we were going back on line.

So we sat in our battle gear—we knew what to do with it now: the antigas envelope and other extras would be thrown into the first convenient ditch—on the concrete airstrip, watching the tow planes warming up, and, more interesting, the gliders. We'd flown in them, but never into battle. The Waco CG-4A glider was made of canvas warped on a wooden frame. It was hardly lifted off the ground by its little wheels; it seemed to be lying down, belly-flat. The extended wings spread out from the top of the frame in a gesture of despair. The only window was where the pilots sat, up front. Some of the gliders, the bow unhinged and thrust up into the air like a jaw, were having heavy weapons and boxes of ammunition thrust down their throats. And they had no engines. Not for the first time, I wondered what I was doing here. Fate had granted my wish to be in the infantry—a simple soldier without responsibilities—but I hadn't seen the small print under her thumb.

"On your feet!"

We marched by platoons to the gliders. The door of our glider yawned open beneath the wing. I clambered through, sat down, and buckled myself in. We sat in two rows facing each other. Then the pilots jumped up lightly (they had nothing to carry but a carbine), looking like sports enthusiasts in their pinks and caps and sunglasses. They shut the door and went forward to the controls.

Now there is a roaring of engines and our glider trembles in blasts of air; the tow planes, having warmed up, are taxiing into position.

A plane to each glider. A cable is run out from the rear of the C-47 and attached to the nose of the glider. The plane takes off and the glider follows, bumping lightly; then smoothly it takes to the air. You are meanwhile praying to your God. Or maybe you're visualizing a disaster, with the trust that anything so clearly foreseen cannot, by some law against coincidence, happen. A draft whirls the glider upside down, and it smashes into the earth; or it crashes on a tree, and as you hang here, fumbling at your belt, bullets hum through the canvas, slicing off the face of the man in front of you.

When we are over the landing area, the glider pilot pulls the lever that releases the cable. For the first time, the kite has a character of its own. It soars like a bird. Then it travels on the air currents in silence. All that we hear is the creaking of struts. Then it slants down, tilting sharply on one wing. Your life is in the hands of the pilots.

At last the glider stops falling and levels out. A few bumps and it rolls to a stop. The men ahead of you are climbing out through the door. Safe!

Now you are in the files of the company in march formation. The land is flat and everywhere gliders are strewn, pointing in every direction. Others are still skimming down. The landscape is filling up with men.

And now you're marching in the route march double files, men staggered apart so that they will be less vulnerable to bullets and shells. It is as though the weeks since Normandy were only a dream. This is reality, the burden of your pack and the pace of the march. But above all, you are once more in the grip of anxiety. How could you ever have forgotten it? Once more you are reduced to nothing; you're not a man, but a vacuum into which move apprehensions and fancies. You are once more dependent on others, at the mercy of chance. Because you could read the past, you thought you had an identity; but the present is all that matters—there is no future.

On the horizon, a windmill, like a Dutch painting.

Somewhere guns are rumbling. The sun is warm; under your woolen shirt you begin to sweat.

At dusk we entered a village. At the entrance a German tank had been blown apart. On it and under it were the blackened forms of the crew; they appeared vulcanized, melted; through the crust of black gleamed streaks of ruby-red flesh. The street beyond was a shambles. There must have been over a dozen bodies sprawled in all the attitudes of shock. Sheets of paper lay in the gutters—letters mostly, as though the pockets of these bodies had been turned out. They had been read by the sky.

Toward us came a company of paratroopers returning from the front. They passed sullenly, in silence. Up ahead the darkening sky was trembling with explosions. A little further on the files divided to left and right. I skirted a pit shaped like a grave. At the end of the pit stood a cross from which hung an American helmet with a bullet hole through it. On the cross was written in Gothic lettering, "Welcome, 101st Airborne Division."

Krauts are strange. Imagine, in the press of battle thinking up a trick like that and putting it into execution! A symbolic grave! Do they think they're frightening children?

We dig in for the night on both sides of the road. Except for the ceaseless, impersonal rumbling of cannon, the night passes without incident.

The next day we captured a jam factory. Rows on rows of preserved apples, pears, and plums. This was only the beginning; it was to be one of those days on which exotic things happen—a surrealist interlude.

As we approached a house set off by itself in an orchard, we came upon a plump mattress dragged out under a tree with a German officer stretched on it. He had been laid there to die in all possible comfort. The mattress feathers were escaping through a tear in the material, littering the grass. And it was as though they were coming loose from Herr Kommandant himself, like a fat goose; for he had swollen, and was continuing to swell. His belt was lost in the balloon of his belly. His legs and arms stuck straight out; his fingers were plump as carrots. His legs were stuffed into the boots that would, it appeared, split at any moment.

A little further on in a field a Messerschmitt had crashed on its nose. Delicately it hung there, the black crosses glaring from the fuselage.

Then, a long concrete ramp, like the track of a trolley aimed at the sky. It was one of the buzz bomb launching platforms.

Our tour came to an end in a straggling wood where the Germans had arranged a few machine guns. We dug into the earth; it sifted with every stroke of my shovel, like sand. I had a devil of a time cutting the regulation hole in that ground. As I was busy, two British planes flew over—Typhoons. They darted to and fro, hunting around until they found what they were after. A hundred yards or so in front of me, they went plunging down. From their wings, rockets streaked. The ground shook and clouds of smoke welled up. End of the machine guns.

I had now become the captain's runner—a distinction I had not sought. As I made my way alone from headquarters section to the platoons or to battalion, I learned to watch out for certain places where I might be under observation, and was friendly with certain banks and screens of trees. Like most of my companions, I could calculate the line of fall of a shell when it was still far away. One field presented a nightmare, and there was no going around it. Here, it seemed, a company of paratroopers had landed among the Germans. The area, perhaps fifty yards across, was strewn with corpses, mostly German, but with a fair scattering of paratroopers. It was a masterpiece of rage. Mutilated bodies, twisted torsos and limbs, hands grasping, teeth grinning, a welter of rotting cloth and rusting weapons. The bodies began to swell; every time I crossed the field, they had become more grotesque. Luckily, the cool October air preserved them. In a while I was accustomed to these sights; they were no more to me than shadows and moonlight.

It began to drizzle, and after that we were never really dry. We drew our shelter-halves over our mud-holes and huddled under them, wrapped in our raincoats, sleeping fitfully; or we stood guard, looking out across the gray flatness that was swept now and then by bursts of small-arms fire or the flash and drifting smoke of a shell. We cooked our rations in the can, and heated mugs of powdered coffee. The company kitchen came up to join us—the cooks trembling in every limb—and the food was improved. Then British tanks came up on line beside us, and we got their sausages for a change. The Limeys brewed up tea at four o'clock, in the open, within a few feet of my hole. A brace of shells came in; they packed up the teapot, popped into the turret, and backed off.

At night buzz bombs wandered across the sky, droning and pulsing with a red flame, on their way to Antwerp and London.

The weather got wetter and colder. We were peevish as hell.

At last we were out of there—packed on the cattle trucks and driven back to France and billeted in tents near Rheims.

Then passes were distributed generously: we could go to Brussels or Paris on three-day passes. We only had to wait our turn. Till it came, there was Rheims—though not much of a town—and we could catch up on the movies we'd missed, and the baths, and the letter writers could catch up on their voluminous task. The first lucky men returned from Paris. My God, the naked women! The cognac and Calvados!

One afternoon, for want of anything to do—after all, you can read just so many detective stories—I wandered out of camp onto the plains of Rheims. There was a slope. I climbed it and sat down under a tree. A blustering wind was harrying clouds through the sky; it was the same sky, after all, that I'd looked at when I was a boy. Then I had dreamed of adventures, of foreign lands and battles. I'd kept the names of history like talismans. Since then I had assisted at great events. I saw the boy standing before me, and wondered what I could say to him about experience. Nothing, perhaps, except that I envied his enthusiasm. For I had lost most of mine.

In the distance, across the plain where the flying cloud shadows heaved like waves, rose the town of Rheims and the great cathedral, traveling the plain.

For the first time in many months I was alone. The camp, from which ant-sized figures emerged now and then, the military life in which I'd been immersed, was apart from me. Interludes like this were, perhaps, to be avoided; for then you began to think. You could only endure the monotony and meet the onsets of danger if you were part of a mass. But to be alone was the essence of my life.

I smoked my pipe and looked around me. Between the trees that sprouted from the crest of the slope wound a shallow ditch no more than a foot deep. I stood up and walked beside it. At intervals there were stumps of rotten wood embedded in the ground, remnants of posts.

It was an old trench. To be filled in like this, it must have been abandoned for years. Had the front in 1914 come this close to Rheims? I knelt and touched one of the stumps. Then as I paused with a dozen fancies, remembering all I had heard of that war, it seemed there were others on this slope, a company of infantry who had been standing there for generations. Before the Marne and before Sedan they had been posted here, above the plain; the men they relieved had gone down the hill, leaving it to them. There they had stayed, with Rheims and the cathedral at their backs, guarding the bare, wind-swept plain. Rain had fallen, and snow; the stubble on their jaws had been caked with mud and covered with frost. They stamped their boots and wrapped their long overcoats around them and propped their long rifles against the parapet and stared into the east. It was too much for flesh to endure—so they murmured. Nevertheless, they had remained. They ceased to murmur; their jaws could no longer move; they were motionless. And gray morning rose, and the sun passed over, and night returned, bringing the pale moon. Their coats turned to rags, and the flesh withered from their arms, and their skeletons leaned against the parapet. And then, gnawed by rats, their bones collapsed into the bottom of the trench. And leaves and dust covered them. Other men were born, and lived, and died. There were other wars and great cannonades; and again the trumpets sounded for peace. But these, and all they endured, were as though they had not been.

The greater part of life has not been expressed. The simple and illiterate, those who sustain the labor and pain of existence, those who carry out the orders, are never themselves heard. History neglects to mention them; most art admits little of their existence. Yet on the hill near Rheims, and at other times in my life, I have seen for a moment into the depth of this life, and it has given me an instinctive distrust of expressed ideas. If most of man's life has passed into silence, is not truth itself silent? What are governments, with their systems of taxation, and cities, with their universities, with their speculations, all that chattering, compared with the silence of all the lives that have been forgotten? The very stars in their silence, and God, if he exists, by his absence, sympathize with what has not been spoken.

But I, by a quirk of chance, belong with those whose task it is to describe the surface of things, to record the gestures of men and women. If I must, then so be it—but I will speak only with reluctance. I will resist any expression that is not the truth. And, rather than say what is not true, I will be silent.

One afternoon as I lay dozing on my cot while a chill December wind snapped the tent flaps and drummed on the canvas, Rumor, in the shape of a private first class, ducked through the door and said, "We're going back on line!"

The soldier who always polished his boots continued to polish them; the letter writer still stared at the tent wall.

"No kidding," said Rumor. "There's a big German breakthrough. I heard it from a guy at headquarters."

"And what about the passes to Paris?"

"Passes!" Rumor laughed sardonically; he was rid of his own fear by sharing it.

By my sinking heart, I knew it was true. But what an injustice! The usual peevish complaints by which the soldier, at least the American soldier, adjusts himself to the task on this occasion were stiffened with anger. After so many weeks in Holland, in the mud and rain and all the shelling, to be put back on line so soon! It was not according to the arithmetic of punishment and reward which each man in his own mind was always calculating. We were beginning to be too meritorious, piling up more marks for good conduct than any number of passes to Paris could repay. A little more, and it would be hard for America, even the most golden future, to meet the exorbitant sum of our deserving.

Such resentment is the privilege of victors. Troops that are running for their lives do not reckon their working hours so nicely. Our war so far had been a series of jobs; though men were killed, as an army we had never been in peril. We had not been asked to assume the responsibility for our fate. Therefore, like men employed by another, we were inclined to knock off work at five, pack up our tools, and go home.

The camp was stirring. Rumor had been supplanted by command; we were to pack our full field kits at once. I rolled up my sleeping bag and pushed a cleaning patch through the muzzle of my gun and looked down it into the whorls of bright steel. Outside, vehicles drew up, returning the men who had been on leave; they had been snatched away in the middle of their pleasures. Most of them, to hear them tell it, were suffering from *coitus interruptus.*

When we emerged from our tents, a line of trucks was waiting on the road. We fell into company formation and answered the roll. The platoons in their winter clothing looked like an assembly of bears. We wore stiff woolen overcoats, our bodies were thickened with sweaters, our hands encased in woolen gloves. In our packs we carried rubber overshoes. Add to this the combat load of bullets, grenades, et cetera.

There was no speech by the captain, no briefing on the assignment. We were not asked to play our part; it was apparent by the somber haste of this assembly that in some way we ourselves were going to be the drama. One by one the squads filed to the trucks; the men climbed in; the tail gates clanged shut behind them. In a few minutes the engines, which had been trembling quietly, all together uttered a roar and moved into gear. From where I sat, pressed by a man on each side, looking over the tail gate, I saw the truck behind and, coming into view on the turns of the road, a convoy that stretched endlessly. The trucks passed through vistas of December farm land and, hardly abating their speed, through the bleak villages of northern France, with their fungus-growing stone walls and shuttered windows. At the crossroads, military policemen waved the convoy on. Here and there by the road, a Frenchman wheeling his bicycle did not pause to raise his head. An old woman in black, her head bound in a kerchief, stared after us with no smile.

Hours passed; the landscape darkened; the trucks switched on their shielded, downward-slanting lights. Cones of light moved on the surface of the road. No other lights were visible in the profound night; not a crack from a cottage window. We nodded and dozed, propped against each other. The wind pried down our necks and grew chilly around our ankles.

Where were we going? We didn't know or care. The line was always the same, wherever it wound. Did the infantry on their way to Gettysburg care about the name? They knew what it would be like when they got there. It is only afterward that these places assume a countenance of their own; as time passes and legends accrue, one place seems clearly unlike another.

Sinking into sleep, or jolted awake, we traveled for hours. Some-times the truck would halt for minutes and there would be a stirring of cramped limbs, a ripple of complaints. Finally at one of these stops, the tail gate clanged down.

"Dismount!"

We climbed down onto a road. In the darkness there was a shuffling of feet and clinking of metal. Someone's helmet tumbled clanging on the road.

"Left face!"

We turned ponderously.

"Forward 'arch!"

Then began a march of somnambulists. The files would telescope and you stepped on the heels of the man in front of you; then, as suddenly, they would extend at a fast pace and you found yourself falling behind.

We had left the road and were climbing a path between trees. To my right a ravine fell away into utter blackness.

On the crest of a slope, the section halted.

"Fall out!"

I lay down, propping myself on my pack. Rivulets of sweat trick-led under the layers of wool; then my feet and hands began to be cold.

"On your feet!"

We set off again over hill and dale. Dead branches broke under-foot. We were in some kind of forest.

"Hold it up!"

Again we collided.

"All right, dig in. Facing down the slope."

I took my place in the usual defensive position, unhitched my pack, got out my entrenching tool, screwed the shovel at right angles to the haft, and picked at the earth, circumscribing a foxhole. As I began to dig, my face was struck by something wet.

Snow!

The flakes continued to fall. When my hole was five feet deep, I dragged a tree branch over it and settled down, pushing my body into my sleeping bag. The sound of the last shovel ceased, and I drifted off to sleep under the hush of the snow.

I was wakened by the guard, to take his place. At once, filling the vault of silence as a dripping tap fills a dark house, I heard the tapping of gunfire. The sky at one edge—to the east? the north?—was flickering red; a pillar of smoke turned there; the clouds were floating on scarlet. The flames extended; the sound of the guns strengthened. One hour, two hours, and there were half a dozen livid spots; the rumbling of cannon was continuous.

Beneath me, at the foot of the slope, snow-wreathed trees appeared reluctantly in the gray light. Between the trees and the crest of the slope, white heaps here and there, where the foxholes were dug, described a rough perimeter. It was not as though morning had come, but rather, that the dark had yielded. The sky was supported by the tops of the trees and wisps of fog were trailing to the ground.

The inhabitants of this landscape began to move. A helmet rose through a roof of leaves and snow, then shoulders and hands. This creature made a mound of dry sticks at the edge of its burrow, added pieces of paper, struck a match, shielding the flame in its gloved paws, and bent over the pile. The twigs caught. With infinite care, the creature mixed a full mug of powdered coffee and snow and balanced it over the flame.

"Duncan!"

I raise my head and peer through the twilight.

"Bell!"

I can just make out Pucci's helmet above the line of the snow, moving like a turtle shell.

"What is it?"

"You're the son of a gun and a hole in the ground!"

With that the head disappears and I'm left to chew on this bit of wisdom. Only Pucci would have the energy to move his jaws in this weather. I am numb with cold. The day, which gave no warmth, is again yielding to night. A freezing wind plays on the slope.

He's right. We are sons of a gun and a hole in the ground. It will be a wise father after this war who knows his own child.

The snow glistens as though every particle is charged with electricity; round the horizon, the clouds which press down on the earth like a headache are lightened by intermittent flashes. The sound of the cannon, unlike the flashes, merges and continues. The sky has turned red, as though it is being pumped full. My head is filled, too, with strange ideas. It would take a lifetime to remember a half hour of the thoughts that come to you during a war till, crouched in the bottom of your hole, you fall asleep.

I had to carry a note to battalion. I took it from the captain, who had installed himself in a barn. In Holland he had begun the practice of finding himself comfortable headquarters. All the company commanders did this, perhaps, but it was bad for his authority with the men in the foxholes. When I delivered his messages to them, they would ask if he was warm and safe.

I set off through the trees in the general direction of battalion. In a few minutes I came onto a road. On my right, where it rose against the sky, there was a Sherman tank reflecting a glow of fire. It was only a few steps out of my way; I walked over. The tank sergeant was seated negligently in the turret, as on the saddle of a horse. Fifty yards down the road, a German tank was burning; it had been knocked slanting into the ditch and the long gun with the muzzle brake was reaching for us in its convulsion. Beyond this, as my eyes grew accustomed to the view, loomed another machine to which something equally violent had happened.

I asked directions and the sergeant gave them. I inquired what had happened. "They tried to get through," he said and turned his head away, having no time to waste on strangers who asked questions.

I continued on my path, considering. If the German tanks had broken through in this place, what would have happened to my company? We would have been cut off. And then? What astonished me was the haphazardness of the affair. It had depended on—a sergeant. True, he had destroyed the German tanks, but he did not look in any way extraordinary. He was appallingly casual. I had no confidence in him. Could the people in command be aware of the danger of the situation?

A fragment of reading I'd nearly forgotten—such memories were submerged in the monotony of purely physical existence—returned. I saw Tolstoy's sergeant at Borodino, with his pipe stuck in his mouth, directing the fire of his battery. On men like this the hinge of battle swung. They did not see themselves in a dramatic role. They would do great tasks, and be abused for not doing them right, and accept this as normal. To what were they committed? Saving their skins, of course. Yet between two men exposed to the same danger, there might be all the difference in the world. What made the difference? It was not in any conventional sense patriotism or religion; the chaplain's office was a subject of humor, and Fourth-of-July oratory was met with silence. Rather, it was as though these men held an unbreakable contract with an employer who was—like themselves—emotionally illiterate.

At the battalion stove, where messengers and other birds of passage warmed their extremities, a technical corporal informed me about the state of affairs.

"We're surrounded," he said. "Up a creek. You hear about Saint-Vith? The Kraut tanks run over our line. They're not taking any prisoners. SS troops. And everybody's pulled out."

"Everybody but us."

"You hear about the Kraut paratroopers?" said another. "They dropped all over. And they got SS men in GI uniforms, with jeeps and everything. They druv through the lines and raised hell. Three was captured over in the 501st."

The somberness of the staff at battalion reinforced these remarks. As I waited, the colonel of the regiment passed in a hurry, trailing a cortege of majors, captains, lieutenants. They plunged outside, as though about to hurl themselves personally into a breach.

When I got back to my hole and let myself down into it, exhausted by the effort of placing one snow-covered boot after the other, Pucci, my neighbor, said: "Welcome home! So what's new?"

"We're surrounded."

"So what's new!"

My feet are going numb; when I walk on them for any distance, they hurt.

Yesterday the slope was blasted by shells of a sinister weight, and the white surface is blotched. Back in the barn, where the aid men bring the wounded, lies the body of a first platoon man. Hit by a shell fragment, he died before he could be removed to the rear. In this cold the life in the wounded is likely to go out like a match.

A freezing wind blows between snowfalls, and the snow on the trees has changed to ice; shiny stalactites hang from boughs, a glittering filigree. Sometimes the snow is lifted in skirts and sweeps to and fro. Then the wind falls, and more flakes drift down.

I am losing count of days and nights. They merge in one colorless dream.

When last did I have a hot meal? Or a meal of any kind, for that matter? We are down to two boxes of K-rations a day. Apparently it is impossible for our supply planes to find us through this overhang. But the German planes have found us. Last night we heard their engines over Bastogne, the town at our backs—they sound like diesels, with their heavy throbbing—hunting to and fro. Then bombs came whistling down.

Yesterday, also, I've been told, the Germans broke through as far as second battalion headquarters. Even the mail clerk had to grab a rifle. A runner whom I know, a towheaded fellow with a pleasant smile, used an automatic rifle to such effect that he is to be awarded the Silver Star.

So far, the company has not been attacked.

First, the sound of the burp guns—short, velvet bursts.

I peer down the slope, trying to see and still keep my head down. In my gloved fingers the rifle is awkward. Why didn't I think of making a hole for my index finger?

Bullets are whining over. To my right, rifles are going off. They must see more than I do.

The snow seems to have come alive and to be moving, detaching itself from the trees at the foot of the slope. The movement increases. And now it is a line of men, most of them covered in white—white cloaks and hoods. Here and there men stand out in the gray-green German overcoats. They walk, run, and flop down on the snow. They rise and come toward us again.

I aim at one, at the belt line, and squeeze the trigger. The M-1 goes off, kicking into my shoulder, and the cartridge case flies into the snow.

I aim at another. He flops down out of sight.

There is a booming of rifles to right and left, and the crackle of a machine gun.

A thunderclap, and a drift of black smoke. Metal goes humming through the air. Their artillery is helping out.

The Germans are shouting. Orders, screams, and threats, mixed together. The sound of voices in this melee is grotesque. From our side, not a word.

It is all over. They have vanished into the trees.

The sound of the wounded. From the foot of the slope a voice is wailing in German. Minutes pass. I find myself still rigidly grasping my rifle. The voice stops. It begins again. Then it trails off and is silent.

I count seven lumps on the slope.

An hour later, beneath the snow flurries they have merged with the surface.

On Christmas Eve we were informed that we could take turns in going to the rear for religious services. Remembering that I was a Christian, I joined the procession of devout men on the path back to Bastogne. The chaplain conducted the service in the open. "Tonight at home our families are praying for us. They are putting presents under the tree and having Christmas dinner. Now, more than ever, here in the Ardennes forest, you feel how much you are missing and the terrible discomfort and danger to which you are exposed. It is for your parents, brothers, and sisters, and for the divine history of the birth of Christ, that you are fighting. Those who are attacking you are the enemies of Christ. It may seem strange to you to be called on to kill men, but . . ."

I return to my foxhole with a sinking heart. When one is reminded of another life, these conditions are doubly hard to endure. Also, his description of our predicament was rather depressing. So long as you don't know that you are in a disaster, you can fool yourself that it doesn't exist, say to yourself that your fears are exaggerated. The chaplain is a good man. It must be difficult for him to reconcile his faith with his occupation.

> And yet, for all his faith could see,
> I would not the good bishop be.

On my message-carrying journeys through the woods I have a greater freedom than is allowed to the ordinary riflemen, who only stir out of their holes to relieve themselves in the slit trench. But under these conditions, they don't go there often.

My feet are getting to be a problem. The toes and heels are sore; I try walking on the sides. This must be incipient trench foot. The trouble is caused by the boots and rubber overshoes. You can't do without the overshoes, for the boots become wet; but with the overshoes your feet perspire and then the moisture freezes. Also, we don't move around enough, and the circulation is bad.

The Russian soldiers massage each other's feet. You're assigned a companion; you massage his feet, and he massages yours. If your buddy's feet go bad, you're shot. At least that's the story I was told by an aid man at battalion. By the gleam in his eye, he wanted to see us put on the same system. Which would be worse—to be shot or to massage Pucci's smelly feet?

One day the sun shone. The slopes were lit with sunlight and the fog lifted.

Then our planes appeared. We saw Thunderbolts darting around the horizon and heard the rattle of their guns as they strafed the German positions. The air was filled with the humming of supply planes and bombers.

Food and medical supplies began to filter through to the forward positions. And we heard that tank columns were fighting their way toward us, breaking the German ring.

It seemed we were heroes. The world was watching the siege of Bastogne.

Perhaps the world had a picture of heroes standing on hilltops, rifle in hand, fighting off hordes of SS men and throwing themselves under tank treads. The battle, as I saw it, was more like Fabrizio's view of the field of Waterloo. Men were dying, of course. On the slope beneath me lay seven relics of the *Wehrmacht*, frozen in their final attitudes. On my comings and goings I would pass a half dozen other bodies at certain places, American and German both, lying out in the wind, snow sifting into the folds of their overcoats, their eyes changed into blue ice.

Now and then the foxholes were swept with shellfire. And in the forward rifle positions there were sporadic bursts of small-arms fire as German patrols probed our position and withdrew again.

But any panoramic idea of battle was false.

The real battle was occurring in every foxhole. There life had to be sustained with slow, painstaking movements of cold fingers. I felt that I was slowly freezing to death. I was preoccupied with saving the vital ember. I was aware that life depended on a motor pump, my heart; on the expansion and contraction of the lungs, drawing in cold air; on threads of blood to my extremities—channels that were being filled with particles of ice.

I heard that the ring had been broken; we were no longer surrounded. In a few days we would be relieved.

But still we remained. The German artillery pounded the line again and again in a fury. They seemed to hate us personally; they wanted to kill us because we existed, not just because we stood in their way.

At this point memory becomes dim. I recall walking into the command post to take another message. The first sergeant looked me up and down from face to feet and said, "Wait there, Bell," pointing to a heap of straw on which were four or five other men. I sat down.

I was plodding with this small group on the path back to Bastogne. We were to be evacuated, it appeared. I was incredulous; it was too good to be true. I pretended to myself that it was a mistake, so that at the last moment, when I was sent back on line, I would be able to bear the disappointment. But the file of disabled men limped on, and no one turned us back. Aid men guided us toward ambulances, and I found myself being helped by careful hands into the rear of one of these vehicles. I climbed onto a stretcher that was suspended against the wall. I removed my boots and lay back. The ambulance started, and I fell into darkness.

Limping along, with a pass in my pocket ... a pass, incidentally, that I've written and signed myself. When I appeared at the outer door of the hospital, holding out this forgery with an ingratiating smile, the guard glanced at it and quickly looked the other way. A gentleman!

To be twenty-one years old, in Paris, with a roll of thousand-franc notes burning a hole in your pocket! Add that you've recently been on line, and you're not going back for a week or two. If this isn't happiness, what is? It's about as close to being absolutely free as I've ever felt. For by being in the Army, I was free of my own life; and for the time I was free of the Army, too. Youth and money, the univer-

sally recognized irresistible powers, were mine. It was the heyday of
the world; the air sparkled—though it was gray weather for the
Parisians. The prospect is always dark when the hero arrives. The
lives of the inhabitants have not been what you would call an unin-
terrupted pleasure. But the hero knows nothing of this. Everything
is trying to attract his attention. The avenues spread themselves for
his inspection. The shopkeeper is winding out his awning only to
add a few stripes of color to the scene. The woman fetching her
child a whack on the ear is not in earnest. The girl lifting her skirt to
cross a puddle is doing so simply to please him. The hero is con-
scious of his power to confer happiness on all these people, and
wishes to give them an opportunity to earn his benevolence. So he
asks them to help him, to tell him the way to a certain place. And
they, who are worried about having no money in the house, and no
coal, and so on—they look at his ignorant, expectant, selfish face,
and—a miracle—are touched by his belief in the importance of his
own immediate pleasure; they smile and inform him: "Walk down
three streets and take the Number 11 bus."

Boots, polished like mirrors, clopping on the fan-shaped cobbles.
Inhaling the air—raw and cold after the tepid soap-and-iodoform
hospital atmosphere.

I turn into a bar and order a brandy. The patron examines the
brand new thousand-franc note. "Don't worry," I tell him. "I have to
worry," he answers. When I tell him, *"Au revoir,"* he says, *"Sans doute."*
The French, cynical before defeat; sullen after rescue. What do the
sons of bitches want?

I come out on an avenue used by noisy motor bicycles and occa-
sional cars and Army trucks, and join a line waiting for a bus. It
arrives at last, belching smoke from the charcoal burner attached to
the roof. I jump on and stand on the rear platform. I spell out the
names over the shops as we pass: *Ciseaux d'Argent, La Maison de la
Chemise, Ressemelage Universel.* All at once we arrive at what I imme-
diately recognize as the Arc de Triomphe. A small ceremony is
taking place. A squad of men in helmets and black gaiters is pre-
senting arms, and an old lady in black, supported by an officer with
a white mustache, is carrying a huge bunch of flowers toward the
arch. The bus swings around the circle and goes down a magnifi-
cent boulevard. I ask the conductor where we are.

"Champs Elysées, evidently," he replies, and repeats it in a loud voice. Several people look at me; I smile at them.

To be in Paris! And with money to burn!

However, you can stand just so much excitement. You're filled with helium and the sky goes on and on upward. You've got to get rid of the burden of ecstasy. So you wind up at Place Blanche, at the foot of Montmartre, where all the soldiers go. Dogged by a Moroccan who wants your cigarettes, you duck into a bistro on one of the alleys. There you have another cognac. The place is swarming with women, drunken soldiers, pimps, and Arabs; there's a smell compounded of alcohol, tobacco, urine, and perfume. Zig-zag is here, and Aphrodisia, her lady-in-waiting. The soldier moves to another bar. The same spirit pervades, only the faces are different. Here he is attached by a pretty brunette—she doesn't look more than eighteen—with a roundish face.

She had a drink and he had a drink. In the mirror above the bar his face looked strangely pale and soft. She complained about the war, but she had a cheerful disposition. She had a friend in Nice, and soon she would be going there *en vacances*. She said something that struck him as very funny: "You could spend your life here like this and never see anything." She was looking forward to her vacation.

His elbow tucked in at her side, she led him out and around a corner or two, and up some stairs, and into a room. She carried on some *chuchotement* with a maid at the door. Meanwhile, in the semi-darkness, on the soft, sagging bed, he was getting out of his boots and shirt and trousers. She closed the door and began to undress. She had a wonderful figure; she couldn't have been over eighteen.

When I got back to the regiment, they were on the frontier of Germany.

We crossed the border in the usual marching order. Was it imagination, or had the landscape suddenly changed? No, it was true enough. There were, all at once, pylons straddling the fields; the *Autobahnen* ran straight and the houses were neat; there was much evidence of concrete, electrification, and modern plumbing. Some of my companions perked up—first symptoms of the postwar infatuation with German *Kultur*. However, over this paradise for automobile mechanics and refrigerator salesmen frolicked a sick devil; he exploded as a shellburst above a chimney; he swept over the *Autobahnen* in a stream of bullets. From a picturesque medieval townhouse, where groups of *Kinder* should have been assembling with flowers in their hands and *Lieder* on their lips, the sickness had to be exorcised with blasts of high explosive. He fled, leaving behind three corpses and a bazooka.

As I sat on a sidewalk of the village eating my K-ration, a German girl of my own age stood on the pavement opposite, staring at me. She was wondering, no doubt, what kind of monster I was. A "Sammy." One of the mongrel people who were invading this land of yellow-pigtailed maidens and kindly old watchmakers for no reason at all, only because we had been persuaded by Roosevelt and the Jews. As I was evidently eating cheese and crackers and had no intention of swallowing her, she stood and stared.

I remember her face. The heart-shaped face of the *Mädchen*. It was the same before the war, and it is the same now. That face has never heard of Dachau, Belsen, Buchenwald. For that matter, six centuries ago, on St. Valentine's Day—when the Jews of Strasbourg were despoiled of their money and packed on a platform and burned alive—the *Mädchen* looked on with the same bland features. That face would not understand such things even if it stared at them. It is framed in flowers, that face. Sometimes it emits snatches of *Lieder;* sometimes it laughs, revealing pearly teeth. The eyes are cornflower blue. And the fact is, the creature to which that face belongs is burning in hell, while the eyelids et cetera are constrained to keep the *gemütlich* smirk of a valentine.

We came to a stop on the Rhine, in Düsseldorf. Headquarters section was billeted in a house overlooking the river. From an attic window I looked across at the German-held half of the city, on the other bank. Occasionally a shell would whistle over from that direction. More frequently shells went over from the batteries to our rear, to stroke out another suspicious bump in the view. In boredom, I turned over the pages of magazines and books left behind by the good burghers in their flight. There were picture magazines which featured the social activities of German officers in Oslo, Paris, and Rome. Everywhere they were escorting beautiful women, wrapped in furs, to the opera; or standing beside other women, dressed in

tweeds, on country estates. There were also illustrations of
Wehrmacht youths waving as they entrained for the winter sports in
Russia or a little sea bathing at Anzio.

One morning this interlude ended. We crossed the Rhine before
dawn in rubber boats. Fortunately, the capture of the bridge at
Remagen had made this crossing purely anticlimactic; there was no
blood bath as we paddled toward the eastern bank. A few miserable
Poles and Italians laid down their arms in a hurry and were gath-
ered in.

Then began a race to the interior. We speeded in truck convoys
over the *Autobahnen*. Miles lapsed behind us. Now and then we
dismounted, formed combat files, and encircled a spot of resistance.
That being cleaned up, we resumed our easy conquest. Down the
sides of the road past the convoy trudged masses of German infan-
try—dusty, unshaven, yellow-faced wretches who muttered, *"Alles ist
kaput!"* They were eager to inform us that some of their mistaken
brothers were holed up in the next village or hiding out in the
woods. And they were all innocent: Hitler and the SS men were to
blame for everything.

We entered the forests of Bavaria. Our destination, it appeared,
was to be none other than the buzzard's nest itself—Berchtesgaden.
When we got there, little remained of the village. It had been
pulverized by bombers. Under the fairy-tale mountains covered
with pines we slept, and without emotion heard the news of the end
of the German war.

Not only our bodies were dissipating, but our imaginations also.
Nothing but alcohol and satisfaction by a whore seemed worth the
trouble. We had been exhausted, degraded, and reduced. War
made you rub shoulders with many kinds of people, forced you to
live intimately with them, with the stink of their bodies and the
dullness of their minds. You ceased to be able to differentiate;
everyone in a while seemed to have the same thresholds of pleasure
and pain. So much raw experience made you lose your curiosity
about shades of feeling. You wanted only to be relieved of other
people; not to be forced to do anything; to sink into blank uncon-
sciousness; to sleep. The difference between one mind and another
and the mysterious difference between man and woman had ceased

to be of interest. What were ideas, after all? They seemed unreal. What remained? One's boots stepping over the pavements of foreign cities; one's profile, with the cap tilted at the right angle, glimpsed covertly in the glass of a window; one's skin, shaved parade-smooth; one's own mind, drab and savage as a rat in a corner.

The redeployment area was situated in the hills overlooking Marseilles. Our tents were pitched on flats of scrub and rock. Rainy gusts howled over the hills and funneled into the valleys. The tents flapped in the wind, the tent ropes twanged, and from between the floor boards where we huddled around the stoves there oozed a black mud that seemed compounded of the excreta of thousands of lives. At night the guards piled wood and broken cardboard cartons into garbage cans and lit them and stood kicking their feet together, close to the flames; these burning spots linked the encampments.

Between these fires, we stumbled through blackness. One night, instead of walking through the tent door, I walked into the canvas; the material billowed inward, and I floated on it, able neither to fall nor to step back. I let myself slip down onto my knees, backed away, circumventing the ropes, and groped through the door to my cot. It seemed in a curious way the climax of the years I had spent in the Army. Someday, I thought, after the professionals have finished with it, I'm going to tell the story of the real war. There won't be anything but cold, rain, and men falling into tent walls in the dark. Why not go further? Tell it from the viewpoint of the materials—the shovel, the mud, the hole in the mud.

Of course, I have not told this story. It would be unendurably monotonous, as war itself is monotonous. But physical discomfort may be the ultimate horror. All that we have so elaborately constructed over the centuries—the roof above our heads, and the roof of ideas—is removed, and there we stand, like so many forked radishes, exposed to rain and wind and snow. It is not only the poor naked wretches under the eye of the Germans, men, women, and children, as they stumble, hand in hand, toward the gas chambers, who have been degraded. All of us have lost our covering. And with it, the mystery that alone keeps men sane.

* * *

We climbed out of the trucks, dragged down our duffel bags after us, carried them to a designated spot, and waited our turn to go on board. The dock area was littered with fragments of concrete and pitted by high explosive. The loading sheds were only shells of walls and mounds of rubble from which protruded parts of machinery and netted wire, fraying and rusting. The area had the gnawed look to which we had become accustomed.

A liberty ship was tied to one of the piers. Platoon by platoon, carrying their duffel bags over their shoulders, a line of men went up the gangplank. Then it was our turn. We hefted our bags and moved off.

From the deck I looked back at the shore. A crane was being driven over the dock by a German prisoner. He maneuvered it skillfully, picking up and transporting the larger fragments of concrete to a central heap. He was the liveliest thing in view.

I went below and found my hammock, stretched out on it, and opened a detective story. The engines hummed, the propeller turned, and the ship was moving to the sea.

And yet, it was an adventure. It was something to be there, at the time, on the landing beaches. In a just war.

Jimmy

Jimmy picked up his portrait and looked at it at arm's length. It showed a young soldier in the uniform of the Rangers. I guess you didn't ever think you'd pick up that picture in this house, thought Jimmy; sure, it had been a common joke about getting home and looking back on it all, but it was just a joke. At that time it was certain they weren't ever going home again. And here he was, looking at himself as he'd been in that summer of forty-three. You were very young, thought Jimmy; that stupid smile you put on for the camera . . . what were you thinking of? I bet you never knew where you were going. Jesus, if you had you'd have gone nuts or gone and got a broad, instead of taking a picture to send home.

And yet, he thought, if they dragged you into it again you'd walk around London or Paris looking just as young again, with a clean chest, till you got on the dirt road it all leads up to, and heard the shells going over again, and then you'd be old, and a lot older than the first time, because although every time is the first for ever and ever, Christ help us, yet the things have a way of piling up on you.

He took the little "Welcome Home" ribbon off the frame. When do you stop being welcome home, he wondered. Well, he took it off so he would never have to find out.

Reprinted from *Columbia Review*. Vol. 26, No. 5. May 1946.

He walked over to the radio, turned it on, and reached for a newspaper. He was careful when he read the news, trying to see what the score was. It was simply a matter of self-protection. He now understood quite clearly that there was a relationship between what people said and what they did to you.

It struck him right between the eyes. A little article saying that some German officer had been hanged for shooting Canadian prisoners.

He laid the paper down and remembered. He didn't have to try to remember. It wasn't a trick like in the movies, or like trying to remember something pleasant like the first time you kissed a girl. These memories followed him around, and he knew he'd never forget them, not for all his hatred of the army. War and peace were together inside him, and though they said one was over he knew it would never be for him. He hadn't known he was getting into that. He'd thought he'd go away and do what they said must be done in a dream country, and then he'd come back and forget it.

But he remembered the day at Carentan. They were coming over the fields in perfect order, feeling lean and sweaty from the fast advancing, and now and then a rifle would pop off and they'd whoop and holler bringing in the snipers. They were winning, and it was easy.

They handed over this prisoner to him. He was a lousy-looking soldier and obviously left there because he was a sad sack. Jimmy had seen others left behind by the retreating Germans because they wanted to stay back. Big blond men with a hole in their head, lying over the rifle among the onions, with a pipe still clenched in their jaws, or under the cider barrels, with cider soaking into the jaeger. Death and apple-cider always went together, it seemed, in Normandy. Other fronts had other smells, but it was cider in Normandy. This sack hadn't wanted to stay behind. Some lieutenant had picked him out, thrown a camouflaged raincoat at him, and said "Hans, you will stay here." In that army they didn't feel sorry for anybody. Hans had stayed. Here he was. Every now and then Hans would look in the ditch at some other members of his fine organization with holes in their heads. Hans was dumb, but he didn't want a hole in the head. He had put up his hands rapidly.

Jimmy gave Hans a cigarette. At this time Jimmy hadn't been in a

German counter-attack, nor had he lain down under the church steeple at Veghel, nor had he been in Belgium. He felt good in giving the cigarette. Only once more did he give a German anything, and that was a stick of gum to a dying soldier at Bastogne who took eight hours to die, right beside Jimmy's hole. But then Jimmy had been through it all and knew why he was giving the stick of gum. In Normandy he would have given his watch away and thought nothing of it. But he thought over the stick of gum a great deal.

Well, here he was with the sad sack. The sad sack had his palms pressed to the top of his head, and was looking at Jimmy as his protector. He dogged his steps. That was the word, dogged. Jimmy wanted to reach over and pat him on his square skull to reassure him. But he just let him stick close by.

They entered Carentan easily. Towards the end of the war it was easy to enter any town, But this was Normandy, and they might have been suspicious. But it wasn't Normandy yet. In half an hour the countryside would begin to be what men mean when they ask you "Were you in Normandy?" but at the moment it was just a piece of ground, with hedgerows and big barns and apple cider. The people were coming up from the cellars and weeping with joy and handing out wine. When the French give away their wine you can tell there's something artificial about the atmosphere and that things will change for the worse. When the price of wine goes up to 500 francs then you know a war is getting down to business. But of course they didn't know it. This was a liberation, and the guys were standing around in the squares asking each other, "Where in hell are the movie cameras?"

Jimmy was doing pretty well with a French girl, when the first shell came over. Maybe the other army's shells always sound worse than they could possibly be, but at once everybody in Carentan had a vision. It was a vision of devilish men piling ammo into gun breeches. But they weren't just firing guns. They were saying, "Here is one for you, Americans, to take with the wine; and here is one for you, you French, who are giving it away."

The Germans always made their weapons have a language of their own, each gun its own line of convincing, and to go through a bombardment was to go through an argument with German ideas, to feel the weight of Teutonic thought on the frail arch of the spine.

At this declaration of purpose all the Americans looked at each other. The French grabbed the bottles and went back down into their cellars.

Jimmy's prisoner began running. He was heading for the nearest hole. Jimmy fired from the hip and caught him neatly in the back of the head. The prisoner fell in the middle of the street and stayed there several days.

Jimmy had fired partly out of surprise and out of his knowledge of duty, which says that a guard is right in shooting an escaping prisoner.

But of course the prisoner hadn't been trying to escape. Jimmy saw that at once, and the longer he thought about it, the more clearly he saw it. The man had simply been acting human, trying to get to a hole. Of course Jimmy didn't feel badly about it then. Now, as he sat reading the newspaper which said a German major had been hanged for ordering the execution of Canadian prisoners, he didn't feel badly about that either.

But the problem presented itself to him in these terms. His act had been, in terms of pure justice, just as criminal as the major's. But there were extenuating circumstances. There was one fact which prevented his being hanged. The fact was that America had, as they said, "won the war." Under a court of pure justice such as God might direct Jimmy would be just as guilty as the German major.

But this guilt was washed away by the crossing of the Atlantic from east to west, by the cheers of the crowds on Fifth Avenue, and by the "Welcome Home" on the framework of his picture, which somehow all added up to saying "Not guilty." He was not expected to feel bad about what he had done; rather, he was to be proud of it.

To know what the score was, to find out the extent of his own guilt and to discover who was guilty and who was not, Jimmy struggled with his confused memories and spent a good part of each day in reading the newspapers.

3

VIEWS FROM A WINDOW

After the war I picked up my studies at Columbia, and wrote furiously . . . short stories and a novel. Some of the stories were published. Then I had a "nervous breakdown" and was sent to King's Park Hospital on Long Island. There the patients hardly ever saw a doctor and were knocked about by the guards.

I had amnesia; much of the war was blotted out, and parts of my life before the war. Then memory returned . . . my memories of combat returned with a vengeance. They still give me bad dreams, and looking at an open field I think, How are we going to get across that?

I grieved for men who had gone to the front and died there. In comparison with these, other men—especially the kind one met in universities—seemed hollow. Ideas were only so many words, they had nothing to do with reality . . . a man spilling his intestines in the road.

On my release from the hospital I applied for readmission to Columbia College. The doctor who interviewed me had my case history mixed up with someone else's, apparently a music student. I thought he was testing my sanity and did not try to correct him—I had recently been exposed to such testing by psychiatrists. He said that I could not be readmitted, and advised me to find some occupation that would bring me in contact with the common man.

But the School of General Studies would admit me. So I went back to school and also worked at odd jobs: as a copyboy on *The New York Herald Tribune,* a packer in an import-export firm.

I was seeing Mona again, and this became a passionate affair. But her parents shipped her off to a school in Boston to study acting.

I had exciting memories of Paris during the war, so I decided to go back. I could afford to—I had a pension for my disabilities as well as the G.I. Bill. I enrolled at the University of Paris in a course for foreign students. In a few weeks I found the classes intolerable— if you didn't speak French like a native they treated you like a child.

155

I dropped out and, with other disaffected Americans, hung around the cafés of Boul' Mich and Saint-Germain-des-Prés.

I had published a few poems in the manner of Wyatt, Marvell, and other English poets. In Paris I wrote other poems that were not so derivative. When I had enough poems to make a book I took them to a printer who for $500 would make 500 copies, and arranged with a man in New York to distribute them.

There was a favorable review of *The Arrivistes* by Randall Jarrell in *The Nation.* I wrote to thank him for it, and he wrote back with some advice. There were good things in my book but it would have been better if they had been organized into a few good poems. About critics . . . "in the long run you benefit from them . . . by the time you're old and grey a couple of good ones have written well about you, and the bad ones have looked up allusions in the *Britannica,* explained them, and ignorantly marveled at you enough for readers to accept you as one more mountain range. Anyway, I trust this happy ending is so."

I married and had a son, but the marriage lasted only a short time.

I worked for a publishing house in New York, reading manuscripts. Sometimes I had to talk to an author. Some were far more interesting than their works. The man who submitted a manuscript bound with a chain . . . When I asked why, he said that Irving Berlin had been entering his apartment and stealing his songs.

The woman with the mating machine . . . She showed me a picture . . . it looked like an electric chair. You had to sit in it and see what the dial registered, and put your prospective mate in the chair, and see how the numbers matched. Then you did some calculations based in astrology. When I said that we couldn't publish it she began to tremble, her elbow rapping on the desk. "I hear you were in California," she said. "What did they tell you about me?"

"Furnished Rooms" and "Literary Life" describe this period. I worked for five years in publishing. At the end of that time I married again, returned to Columbia, and published a second book of poems.

Dogface Poetics

       I got through the war all right, but afterwards, when I was back in the States, I had a nervous breakdown and was hospitalized. I had amnesia; the war was blacked out in my mind, and so were episodes of my life before the war. When I left the hospital I found that I could hardly read or write. In these circumstances I began writing poems.

Before the war I had written a few poems and some prose. Now I found that poetry was the only kind of writing in which I could express my thoughts. Through poems I could release the irrational, grotesque images I had accumulated during the war; and imposing order on these images enabled me to recover my identity. In 1948, when I was living in Paris, one night I dreamed that I was lying on the bank of a canal, under machine gun and mortar fire. The next morning I wrote it out, in the poem "Carentan O Carentan," and as I wrote I realized that it wasn't a dream, but the memory of my first time under fire. So I began piecing the war together, and wrote other poems. "Memories of a Lost War" describes the early days of the fighting in Normandy; "The Battle," the fighting at Bastogne.

Twelve years after the war I wrote a long poem, "The Runner,"

Reprinted from *A Company of Poets*. Ann Arbor: The University of Michigan Press, 1981. This essay first appeared in *The Poetry of War*, ed. Ian Hamilton. London: Alan Ross, 1965.

157

which was devoted to the dogface soldier's war. I wanted to represent the drudgery of that life, the numbing of intellect and emotion, and the endurance of the American infantry soldier. I wanted to write a poem that would be abrasive, like a pebble in a shoe. Some readers thought this flat poem a mistake, but other readers, who were infantrymen, appreciated the details. To a footsoldier, war is almost entirely physical. That is why some men, when they think about war, fall silent. Language seems to falsify physical life and to betray those who have experienced it absolutely—the dead. As Hemingway remarked, to such men the names on a map are more significant than works of imagination.

However, in a postwar world there are limitations to the dogface way of looking at things. Love, for example, is not best written about by a man who is trying to avoid extra duty. And a country cannot be governed by silence and inertia. In recent years the closemouthed, almost sullen, manner of my early poems has given way to qualities that are quite different. Like other men of the war generation, I began with middle age; youth came later. Nowadays in my poems I try to generate mystery and excitement: I have even dealt in general ideas. But I retain the dogface's suspicion of the officer class, with their abstract language and indifference to individual, human suffering. You might say that the war made me a footsoldier for the rest of my life.

What, in these poems, was I trying to do that had not already been done? I did not wish to protest against war. Any true description of modern warfare is a protest, but many have written against war with satire or indignation, and it still goes on. My object was to remember. I wished to show the war exactly, as though I were painting a landscape or a face. I wanted people to find in my poems the truth of what it had been like to be an American infantry soldier. Now I see that I was writing a memorial of those years for the men I had known, who were silent. I was trying to write poems that I would not be ashamed to have them read—poems that would be, in their laconic and simple manner, tolerable to men who had seen a good deal of combat and had no illusions.

"Baudelaire, three injections!"

The Veterans' Administration decided that my breakdown had been due to combat fatigue. They gave me a pension and I bought a ship ticket to France. I wanted to put an ocean between myself and my illness. Besides, all American writers went to Paris, and I had a longing to see the city again—the days I spent there during the war had been just enough to whet my appetite.

When I arrived I registered for the Course in Civilization at the University of Paris. This would give me something to do.

The course was designed for Americans, especially ex-soldiers, whose dollars were needed immediately by the French. One part of the course was French composition, taught by a professor whose method was a triumph of that logic on which the French pride themselves. The professor would translate passages from French novels into English. The professor's English. Then we translated the passages back into French. Then he marked our efforts wrong, because they did not correspond, word for word, with the original, *le mot juste*.

I protested that the method, though logical, did not allow for the

Reprinted from Louis Simpson, *North of Jamaica*. New York: Harper and Row, 1972.

use of intelligence. The professor replied that Americans had no training in logic or taste, and moreover he was a professor of the University of Paris.

If I try, I can still hear him expounding the beauties of a passage by Anatole France. What made it beautiful? Could no one tell? It was a description of Paris, viewed from the famous author's window on the Seine. This was the art, that in describing things far away France had used fifty-seven syllables. Did anyone dispute the computation? No. Well, now look! In describing things seen close at hand, France had used twenty-two syllables, only twenty-two. What was the reason? Could no one tell? Mees Brown? Meester Smeeth? Meester . . . No one? Ah, there was a hand! A miracle. What, what was that? Yes, of course. The great author had used more syllables for things seen far away than for things seen close at hand because at a distance one sees many, many more things.

What seems to be the trouble? You seem to have an objection, Meester Smeeth. Well, if Meester Smeeth wishes to correct the method of the French masters, we should all give him our attention. What's that? I don't understand. No, not "oo" but "eou", with the lips held so. Not "et," Meester Smeeth, but "ay." You are saying?

"Suppose France was describing a house ten feet away, and the same house a kilometer away . . . I mean, isn't it possible that you see more details close at hand than at a distance? Or suppose he was describing a locomotive right in front of him, and an empty field. Wouldn't the locomotive get more syllables?"

"Meester Smeeth, no nonsense, please. This is the way Anatole France has written it. Listen."

The professor reads through the passage, giving full expression to every word. Any questions? There are no more questions. Nevertheless, he has it in for Smith, and twenty minutes later swoops down to surprise him reading a book under the desk. The professor holds the book up and shakes it.

"Ah, very good! It is not even in French! *Lif on Ze Meeseeseepi!* Very good, reading Engleesh novels during ze class!"

Afterwards, Smith is called to the department office, where he is warned that such behavior, coupled with his absences, may have a dire consequence—the cutting-off of his GI Bill. . . .

Besides composition, we were taught Method. The class was in the hands of a portly dame. She said that the classical method of criticism was based on Taine. But before one could approach Taine it would be necessary to review French grammar. And before one could approach grammar it would be necessary to learn the proper pronunciation of the language. She approached with a lighted candle and held it in front of a student's mouth. She asked him to pronounce the vowels. If he exhaled while uttering the vowels, the flame flickered. If his pronunciation was atrocious, the flame went out.

"The lips like this . . . ooh! ooh! The tongue back so."

In front of me the flame writhed like a tortured creature and died. I was reduced from an enthusiasm for French literature to stuttering, and then to silence. Smith and I spent more time at a table with a view of the Boul' Mich than we did in the classroom. However, once a week I revisited Mademoiselle's class, and there they would be, more than a score of adults groaning the vowels in unison or chanting the sentences of a primer for six-year-olds. Paris is worth a mass. These visits were necessary for me to be nominally included on the list of students and kept on the payroll at the American consulate.

Then I had an idea. Maybe I should quit the course for Americans and get into the classes for French students. I had noticed a course in Baudelaire advertised on the bulletin board. Baudelaire would be fun. There's no time like the present—why didn't I go over to the university and register for Baudelaire right now?

I went to the building where one registered. It was full of French and foreign students, but no Americans. The waiting line wound up a staircase. I took a place on the lowest stair. How earnest these students seemed! This was the real Sorbonne, certainly. The French students, in particular, looked in earnest. They made jokes among themselves—they'd probably known one another in the *lycée*—but whenever anything official happened—a door opening at the top of the stairs, a name being called—they grasped their books and riffled to attention. Going to school was very serious for French students. Their whole life could depend on the results of examinations.

At last I arrived at the top of the stairs, facing the door. A voice said, *"Entrez!"* I entered. A man in white, evidently a doctor, walked up to me. "Certificate of inoculation," he said.

"I beg your pardon?"

"The certificate of inoculation. It is necessary to have a certificate of inoculation in order to register. This is an institution of the state. Have you been inoculated against typhus and diphtheria?"

"I don't know," I said. "I suppose I must have been. At some time. I only want to take a course in Baudelaire."

"Then it is absolutely necessary that you be inoculated."

"Very well," I said.

The doctor filled a hypodermic needle. "Take off your jacket and shirt, if you please."

I did as I was told. He stepped behind me, and a moment later I felt as if I'd been shot with a gun.

"Jesus Christ!"

He stepped in front of me again. "You will return tomorrow."

I put on my shirt and jacket and went downstairs. In half an hour I was lying on my bed in my hotel room. My temperature was rising, and when I dozed off I had the fitful dreams of fever. My back, where the doctor had driven the needle in, was throbbing. I dreamed of water and ice, pitchers of lemonade. I woke with a parched mouth and throbbing head, to see night falling outside. At a window opposite, an old woman was gazing out at the dusk like some terrible bird of prey. I'll bet they live on soup, she and her family; the soup of horse bones. I need iced lemonade.

It was a bad night, but the next morning my temperature was down. Once more I set off for the Sorbonne, to complete my registration.

Again I stood in line on the staircase. When I arrived at the top, the same voice said, *"Entrez."*

"Ah yes," said the doctor. "Now, the inoculation, eh?"

"Wait a moment," I said. "I had an injection yesterday."

"There are three injections. This is the second."

He filled the hypodermic needle and I took off my jacket and shirt. This time, when he stepped behind me, I thought I knew what to expect and braced myself accordingly. But the shock was no less, nor the pain.

"Holy Mother of God!"

Three hours later I was tossing on my bed in delirium. The Sahara, dry as a bone, stretched to the horizon. An Arab on a camel came riding by. He had a big goatskin of cold water flapping at his side. When I asked him for a drink he stopped obligingly. But, just as I was raising the goatskin to my lips, the camel put his head round and tried to take a bite out of my back. The camel and rider vanished. I was standing on the staircase, next to a French student who had his face in a book. "How many inoculations are there?" I asked him. Without taking his head out of the text he said, "What course do you wish to take?" "Baudelaire," I said. He did not answer, but whispered to someone standing on the other side. The whisper traveled up the staircase. The door at the top flew open and a voice shouted, "Baudelaire, three injections!"

The next day, instead of going to the university, I sat down at a table at the Flore and thought things over. Then I tore up the application forms.

After all, this was what Baudelaire would have done. Or was it? French writers, even the decadents, are sticklers for rules; *au fond,* most of them are middle-class. In fact, France has no poets of the first rank. I decided to give up French poetry and read the Russians in translation.

Furnished Rooms

Furnished rooms.

Someday I'll write a history of furnished rooms and landladies—the crazy women who sit on the other side of a partition listening for suspicious noises.

I found a room for ten dollars a week in Chelsea, below street level, across from the seminary, a soot-black building resembling a prison. The top of my window truncated the passers-by; they were cut off at the waist, as though a universal calamity had left only legs, legs of every shape, ambulating by themselves. The garbage can stood outside my window; famished dogs sometimes sent the cover clattering down in the middle of the night; cats lurked along the railing that projected a few feet out from the building, and in the dawn, when they mated, their howling brought me bolt upright.

Through the window dust sifted into my room, covering everything—the marble fireplace that had been boarded up; the stuffed chair and the straight wooden chair, the table, with my secondhand typewriter on it; the bookshelves and half-dozen books. If I wiped the dust off, an hour later it had started to settle again. I felt this dust—though dust is too dignified a name for the substances in the air of New York—in my hair, my nostrils, my skin; under my

Reprinted from Louis Simpson, *Riverside Drive*. New York: Atheneum, 1962.

fingernails it formed black rims, and I imagined it lining the walls of my lungs with carbon.

One door of my room opened on a corridor; the other on the bathroom I shared with the landlady. The bathroom became one source of quarrels between us. She wanted the air vent opened whenever I ran hot water; it was a regulation of the Fire Department, she screamed; why didn't I observe it? Then turn in a fire alarm, I told her. But I am anticipating. It took three months for things to come to this pass. At the beginning she was as sweet as the pot of mildewed honey she kept in her refrigerator. She showed me the shelf in the refrigerator where I could keep a carton of milk, eggs, and a butter dish; she showed me how to operate the stove— for I had "kitchen privileges." She told me about the couple upstairs whom she was having evicted because they were noisy. She told me about her years on the staff of a liberal weekly, about her psycho-analysis, about the refusal of the government to grant her pension claim. When both doors to the bathroom were open I could hear her singing *Die Fledermaus,* and I found her gray hairs in the bath-room sink. She was so happy to have me staying there, for the last roomer had set fire to his furniture in the middle of the floor; and sure enough, there was a charred spot three feet across, in the middle of the floor, to prove it.

The woman, had she lived three centuries before, would have been burned as a witch, and I, for one, would have been happy to see it. The trouble began with my kitchen privileges. If I turned up the flame of the gas range a few millimeters beyond what she considered necessary to boil an egg, she came complaining in. One night when the man upstairs was putting his garbage in the can outside my window, she flew out to intercept him, shrieking that he had woken her with his noise, and she practically had a fit when he told her to shut her big mouth. When she had a workman in to attend to the plumbing, I heard her pleading with him for half an hour not to charge her for his labor. Then she began whining about the air vent in the bathroom and in a week or so I wasn't talking to her.

She was typical of her breed. Let her stand, in this chronicle, for landladies in general; and let the room, with its perpetually down-sifting dust, broken furniture, and boarded-up fireplace, stand for all the rooms into which, heavily, I carried my suitcases and type-writer, and out of which, three months or so later, I carried them again.

Living in these conditions, I took my job more seriously than ever; routine was a float that kept my head above the tide threatening to engulf me—falling buttons, torn shirt sleeves, bad food, a gasping bank account. I held to my desk desperately. In order to combat the currents that swirled about me, I conserved my strength. Between the dusty walls of a furnished room I made out a budget like Hannibal planning a campaign in Italy. There were heroic struggles to which only angels were witness. At the end of a hard day at the office, when I had rewritten somebody else's book, I sat down and wrote a few pages of my life of Racine. With hunger gnawing at my belly, I read the plays of Molière from beginning to end, rising now and then to pace around the room, gleefully reciting his lines. Or, if the December night was not too cold, I'd walk around ten blocks. Often I was filled with a strange joy; I was free. My shirts might be falling apart, but I was free.

I speak of December because it was then, in the nadir of the year, that extraordinary things began to happen. I am not superstitious, but I have seen, particularly in New York, coincidences so striking that they seem supernatural. I never see a black dog but on the same day I see another, or an albino but within a short time I meet another. There are days that are nothing but Armenian restaurants, and days on which at every corner a red-haired woman is visible. No doubt these coincidences are only a psychological condition in the observer; on one day he happens to be particularly alert to black dogs, whereas on any other he would not notice them. No doubt, in cities the same things happen over and over again. Be that as it may, these coincidences, when they are perceived, seem to be on the verge of formulating a law by which the whole of life may be understood in a flash. All the syllables of confusion are trying to utter one word.

The sequence began with a dream. I got out of bed and wrote the dream down, for at the time I was keeping a journal—it was one of my resolves. I have lost the journal and the dream, but Mona figured in it, in the way she usually did—smiling, caressing, and vanishing—so that I woke between happiness and grief.

On the evening of the next day, at a party in the Village—for I went to parties, casual gatherings of people who didn't know each other, where nothing was expected of you—I met a young woman who looked very much like Mona. Or was this an illusion? For more than once, with a suddenly pounding heart, I had imagined that a woman coming toward me was Mona, only to discover a moment later that she was a stranger; and the woman passed by, puzzled by my searching glance. But no—it was true; this girl, particularly about the eyes, resembled Mona. After the party I took her to a coffee shop, where I told her what had attracted me to her. She wasn't flattered, but she smiled with good humor and asked me why, if the girl meant so much to me, I didn't call her up.

Why not, indeed? It is difficult to understand my reluctance to see in the flesh the person I desired in my dreams. Perhaps I preferred the dream to the reality. I was afraid that if I saw Mona again I would be shaken with the old fever.

On the third day, as I was going home by walking across Forty-second Street to the west side subway, I paused on a corner waiting for the light to change. A girl standing in front of me turned around, and this time when my heart leaped it did not fall. We stared for a moment, then I found her hands between mine, and I pulled her out of the crowd streaming around us.

"I had a dream about you," I said.

"So have I."

We walked together, not noticing the direction. I was trying to tell her, all at once, about my life: my separation from Libby—"I'm practically divorced"—and my work.

"Was Libby the woman I saw you with that day?"

I knew the day she meant; it was when I'd seen her modeling in the window.

"And are you still modeling?"

"Oh, no. That was only for a while. I'm in show business."

"What kind of show business?"

"TV. Haven't you ever seen me? I'm on . . ." She named a show I'd heard about—an hour-long revue of songs, dances, and comic sketches riddled with commercials.

"What on earth do you do?" I said. "You don't sing and dance."

"I look pretty," she said. "I'm part of the scenery."

She said this with a touch of bitterness, and as I talked to her, I thought she looked, though more beautiful than ever, a little changed. How old was she? I was on the edge of thirty, and there was a gap of five years between us—she must be twenty-four. In the moment on the corner when she turned, before she recognized me, she seemed fatigued, and almost bewildered, as though not knowing where she was going or what she meant to do. And now, as I searched her face—so much more beautiful, and in detail so different from the face I had imagined—I thought I discerned traces of weariness and at the corners of her mouth slight down-turning marks. But, if anything, these traces improved her beauty; her features were touched by experience.

"I'm just a dummy," she said, "going no place fast. Once I had an acting part with two other girls. And do you know what? We had to wear masks."

Apparently show business wasn't a picnic. Not what she'd thought it would be when she was at school in Philadelphia.

"Then why do you do it?"

"What else can I do? I'm not a star, you know. Oh, I know, you always thought I was something wonderful, but a lot of people don't. And there are things in the business you can't imagine."

I asked her about her family.

"Daddy died," she said. "We live at the same place."

She had to be home soon, so we said good-by. I took her hand to shake it, but this seemed absurd, so instead I took her in my arms and kissed her on the mouth. When I released her, she laughed.

"I'll call you tomorrow," I said.

I left her at a bus stop. When I looked back, she was still there; she smiled and waved. I waved and, as I turned round again, collided with a man carrying a brief case.

"Why don't you look where you're going?" he snapped.

"The same to you, Jack!"

At ten o'clock I phoned Mona. "Don't call me early," she'd said. "I sleep late." When she came to the phone she was still sleepy; she slept very late indeed. "I'll meet you at eleven," she said. "On the corner of Forty-second and Park."

One of the advantages of my job was that no one questioned my coming and going. I wasn't essential to the business of the firm; so long as I read manuscripts, corrected copy, and wrote jacket blurbs, I was left to my own devices. The vice president in charge of sales, the head editor, and the office manager took agents out to lunch, conferred with authors, drew up contracts, planned the format of books, launched the advertising, attended publishers' meetings, and decided the policy of the firm *in camera*. So at 10:45 I simply walked out, and ten minutes later was waiting for Mona.

She was late, as she always had been. But how could I be angry with her? She was dressed to turn heads—costumed would be a better word—and when she came trotting up on high heels, taking short steps, in her fashionably long skirt, leaning slightly forward from the waist—because she was myopic—and put her hand on my arm and tucked it into her side, I forgot my annoyance. One or two people paused to glance at our meeting.

"Am I very late?" she said.

"Just a few minutes."

"I'm sorry. I had to call my agent. And I've got to call the studio."

Then off she went again, into a restaurant, to use the telephone, while I waited for her outside. The call took all of ten minutes, and I began to feel ridiculous. What was I doing waiting for her? I'd made a clean break with my former life; I was living well enough. Why was I waiting for a woman on a street corner?

Finally she came out.

"That's that," she said. "I had to talk to one of the directors. He doesn't like me, so I have to be nice to him."

"What shall we do?" I said.

"Couldn't we just sit somewhere?"

"We could go to my place."

She didn't answer at once. Then she said, "No."

"Why not?"

"No."

"Look," I said. "I promise to be a gentleman, if that's what's worrying you. Honestly, I just want to talk, and I don't like trying to talk in restaurants, especially in the lunch hour."

"All right."

I hailed a cab, and we went bowling down Fourth Avenue and across town and descended in front of my apartment. I handed the cabbie a dollar tip; Mona always had that effect on me. There went tomorrow's lunch.

"Watch out for the garbage," I said, and led the way, three steps down and a turn to the right through the hall door. Then I opened my door, and there we were. I shut it behind us. There she stood, where she had been in my dream. It was incredible.

"It's very nice," she said.

"Nice!"

"The old fireplace. And the pipe rack. I remember your pipe rack."

She walked around the room and found more things to enjoy in that space than Libby would have in the Taj Mahal. The room began to look different to me; it was no longer just a dust box. I thought that after Mona left enough of her would remain to make it glow a little. I'd not be able to see the old chair again without visualizing her in it. So it is we enrich the pale shells we inhabit; and so temples are built. The changes she had wrought in that room in five minutes were enough to make a man believe in ghosts; at least, I saw that the dull materials of existence could be changed by another kind of physics, and if the physics was only in my head, it was no less real for that.

She wanted to know about my job and my work. I talked, and in my narrative the penny-pinching firm of Hancock-Williams became Dickensian, a wonderfully funny place. My laborious, ill-fated life of Racine became a jewel of biography; by her eyes and mouth she made me think so. But more than this, as I talked to her, the limits of my world, which had seemed immovable, began to move, and I was aware that I was cut out for better things. I began to feel again that the world was romantic, that my strength was in yielding to the destructive element, following my own crazy impulses. I'd been limping along in the ranks to other people's music. Like Baudelaire's albatross, I had been flopping on the deck instead of sailing in the wind. Why? Why? What did I have to lose? I found myself telling her that I was going to chuck it all—the ephemeral, money-grubbing, sycophantic world of business and Madison Avenue, and do something brave. Teach in a high school in California, perhaps, under the redwoods, while I wrote a real book, a book that would be filled with all the rumors of the years.

As I ranted on, I was standing a foot in front of her. The air began to thicken. My voice faltered; she said nothing. I continued talking, but the noise of words had nothing to do with what was actually happening, what was bound to happen, given her and me and the place. It was as though another were in the room with us, a creature that sought only its own satisfaction, that came in where the circumstances were right, paying no heed to locks or promises. The air was thickening, and at last I found it absurd to speak. She put her arms around my waist in the moment that I began to bend toward her. So we kissed, and five years vanished.

A few minutes later, as she lay on the counterpane, which in our haste we hadn't bothered to turn down, with her skirt up, her flesh parted like a flower in the ruffles of the petticoat that, it seemed, was also fashionable this season, she put the back of her hand to her mouth and said between clenched teeth, "I didn't mean this to happen."

I hadn't meant it to, either. At least not consciously. So there we were, right back where we'd started. As I touched the curve of her cheek and looked into the mirrors of her eyes, I knew this was reality, that all the improbable stories were true, and the world is what you want to make it. Here we were again, in spite of marriages and jobs, in spite of time. If this could happen, anything could.

Annus Mirabilis! And how to describe it? Where to start?

Once we calculated how many times we'd made love; it was an astonishing figure, considering that we weren't living together. One episode merges into another; in the room there is a continuous mingling of arms and legs, scarcely interrupted by flickers of the light outside. After these interruptions, she soon returned, with a knock on the door, to revenge herself on the world. When she had had to spend an afternoon with her mother at a tea party, with old biddies and their husbands, men from the cosmetics factory where her father had worked, on the next afternoon she turned up at my place wearing her party clothes, long gloves, and a hat as broad as a cake. She borrowed my landlady's teapot. She had bought sandwiches on the way over. "We'll have our own tea party," she said. And nothing would do but that I must dress up and take her into the garden, the plot of dirt behind the building, overlooked on every side by neighboring windows. There, while the slatterns with their dustmops hung staring out of windows, she served tea. "One lump or two? Cream or lemon?" Then we returned to my room, leaving the neighbors wondering what on earth this vision was doing among the ash cans. She kicked the door shut behind her and peeled off her gloves. She removed the party dress and tossed it on the floor. Petticoat, brassière, shoes, stockings, and pants followed. "How do you like my hat?" she said. And a little later in her best home-counties accent, "I'm so happy you came."

Sometimes when we made love, she seemed to be revenging herself on the world that, as she told me, though I found it hard to believe, disliked her. If she was having a bad time at the studio, she held to me like a drowning soul until I kissed away the frowns and the sullen corners of her mouth. There was a woman in a position of power at the studio who hated her, she said, and one of the directors, the woman's toady, made every attempt to put her in the wrong. "I can't get ahead," she said. "Most of the actresses who get ahead sleep with everybody. I can't do that. And besides, I don't have the drive you need. It's dog eat dog; you've got to be willing to starve, to do anything, to make out in show business. It just doesn't matter enough to me." When she spoke of show business, she adopted the language of show business—the vulgar, knowing phrases that, coming from her mouth, seemed affected. At such moments, she was far from the girl I'd first fallen in love with. On one occasion, as she described an episode at the studio, she seemed almost a stranger. She was talking about a famous actor, now in his fifties, who had been given a leading part in a sketch. It seemed that he kept putting his hands on the girls' backsides. During rehearsal, in a break when the girls were chatting near a mike they thought dead, the voice of one of them filled the studio, amplified and clear as a bell: "I say, if he wants to feel, let him feel!" Mona told this story with an expression of distaste, and yet, as she told it, I could see she thought there was something fine about the girl's attitude.

She had one friend among the girls, a tall blonde who, in Mona's own words, had the kind of body she admired. "I'm too short," she said. "But you ought to see Belle. When she lies down on a couch, she looks so damned sexy. She has the long-legged look men admire."

As she described Belle, she herself was lying aslant my bed, with her feet flat against the wall, so that her calves and thighs had long, tapering contours. I saw nothing wrong with them and told her so. Indeed, I wondered why, long ago, I had thought her legs fat. Trotting up and down New York, or making love so often, had changed their appearance. In fact, I thought our love-making was making her more attractive every day. And this was no illusion. She told me herself that nowadays people were remarking on her looks. Her face had a delicacy, her body a slender undulance, that could only be the results of love.

She and Belle had decided they were the only two girls in the show who weren't "dawgs." At least Belle had said so, and Mona was so tickled to be picked out by Belle in this way, you'd think she had been nominated for an Academy Award. Belle, by Mona's account, sounded like a tin-plated bitch, and there was something peculiarly repulsive about her vocabulary—"dawgs" was the least of it—but Mona admired her unreservedly.

From what she said, she wasn't any too popular at the studio. They thought she was stuck up; they didn't understand her refusal to participate in kaffee klatsches when the girls raked other people's reputations over the coals. One day when they were all discussing the lesbianism of a famous actress, Mona had stepped out of the circle, saying, "How do you know?" Her remark struck them dumb. Then one of them said, "What are you defending her for?" "I just don't believe in gossip," Mona replied. Remarks like this hadn't endeared her to the bunch.

I could see that, in her lowly position, having so many reservations about that kind of life, she must find the way she'd chosen to go full of thorns. Yet, and I was ashamed of myself when I thought so, sometimes it seemed she was not as far removed from the vulgarity of that life as she said she was. Though she painted a picture of herself as innocent, her anecdotes would reveal a sympathy with the promiscuous, hard-boiled, empty-headed life of theater people. Sometimes I thought she was telling me what she knew I wanted to hear, and only betraying her real feelings now and then by a slip of the tongue. This suspicion would be strengthened by the look, almost of fear, in her eyes and by her rapid attempt to qualify what she had just said.

Her off-guard remarks, reeking as they did of show business, the market of beautiful, charming, vicious women and men without character, all consumed with vanity and pretension, a pit where indeed dog ate dog, came more and more to acerbate my intelligence. It was as much as I could do to keep from puncturing the pretty balloons she sent up—for in spite of her complaining about show business, it was her life, and she was still taken with the glamour of acting. But I couldn't always, in fear of chilling her spirits and throwing a shadow over our love, restrain myself from saying what I thought. When a Hollywood actress, a notorious tart, by another marriage got herself a European title, Mona said, wagging her head, "You've got to give the devil her due!"

"What does that mean?"

"Say what you like, you've got to give the devil her due."

"Must you really? I suppose Belle said that. It sounds like one of her bits of advice."

But this wasn't as bad as the time Mona, having been unreachable by telephone for a whole weekend, turned up at ten o'clock on Sunday night, threw herself in my arms, and announced that she had had the honor of meeting at a country club an actress who was just as notorious as "the devil" for her affairs and the amount of money and jewelry she had salted away. They had gone swimming together, and the actress questioned Mona and told her that, with her body and looks, she was a fool if she didn't make a million dollars. As Mona told me this, with lights dancing in her eyes, my heart sank; I visualized the older woman clearly—one of those makers of assignations, dope peddlers, God knows what, who would arrange any corruption. If rumors were true, that woman had begun her career in a brothel, and now, apparently, she was a procurer.

Seeing my expression, Mona was suddenly silent. Then she changed her tack. "It's really terrible," she said. "A woman like that. She's nothing but a . . . a war."

Poor Mona, she was still so innocent she couldn't pronounce "whore" properly. Or did she want me to think she was innocent? Weren't those the lights of a million dollars dancing in her eyes?

One night Mona telephoned to say that she didn't feel well. She was alone at home and wanted to see me.

"What about your mother?"

"She's visiting friends in Syracuse."

Mona hadn't told her mother that she was seeing me again. "Why don't you tell her?" I said. "She's bound to know sooner or later." But Mona said she wanted to break the news gradually.

I traveled uptown on the subway and got off in the neighborhood that had been so familiar when I used to take her home. It was a strange feeling, walking again on the side street down to the Hudson. The block had deteriorated; the lobbies I passed were unswept and garbage littered the gutters. There was the recess between two buildings where I remembered we had held each other and kissed before I took her upstairs. The lobby of the residence hotel had the same worn carpeting, the same marble copy of a bust by Houdon— relic of the period thirty years ago when the neighborhood had had pretensions to elegance. Through this lobby the body of Mona's father had been carried, no doubt in the middle of the night so as not to frighten the tenants. Death was invisible in New York, but time, in the holes in the carpet, in the chipped nose of the bust on the pedestal, was all too visible. The elevator man asked me what floor I wanted. There had been a time when he hadn't had to ask; I'd brought Mona home so often, waking him from his cat-naps, that he had known me well. His face had been old then; now a hundred wrinkles had been added and his hand shook on the lever.

Mona let me in. She was in a dressing gown and looking sallow. She led me into her mother's bedroom and settled down again in the middle of the big bed, with two pillows at her back, a box of tissues on the side table, a pink bottle of medicine, and a scattering of magazines.

"What's wrong?" I said.

"I have a cold and fever." She tucked the blanket around her and drew up her feet. "Sit here and keep my feet warm. Keep me company. Why don't you read to me?"

I sat on the bed and read to her. I was still reading to her when we heard a key turn in the lock of the outer door.

"Mother!" Mona said. She was as white as a ghost. I didn't feel happy, either; my mind was racing. Our positions were innocent, but her mother was in for the shock of her life. Her precious daughter in her bedroom with a man! A married man. Me! I looked around. There wasn't a chance of escape; the windows opened on a sheer drop of twelve floors, and much as I wanted to protect Mona, I couldn't see myself making that sacrifice. The closet? I might stand there among old shoes and dresses for the next twenty-four hours, or be uncovered by a sweep of Mrs. Jocelyn's arm.

Mona got out of bed and drew her dressing gown around her, her arms crossed over her breast like a Christian virgin going to the lions, and said, "Come on."

We walked into the living room.

"Hello, dear," said Mrs. Jocelyn. "What!"

The cry was torn from the depths of her being. Then she turned red. I feared she was going to have a heart attack.

"Mona, what is this?"

"I'm not feeling well. I asked Duncan to come up and keep me company."

Mrs. Jocelyn's mouth was open. Her complexion went through the colors of the spectrum, settling finally in a shade of purple.

"Come into the bedroom," she said. "I want to talk to you."

She picked up her suitcase and marched into the bedroom. Mona followed. I tried to catch her eye, but she was looking straight ahead, with a hard set to her mouth I'd not seen before. Then I heard their voices in the bedroom. Mona seemed to be giving as good as she got. Then Mona came out again, alone.

"I suppose I ought to go," I said.

"Why? You stay right here. Do you think I worry about *her*?"

So I stayed, and in a few minutes Mrs. Jocelyn returned. She looked at me with hatred. I had an idea of how she felt about me in general; now she must be wishing me dead.

Mona had told me, "Mother thinks you treated me badly, going off and getting married. I can't tell her about us."

"If she didn't want me to marry somebody else, why did she always stand in the way of our getting married?"

"It isn't only that."

"What else?"

"She wants me to marry a rich man."

"Any rich man? Or somebody in particular?"

"Don't blame me, Duncan. I'm just telling you how she feels.

Someday I'll tell her about us, I really will. We're so happy now, why spoil it?"

Mona wouldn't have to tell her mother about us now. Mrs. Jocelyn could see for herself.

"Did you have a nice trip?" I said politely.

Mrs. Jocelyn snorted.

"It must be very nice up there at this time of the year. Syracuse."

"Yes," said Mrs. Jocelyn, "very nice."

She stopped pacing and stood at the fireplace—the imitation marble fireplace with a glass log that was lit up by electricity, typical of the pretensions of Mrs. Jocelyn and the whole West End Avenue-Riverside Drive middle class. But they had beautiful daughters. Daughters who looked desirable even in an old dressing gown, with a red nose and fever, with their hair tumbled over their eyes and a set to their jaw; whose feet in bed were like animals, their breasts as round as melons, their navels like goblets of wine, their knees more cunning than silver and gold, and the liquor of their tongues stronger than brandy.

Maybe Mrs. Jocelyn was reading my thoughts. She gathered herself together and began, with what she must have considered exquisite indirection, talking about a young man to whom she'd been introduced in Syracuse. I thought she had lost her mind. What was she leading up to?

"There's a very interesting thing about the young man," she said. "Everyone was talking about it one evening. You remember Mrs. Samuels, Mona?"

Mona nodded.

"She told me the young man had been married for a year. Then he met another woman, and just ran off and left his wife. Everyone was sorry for the wife. She was crying all the time. But the other woman seemed glamorous to him, I suppose, and he just went away with her. It was a terrible thing."

"Terrible," I said. "It's a very sad story. But surely you didn't let it spoil your stay? Didn't anything nice happen?"

Mrs. Jocelyn looked at me in silence. Apparently I was too stupid to get the point of the story.

"If he'd only realize that glamour isn't everything," she said, "and go back to his wife."

I laughed out loud. I couldn't help it.

Mrs. Jocelyn stared at me. Then she raised her arm and looked at her watch. I made no move to leave. I was going to make the old bag come right out and say what she meant for once.

"It's very late," she said.

Then I got up and left. Mona let me out the door. I bent to kiss her good night, but she averted her face. The door closed.

Going down in the elevator, I thought, That's that! Now everything's out in the open. Poor Mona, she must be knocked out! But I was proud of her, the way she'd stood up to her mother.

After this confrontation, I would bring Mona home instead of putting her in a taxi. If Mrs. Jocelyn was still up when we appeared, she would gather her sewing box, letter-writing apparatus, or whatever other articles she occupied her mind with, and leave the room, abandoning the field. Usually I brought Mona home after midnight, and her mother was already in bed.

"She doesn't warn me against you any more," Mona said. "She knows it's no use."

I was glad this barrier was passed. Someday, when my divorce went through, Mona and I would be married. It was time we started moving in the world together. I wanted the whole of my life, not just the room in which I slept and ate, to be illuminated by our love. I wanted her to meet my friends and go to parties with me.

"But your friends are intellectuals," she said. "They're going to think I'm stupid."

"Intellectuals! Don't be silly. If you mean writers and so on, you'd be surprised how unintellectual they are. It's just another kind of show business, that's all."

"That's easy for you to say. You know how to talk to people. But I can't."

"You talk beautifully to me."

"That's just it." She sat up and put a finger to my chest. "I can talk to *you*. Duncan, that's why I love you. But I can't talk to other people. They hate me!"

"What are you talking about?"

"You don't know, you just don't know. They think I'm stuck up or neurotic, or something. Look, I'm going to tell you something that will surprise you. Do you know that for the last two years I've been seeing a psychiatrist?"

"What on earth for?"

"I told you about Jim, remember?"

I remembered. When we met again, the day I brought her to my apartment and we resumed our lovemaking, she explained as the reason for her reluctance to be alone with me that she was engaged to a man named Jim. "Engaged to be married?" I said foolishly. "Yes. No. I don't know. He's been asking me to marry him for two years. And he's angry with me because I won't." A few days later she said that she'd told Jim that she was seeing me again and he had broken off their "engagement."

"Yes," I said. "I remember old Jim. Is he trying again?"

"He phoned me last week. But that's not the point. It was Jim who arranged for me to go to a psychiatrist. But," she said happily, "since I've been seeing you, I've given it up."

"Fine. It's a lot of foolishness, for you at any rate."

"Sometimes I think you don't know anything about me at all," she said.

"Are you going to turn into another of these New York women," I said, "with problems? I've just been married to a woman with problems."

"Then I won't ever tell you a thing," she said. And before I could protest, she was off on another tack. "And there's another thing. A lot of your friends aren't Jewish."

"What?"

"I am," she said.

"My friends don't go around asking each other what they are."

"Mother says you married Libby because she wasn't Jewish. And you didn't marry me because I am."

"Hold on! What does your mother know about my marriage?"

"She asked me about it."

"She did, did she?"

I hadn't given Mrs. Jocelyn enough credit. I'd thought she had admitted defeat. But she obviously hadn't; if she was no longer warning Mona against me, she was making insinuations. Once upon a time she had suggested to Mona that I was tainted with hereditary insanity. Now she was trying the racist angle. The old

woman was a viscous fluid that kept creeping under the door;
a vine that poked its tendrils in at one window or the other; a fat
hydra—no sooner did I chop off one head than up grew
another. . . .

"I suppose," I said, "I'm anti-Semitic. Don't you realize my own
mother was a Jewess?"

"There you are!" she said.

"What? What have I said now?"

"That word, Jewess. No Jew would ever use it. You see?"

I looked down at her, at the shape of her face, her neck, her
breasts, and thought, with a kind of bitter sadness, of all the time
that words waste, of the joy of life that is so sadly marred by the
ideas people have in their heads. Ever since Eden, love has not been
simple. Ever since Eve reached out her hand and plucked the fruit
and had her first idea, the natural world has been spoiled. What
did a girl like Mona, a girl with the kind of beauty I'd dreamed
about when I was a soldier in all those lonely nights in barracks,
a beauty that at this very moment millions of men were imagin-
ing in furnished rooms—what did a piece like this want to
have ideas for?

However, there was some truth in Mona's apprehensions. Some of
the people I knew, or rather had known when I was living with
Libby, were anti-Semitic. They wouldn't approve of Mona. They
would find her gestures not merely a trifle too theatrical, but Jewish;
they would think her laughter not spontaneous, but "noisy." Well, so
much the worse for them! If I ran into any of them when I was out
with Mona and they betrayed by so much as a flicker of an eyelash
the prejudices I was so superbly equipped to recognize—for I had
been in all the camps—I would cease to see them without a
moment's regret. I had had my bellyful of good society, and it didn't
warm your feet on a cold night.

It was time we began going out together. If Mona had fears about
the opinions of my "intellectual" friends, I could dispel them by
having her meet my friends. If she thought I lived in some world of
White Anglo-Saxon Protestants, Wasps for short, I could remove
that illusion by showing her the vapidity of the gentiles—how uncer-
tain they themselves were about what they believed, how they took
their cues from one another and were thrown off balance by a
stranger who had self-assurance.

"There is one thing you ought to remember," I told her. "It's one of the few remarks about life I've ever believed in. Fitzgerald said you think other people are thinking about you all the time, judging you for better or worse, but it isn't true. You're less important to other people than you think you are. People are preoccupied with themselves. Don't go getting fantasies about your stock fluctuating every day with everything you do. Just take it easy."

"Duncan," she said, "I don't know what I'd do without you."

"Don't worry about that. There's one problem you won't have."

"I love it when you're in earnest," she said. "Your eyes are so bright."

I began taking Mona out. But I put off introducing her to my friends. We were so happy together, being with other people would only have been an annoyance. We went to night clubs, cocktail bars, plays, and musicals. I realized that on her job she met people who spent a great deal of money on entertainment, and I was spurred to compete in this area, to show her that I could spend ten dollars on dinner with as little compunction as anyone in show business, or her last boy friend, Jim. But Jim was a producer, and though by Mona's account he was not a very successful producer, he probably made twice as much money as I.

Mona was oblivious of the figures on the bill. Sometimes when the waiter put down the check in some dimly lit trap where she had heard there was a "marvelous" chanteuse—who turned out to be an aging woman who sang dirty songs—or a new comic genius or horn player, while Mona powdered her nose, I nervously counted my money. On two or three occasions I ran out of money and told her so, whereupon she simply handed her purse to me. Though she was only a stage prop, "part of the scenery," as she described herself, she was well paid. Besides, her room and board were taken care of at home; Mr. Jocelyn had left his widow and daughter well provided for by the insurance.

She gave me presents. On my birthday she entered my room with a beaming smile and her arms filled with packages—a bottle of champagne, a bathrobe, a pair of gold cuff links with my initials on them. I retaliated by buying her a necklace and gloves and taking her dancing at night clubs. As a result of this lavish prodigality, not to mention our physical activity, I grew lean as a rail. But I'd never felt healthier or so lighthearted.

At two or three in the morning we would leave my room and hail a late-prowling taxi and ride up the West Side Highway. To our left moonlight shone on the ships, the dusky red funnels of the *Elizabeth* or *Mary,* the *Ile de France,* the slender white bows of the Grace Line steamers, all seeming magically dwindled in their berths. It was odd, I told her, how enormous a ship seemed when you were on it; and at a distance, across the water, it had majesty. But in the docks ships lost their proportions; you couldn't judge how big they were. Perhaps it was the foreshortening. It was one of the inexplicable illusions.

The river glittered in moonlight. The dark Palisades loomed against the sky and the moon paced through heaven, conspiring.

We woke the elevator man. He seemed to be getting older every day; no wonder, we never gave him an uninterrupted night's sleep.

Mona turned the key in the lock and pushed the door open. Then she held me for a last kiss.

But one night she said, "Come in."

I entered. She switched on a lamp in the living room. Then she went to the arch dividing the living room from the corridor at the end of which was her mother's bedroom, and stood listening. She returned and sat beside me on the couch.

"Give me a cigarette," she said.

She smoked for a minute. Then she stubbed out the cigarette in an ash tray, and leaning against me, put her hand on the buttons of my shirt, undid them, and began caressing me.

In a little while she stood up and slipped out of her pants, balancing on one foot, then on the other. Then she threw one of the couch pillows on the floor.

She came back to me with a glitter in her eyes, as though she were running a fever, and pulled me toward her. It was crazy, but we made love on the rug. We were directly beneath the picture of her father—an oil painting of Mr. Jocelyn in his glasses, one hand grasping a lapel of his coat. Mona stared up with wide eyes, biting her knuckles, her mouth turned down at the corners. She seemed in agony. But she didn't utter a sound.

On the way home, standing on the subway platform at three in the morning—for I couldn't afford to take a taxi both ways—waiting for the train that, at this hour, took forty minutes to arrive, I thought of the incident with wonder. What if her mother had come in? Why did Mona do it?

Apparently she had problems, as she had tried to tell me. And what about me? I had problems, too.

Literary Life

It may be true, as Nick says in *Gatsby,* that the world is best looked at from a single window, but the writer's life is a very narrow window.

Writers are not the best company, they are too full of themselves; nor are they even good conversationalists, for they are preoccupied with the ideas they will be able to use. And among writers, poets are the least interesting company of all, for they are usually daydreaming. Yet I have found myself over and over again in the company of writers and especially poets, simply because I was a writer, when I would much rather have been somewhere else. It's too bad that the love of books brings you into contact with the people who write them.

In America it is common for a writer, after his first book, to have nothing more to say, because he has had no new experiences of any importance and has just hung around with other writers. By importance I mean emotional and intellectual content. In this fix the writer is likely to look for adventures, go to the Brazilian jungle, become interested in science or politics, travel around with a candidate for the presidency, but these activities—the "real world" that magazines commission writers to write articles about—have no con-

Reprinted from Louis Simpson, *North of Jamaica.* New York: Harper and Row, 1972.

184

nection with his own individual artistic character. So he is trapped in a career, and his life is not different from the professional life of lawyers, actors or baseball players. The man is distorted by the profession.

Looking back, the people I have known best have been writers. With the exception of women. But they would require another book and I am not prepared to write it. As Tolstoy said, I will tell what I think about women when my coffin is open and I can jump in and slam it shut.

So for the present I shall continue to talk about writing. It is a narrow window, but as wide as others.

In the early 1950s poetry was at a low ebb. The best-known younger poets—men such as Christopher Green—were the products of universities and writers' conferences. They published in established literary magazines, *The Hudson Review* and so on, and were awarded prizes and fellowships. When I had spent any time in the company of such people I found myself depressed; there was nothing to talk about, only mild gossip punctuated with the eternal question, "Have you read?"—meaning some new volume of verse or a critical article. These people had no subject, least of all themselves. Their existence seemed real only when their name appeared in print, most real when it was in an anthology with the date of birth next to it and a blank for the date of death. You felt that they could hardly wait for the terminal date to be filled in.

My dissatisfaction with the literary world began to be acute. For some time I had been publishing poems in the quarterlies, and had a contract with *The New Yorker* stipulating that I was to let them have the first look at anything I wrote. My poems came out in *The New Yorker,* and if a large public means anything—and some people think it does—then I should have been satisfied. But, to the contrary, when I saw one of my poems in thin type next to the ads for shirts and whisky and sports cars, I was depressed. I was sure that no one would read the poem, or if they did, anything intelligent that it might say would be immediately overwhelmed by the fatuous thoughts rising out of the advertisements.

Moreover, the close-editing policy of *The New Yorker* was annoying. They queried every fact and were always recommending changes for the better. This might be tolerable in prose—though some fiction writers found it less and less tolerable—but in poetry it was ludicrous. On one occasion I sent them a poem that mentioned the Conquistadors in the lines,

> And murdering, in a religious way,
> Brings Jesus to the Gulf of Mexico.

I got back a three-page single-spaced letter from the editors, apparently the result of research and consultation, informing me that Jesus had never gone to the Gulf of Mexico. But Cortez had, and as his name contained the same number of syllables, the meter wouldn't be upset if I said Cortez instead of Jesus. What irritated me about this was not so much the censorship as the hypocrisy: why couldn't they just say they didn't want any mention of Jesus, good or bad? I came to understand their editorial policy—any writing that might really disturb anyone was out. Over the magazine there hung a tiresome air of facetiousness; at the same time there was a pretence of being serious. Stories about the neuroses of well-to-do people living in the suburbs were acceptable and they printed them all the time, for these of course disturbed no one, they were just more of the pseudo self-criticism the middle class indulges in, that enables them to think that they are thinking.

The New Yorker put great stress on the checking of facts, and the finished story or poem presented an entirely smooth, impenetrable surface. In one poem I mentioned a well-known photograph by Matthew Brady, depicting a dead Confederate soldier in the Devil's Den at Gettysburg. They wanted to know the number of the plate in the Brady collection. On another occasion I referred to a place named Beaulieu and an Irishman who had lived there. They wanted me to clarify this; Beaulieu, they told me was in England, not far from Stonehenge. The Irishman, of course, would be Yeats. Would I explain exactly what I intended to imply by all this? I wrote back that my Beaulieu was in France on the Mediterranean, and the Irishman I had in mind was more like Scott Fitzgerald. In a return letter they suggested that I would find Yeats better suited to my purpose.

I have tried to imagine what it would have been like if Coleridge had submitted "Kubla Khan" to *The New Yorker*.

In Xanadu did Kubla Khan
A stately pleasure-dome decree:
Where Alph, the sacred river, ran
Through caverns measureless to man
Down to a sunless sea.
So twice five miles of fertile ground
With walls and towers were girdled round:
And there were gardens bright with sinuous rills,
Where blossomed many an incense-bearing tree;
And here were forests ancient as the hills,
Enfolding sunny spots of greenery . . .

The New Yorker might have written to Coleridge as follows.

Dear Sam:

We liked "Kubla Khan" very much and want to take it. Our readers, however, have some queries that we hope you can clear up.

"Xanadu." One of our readers points out that this name is unfamiliar to the general reader, and that the poem would get off to a much better start if you simply said China. You would lose a syllable this way, but you could keep the meter if you added another word. For example:

In China once did Kubla Khan . . .

"pleasure-dome." We don't visualize this clearly. Do you mean hanging gardens, as in Babylon, or are you maybe thinking of the Crystal Palace Exhibition?

"Alph . . . Down to a sunless sea." This presents a real problem. If the caverns are, as you say, "measureless to man," how can we know that the sea is "sunless"? No one will ever have seen it. I hate to be Johnsonian about this, but some of our readers are sure to pick it up.

"twice five miles." This seems rather unnecessarily specific and also long-winded. If you must, couldn't you just say "ten"?

Best wishes,
Gerald

I was invited to a party being held by the editors of a new literary magazine. Arriving at an address on the East Side I found myself among the most successful first-novelists of the time. Their first novels had been handled by leading literary agents and acclaimed at length in such places as *Time* and *The New York Times*. Their conversation was all about agents and reviews. They seemed not at all interested in ideas, not even in writing novels, but only in plays they had seen and houses they were renting for the summer. They were what would be called a few years later "the beautiful people." Listening to them I was filled with the kind of despair I felt when I read a poem in *The New Yorker*. I had a feeling of panic and broke out in a cold sweat. I went for my overcoat and plunged out through the door just as the main party was arriving, more first-novelists with their wives. I got on a bus going down Fifth Avenue, and remember thinking, That's finished. If that's what it takes to be an up-and-coming writer in New York, I'll never make it.

Everyone seemed to be at loose ends. One day Ginsberg came to see me at the publishing house. He showed me a few poems in free verse—flat, feeble little things—and said he had been reading William Carlos Williams. We had little to say to each other. He said he was going away to Mexico. I watched him leave and turned back to reading another manuscript.

At this time, luckily, I met one man from whom I could learn something. This was Saul Bellow. He himself was a product of literary milieux, and had written for *The Partisan Review* and that gang. His early novels, tightly constructed and limited in their objectives, had pleased the critics. His future seemed assured if only he were willing to take one step at a time. The people who keep an eye on such things are not averse to helping young writers if they progress in an agreeable manner—that is, according to the rules. It is necessary at every step for the young novelist to approach his elders, who are presumably his betters, and to enlist their help and advice. But Bellow suddenly took a giant step. He had discovered his subject: being a Jew in America—not the Jew trying to be an American but the American Jew learning to be himself—and in *The Adventures of Augie March* he wrote an expansive, eccentric novel about such a man. Moreover, it was not a New York novel, it was situated in Chicago. Some of the critics thought he had gone too far, but when the reports started coming in and it was evident that *Augie* was a band-wagon, they hastened to get on it. In spite of their praise, and though *Augie* was not the masterpiece they then said it was—for it was too long and rambling and the boisterousness of the main character often rang false—nevertheless Bellow had done something new. In fact he had created a *genre* of fiction that would in the coming decade be practised by other "Jewish" writers, Malamud and Roth being the most successful.

I was visiting friends in the Village when Bellow came in, carrying a briefcase. His overcoat was sprinkled with snow; he had been giving a talk at the New School for Social Research, and had come through a snow storm. It is a strange thing about the New School, you always get snowed or rained upon, the nights you teach there. But it wasn't the weather that was bothering Bellow, it was a man who had followed him up the street after his lecture to tell him he didn't know anything about novels really, for he was only a novelist. Finally, in order to get rid of this example of a critic, Bellow had swung at him in self-defence with his briefcase. He hadn't connected, but he was still disheveled and excited. He felt this was a symbolic encounter, everything he was trying to accomplish being threatened by a fool. He was exhilarated; there is nothing like opposition, driving a man against the wall, to make him believe in the reality of his ideas.

Over the next three years I got to know Bellow, but here I must mention a curious thing. There were many people who knew him, and each had a different idea of the man. One saw him as a tough guy; another saw him as *ein mensch,* sympathetic and full of wisdom. For my part, I saw Bellow as a man who had a magnificent original prose style and who, moreover, had fared ahead of me in a world of marital troubles, alimony payments, visiting hours—the whole tangled, perplexing world of divorce that I myself, along with many other Americans, had begun to explore.

Divorce was the last frontier of an American turning toward suburbia. Paying alimony was the middle-class American's substitute for cutting his throat. Visiting hours were his equivalent for purgatory. Bellow was going through them all with expressions of grief and rage, but he survived and, moreover, had hitched up with a new wife who was young and devoted to him, who stood by his side at the helm on those rough seas where the next wave, a telephone call from "her" lawyer demanding more money, would crash on the deck and nearly swamp the boat. But they steered through, and Bellow continued to write, planning novels, plays, stories, and writing reviews besides. His study was a welter of books and long sheets of paper piled on a table. He complained about being distracted. He had an idea that not only business people but also people who asked you to write reviews and the people who ran universities were engaged in a kind of conspiracy to stop you writing. Not to mention lawyers and ex-wives. It was poetry they were all against. They were all trying to distract you from writing poetry. By which, of course, he meant prose, and indeed I thought his prose was more poetic than the verse of the poets I knew.

One day at Tivoli he showed me pages of a short novel he was finishing. I sat on the lawn reading after he had gone back into the house. As I read time was suspended, and when I came to the end I had a feeling I have had only two or three times in my life—that I was witnessing at first hand the creation of a masterpiece. The man who'd first seen the manuscript of a story by Gogol or Dostoyevski might have had the same feeling.

> He, alone of all the people in the chapel, was sobbing. No one knew who he was.
>
> One woman said, "Is that perhaps the cousin from New Orleans they were expecting?"
>
> "It must be somebody real close to carry on so."
>
> "Oh my, oh my! To be mourned like that," said one man and looked at Wilhelm's heavy shaken shoulders, his clutched face and whitened fair hair, with wide, glinting, jealous eyes.
>
> "The man's brother, maybe?"
>
> "Oh, I doubt that very much," said another bystander. "They're not alike at all. Night and day."
>
> The flowers and lights fused ecstatically in Wilhelm's blind, wet eyes; the heavy sea-like music came up to his ears. It poured into him where he had hidden himself in the center of a crowd by the great and happy oblivion of tears. He heard it and sank deeper than sorrow, through torn sobs and cries toward the consummation of his heart's ultimate need.

I ran into the house with the manuscript and told Bellow, "It's great. And the part where Tommy is in the phone booth . . ."

He smiled and had a cunning look in his eyes. As with all first-rate writers at the height of their power, he knew very well what he had done.

I showed Saul a bunch of my poems. He said nothing about the poems that had been published by *The New Yorker, The Hudson Review,* and *The Paris Review,* but put his finger on a few lines, a fragment I did not understand myself.

> Though mad Columbus follows the sun
> Into the sea, we cannot follow.
> We must remain, to serve the returning sun,
> And to set tables for death . . .

"I like this," he said. "It shows a direction."

What the direction was, he did not say. But I often returned to look at the fragment, and years later when I began writing poems that meant something to me and had some of the same quality, I thought he had been astonishingly perceptive.

Grigoryev and I

Apollon Grigoryev writes: "It is easy to believe in theories—and I cannot, no matter how I try." These words could serve for me as well, and for others who go through life with a constant uneasiness, a sense of being tossed about, verging on an explanation and never quite reaching it—while other people seem to have so much certainty, seizing on politics, art or religion with both hands, making themselves a definite place in the world. For Grigoryev and myself and other "unnecessary men" the explanation is never quite right, the answer eludes us, until we give up the struggle in despair or discover that we are old. Besides, there is always the hope that the longer you put off deciding, the greater, the more inclusive and profound the answer will be when it comes—until it is too late. Some of these "unnecessary men" are fortunate; at the last moment they do cross over and join the ranks of the "saved." Proust comes to mind; he was at the mercy of impressions—gestures, anecdotes, odors, pieces of furniture; then he discovered a theory of time. But for the most part such people merely drift; they inhabit the penumbra; they vanish, leaving no trace on thought or history. Wouldn't it be better to have a place in the Paradise of Fools, among the true believers in wrong theories, than to have no place at all?

Reprinted from Louis Simpson, *North of Jamaica*. New York: Harper and Row, 1972.

Like Grigoryev's, my head is full of seemingly significant scenes, gestures, faces, words spoken, that have no significance because they are not connected and serve no purpose. "Experience," said Johnson, "is a hard school, but fools will learn in no other." And what if you don't learn anything?

Moreover, it isn't just my own experiences that are obsessive, that come to me day and night as though this time surely they have something to declare, and then like the others don't "turn out," drifting into chaos, but also the experiences of other people. My mother tells a story about something she saw as a child, and this torments me as though it happened to myself. One night in Russia she looked out a window and saw a man being taken away in chains. It was one of her relatives, an old man with white hair. He had quarreled with a neighbor over a piece of property and the neighbor denounced him to the police for "subversive political activity." He was innocent, yet he was sent to Siberia and never returned. I can hear the shuffling feet and see the head and shoulders of the prisoner and his shadow cast on a wall. So I rush out to buy a copy of Chekhov's book on the penal colonies. At the present time, seventy years after the event, I am concerned with the administration of justice in Tsarist Russia. A fat lot of use that is!

Or I read a book about the Communist uprising in Paris in 1871. When the Communists surrendered they were roped together and marched, men, women and children, to the outskirts of the city. Too bad for the workingman who had the mark of a rifle butt on his shoulder, or hands blackened with powder! The Government troops stopped a chimney sweep, and his hands were black, so they shot him. They brought the prisoners in front of a table where General Galliffet was presiding, the hero of Sedan, and Galliffet said, "You have heard that I am merciless. Well, I am worse than you could imagine." Then the prisoners were taken out and shot. Don't Galliffet's words make your blood curdle? But what good is that?

It's not that I don't have ideas. For example, the matter of the Commune . . . if I were a professor, a real one, I'd work up a thesis explaining that the origins of the struggle between Communism and Capitalism in the twentieth century are not economic, as has been thought, but personal, a blood feud, the kind of hatred that starts between families and goes on for its own sake, with incidents always being found to justify it. The rich and poor hate each other in their guts; it's a physical reason, based on the way people talk and blow their noses. When the Communists came to power in Russia they had all those people shot in order to wipe away the memory of Galliffet's smirk. So they perpetuated the blood feud. I can see the thesis standing on a shelf: *Notes Toward a Study of the Psychological and Cultural Origins of the Capitalist-Communist Struggle.* I can even see the footnotes. And as I can see them, why should I write the thesis?

Having a belief is not so much a matter of being intelligent as of being hungry. Some people, whom Grigoryev calls *hommes forts*, have strong appetites for fame, money, women. In order to serve their appetites they seize life with both hands. They glut themselves, and to justify this they get up a theory, they say that they believe. The rest of us have weak appetites, and so we are always thinking "yes—but." For an excuse we say that we are intelligent. But the universe has enough intelligence. What the universe wants is something to happen, in any form whatsoever, a little excitement—explosion of gases, liquefaction, solidification, formation of rocks, solid heads. From the viewpoint of the universe, thought is nothing and vacuity is terribly boring. From there even a dinosaur looks good and any theory is better than no theory at all.

Of course, artistic people think they are more than merely intelligent. Even a Grigoryev says, "I am greedy for life." Artistic people have to think so, for their vocation is providing nourishment for others, so they think that they themselves are capable of consuming and regurgitating masses of material. But in comparison with your real, full-grown meat eaters they are only children. People with artistic temperament, "sensitive" people, overrate their capacity. They don't have enough experience; they simply have no idea what goes on in the way of consumption in normal middle-class families.

People such as Grigoryev and myself who have no convictions are likely to be superstitious. *Déjà vu*—we think we have been here before. Prophecy—we have a vision of a strange room, and twenty years later we find ourselves inside it. Spilled salt, a ring around the moon, a line of poetry read by accident, strike us as having an ominous, personal application. We are always brooding over coincidences. Three times in the same day a man walks past carrying a ladder, and we think there is some significance in ladders. So we sit down to write a poem, "Ladders," and of course it doesn't work out. A practical man would think they are painting a house on the next corner. He might be mistaken, but at least he wouldn't cut himself shaving. Or we see pregnant women everywhere, and surely this is a manifestation of some great change in the world. We do not consider that there are always pregnant women. The difference is in our own psychological condition; on this day we happen to have, for personal reasons, an unusual interest in pregnancies.

Poets are particularly sensitive to things happening over and over again, and to juxtapositions of different things. These are rhythm and metaphor, and they comprise the better part of most poets' writings. It would be enough to write lines with rhythm and metaphor, but everyone else has a theory, so we must have one too, and then we write philosophy. The philosophy of poets is the despair of philosophers. The poet speaks of time and reality, but his explanation is only a means of justifying himself, of organizing and using the materials.

This is what happened to Proust. When his parents died he discovered that he, too, had a digestive system. He too was a weight lifter, a strong man with an enormous appetite, incredible willpower. And this had been true from the beginning. He had even developed asthma in order to put people off and not be interrupted in his gathering of materials. Now that his parents were dead, he could let himself go. And now, if the reader will go back a few pages where I was talking about Proust, he will see what I mean when I say that I have no consistency, that like Grigoryev, "I can never contemplate an object from any single aspect." I cannot even think about Proust with any consistency for a few minutes. "My thinking is somehow kaleidoscopic. That's just the word!"

As I've said, we are troubled by coincidences. What, for example, am I to make of Ginsberg, who comes into my life again and again, and always at a crucial moment? Or is it his coming that makes the moment seem crucial? Our paths keep meeting and diverging. I meet him in New York when we are both young and "neurasthenic"—the doctor's very word. Then I am working in a publishing house and Ginsberg comes to see me because he is leaving for Mexico. We have nothing, really, to say to each other, we just stare. Yet his departure seems significant, as does my continuing to sit there reading bad manuscripts. Years pass and I hear that he has written a famous poem. I read it, and run to the typewriter to write a parody of it, and just as I'm licking the envelope there's a knock on the door. It's Ginsberg! At this moment of all moments! More years go by. I am living in Rome, and one day I decide to go and see the Sistine Chapel. I have never been here before, and here is Ginsberg coming toward me, from the middle of the Last Judgment. Years later, in California, I am asked to read poems protesting against the war in Vietnam, and I find myself side by side with Ginsberg on a platform. He now has a beard and a potbelly, like Socrates. A few years more, and I see him sitting on the steps of a house at Port Jefferson, ringing bells and chanting an Indian song to calm two men who are fighting on the lawn. Should I write an article about all this? Or a fictionalized version in the manner of Beerbohm? Nobody cares about such things nowadays, and besides, what would it prove? So instead of writing I go fishing.

> letting the line drift with the current,
> skirting the shadows of rocks . . .

Grigoryev and I are hoping to be convinced. We hope that one night when the moon has risen an angel will appear and say, "Take this down." According to Rilke this is what happened to him at Duino. An angel gave him the elegies. But with us it happens otherwise. The angel appears, dictates a few lines, looks at his watch, and vanishes. And there we are, with a handful of words. The worst of it is, these fragments don't vanish; they keep repeating themselves like a damaged record. They keep creeping into any new thing we are trying to write, where they don't belong, spoiling any new idea we may have. For example:

> I am swept in a taxi
> to the door of a friend.
> He greets me like a statue
> fixed in the position of a man
> who always marries the wrong woman.

These lines came to me three years ago, and have been returning ever since, and I can't exorcize them. They are the beginning of a poem about New York, the comedy of Chekhov brought over to verse, that will never be written.

But how can I tell? Maybe it will be written. For I've had other fragments that managed to come together, one day when I wasn't thinking about them too hard. Also, sometimes by sheer hard work I've managed to make sense out of such things. So just waiting isn't an answer—it's necessary to try. Yet, as I've said, there's no guarantee that if you keep trying anything will come of it.

Grigoryev and I keep looking out of the window when we should be listening to the lecture. I remember, when I was a schoolboy, three lines gouged in the desk along which you could run a pencil point like a locomotive, switching from one line to another, but I don't remember how to use a slide rule. I can remember the chapel floor under my knees but I don't remember the sermon. As for scenery—to people of our sort a landscape can be a disaster. Really you ought to keep your eyes closed to trees, mountains and so on, if you want to get ahead in the world. It may be that my whole life has been "conditioned" by the view from my window when I was a boy— curtains stirring, waves rushing toward me, coconuts thumping in the wind, sea gulls. Even when I was asleep I could hear the sea.

Sense perceptions are a hindrance to anyone who wants to make a career. Take literature, for example. Whenever by chance I come across *The New York Review of Books* I am amazed at the certainty those writers have, their ability to generalize, the clarity of their ideas, their lack of sense perception. They are informed about everything—the latest news of politics, art, the theater—and they go straight to the point. Reading those writers I understand how they can say that storytelling and poetry are dead and journalism is the only thing that matters. Grigoryev and I could never write like that. We are obsessed with a handful of words, the way a branch keeps tapping against the window. If history were left to people like us, what a botch we'd make of it! I was once involved in a revolution, and what I remember best is the bicycle I rode from place to place. I lived for a year in Italy, visiting the cathedrals, and what I remember most clearly is a patch of wall—earth-color, with a poster, one corner of which had been torn off—on the *Via* Something or Other.

4

LIVES AND WORKS

W. B. Yeats

Yeats's "Byzantium" is the city where all the artifices of eternity are found. Every image exists there; every idea; everything that can be made. It is an entirely artificial place; nothing is natural; man is the cause of everything there, and man must live or die as these images live or die. These things are his only proofs of his own existence. By Byzantium man must justify himself to the world: (Yeats, with an ignoring which is profound, does not suggest that God should justify himself to man; nor does Shakespeare; it remains for Milton to make the blasphemous hint).

Byzantium represents the best of man. That best, including everything, is seen at midnight, when the confusion of the day's action is past; it is that hour when action may be evaluated properly. All action, ideas, images, are seen as purged forms, flitting like flames on the Emperor's floor. Everything assumes its perfect form; one might say that the Platonic image, the ideal, had been given life. The ideal form scorns the confusion of natural life; the ideal is artifice, the art of the human mind.

The ideal human form present among these images is "Shade more than man, more image than a shade . . . death-in-life and life-in-death" . . . it is the mummy given life, the Lazarus risen from

Reprinted from *Columbia Review*. XXIV. Autumn 1942.

Hades. The ideal human being is preserved like a mummy, with the balms of wisdom.

The scene beneath the Dome, so far, is tranquil. Yeats sings like a golden bird his scorn of "common bird or petal/And all complexities of mire and blood."

The images are Platonic in the first four stanzas; they are artificial images, quiet as metal. But in the last line of the fourth stanza one word causes the earth to quake:

"An *agony* of flame that cannot singe a sleeve."

Agony is the great paradox which we would not have expected. Why agony? Byzantium is a cold and tranquil city; perfection is satisfying, not painful.

But it is as though the very energy of life were injected into the images at this point; they are galvanized, they fall apart like shells from the emerging life force, they burst like wombs in conception. The metal breaks, the artificial breaks, to let the force of life emerge. That nature, which has been so scorned in the accumulating poem, now forces itself as though inevitable upon the poet. It is as though Yeats has been forced, by a vision of the vast power of nature, to acknowledge that power which he would rather *not* acknowledge. The poem has got out of hand. Artificial Byzantium is a comfortable place; to be a golden bird is a comfortable role; but this brute injection of high animal spirits wrecks all that careful quiet, that artifice of the centuries. The Platonic images split, swell, disgorge fresh images; the life force is here; an animal evolution takes places. The last stanza becomes a struggle, a smashing across the Emperor's pavement. Complexity, which was assumed to have disappeared with daylight, returns with almost devilish fury; for this new complexity is the complexity not of Nature only, but of Nature plus Artifice. Yeats, in substituting Artifice for Nature, has only formed a new political party which will in turn revolt against him; he, the poet, in himself, will suffer a redoubled battle. "Byzantium" ends with the infinite suggestion that every achievement adds new complexities, new confusions. The artificial becomes natural. The poet has desired the artificial to bring peace, but it becomes natural, life seizes upon it. The poet suffers this counter-revolution inside himself. A vast vista of unachievement opens before him. He must repeat the struggle, he must:

1. make the Natural Artificial, seize Art from Nature;
2. see the Artificial taken back by Nature, and changed into life.
3. Once more the poet must seize this life from Nature, in the form of Art . . .

and the process is infinite. The frenzy of this final stanza is a frenzy of the mind at the contemplation of the infinite labors of man, and his infinite dignity.

After this triumph of the intellect, Yeats deliberately turned his back on the "Byzantium" type of poem, because it represented a victory over Time, and he did not want a victory . . . he wanted to suffer a tragic defeat. He chose to become a sort of saint, crucified by Time in the flesh, rather than a victorious intellect. He deliberately stressed his immortality, that part of man which is weakest. It was the saint's choice. The Rocky Face of the saint accompanies bodily suffering.

The voluntary and heroic acceptance of lust and rage as weapons to fight Time with is declared in:

A Last Confession

What lively lad most pleasured me
Of all that with me lay?
I answer that I gave my soul
And loved in misery,
But had great pleasure with a lad
That I loved bodily.

(It would be well to pause here, for the poem changes. Notice the self-mortification of the saint, the pride that the saint has in humbling himself to the beast's level, through physical torture. For the woman's laugh is bitter, certainly. The saint suffers in the flesh to test his spirit, to divide the spirit from the flesh. Yeats, at the end of his life, dealt in lust and rage because he could afford to . . . he had already achieved sainthood of the spirit. Only great men can attempt a separation of spirit and flesh.)

I gave what other women gave
That stepped out of their clothes,
But when this soul, its body off,

> Naked to naked goes,
> He it has found shall find therein
> What none other knows.
>
> And give his own and take his own
> And rule in his own right;
> And though it loved in misery
> Close and cling so tight,
> There's not a bird of day that dare
> Extinguish that delight.

The two lines:

> But when this soul, its body off,
> Naked to naked goes . . .

show that Yeats is repudiating the flesh for the soul, and at the same time stating that the soul is flesh. The divine union (I incline to think that the woman in the poem will not be satisfied until, like the Virgin Mary, God is her lover) is a "naked" union. That is, to use words from another poem, everything stands in God's eye in the vigor of its blood. The soul's union will be more delightful than the flesh's union, but it will be along fleshly lines. Just as, in "Byzantium," Nature becomes Art becomes Nature; here, Flesh becomes Soul becomes Flesh.

The Santa Claus of
Loneliness

God is dead, said Nietzsche. Abandoned by God, philosophers and poets turned to expressing their psyches. Freud invented psychoanalysis, and Rainer Maria Rilke wrote poems about the Inner Life.

Literary history makes for these scenarios; authors are seen as embodying ideas and setting out to express their times. But biography suggests that it happens the other way round: the life we have determines the ideas by which we live. Rilke is a case in point. He was born into one of those socially aspiring and ineffectual bourgeois families that have provided the substance of a hundred plays and novels. Prague, where he grew up, Rilke described as a "miserable city of subordinate existences." His father had declined from an army officer to a petty clerk for the railroad. Rilke's mother was by turns religious and ambitious to get on in society. Her infant daughter died, so that when Rilke was a small child she dressed him

Reprinted from Louis Simpson, *The Character of the Poet*. Ann Arbor: The University of Michigan Press, 1986. This review of *The Selected Poetry of Rainer Maria Rilke*, ed. and trans. by Stephen Mitchell, and *The Roses and The Windows, The Astonishment of Origins, Orchards* by Rainer Maria Rilke, trans. by A. Poulin, Jr., appeared in the *Washington Post Book World*, Dec. 5, 1982.

as a girl and called him "Miss." Like Proust, Rilke never knew that domestic happiness toward which the middle class directed its energy and by which it justified the punishments inflicted on its members. Rilke's early sorrows forced him into a premature retirement—he may be said to have never truly lived. His life went into his poetry, where it vibrated with energy.

Much of his life was spent waiting for visitations of the power that enabled him to write. He paid little attention to the world, had none of the fascination with men and women that one finds in Homer and Chaucer, even in Baudelaire. Rilke thought about "things"—the "Santa Claus of loneliness," Auden calls him. To Rilke things were masks through which another world was striving to be seen and heard. Baudelaire said it long ago: we walk through a forest of symbols that watch us with knowing eyes. Our part is to enter into things and meet the other world halfway. Rilke wrote, "Perhaps we are *here,* in order to say: house/bridge, fountain, gate, pitcher, fruit-tree, window."

Our deprivations, the powers we do not have, are seen as existing in the antiworld—absences here become presences there. Rilke calls them angels, and calls upon them to listen to his poems, the voice that expresses things of this world. But he does not know if they are listening: "Who, if I cried, would hear me among the angelic orders?" And if an angel did respond, would the poet be able to withstand contact with the angel's stronger existence? The end to which the poet strives is annihilation of the poet. And so he holds back, repressing the "call-note." For years Rilke held back until at Duino the angel came flooding in.

"Who, if I cried, would hear me among the angelic orders?" This trumpet call launches the *Duino Elegies.* The *Elegies,* together with *Sonnets to Orpheus,* which were written directly afterwards, are Rilke's most astonishing poetry—it makes other poetry seem earth-bound in comparison. I have quoted the line in the 1939 translation by J. B. Leishman and Stephen Spender, the only translation available at the time. One's first reading of a poem, like first love, leaves an ineffaceable impression, and though I have been told by people expert in German that the Leishman-Spender version is too smooth, even soft, I still keep hearing it.

Rilke wrote: "Wer, wenn ich schriee, hörte mich denn aus der

Engel/Ordnungen?" Stephen Mitchell has given us the German text on facing pages, as every translator of poetry should. He translates the lines as follows: "Who, if I cried out, would hear me among the angels'/hierarchies?" The Leishman-Spender "orders" is surely closer than "hierarchies" to the sound of "ordnungen." I do not find anything particularly attractive about "hierarchies"—on the contrary, it seems professorial. Perhaps translators do not always use the most suitable words—they put aside the most suitable words because they have been used by other translators, and choose other words.

I own three previous translations of the *Duino Elegies:* the Leishman-Spender translation; a translation by Stephen Garmey and Jay Wilson, published in 1972; and a translation by A. Poulin Jr., published in 1977. In order to compare Mitchell's translation with these other, older versions, I chose his translation of a passage by Rilke that is, for me, the best thing he ever said:

> Perhaps we are *here* in order to say: house,
> bridge, fountain, gate, pitcher, fruit-tree, window—
> at most: column, tower. . . . But to *say* them, you must understand,
> oh to say them *more* intensely than the Things themselves
> ever dreamed of existing.

There is trouble here with the understanding. One has to search to find the connection between "dreamed of existing" and "to say . . . more intensely." And when one has found it, the syntax is slightly askew—certainly one has to force it into sense. A second fault is the sound of the lines. They are prosaic. The German is as follows:

> aber zu *sagen*, verstehs,
> oh zu sagen *so*, wie selber die Dinge niemals
> innig meinten zu sein.

My German exists in a Rilkean antiworld; still, I can make this out, and it is far more poetic than the translation. The German words are short and resonant. The translator's "ever dreamed of existing" makes the passage topple over heavily at the end.

Leishman and Spender translated these lines:

> but for saying, remember,
> oh, for such saying as never the things themselves
> hoped so intensely to be.

The meaning here is clearer than in the Mitchell version, but not much, and "to be . . . such saying" is not idiomatic. As for style, it is breathless, a bit gushy.

Stephen Garmey and Jay Wilson wrote:

> but to say them, understand me,
> *so* to say them as the things within themselves never
> thought to be.

This pushes the fault of the Leishman-Spender translation one step further, so that the passage doesn't make sense: "to be" requires an object, and "to say them" is not it.

Turning to A. Poulin Jr.:

> but to say them, remember,
> oh, to say them in a way that the things themselves
> never dreamed of existing so intensely.

For clarity I would give this first place. We can see what it is that things never dreamed of: "a way," and that they never dreamed it could exist so intensely. The lines, however, are no closer to the poetic sounds of the original than Mitchell's version.

Taking one thing with another, I prefer the translations by Mitchell and Poulin. The lines I chose to compare are difficult—in other places Mitchell conveys Rilke's meaning clearly. As for the sound of his translations, it would be ill-natured to find fault with him for failing to sound as interesting in English as Rilke does in German. I would rather have his accurate translations than the kind in which the translator writes his own poetry at the expense of the author.

Mitchell has selected from the entire range of Rilke's poetry: from *The Book of Hours, The Book of Pictures, New Poems, Requiem, Uncollected Poems,* and the *Sonnets to Orpheus,* as well as the *Duino Elegies.* There is a selection from the prose *Notebooks of Malte Laurids Brigge.* I don't know of any other selection of Rilke's writing that is so representative, and it is portable, convenient to take with you. The *Cornet* is not represented, nor Rilke's *Letters to a Young Poet,* but I suppose you can't have everything in one easy volume.

Robert Hass has a fairly long introduction to Mitchell's selection of Rilke's poetry. I rather dislike Hass's chatty touches: telling us how, in Paris, he went looking for a café where Rilke had breakfast, and about a friend named Fred who was hungry "and could not have cared less where Rilke ate breakfast." Fred showed good sense: information about such matters may have some bearing on the life of a hip poet, the kind who hangs out, but it can tell us nothing about Rilke, whose life, in his own eyes, was of no importance, the poetry everything. Hass is much better when he explains that poetry, and very good indeed when he tells us how the *Elegies* were put together and describes their effect on the reader: "The author of these poems is everywhere. Really, they are the nearest thing in the writing of the twentieth century to the flight of birds. They dive, soar, swoop, belly up, loop over. . . . The subject is the volatility of emotion."

Between February 1922 when he completed the *Duino Elegies* and *Sonnets to Orpheus* and December 1926 when he died, Rilke wrote nearly four hundred poems in French. In a poem titled "Verger" he says that he wrote in French in order to use the word "verger" (orchard). This is the kind of witticism Oscar Wilde might have made, but though it is witty it may be true: Rilke may have written in French because he liked the sound of the words.

His French poems sound like Verlaine. They are lighter in tone than his poems in German. The content also seems lighter, perhaps because it is familiar: we have known these angels, loaves of bread, and windows. But Rilke is always capable of astonishing, as in these lines from *The Astonishment of Origins.* The translation is again by Poulin, who translated the *Duino Elegies* and has also translated the *Sonnets to Orpheus.*

> Look at a child's index and thumb—
> so gentle a vise,
> even bread is astonished.

And these lines from *Orchards:* "None of us advances/but towards a silent god." Had anyone thought of this before? Or said it so memorably?

These poems, however, must have seemed old-fashioned in Paris of the twenties. Symbolist poetry was old hat. The Futurists had heaped ridicule upon Symbolism—the poetry of the future would speak of racing cars, airplanes, and battleships. Dadaists turned all writing into a joke, and Surrealists were inventing images, not exploring an inner world. A German poet, Walter Mehring, who read poems in cabarets, told me that one day, strolling with Rilke in Paris, he told Rilke that his poems in French were awful. But everything passes, and Rilke's poems are no more old-fashioned now than the writings of the Futurists, Dadaists, and Surrealists. They do strike me, however, as delicate. I miss the ruggedness of Rilke's poems in German, the cragginess of his style and his formidable subjects. In German Rilke may write about a drunkard, a blind man or a panther. In French he writes a great deal about roses.

Poulin has translated the French poems in four volumes, and there is another still to come. He is a deft translator, with sympathy for Rilke's ideas and a nice sense of the rhythm of lines. I doubt that anyone could have done the job better, and until now, it appears, no one thought of doing it.

The books, by the Graywolf Press, are attractively bound and printed. They fit in the pocket—just the thing to read at a play or concert during the intermissions.

Apollinaire! The Perfect Romantic

Fifty years after his death a prophet is being honored—in another country. The life and works of Guillaume Apollinaire, French poet, art critic, editor, writer of erotic novels, lover, soldier, patriot and, above all, spokesman for modernism—or as they called it in those days, *L'Esprit Nouveau*—this phenomenon is being honored with an exhibition in London, at the Institute of Contemporary Arts. On the other hand, though Apollinaire is a hero of modern French letters, and a street has been named after him in Paris, the anniversary is not being celebrated in France. It may be that Apollinaire has remained so continuously present to the French that it has not been thought necessary to revive him. Or it may be that Apollinaire's bohemian life and attitudes do not appeal to General de Gaulle and André Malraux, guardians of the national monuments.

Though in his own time he was known also as an art critic and writer of prose tales, Apollinaire's reputation today rests on his

This essay first appeared in *The New York Times Magazine*, Jan. 19, 1969. Reprinted in *A Company of Poets*. Ann Arbor: The University of Michigan Press, 1981.

poetry. The earlier poems are somewhat old-fashioned, with sym-
bolist echoes:

> The days pass and the weeks together flow
>   None none return
>   Nor loves of long ago
> The Seine runs under the Pont Mirabeau . . .

Then, with "Zone," he leaped into modernism:

> And you drink this alcohol that burns like life
> Your life that you are drinking like a brandy
> Toward Auteuil bedward you home on foot
> To fetishes of Oceana Guinea
> Christs of another form and other culture . . .

It is to the later, experimental poems that men turn these days.
They look to the Apollinaire who hailed a fusion of science and
metaphysics; who, in *Calligrammes,* found images for a new poetry
in airplanes, submarine cables, bombs, the telephone, and the pho-
nograph; who placed images in sudden, illogical juxtapositions,
thereby achieving "simultaneity"—representing several points of
view at the same time, the actual flow and confusion of sense per-
ceptions. After Apollinaire's death André Breton, leader of the
surrealist movement, called him the "re-inventor" of poetry and
pointed to the apparent disorder of his writings as the major char-
acteristic of modern poetry in France.

"Each of my poems," said Apollinaire, "commemorates an event
in my life," and the reader of the poems is immediately involved in
the atmosphere of the pre-1914 years and the "mystifications" of
Apollinaire's existence. His life was a series of misfortunes—espe-
cially in love—that were not tragic only because he had an appetite
for further misfortunes and the ability to transform them into
poetry. Apollinaire was romantic. "He seemed always to be playing
the parts of several characters simultaneously," said a man who
knew him. "Even his handwriting was affected by this, and his bank
required him to supply five or six specimens of his signature." This
suggests the "criminal" tendency of the artist's life in the twentieth

century, described by Thomas Mann and others. I do not mean that
Apollinaire was a criminal—though in fact he was arrested "and
dragged to justice like a criminal." I mean that he had a confidence
man's charm and was always decamping from one role to another.
On the one hand, a Bohemian; on the other, a man who joins the
colors in order to establish himself as a French citizen and, more-
over, writes happy poems about the front:

> In the days when I was in the artillery
> On the northern front commanding my battery
> One night when the gazing of the stars in heaven
> Pulsated like the eyes of the newborn
> A thousand rockets that rose from the opposite trench . . .

It is clear that we are dealing with a perfect romantic specimen. If
we consider, also, that Apollinaire hinted that he was descended
from Napoleon and his father was a cardinal; that he called himself
mal-aimé, unlucky in love, yet was always chasing women—we are
dealing with a romantic who is not entirely responsible for his
actions and not strictly accountable for his ideas, leaving us to
discover the truth and put everything in order. The type is espe-
cially sympathetic nowadays, for we suspect that the opposite type,
the man who is in control of his life, is intending to control ours. The
Apollinairean life is permissive, and at the center of the permissive
life there is a child.

The child, in this case, was illegitimate. There were two children,
born of a woman named Angelica Alexandrine Kostrowitzky. Her
parents were Poles who had taken part in an anti-Russian insurrec-
tion and had been forced to leave Poland. They settled in Rome,
where Angelica's father was appointed papal chamberlain.
Angelica was placed at school in the French Convent of the Sacred
Heart. At sixteen she was expelled. She would not be obedient; one
biographer speaks of "precocious sensuality." Six years later, in
1880, Angelica gave birth—out of wedlock—to a male child, listed
in the register as being of a "father N. N." (*non noto,* unknown). This
child would be Apollinaire the poet.

Biographers think that one Francesco Flugi d'Aspermont has the
best claim to being Apollinaire's father, but this is uncertain. Two

years later Angelica bore another son, also listed as being "of father N. N." Then we find Angelica—who has changed her name to Olga—living with her two children in Monaco, where she is employed as an *entraîneuse*—we call them B-girls. She is invited by the police to leave, but manages to hang on. Then we find her in a more stable relationship, being protected by a man named Jules Weil. It is worth considering Olga, for her way of life determines that of her son Guillaume. Having cut herself off from bourgeois society, she assumes the extravagant manners of a royal personage, a dragon, ridiculous but formidable. It is she who teaches the poet how to decamp, moving from one place to another.

When Apollinaire was nineteen he and his brother stayed with Jules Weil at Stavelot, in eastern Belgium. Weil went away, and then, after running up a long bill, the brothers slipped off too, without paying it. Throughout this episode Guillaume told people that their mother was coming to pay the bill. When he was brought before a magistrate in Paris, Olga came to his defense with a great deal of aristocratic hauteur. But though she acknowledged him, it is clear that all her life Olga thought him a nonentity. After Apollinaire's death, having learned from the newspapers that he was a famous poet, Olga Kostrowitzky appeared at the offices of the *Mercure de France* and asked for an explanation. Paul Léautaud told her about Apollinaire's works. Olga listened, then she remarked, "My other son is a writer, too. He writes financial articles for an important paper in New York."

Apollinaire's illegitimacy and Olga's influence may account for his Bohemian life, his womanizing, his pursuit of novelty in art. On the other hand, it could just as well be argued that his doubtful origins account for Apollinaire's sporadic attempts to be respectable. Psychoanalysis can tell us some of the reasons that men act as they do, but psychoanalysis cannot analyze or evaluate the work of art itself, and it is a relief to turn from explanations of Apollinaire's behavior to the poetry that he made out of it.

The poet began with a good education—enrolled in 1889 at the College of Saint Charles in Monaco. Guillaume had a strong religious and mystical side to his nature, and at Saint Charles he was instructed by nuns. He developed a taste for literature and planned to write a novel in the manner of Jules Verne. In 1891 he took seven prizes and received five honorable mentions at the prize distribution presided over by the Bishop of Monaco. Then the college was closed, and the schoolboy commuted every day by train along the Côte d'Azur to the Stanislas College at Cannes. In February, 1897, he transferred to the lycée at Nice.

By this time he was reading the poets Henri de Régnier and Mallarmé and the prose of Remy de Gourmont. He was fond of bizarre anecdotes. He delved into rare texts and collected esoteric information, particularly Gothic mythology, with which he impressed his companions. He was taking note of the fabulous creatures that would later flash into his poems, along with the planes and submarine cables:

> . . . the pihis, long and supple,
> They each have one wing only and fly in a couple.

For some reason the student failed his *baccalauréat.* In June, 1897, he returned to Monaco, and from then on he studied or idled as he wished. He had already tried writing verse in classical Alexandrines. The themes, too, were traditional:

> Flora and warm Phoebus were returning to earth
> And the murmuring waves were breaking on Cytherea
> And the golden Venus, adored in those places
> In her temple listened . . .

Soon, however, he tried his hand at free verse, describing the carnival at Nice:

> Songs! Bengal fires!
> Champagne! Dithyramb!
> The Carnival King is burning! . . .
> And the cannon down there tolling.
> And the moon, pale golden watcher,
> Lighting the sky starred with pale gems
> (Ruby, emerald, opal)
> Seems the wonderful lamp
> Of gigantic Aladdins. . . .

In April, 1899, the Kostrowitzky ménage, including Jules Weil, moved to Paris, where they settled in the Avenue MacMahon. Apol-

linaire delighted in Paris. He rummaged every day in the book-
sellers' boxes along the quays. "I imagined myself meeting one or
another of the poets I loved, a prose writer I admired, a pedant I
hated."

It was then, when Apollinaire was nineteen, that he traveled with
his brother and their "uncle" Weil to Stavelot, in Belgium, with the
result we have seen. But there was another, happier result. At
Stavelot, Apollinaire began writing seriously. He walked the roads,
talking to the peasants and observing Walloon customs. He rambled
about the heath and rocks and fell in love with an innkeeper's
daughter. Out of these experiences he wrote poems—love poems,
of course—and stocked his mind with images and legends of the
Ardennes countryside. He wrote the greater part of a prose story,
"L'Enchanteur Pourrissant"—"The Putrefying Wizard"—a medi-
eval tale about Merlin, depicted as the son of a virgin and a devil,
who esteems man above Christ.

After Stavelot the next milestone for Apollinaire, both as man
and poet, was his love for Annie Playden. She was an English girl
employed as governess by a German family. After one look at the
governess, Apollinaire took a position as tutor with the family and
accompanied them to Oberpleis in the Rhineland. But it didn't
work out. Annie Playden was straitlaced, and "Kostro's" manner of
wooing terrified her. On one occasion he proposed marriage to her
on a mountain top, the Drachenfels, where Siegfried was reputed to
have slain the dragon. He offered to make her a countess—"he
came of a noble Russian family, full of generals and heaven knows
what." He offered her his huge fortune. The governess declined.
Whereupon Kostro pointed to the precipice at their feet and said
that he could easily explain the accident when her body was discov-
ered.

A year later he came to see Annie in London. This muse lived in
Landor Road, Clapham. While renewing his attentions Apollinaire
stayed with an Albanian friend, Faïk beg Konitza, and he rang the
Playden doorbell late at night, and flew into rages. The courtship
was not a success. Annie escaped by the desperate expedient of
going to America. Out of this, however, Kostro made a ballad, "La
Chanson du Mal-Aimé," and some poems about the Rhine.

In 1951 a lady named Mrs. Annie Playden Postings was interviewed in New York by LeRoy Breunig. She remembered Kostro, but in those days on the Rhine she had not known that he wrote verse. For fifty years she had not heard his name; she had been living in Texas; only recently had she discovered that he had become a famous poet named Apollinaire. She thought, in retrospect, that she had been prudish; it was the result of her puritan upbringing. But, she said, if she had been more generous maybe Kostro wouldn't have written the poems. During the interview she gave the impression that if she had to do it all over she would have been more romantic.

In the years when Apollinaire was writing the poems that would appear in *Alcools* and make him famous, he supported himself by writing for magazines and editing. He was the editor of his own magazine, *Le Festin d'Esope* (Aesop's Feast), from November, 1903, to August, 1904. In order to make money he wrote two erotic novels, *Les onze mille verges* and *Les exploits d'un jeune don Juan.*

The first—*The Eleven Thousand Strokes*—has been described by Francis Steegmuller as a "high-spirited parody of a holocaust by the Marquis de Sade . . . and indeed Picasso once owlishly pronounced it Apollinaire's masterpiece." *The Exploits of a Young Don Juan* is "limpidly perverse . . . fragrant with young private perfumes." These novels are finding new readers today, for what used to be called pornography and read for its aphrodisiac effect is now being taken seriously, and there are even courses in it.

Apollinaire made a more conventional bid for fame in 1910, when he published a collection of short stories, *L'Hérésiarche et Cie.* "The author of all these inventions," said the jacket blurb, which Apollinaire wrote himself, "is intoxicated by a charming erudition, which he makes use of to charm his readers as well." This was one of the books voted on for the Prix Goncourt that year.

Besides his poetry and stories Apollinaire was also busy with art criticism. He wrote about exhibitions and painters in magazines and newspapers; from 1910 to 1914 he occasionally wrote about art for the newspaper, *L'Intransigeant.* Today this second string of his reputation is somewhat frayed. To appreciate Apollinaire's role in modern painting we must concentrate not on what he wrote about painting, but his activity, buzzing about in the ateliers of Montmartre, bringing one artist to meet another, issuing manifestoes:

L'Antitradition Futuriste

> Manifeste-synthèse ... ce moteur à toutes tendances impres-
> sionisme fauvisme cubisme expressionisme pathétisme dra-
> matisme orphisme paroxysme.... "Mer ... de,"

he says, accompanying the word with notes of music, "to critics,
pedagogues, professors. A rose to ... Marinetti, Picasso, Boccioni,
Apollinaire...."

It was a significant moment in both modern painting and poetry
when the young Apollinaire, walking along the Seine, stopped to
observe a man dabbing at a canvas. This was André Derain. They
became friends, and then Apollinaire met the *fauve* Vlaminck. From
these friendships Apollinaire emerged as an art critic. Then one
day "Baron" Mollet—Jean Mollet, managing editor of *Le Festin
d'Esope,* nicknamed "Baron" by Apollinaire because he was so ele-
gant—brought his friend Picasso to the Criterion bar to meet Apol-
linaire, who at that moment was holding forth on the comparative
merits of English and German beer. In his turn Picasso brought the
poet Max Jacob—and the character of artistic and poetic life in
Paris was established for the following decade. It was a time for
cross-fertilization of the arts—painting affecting poetry (the
painters were insistent on this point—they had changed the poets,
not vice versa), a time of conversation, theorizing, innovation, and
hard work.

Apollinaire was also enjoying himself vastly. Who would not, in
Paris and with friends such as Picasso and Max Jacob, whose spe-
cialty was a dance called "the barefoot dancing girl"? Jacob, who had
once actually seen Christ ... Jacob was hairy all over, except his
head, which was bald, and he never took off his glasses. He would
dance "with airs and graces that made it impossible not to laugh and
that were a perfect burlesque—his steps, his manipulations on tip-
toe." (At about the same time by my calculations, in another street
James Joyce might have been doing his "spider dance" for *his*
friends.)

These Bohemian types would gather in the bars opposite the
Gare Saint-Lazare. There Apollinaire ate and drank large quan-
tities. Photographs of him at that time show a stout man with a pear-
shaped head; he needed quantities to sustain this frame. Sometimes

the painters and poets gathered to feast (these, as Roger Shattuck has said, were the "banquet years"). One night they held a banquet in honor of the painting of the *Douanier* Rousseau. It was half a joke; some of the celebrants thought Rousseau an old idiot who had tried to draw correctly, like an academy painter, and had failed. So much for primitivism! But they celebrated nevertheless, and the old man sat above it all with tears running down his cheeks, delighted as a child.

As a critic of art Apollinaire has been harshly criticized. "It is difficult," says Steegmuller, "to discover in all of Apollinaire's art writings, a mention of a picture that has been seen—let alone seen as an artist's image." When we turn to Apollinaire's book, *The Cubist Painters*, the harshness seems justified. Here is Apollinaire on some precubist paintings by Picasso: "Picasso's predilection for the fugitive line changes and penetrates and produces almost unique examples of linear etchings in which the general aspect of the world is unaltered by the light which modifies its form by changing its colors."

Apollinaire uses paintings as a point of departure for his own lyrical flights. In this, however, he strikes me as no better or worse than other art critics, for most art criticism is nonsense—attempting to represent paintings and sculpture in the medium of language. Finally, one can forgive Apollinaire his shortcomings as an art critic when one considers his usefulness as a publicist. He knew them all—Pablo Picasso, Georges Braque, Juan Gris, Jean Metzinger, Albert Gleizes, Marie Laurencin, Fernand Léger, Francis Picabia, Marcel Duchamp, Robert Delaunay, Henri Matisse, André Derain, Maurice de Vlaminck, Raoul Dufy, Henri Rousseau, Marc Chagall, Giorgio de Chirico. . . . The list stretches on; in fact, it is difficult to think of an important artist living in Paris before World War I whose later fame does not owe something to Apollinaire's friendship and his writings about art. Cubists, Orphists, fauvists, independents—Apollinaire had something to say in praise of them all. The recipients of his publicity were grateful, though a few of them sniggered. It was evident that their torchbearer didn't know a damned thing about art, really.

This is true if we look at Apollinaire's ideas about art as only art criticism. But if we regard them as ideas for poetry they are a great deal more important. Out of his studies of the new painting Apollinaire envisioned techniques that could be applied to poetry. Reality has nothing to do with "realism." Chronology, logic, rational connections are not important. What matters is to seize a feeling and get it across. The artist must be bold—audacity above all!—reducing experience to the essential elements and representing them according to the importance they have in his mind. Today, these ideas are a cliché in poetry, and in art they are a doctrine—excluding Pop Art—of the academy, but in 1913 they were new.

He deduced an idea of cubist poetry. "Cubist poetry?" said Pierre Reverdy. "A ridiculous term!" What Apollinaire meant, however, was not ridiculous—it was simultaneity of points of view, juxtaposition of images, the stream of consciousness. Applying this technique in his poem "Lundi Rue Christine" and elsewhere, Apollinaire anticipated Pound's *Cantos,* and by about fifty years anticipated the theories of Marshall McLuhan.

> Three gas lamps lighted
> The boss has T. B.
> When you've finished we'll play backgammon
> A conductor who has a sore throat
> When you come to Tunis I'll show you how to smoke kief
> That seems to make sense . . .

Above all, in Apollinaire's art criticism, and then in his statements about poetry, he insists on innovation. Here he is certainly up-to-date. Modernism could be defined as the belief that novelty is a virtue. "Make it new," says Ezra Pound, and in most serious art and writing of the twentieth century the assumption is made that if a thing is new it is good. This belief would have astonished artists of former periods, and a hundred years from now it may again seem unfounded, but today the creed is everywhere, and no one promulgated it more forcefully than Apollinaire, or demonstrated it more clearly than he in his pleadings for the new painters and in his own works.

In 1913, when *Alcools* finally was going to press, Apollinaire wrote a new poem, "Zone," to introduce the book and give the whole of it a modernist cast and emphasize the importance originality had assumed in his mind. (At the same time he struck out all the punctuation in the galleys.) "Zone" was one of the seminal poems of the new century—worthy to stand beside the poems of Eliot and Pound and Rilke—though the influence of "Zone" is only now beginning to be apparent. In the free flow of images "Zone" anticipates surrealism:

> Christ surpasses pilots in his flight
> He holds the record of the world for height
> Christ apple of the eye
> Fruit of twenty centuries he can fly
> And changed to a bird this age like Jesus rises
> The devils look up at him from the abysses
> They say he imitates Simon Mage in Judea
> They cry since he is stellar call him stealer
> The angels stunt around the pretty stunter
> Icare Enoch Elie Apollonius of Thyane
> Float around the first aeroplane . . .

And fifty years in advance, "Zone" anticipated the confessional poetry of the 1960s. The poem is a promenade through the splendors and glooms of cities. In every place there rises the lament of the "ill-beloved":

> Today you walk in Paris the women are bloodstained
> It was and I would wish to forget it was then beauty waned
> Surrounded with leaping flames Notre Dame at Chartres
>   looked down on me
> The blood of your Sacré Coeur at Montmartre drowned me
> I'm sick of hearing the windy pieties
> The love from which I suffer is a shameful disease
> The image possessing you makes life a sleepless woe
> This fugitive image is with you wherever you go.

In "Zone," Apollinaire has fulfilled his own prescription of a new form, "a supple line, based on rhythm, subject matter, and breathing." Even in translation Apollinaire's audacity comes through. The opening line is a clarion call; the young men of 1913 went around repeating these words like a charm:

Finally you're tired of this ancient world

The poem proceeds:

> O Eiffel Shepherdess the flock of bridges bawls this
>   morning

"O Eiffel Shepherdess. . . ." Apollinaire is never free of tradition; indeed, he believes that it is necessary to incorporate "the classical heritage" if anything new is to be done—and, like Eliot, he has been criticized for being too knowledgeable.

> You're tired of living in Greek and Roman styles
>
> Antiquity has touched the automobiles
> Only religion is still new Religion
> Still simple as the hangars at the airport. . . .

In this poem about his wandering years Apollinaire speaks of "a picture hanging in a somber museum," and no account of his life would be complete without the episode of the Mona Lisa. On August 23, 1911, the *Paris-Journal* revealed that the Mona Lisa had been stolen from the Louvre. A reward was offered for the return of the painting. Then the newspaper received a letter from a young man who offered to return, not the Mona Lisa, but a "Phoenician statuette" he had stolen from the Louvre. Sensation! "An edifying story—our Museum is a supply center for unscrupulous individuals."

It turned out that the man who lifted the statue had been Apollinaire's secretary. Moreover, on a previous occasion he had stolen two other statuettes. These he had given to Apollinaire, who had passed them on to Picasso, who still had them. (If you look at Picasso's "Les Demoiselles d'Avignon," the ears of the two central figures are modeled on these stolen statuettes.) Threatened with exposure, Picasso and Apollinaire debated throwing the statuettes in the Seine, but thought better of it, and turned them in at the offices of the *Paris-Journal*.

Then Apollinaire was arrested and taken to prison. He was interrogated by a magistrate who evidently enjoyed humiliating the

Bohemian poet and friend of artists. It was clear, however, that Apollinaire had been guilty only of harboring a thief, and he was released. But he was profoundly disturbed—his photograph, in handcuffs, had appeared in the papers. He was shaken by the treachery of Picasso. Brought to the prison to confront Apollinaire, Picasso had denied knowing him. Apollinaire was disturbed, also, by the outcry of the rightists, who demanded his expulsion as an undesirable alien. Some of these people were anti-Semites who supposed that, being a Pole, Apollinaire must be a Jew. Six brief, agonized poems in *Alcools* record the experience:

> Before I entered my cell
> I had to strip myself naked
> What sinister voice resounding
> Guillaume, what has become of you?
>
> Lazarus entering the tomb
> Instead of emerging . . .
> Adieu adieu . . .
> O my life O young women

The Mona Lisa, as it turned out, had been taken back to Italy by a patriotic Italian, and of course was safely recovered. The sadness of the episode for Apollinaire was that this was how he became famous. Louise Faure Favier remarks: "Guillaume Apollinaire abruptly became famous throughout the entire world. He was thought of as the man who had stolen the Mona Lisa. Even today there are Parisians who believe it, and who are a little disappointed to learn that Apollinaire had nothing to do with the theft."

"O my life O young women. . . ." I believe it is Camus who, writing about life in prison, has a character remark that when we say freedom has been lost we mean sexual freedom. The imprisonment in La Santé, for Apollinaire, presented itself immediately as a kind of castration, reinforcing his history of sexual failure. Not incapacity—he was always trying to seduce some woman and frequently succeeding—but he never could attach a woman permanently.

After Annie Playden his next major love was Marie Laurencin. It is hard to discover the right and wrong of this affair, which ended in bitterness on his side. My impression is that, although Apollinaire was possessive and even violent, and was not faithful, yet he seems ingenuous, while Marie Laurencin was a nasty, calculating type. She met Apollinaire when he was making a name for himself as an art critic, and then when she had made a little name for herself as a painter she broke the connection. She strikes me as an all-too-familiar type of young woman, with a little talent and less sincerity. The portraits of Marie Laurencin give me a bad feeling—those beady eyes. . . .

Apollinaire's third passion was "Lou"—Louise de Coligny-Chatillon, a member of the aristocracy whom he picked up at an opium party in Nice. She kept him dangling for a while. He enlisted, in the fashion of rejected lovers, to ride off to war. Then she threw herself at him, and for a week Apollinaire was swept beyond his depth by a woman of considerable sexual inventiveness, with pronounced sadomasochistic tastes.

From the front he wrote her letters; Lou answered. Then she stopped answering; she had taken another lover. Apollinaire wrote her erotic letters, and she wrote back describing her new affair—more erotica. The thing becomes a case history, reminiscent of Aldous Huxley's bitch, Lucy Tantamount. A further complication—returning from a visit with Lou, Apollinaire had met a young lady on a train. Out of his reminiscences and masochistic fantasies of Lou he was writing erotic poems—it is terribly chaste at the front—and copies of these poems he sent also to his new friend, Madeleine.

The end of Apollinaire's life is melancholy, from one point of view. In the trenches, having been transferred at his own request from the artillery to the infantry, he was wounded by a shell fragment in the head. At first the wound seemed superficial; then it was found necessary to trepan—to cut into the bone. He was discharged from the hospital to a desk job, censoring mail, which he did with a scrupulous sense of his patriotic obligations.

The wound had changed him physically; he was more corpulent, drowsy, given to irrational outbursts of anger. In 1918 he married Jacqueline Kolb (the "pretty redhead" of a poem). Then, a few days before the Armistice, he contracted influenza and died. His body was laid out. His friends tiptoed in to gaze at the decomposing modernist. His mother, the dragon Olga, arrived and began a furious quarrel with his widow. Final touch of the ridiculous: outside in the streets people were shouting, *"A bas Guillaume!"*—meaning down with Kaiser Wilhelm, but dreadfully ironic in these circumstances.

On the other hand, toward the end of his life Apollinaire was writing with increasing gaiety and freedom, and moving into a new field, the theater. He invented the word surrealism, and in his play *The Breasts of Tiresias* and in statements about esthetics he made at this time—urgently, as though he sensed his approaching death—he was predicting new forms of art.

In *Calligrammes,* a collection of poems published in the last year of his life, he discovered what could be done with typography, making the poem on the page look like an object. So he anticipated the present fashion of concrete poetry. Recently in the *New Republic,* a writer said that Apollinaire "invented a new poetic form ... a mixed-media type of poem where letters, words and images were graphically intermingled." Actually, the form is as old as the hills, but Apollinaire deserves credit for reinventing it.

He welcomed the phonograph and the cinema, and predicted and wrote for a theater in which several media would be used simultaneously to achieve astounding effects. Indeed, Apollinaire went beyond theater in his prediction of a "new art ... an orchestra that will include the entire world, its sights and sounds, human thought and language, song, dance, all the arts and all the artifices—more mirages than Morgan le Fay conjured up on Mongibel to compose the book seen and heard by the future." He sounds positively psychedelic as he foresees:

> The full unfolding of our modern art
> Often connecting in unseen ways as in life
> Sounds gestures colors cries tumults
> Music dancing acrobatics poetry painting
> Choruses actions and multiple sets

In one respect, Apollinaire is not typical of modern times. He is full of enthusiasm. He would not have felt at home in the Waste Land of the twenties, nor would he be happy in the present circles where paranoia reigns. Apollinaire was fundamentally innocent.

Under the masks—melancholy being only another mask—there is a childlike confidence in love and in art. I think that as we get bored with pessimistic poetry, novels, painting, and theater—and surely the creators of boredom must be beginning to bore themselves, as well as the public—Apollinaire's writings will flourish and his influence will increase. In every generation there will be those who respond to his appeal for "a new spirit":

A joyfulness voluptuousness virtue
Instead of that pessimism more than a hundred years old
And that's pretty old for such a boring thing. . . .

Cloud's Processional

Tweedledum says that style isn't as important as content. Tweedledee on the other hand says that what you say doesn't matter but only how well you say it. On 20 February 1949 the Fellows of the Library of Congress voted with Tweedledee for style and awarded the first Bollingen Prize for poetry to Ezra Pound. The prize was one thousand dollars, for the best book of "American verse" published during the year. It was awarded for *The Pisan Cantos.*

Pound was under an indictment by the government of the United States for "knowingly, intentionally, wilfully, unlawfully, feloniously, traitorously and treasonably" adhering to the enemies of the United States and giving "aid and comfort" to these "enemies." There seemed to be a great difference between the opinion of Pound held by American intellectuals and that held by the government.

The poet Robert Hillyer wrote articles in *The Saturday Review of Literature* attacking Pound and the jury that had given him the prize. People took sides, some congratulating Hillyer on the stand he was taking, others defending the jury. The jurors were well-known "modern" poets—Eliot and Auden among them—so that the controversy went beyond the question of Pound's guilt and the prize, it became a quarrel between those who were for "modern

Reprinted from Louis Simpson, *Three on the Tower: The Lives and Works of Ezra Pound, T. S. Eliot and William Carlos Williams.* New York: William Morrow and Company, 1975.

poetry"—Pound, Eliot and their followers—and those who were for some other kind of poetry that would speak to and for the American people. The proponents of this other kind of poetry named Robert Frost as an example.

One night the members of the Poetry Society of America gathered at the Waldorf Astoria to dine and reassure one another. Speaking from the platform Robert Hillyer compared Pound's *Cantos* to the scribblings of a lunatic. He also criticized Archibald MacLeish. MacLeish too, it seemed, was part of the conspiracy Hillyer was exposing. Then John Ciardi took the microphone away from Hillyer and said that he was a friend of MacLeish and was ashamed to have sat at the same table with Robert Hillyer. W. H. Auden, who was also at the speakers' table, began to cough in his handkerchief. He slipped away behind a screen—one moment he was there, the next he wasn't. The members of the Poetry Society were thunderstruck, their pistachio ice cream melting on their plates. They were accustomed to complaining about modern poetry, and they thought Pound was tucked away safely in a mental hospital. Who would have thought the old man to have had so much blood in him?

The cause of the controversy was in St. Elizabeth's Hospital in the District of Columbia, within arm's reach of the government he had offended. Doctors had decided that he wasn't competent to stand trial. "In our opinion, with advancing years his personality, for many years abnormal, has undergone further distortion to the extent that he is now suffering from a paranoid state which renders him mentally unfit to advise properly with counsel or to participate intelligently and reasonably in his own defense." The indictment remained on the books and Pound was kept in an insane asylum. It was agreed that he wasn't really crazy but if he behaved himself the government would pretend that he was.

Pound's wife came to visit him every day. He had a supply of books and magazines. And he had many visitors. Whenever Eliot was in the States he would make a special journey to St. Elizabeth's. There were other poets and critics who came to pay their respects to the Old Man Mad About Letters. Delighted to have their company Pound bustled about, making tea. Sometimes he would lecture them on economics. At other times, disconcertingly, he would be silent and stare them in the eye.

There were also disciples such as John Kasper, who came to see him and then went forth to preach hatred against Negroes and Jews. For a man who claimed that he was not a racist Pound was remarkably unfortunate. He was more unfortunate than the man in Molière's play, for he kept getting into the same galley. When Kasper began making a name for himself as a rabble-rouser the newspapers revealed that he was Pound's disciple. A businessman and poet named Harry Meacham went to see Pound. He reminded Pound that his friends were trying to persuade the government to release him, and asked him to state publicly that he did not approve of Kasper. "Well," Pound said, "at least he's a man of action and don't sit around looking at his navel."

Thirteen years after the partisans knocked on his door and said, "Come along, traitor," Pound was set free. He sailed back to Italy, and the first thing he did on arriving was to give the Fascist salute and tell the reporters that America was a lunatic asylum.

There is a passage denouncing Vanity in *The Pisan Cantos.*

> How mean thy hates
> Fostered in falsity,
> Pull down thy vanity,

The passage is dear to anthologists, for it is a quotable whole in an unquotably long poem. It is especially valued as evidence of Pound's change of heart—he has stopped railing and is reconciled to the world. On consideration, however, this is not what happened. The line, "The total dirt that was Roosevelt," appears in Canto LXXXVII, a long time after Pisa.

It is not even clear that Pound includes himself in his denunciation of vanity. The passage says, "Pull down thy vanity," it does not say, "I am pulling down mine."

Pound on Vanity had been, as usual, a dramatic impersonation, a monologue in the style of a period. Pound did not change his opinions when he wrote about vanity, any more than he had renounced a part of himself when he created the character Bertrand de Born, "stirrer up of strife," or Mauberley the aesthete and follower of the cult of Beauty. The role of humility, if we assume that Pound does include himself among those to whom the Canto is addressed, was just another of his *personae*. He himself was not to be reconstructed, either by doctors or the state. His discontents were "unremovably/Coupled to nature."

For a time the barbarians had been stronger. They had placed him in a cage, six feet by six and a half. Through wire mesh with metal strips welded over the wire he looked out on other cages containing murderers, rapists, deserters from the Army of the United States. The Disciplinary Training Center was surrounded with barbed wire that slanted out at the top, supported on what looked like gibbets. It was possible that he would be hanged or at least die of pneumonia. Dust blew into the cage and he was wet when it rained. He slept on concrete, wrapped in two blankets. His cage was lit by the glare of a reflector. In the hours before dawn the cold mist made his teeth chatter and his limbs to shake. During the day he was not allowed out for exercise though other prisoners were. He paced to and fro in the cage, striking with an imaginary tennis racket, shadowboxing. Then they gave him more blankets and a pup tent to keep out the rain.

He began to have bouts of panic. He suffered from amnesia. The top of his head felt empty. So they moved him from the cage to a tent in the dispensary.

For a time he was held in one place. Then he saw that there were creatures for whom this time was all, this place the whole world. At dawn he observed the ants.

> And now the ants seem to stagger
>   as the dawn sun has trapped their shadows,

One of the qualities he had admired in Arnaut Daniel was his exact observation of nature. Yeats on the other hand saw everything as a symbol—gazing at Notre Dame he saw it enclosed in a larger significance. For one man who could look at nature and report what he saw, there were a hundred who were purblind, saw trees as men walking. But

> When the mind swings by a grass-blade
> an ant's forefoot shall save you

Now a wasp had built her cell on the roof of his tent. As he watched a new wasp emerged, the color of grass, climbed down to the earth, "to carry our news/to them that dwell under earth." The newborn wasp would sing in the bower of Kore and have speech with Tiresias.

It had taken the mother wasp half a day to make her cell out of mud. It had been a devil of a time before Ezra Pound hit on the right way to make his first Canto. He found it in Andreas Divus's translation of Homer, picked up in a bookstall on the Seine. Divus had translated Greek into Latin. As the Greek sounded to Divus, primitive and heroic, so would Anglo-Saxon, the sound of "The Seafarer," be to twentieth-century readers who spoke English. He began the first, Homeric Canto with the sound of Anglo-Saxon.

> Circe's this craft, the trim-coifed goddess.

He had gone with Odysseus under the earth and poured the libation of blood. The dead rose and their spirits drank of the blood—they spoke to him and through him. The *Cantos* were a history of ghosts, with many crowding round him—the helmeted ghost of Sigismondo Malatesta, the white ghost of Helen, the ghost of John Adams. They spoke together, a confusion of tongues. In the midst of their conversing one would vanish and another take his place.

Last of all came Mussolini, his eyes staring, his mouth hanging open. His naked feet were covered with blood.

> the twice crucified
> where in history will you find it?

Roosevelt had made war on Mussolini. Pound had done his best to prevent it. He had tried to tell people in America about usury, warn them against Roosevelt and the Jews. They had chosen to ignore his warnings. Well, it was no longer his responsibility—they would have to suffer the consequences.

He wrote at night the bits of poetry he composed during the day. They let him use the typewriter in the dispensary. They let him keep his copy of Confucius and his dictionary of Chinese. He also had a Bible—Jehovah was okay with the officials. He had *The Pocket Book of Verse*—this last found in the john.

He was getting back the sound of American, listening to the

guards. " 'If you had a f . . . . n' brain you'd be dangerous.' " Not having lived Stateside as they called it so many years he had lost touch with demotic American. Someone said that when he tried to write American it sounded like *Our American Cousin,* the play Lincoln saw the night he was shot. As Hem used to say, they said many things.

He had been out of touch. But he wouldn't, to save his life, have spent it like Bill Williams in a town in New Jersey. There was a defect there. Doting on the plain and ugly. Puritanism. Williams was like one of the spirits in Dante that walked with eyes fixed on the ground, by preference. Nor would he have wanted to stay in London like Eliot, getting timider and timider. The Possum had taken to religion—he was some sort of deacon in his church. There was a defect there. Of courage. A lack of joy. No, even if he hanged for it he preferred the view from his tent, the morning sun rising, the shadows of the ants, like centaurs, having disappeared.

A group of prisoners was being run over to the obstacle course. In the distance he could see the *"torre qui pende,"* the leaning—no, hanging—tower. He could see a patch of white, the *battistero.* And above Pisa the clouds. They were as fine as any in the Peninsula.

The tower was of white Carrara marble. Beauty formed out of chaos, the female. "By prong have I entered these hills."

He was being compelled to think about his life. There was nothing else to do, no access to a library. His life was in the past. Well, the muses were daughters of memory, and what he had seen and heard was indisputable fact. When he spoke about what he himself had witnessed no one could question his authority. When he wrote about the past, even his ideas took on a feeling of reality—for they were part of his life. In themselves neither valid nor invalid, ideas became believable when they were treated as part of the story of his life— when, so to speak, they became fiction. Then everything seemed to fit—the shadow of the guard, the shouting of the drill instructor, the sow on the other side of the barbed wire with her farrow, "matronly as any duchess at Claridge's." The black man, Walls, had lent him a razor to shave with. It seemed perfectly natural. There was a man named Clower he remembered he might owe money to. That too seemed natural and went into the poem.

In former days when he wrote about present matters he would

harangue the reader. But now there was nothing more to be gained. As Chaucer said, "Wrestling for the world asks for a fall." So now he just wrote about life—London, for example, the gulls on the Serpentine, the sunken garden. He wrote about people he had known before the war. Before which war? The war before which everything. He recalled "Uncle William/labouring a sonnet of Ronsard." And there were lesser men and women. He had a hundred ghosts.

When he was old he lived with Olga Rudge—in winter at her small house on Calle Querini in Venice, in summer at her house at Sant' Ambrogio in the hills above Rapallo. "Down below lived Dorothy."

He was famous—some thought him a great poet and in any case he was a monument. As the years passed he became more and more silent; visitors might be confronted with a man who sat the whole time saying nothing. "He was just out of it," said one who had been through the experience.

When Eliot died Pound traveled to England to attend the memorial service in Westminster Abbey.

Every year he visited the music festival at Spoleto, the most famous person there. He was invited back to the States to be honored and gazed at. His peculiar views didn't seem to matter to young men who had learned about poetry in the university. They were taught that the poem was a thing complete in itself, existing apart from history. The poet's intentions didn't matter—to think they did would be the "intentional fallacy."

To the young American who came to interview him and who asked about his "devotion to technique" he replied that "the *what*" was much more important than how. The interviewer listened to this without turning a hair. It seemed that these days Ezra Pound could say anything and it would go into print without anyone's turning a hair. The world had changed—people took for granted attitudes that, when he was young, had to be fought for. When he was a young man poetry had been dying of sentimentality. So he had insisted on "objectivity." Now poetry seemed to be dying of objectivity. Poetry had always been dying of something as far back as he could remember.

Looking at the clouds he saw his life receding. "In the 'search for oneself,' in the search for 'sincere self-expression,' one gropes, one finds some seeming verity. One says 'I am' this, that, or the other, and with the words scarcely uttered one ceases to be that thing."

There was a man walking on a road lined with poplars. There was a man in a London street, wearing a broad hat and a cape—he looked bohemian, a "Latin Quarter" type. There was a man in a restaurant reading a poem in a loud voice to a table full of people. The manager came up with the waiter, carrying a screen—they placed it around the table to hide the poetry readers from the other people in the restaurant. There was a man sitting in a cage near Pisa, his red hair covered with dust.

He had been a vagabond all his life. He had not been willing to stay in one place, settle for one style.

> One dull man, dulling and uxorious,
> One average mind—with one thought less, each year.

He hadn't been willing to be dull, but had kept slipping from one role into another, "casting off, as it were, complete masks of the self in each poem."

He watched his many selves take shape and fade. Seeing them fade was his life.

> Nothing that's quite your own.
> Yet this is you.

The Author of Prufrock

In 1669 an Englishman named Andrew Eliot, a leather-worker by trade, came to Massachusetts from the village of East Coker in Somerset. His name is in the register of the First Church at Beverly. He was a witness at the Salem witch trials, but afterwards he recanted, and it is said that for the rest of his life he regretted having taken part. Andrew Eliot's descendants were prominent in New England history. They were Presbyterians, then they were converted to Unitarianism.

In 1834, William Greenleaf Eliot, having graduated from the Harvard Divinity School, went out to St. Louis, Missouri, where he founded the first Unitarian chapel and, in 1857, founded Washington University. He was a writer on "ethical and philosophical questions," and set the standard of conduct for his descendants, any deviation from which would be sinful. They had a sense of public service described by the poet T. S. Eliot as "an uncomfortable and very inconvenient obligation to serve upon committees." Robert Sencourt, in his memoir of Eliot's life, says that William Greenleaf's descendants "admired him as a hero, they worshipped him as a saint, and they loved him for the fine old gentleman he was." At the

Reprinted from Louis Simpson, *Three on the Tower: The Lives and Works of Ezra Pound, T. S. Eliot and William Carlos Williams*. New York: William Morrow and Company, 1975.

same time we are told that he "towered over his family as over his congregation," and that his daughter-in-law, Charlotte Eliot, "lived in his shadow." This is the familiar picture of a Victorian patriarch, righteous, awe-inspiring and, it is to be hoped, benevolent. Of the fourteen children born to William Greenleaf Eliot's wife, five survived. The second son, Henry Ware Eliot, graduated from Washington University, of which his father was president, but instead of going into the ministry he went into business as a wholesale grocer. When this failed he became a partner in the Hydraulic Press Brick Company. He rose to be president, collected paintings, was active in the St. Louis Philharmonic and Choral Societies, and served on the governing board of the University. Henry Ware Eliot married Charlotte Chauncey Sterns. She too came of a Boston family that had been among the early settlers. Charlotte Eliot wrote a life of her father-in-law, William Greenleaf Eliot. She also wrote a poem— rather, a series of short verses with prose in between—to which she gave the title, *Savonarola, A Dramatic Poem.*

The poet T. S. Eliot was their seventh child. He was born on 26 September 1888, and christened Thomas Stearns Eliot.

He seems to have been a delicate child. We are told by Sencourt that as a child Eliot suffered from hernia "and so was rather coddled." Also, there was an Irish nurse "who frequently talked to the child about God." She took Tom with her to her church, which was Catholic. In this way, says Sencourt, Eliot was exposed to the Catholicism that he would come to prefer to the "prim moralizing Unitarianism which he had learned at home as the religion of a model grandfather." T. S. Matthews in his biography of Eliot says that the nurse, Annie Dunne, was "the first exciting woman in Tom Eliot's life," and that the child saw the difference between the "liturgical order and richness of the Mass" and the "bloodless prolixities of Unitarian prayer meetings." This may have been true, but a man has many experiences in the course of his life and what matters is his thinking, that is, the way the mind works through the data presented to it and the way it arrives at a conclusion. This process, however, can only be suggested and may hold no attraction for the general public. An Irish nurse is more appealing.

Eliot's father was a Unitarian, a teetotaler, a nonsmoker, and a model citizen. We are told, however, that he was "stone deaf, middle-aged, and remote." To entertain the children he would draw faces on their boiled eggs. He also drew cats, and he made a point of calling nasturtiums "nestertians" in the hope that one of them would correct him. He was a good chess player and his handwriting was untidy. He seems to have been an Edward Learish character whose love of cats and untidy handwriting, at least, were inherited by the poet.

Eliot's mother, Charlotte, was forty-five when he was born (his father was forty-seven). Matthews tells us that she was "one of those admirable women who have strict standards of conduct and no intimate friends, and who are admired, disliked, and feared by all who know them." Matthews tells us that her handwriting was "uncompromisingly ugly." He has an ever harsher judgment: Eliot's mother "did not like children. She never said so; she bore seven and did her maternal duty by them, but none of them needed to be told how she felt." She kept a watch over the children's reading and there were certain "vulgar" books, *Tom Sawyer* and *Huckleberry Finn* among them, that Tom was forbidden to read.

Next to the Eliot house was a girls' school called Mary Institute—this too had been founded by his grandfather—which Eliot's sisters attended. A high brick wall separated the schoolyard from the Eliots' back garden. The wall had a door in it and there was a key to the door. If he stood in the back garden he could hear the voices of the children playing in the schoolyard. At the end of the day when they had gone he would enter the schoolyard and sometimes venture into the building.

The Mississippi, the "strong brown god—sullen, untamed and intractable," the scent of ailanthus in the spring, and voices of children who, when he arrives on the scene, have vanished, are in the poems Eliot wrote many years later. So is the sea, for Henry Ware Eliot built a house at Gloucester, Massachusetts, and the family spent summer vacations there. Eliot would recall "peering through sea-water in a rock-pool, and finding a sea-anemone for the first time."

He began early as a writer. He wrote a life of George Washington in ten lines, and before he was ten founded, edited, and distributed to members of his family a periodical titled *Fireside*. He liked "martial and sanguinary" poetry such as "Horatius," "The Burial of Sir

John Moore," "Bannockburn," Tennyson's "Revenge," and the border ballads. Then for three years he lost his liking for poetry altogether; the only pleasure he derived from Shakespeare was "the pleasure of being recommended for reading him." At the age of fourteen, however, he saw an extract from Fitzgerald's *Omar Khayyam* and had the overwhelming sensation of entering a new world of feeling. "It was like a sudden conversion; the world appeared anew, painted with bright, delicious and painful colours. Thereupon I took the usual adolescent course with Byron, Shelley, Keats, Rossetti, Swinburne." This period persisted until he was nineteen or twenty.

But only a part of an author's imagery comes from his reading. It comes, says Eliot, "from the whole of his sensitive life since early childhood."

> Why, for all of us, out of all that we have heard, seen, felt, in a lifetime, do certain images recur, charged with emotion, rather than others? The song of one bird, the leap of one fish, at a particular place and time, the scent of one flower, an old woman on a German mountain path, six ruffians seen through an open window playing cards at night at a small French railway junction where there was a water-mill; such memories may have symbolic value, but of what we cannot tell, for they come to represent the depths of feeling into which we cannot peer.

He was sent to school at Smith Academy in St. Louis. The hernia prevented his participating fully in games, so he studied and read for pleasure. He was taught Greek and Latin, the history of Greece and Rome, English and American history, elementary mathematics, French and German. "Also English! I am happy to remember that in those days English composition was still called *Rhetoric*." After his discovery of *Omar Khayyam* he wrote some gloomy quatrains. At sixteen he published a few pieces of verse and prose in the *Smith Academy Record*. "A Fable for Feasters" is in the graveyard humor of *The Ingoldsby Legends,* telling of monks and a ghost. In "A Lyric" he was imitating Ben Jonson:

> The flowers I gave thee when the dew
>   Was trembling on the vine,
> Were withered ere the wild bee flew
>   To suck the eglantine.

This was better poetry, his mother told him, than any she had written herself. Eliot comments, "I knew what her verse meant to her. We did not discuss the matter further." He also composed a valedictory poem and read it on Graduation Day.

From Smith he went to Milton Academy in Massachusetts, where he received further grounding in basic subjects, including Greek and Latin.

In 1906 Eliot entered Harvard College. At this time the president was Charles William Eliot, a distant cousin of Eliot's grandfather, William Greenleaf Eliot. President Eliot was a Unitarian and a man for the new century, liberal and progressive in his views. He did not hold with the anthropomorphic view of religion, with references to a Holy Ghost or a Mother of God. He was against morbidly dwelling on sin. The religion of the future would seek to prevent disease and would lead to universal good-will. It was "benevolent materialism." The teachings of Jesus would be brought in line with education, social service, research in medicine and, as Gatsby might have said, "needed inventions."

In his reading in modern languages and literature Eliot came across Flaubert's portrait of the chemist Homais, whose ideas about religion were similar to President Eliot's: "My God is the God of Socrates, of Franklin, Voltaire and Beranger! . . . I cannot worship an old fogey of a God who walks round his garden with a stick in his hand, lodges his friends in the bellies of whales . . ." He was reading French poets; he had discovered Baudelaire, who had a better style than President Eliot and who loathed materialism. Moreover, in his browsings at the Union he had picked up a copy of Arthur Symons' *The Symbolist Movement in French Literature.*

Conrad Aiken, who was at Harvard with Eliot, remembers him as an undergraduate: "a singularly attractive, tall, and rather dapper young man, with a somewhat Lamian smile." Eliot was painfully shy but tried to overcome this by going to dances and parties. He felt very much out of place. He had been born in the South—St. Louis being practically the South in its atmosphere and way of life. He himself had what he called a "nigger drawl" (people in St. Louis said "nigger" and spoke contemptuously of Jews and other strangers). But he wasn't really a Southerner, for his family came from the North and looked down on all Southerners. So he was never really anything anywhere. He thought he was more of a Frenchman than an American, and more of an Englishman than an American. Yet, the United States of America up to a hundred years ago had been "a family extension."

During these years he continued to spend his summer vacations at Gloucester. Samuel Eliot Morison, the historian who was Eliot's cousin, says that "Tom was not only steeped in the lore of Cape Ann; he became familiar with the encompassing ocean." Eliot would sail with a friend named Harold Peters out beyond the rocks known as the Dry Salvages. When there was fog they would listen for the "groaner," the whistling buoy east of Thacher Island, and the "wailing warning" of the diaphone on the island. They grew familiar with "The sea howl/And the sea yelp," "The distant rote in the granite teeth."

He was beginning to write poetry, and contributed poems to the *Harvard Advocate* of which he was an associate editor. They were what might be expected of an adolescent who had been reading Romantic and Victorian poets. The writing shows a sense of rhythm and sound. But there is something more, a quality described years later by a character in one of Eliot's plays:

> a sudden intuition, in certain minds,
> May tend to express itself at once in a picture.

The ability to render thought in images is evident in lines Eliot wrote when he was still an undergraduate.

> The peacocks walk, stately and slow,
> And they look at us with the eyes
> Of men whom we knew long ago.

Suddenly his manner changes—it is no longer Tennyson and Swinburne, it is Jules Laforgue. "Laforgue," says Eliot, "was the first to teach me how to speak, to teach me the possibilities of my own idiom of speech." As Sencourt says, it was as though Eliot had met Laforgue in person; he submitted not only to Laforgue's way of writing but his way of life. When he sat down to write it was as though he were the reincarnation of Laforgue. He now wrote as a man of the world, speaking with irony. In one poem he describes Romeo and Juliet

in the usual debate
Of love, beneath a bored but courteous moon . . .

Romeo is stabbed by a servant and thus spared the longueurs of life, the disenchantment. The narrator remarks that "Blood looks effective on the moonlit ground," and that this is "The perfect climax all true lovers seek!"

It is curious how authors find their affinities. The writer a writer needs may not be a grand figure: to the contrary, he may only strike a certain note. Laforgue is no great figure in the literature of France, but to Eliot he was all-important.

When he writes in the manner of Laforgue he expresses his boredom and sometimes he gives vent to spleen—a vague, nervous irritability. If irritability is too strong a word, let us say a gnawing sense of the ridiculous. With spleen he regards a "satisfied procession/Of definite Sunday faces" on their way to church. Everything about ordinary life—teatime, children and cats in the alley— increases his dejection. He visualizes the arrival of the procession, Life, with hat and gloves in hand, impatient at being kept waiting "On the doorstep of the Absolute." The poem "Spleen" marks an advance: Eliot is beginning to deal with people and ideas rather than flowers, peacocks, and marionettes.

Between Laforgue's life and Eliot's there are resemblances; this is not surprising, for Eliot imitated Laforgue. They were both expatriates: Laforgue was born in Uruguay in 1860 but moved to France at an early age. Laforgue dressed like an Englishman and carried an umbrella. He kept his personal life out of his work and very little is known about him. One further fact should be mentioned: Laforgue was married in London at St. Barnabas's Church. Shortly before Eliot married for the second time he discovered that he was to be married in the same church as Laforgue. This is one of the coincidences in a man's life that prove nothing yet demand to be noticed. Coincidences such as this drive men to art, where facts have some significance.

Eliot turned to Laforgue and the French Symbolists because, he says, there was no poet in England or America who could be of use to a beginner in 1908. The poetry being written at this time was watered-down Romanticism. It was necessary to go to another language or another age for models. The Symbolists taught that poetry "must transmute life into a new incarnation of thought and rhythm." So did the Jacobean dramatists, instinctively. In both the appeal was to mind through sense perception. "In both, too, the interest was dramatic, in contrast to the reflective and descriptive modes of the eighteenth and nineteenth centuries, and to that of the subjective lyric." In dramatic poetry there was a distance between the author and the subject, therefore the poet was able to view life all around, himself included. He was not carried away by his own emotions.

Eliot says that he does not know of any other writer who formed his style by studying Laforgue and the Jacobean dramatists. It was an original place to start. "He has actually trained himself *and* modernized himself *on his own,*" Pound would say after meeting Eliot.

He had been reading Dante, who remained for him a supreme poet. He read Donne and the Metaphysicals. He had come across odd authors such as John Davidson whose "Thirty Bob a Week" with its colloquial speech and imagery taken from mean streets indicated what might be done in the way of realism.

After receiving the BA he continued at Harvard as a graduate student working toward the Master's. He enrolled in a course taught by Irving Babbitt: "Literary Criticism in France with Special Reference to the Nineteenth Century." This was more than a course in French literature, it was confirmation for Eliot of attitudes he already held. Babbitt disliked the liberal mind; he was against the free-elective system at Harvard and in life. "The function of the college . . . should be to insist on the idea of quality." Babbitt wanted a sense of authority and claimed to have found it in the classics, the "unbroken chain of literary and intellectual tradition which extends from the ancient to the modern world." The classics appealed to man's higher reason and imagination and enabled him to participate in "the universal life." The classical spirit was marked by restraint, discipline, proportion and law.

Babbitt called his position humanism. The humanist believed that "the man of today, if he does not, like the man of the past, take on the yoke of a definite doctrine and discipline, must at least do inner obeisance to something higher than his ordinary self, whether he calls this something God, or, like the man of the Far East, calls it his higher self, or simply the Law."

Babbitt thought that most of the harm in the world was caused by people who trusted to their feelings. "In the name of feeling Rousseau headed the most powerful insurrection the world has ever seen against every kind of authority." Romanticism was the father of lies and Rousseau was its prophet. Romanticism meant lack of discipline, individualism, stress on sensation, primitivism and the glorification of spontaneity. Romanticism was the cause of the excesses of modern life—humanism the corrective.

Much of Eliot's later writing, especially his attack on Romantic attitudes, is consistent with the teachings of Babbitt. He continued to respect Babbitt after he himself had decided that humanism was too vague, that he needed the dogma of the church.

Conrad Aiken speaks of a lady in Boston whom Eliot visited: "The oh so precious, the oh so exquisite, the Jamesian lady of ladies, the enchantress of the Beacon Hill drawing room . . . afterwards to be essentialized and ridiculed (and his own pose with it) in the Tsetse's *'Portrait d'une Femme.'*" Eliot seems to have found a situation in real life that could be dealt with in the style of Laforgue: a woman demanding greater intimacy and a man who is unwilling or unable to give it. He squirms under her reproaches; he feels that he is craven and ridiculous; but he keeps returning nevertheless. The Circe of the drawing room takes her place in Eliot's poetry with the punctiliously dressed, balding middle-aged man.

In 1910 he wrote the "Portrait of a Lady." He also wrote two "Preludes" and the first part of "The Love Song of J. Alfred Prufrock."

After receiving the MA he decided to pursue his studies in France, at the University of Paris. He was there in the autumn of 1910, attending lectures by Henri Bergson. He was "at odds with Bergson's optimism from the outset," but Bergson's idea of instinctive consciousness, breaking down orderly thought into a stream of disconnected impressions, may have contributed to the seemingly free flow of thought in Eliot's "Rhapsody on a Windy Night" and other poems.

He was tutored by the novelist Alain-Fournier, whose enthusiasm for Dostoyevski led him to read that author—another possible cause of the breaking down of orderly thought. He met the critic Jacques Rivière, who later became the editor of *Nouvelle Revue Française*. He came to know Charles Maurras, the leader of *Action Française*, a movement dedicated to nationalism, the Catholic church, and anti-Semitism. He read novels by Charles Louis Philippe. *Bubu de Montparnasse*, an account of the lives of prostitutes and pimps, made a strong impression; it was not like anything he had known in Cambridge or St. Louis. From this novel he borrowed the scene for his own third "Prelude," a woman's getting out of bed in a dirty room. Another novel by Philippe, *Marie Donadieu*, supplied Eliot with more ideas about low life and more phrases for poems.

He made a friend, Jean Verdenal. This is the man to whom his first book is dedicated:

> For Jean Verdenal, 1889–1915
> mort aux Dardanelles

There follows a passage of four lines from Dante's *Purgatorio*. Dante is being guided through purgatory by Virgil. They meet the spirit of the Roman poet Statius, who stoops and tries to clasp Virgil's feet in homage. Virgil stops him with the reminder that they are both only shadows. Statius replies, and these are the lines Eliot uses, "Now you can understand the quantity and warmth of the love I have for you, so that I forget how unreal we are and treat shadows as though they were solid."

In an essay that at Eliot's insistence had to be withdrawn from circulation, the critic John Peter has proposed that the relationship between Eliot and Jean Verdenal was more than friendship, it was a "close romantic attachment." There is no way to discover whether this is true or not. Eliot reacted to the mention of this critic's name with "acute sensitivity." If, as Swift imagines in *Gulliver's Travels*, there is a place in another life where critics meet authors, it would be edifying to be present when Thomas Stearns Eliot meets John Peter.

During this year Eliot wrote the third and fourth "Preludes" and "Rhapsody on a Windy Night." It is possible that "La Figlia Che Piange" also belongs to this period. Then, in the summer of 1911, he traveled in Northern Italy and in Germany as far as Munich. There he finished "The Love Song of J. Alfred Prufrock."

Writing is not always a pleasure, it may be a burden and obsession. The poet "has something germinating in him for which he must find words; but he cannot know what words he wants until he has found the words. . . . He is oppressed by a burden which he must bring to birth in order to obtain relief . . . he is going to all that trouble, not in order to communicate with anyone, but to gain relief from acute discomfort."

The poet's mind is "a receptacle for seizing and storing up numberless feelings, phrases, images, which remain there until all the particles which can unite to form a new compound are present together." The coming together of particles cannot be willed, there must be a "passive attending upon the event." When the event occurs, however, the poet consciously finds the right words in which to make his communication. This requires "frightful toil," mainly the labor of self-criticism.

The impulse to create is not the same as merely feeling. Eliot agrees with Flaubert's idea of the impersonality of art: the artist is a man who feels, but he knows how to separate himself from his feelings and use what he needs in order to create a work that will mean something to other people. "The more perfect the artist the more completely separate in him will be the man who suffers and the mind which creates; the more perfectly will the mind digest and transmute the passions which are its material." In a sense one cannot be an artist until one has ceased, oneself, to live. "One is prepared for art when one has ceased to be interested in one's own emotions and experiences except as material . . . Personal emotion, personal experience is extended and completed in something impersonal—not in the sense of something divorced from personal experience and passion. No good poetry is the latter . . . Not our feelings, but the pattern we make of our feelings is the centre of value."

Such are Eliot's views of the process of artistic creation. He had not yet set them down in words, but when he did the process he described was that which had led to the creation of *Prufrock and Other Observations,* and to the creation of all his poems, with the possible exception of *Four Quartets,* which seems the result of having decided to write rather than having been driven to it by an obsession.

In Munich he sat at a table looking at chestnut trees and finishing "Prufrock." The citizens walked by with an air of bourgeois respectability. There were children in sailor suits—German dreadnoughts were being built as rapidly as possible in order to match the British navy—and officers in resplendent uniform escorting blonde women, future mothers of the race. Here were strength, vigor, and the consciousness of a national destiny. In the midst sat a tall young American with a Roman nose and placid eyes—a face somewhat lacking in color, rather gray in fact—composing a poem that expressed disenchantment.

It may have begun as a rhythm. In poetry sometimes, and in some poets a great deal of the time, there is a feeling of rhythm before there is anything else—before the precise words, sounds, images, or ideas. "I know," says Eliot, "that a poem, or a passage in a poem, may tend to realize itself first as a particular rhythm before it reaches expression in words, and that this rhythm may bring to birth the idea and the image: and I do not believe that this is an experience peculiar to myself."

He speaks of the poet as a person with "auditory imagination . . . the feeling for syllable and rhythm, penetrating far below the conscious levels of thought and feeling, invigorating every word; sinking to the most primitive and forgotten, returning to the origin and bringing something back, seeking the beginning and the end."

"Prufrock" has a pleasant rhythm, lines of varying length with an iambic beat—it is not free verse by any means—and there are plenty of rhymes to tie the lines together, even for people who like poetry to be the way it used to be, regular and predictable. "Prufrock" moves with a semblance of freedom, but it is freedom within familiar patterns of rhyme and meter. What is the poem about? It is not far from being the work Flaubert said he wished to compose, that would be about nothing at all, sustained only by its style. As Prufrock describes the uselessness of doing anything, his inability to communicate his meaning to anyone, as he visualizes what the evening would be like if he went, without actually going, Prufrock—like Pyrrhus in the play, "like a neutral to his will and matter"—does nothing. Then, lest we should think that his indecisiveness has heroic proportions, he rids us of this hope too. "No! I am not Prince Hamlet, nor was meant to be."

The poem is practically a demonstration of the "modernist" theory that style is everything, subject unimportant. "It is never what a poem *says* that matters, but what it *is*." This remark by I. A. Richards is quoted by Eliot in *The Use of Poetry and the Use of Criticism;* the New Criticism that prevailed in academic circles from the nineteen-thirties until only yesterday was founded on this belief. Art does not depend on the world, nor does it seek to change it. Poetry is about itself, the experience we have when we are reading the poem. The poem is about what it will be—the poem has a vision of itself in accordance with which it starts and proceeds, arranging matters in detail—rhythm, the choice and order of words, images and ideas—in order to arrive at the result foreseen. What Eliot says of his life in *Four Quartets* is true of the life of the poem: "The end is where we start from."

The poem, however, takes its material from the world, for we think best in images. "Prufrock" begins with an image of the evening "spread out against the sky/Like a patient etherised upon a table." This observation is now as famous, in the United States at any rate, as the remark made by Keats's urn. To the first readers it must have been startling. It was not the kind of thing they were accustomed to finding in poems. You could see the operating table and you could almost see the slops. Things didn't get any better as you went through dingy streets looking into cheap hotels and restaurants. This was followed by a remark about women in a room talking about Michelangelo. Then there was a fog, and mumbo jumbo, highbrow talk about preparing a face "to meet the faces that you meet." It was confusing and to some readers it was pretentious; Eliot was obviously pulling the public's leg, like the fellow in France who painted people with two noses.

If they had been readers of French poetry they would not have been surprised. They would have met with references to hospitals and street scenes in the poetry of Baudelaire. In Laforgue they would have found the tone of self-deprecation, the hesitations and withdrawals, the pondering over motives, Prufrock's inability to speak out, his feeling—it almost amounts to a faith—that life is a dead end.

Prufrock says, "I am Lazarus, come from the dead." Hugh Kenner remarks: "Eliot's unvarying dramatic method is to set loose, in a drawing room full of masks, some Lazarus." What Lazarus knows is death. How Eliot came at an early age by the knowledge of the fear of death is anyone's guess, but he had this knowledge and it gave him authority. The knowledge of fear, and his capacity for transferring it by means of an image to the reader's senses, enabled him to move immediately to the front of living poets.

The other thing Prufrock knows is that we cannot tell each other exactly what we mean. Each of us is enclosed by his experience of the world. At best we see only bits of other people, the mere externals, and the words that consciousness prepares may be the least revealing aspect of ourselves. We see a pair of arms "braceleted and white and bare/(But in the lamplight downed with light brown hair!)." The arms are not attached to a person. Someone asks us a question, and we try to think of an answer—but in order to know what the question meant we would have to be the person who asked it, and any answer we gave would be misunderstood. When we walk through a street we see men as shirt sleeves smoking pipes. The word surrealism has not yet been invented, but there is an air of surrealism in this poetry: the deserted street winds into the emptiness of a dream; the man truncated by the window is like a man by Magritte standing in a reverie. Magritte likes to put a lion in a room, and so does Eliot: the evening enters and stretches out like a cat beside Prufrock.

If we wish to explain what is meant by "modern poetry" we have to reckon with the idea of intensity. Ever since Poe declared that poetry must be short and intense, that in effect there could be no such thing as a long poem, a certain kind of poet—we must be on guard against trying to include everyone in these generalities—has been putting a premium on intensity. The aim is to excite or astonish the reader. Ezra Pound elevates this intention into a rule: "Incompetence will show in the use of too many words." The object is "to charge language with meaning to the utmost possible degree. . . ." This is done by "throwing the object (fixed or moving) on to the visual imagination," and "inducing emotional correlations by the sound and rhythm of the speech." It is well that he mentions rhythm and sound, for this description of intensity would lead the reader to think that it is to be arrived at by means of visual images alone. But there may be images that evoke rhythms or sounds.

"Prufrock" is especially rich in visual images. Prufrock's behavior is concentrated by the bald spot in the middle of his hair, his tie-pin, his possible trouser cuffs. His life, as everyone knows, is measured out with coffee spoons. His cogitating is pinned to the wall like a moth or butterfly. His profoundest self is hidden beneath the sill of consciousness; it is seen from the side of the boat as

> a pair of ragged claws
> Scuttling across the floors of silent seas.

Eliot carried this crab a long way from Gloucester where he saw it, to deposit it in just the right place. But was this the right place? Was his decision to put the crab in right or wrong?

He was to say later,

> I pray that I may forget
> These matters that with myself I too much discuss
> Too much explain.

This is read as a statement about Eliot's struggle to believe, and it is so by the context. We are inclined to think that the most important thing in a poet's life is what he believes, or else we look for an Irish nurse. The poet is likely to do so himself. But the most important thing may be his wanting to set things right, to put them exactly where they belong in order to finish a poem.

Words and Their Intervals

Those were the days. "I can see old Marsden now. . . ."
After the war intellectuals started moving into the territory opened
up by the "lunatic fringe" of the prewar years. New faces appeared:
Wallace Gould and Charles Henri Ford, Matthew Josephson, Djuna
Barnes, Hart Crane. *The Dial* started publishing. Margaret Ander-
son and Jane Heap edited *The Little Review,* which published Joyce's
Ulysses.

Charlie Demuth was around, and in the mid-twenties Williams
came to know Charles Sheeler. These painters had been born in the
same year as Williams. They came from similar backgrounds—they
had been at the Philadelphia Academy of Fine Arts when he was in
medical school. They had broken with their early work as he had—
Sheeler stopped painting Fauvist landscapes, Demuth his "vaude-
ville watercolors"—in order to paint their subjects in a more natu-
ralistic way. They adapted the techniques of international move-
ments, Futurism, Cubism, and Imagism, in order to develop their
own Precisionist school of painting. The painters and the poet were
close friends; they frequented the art gallery in New York run

Louis Simpson, *Three on the Tower: The Lives and Works of Ezra Pound, T. S. Eliot and William Carlos Williams.* New York: William Morrow and Company, 1975.

250

by the photographer Alfred Stieglitz at 291 Fifth Avenue, later An American Place.

Demuth, Sheeler and Williams shared the same attitudes; it was not influence in the common meaning of the term—they painted and wrote alike because they thought alike. Williams thought of poetry as though it were painting. The poem was not a vehicle for thought but a physical object, an organization of sounds and rhythms. Painting, in the modern period so far removed from representation, enabled poetry to see its aims more clearly. "Such a painting as that of Juan Gris," Williams wrote in *Spring and All*," . . . is important as marking more clearly than any I have seen what the modern trend is: the attempt is being made to separate things of the imagination from life, and obviously, by using the forms common to experience so as not to frighten the onlooker away but to invite him." In the *Autobiography* he says that it was the step of using words for their tactile qualities, "the words themselves beyond the mere thought expressed," that distinguished modern writing.

James Guimond points to similarities between Williams's poems and the paintings of Demuth and Sheeler. Demuth was the enemy of stupidity and drabness; he gave witty titles to his paintings. There is a Demuth painting of a grim water tower and chimney titled "Aucassin and Nicolette." Sheeler is "the man of integrity, full of respect for the commonplace, which he clarifies and organizes so that each object's identity is based upon a fresh perception of its unique qualities, its denotations, rather than its utilitarian or sentimental connotations." Both painters used local materials: "Demuth decorated barns near Lancaster with Pennsylvania Dutch hex signs; one of Sheeler's best works is his tempera and crayon 'Bucks County Barns,' an exquisitely precise rendition of contrasting native materials, weathered grey wood and sandy yellow stone." As Williams says in *Spring and All*, " 'Beauty' is related not to 'loveliness' but to a state in which reality plays a part."

The arts were flourishing. Extraordinary talents would appear and cause a sensation. "Once, Mayakofsky read aloud for us his 'Willie the Havana Street Cleaner.' A big man, he rested one foot on top of the studio table as he read. It was the perfect gesture." No one could understand a word of the reading, but they were impressed with the sounds and the intense seriousness of the Russian poet.

At that time artists and writers lived, as in the opinion of Monsieur Homais, artists and writers always do. "These great artists are all night-birds. They need to lead rackety lives, to stimulate their imagination. They die in the workhouse, though, not having the sense to put a bit by when young."

The Baroness Elsa von Freytag Loringhoven, for example . . . She was a sculptor and an artists' model, now fifty years old. She sent Williams a photograph of herself, "8 × 10, nude, a fine portrait." She pursued him, and several others—Wallace Stevens was afraid to come below Fourteenth Street because of her. She had an intimate talk with Williams and advised him that what he needed to make him great was to contract syphilis from her and so free his mind for serious art. She pursued him to Rutherford. One night he was called out to attend a sick baby. When he stepped outside it was the Baroness—she grabbed his wrist and said, "You must come with me." He refused, so she hauled off and hit him with all her strength. A few months later she waylaid him again, but this time he flattened her with a punch. Then he had her arrested. "What are you in this town?" she yelled, as the police took her away. "Napoleon?"

He was really crazy about her. He gave her money to get out of the country—which someone stole. He gave her some more and she went. Then he heard she had been killed. As a practical joke some Frenchman turned on the gas jet while she slept.

Between 1920 and 1923 Williams was associated with Robert McAlmon on the magazine *Contact*. McAlmon had served in the Canadian army during the war. Then he was a flyer out on the Coast. Then he lived on a scow in New York harbor. He was a "coldly intense young man with hard blue eyes" who, when Williams met him, was making a living posing nude for mixed classes at Cooper Union. McAlmon had a fierce belief in the need for contact with the soil, due perhaps to his experiences in the air and on the scow. "Contact meant coming in to land or stepping ashore." He wrote a fable for *The Ace,* a magazine of aviation, describing how glad he had been to return to earth, "something that had been and would continue to be," after his flights in the sky. A subsequent issue of *The Ace* presented a manifesto on the influence of aviation on art: the "air-centaur" would scorn earthbound thinkers who built reputations upon "the little ripples of character accentuation, native to all

men, but with them displayed in the spotlight of self-adoration."
Through his experience in the air the flyer would develop his
individuality. This was the kind of thing Futurists had been saying
in Europe for some time. McAlmon agreed with the manifesto in its
contempt for New York artists and writers who herded together. He
disagreed, however, with the idea that art must be disconnected
from nature and that "we must forget the specific in our contempla-
tion of the general." McAlmon's creed was contact with the soil.

This suited Williams, who had his own theory of locality, and
there was another aspect of McAlmon's thinking he found conge-
nial. McAlmon drew his attention to an article by Mary Austin at-
tacking certain New York Jews—Stieglitz, Stein, Orenstein, Rosen-
feld and Oppenheim, friends of Waldo Frank, whose book, *Our
America,* she was reviewing. These Jews believed that literature must
be Americanized. The mystique came of their familiarity with the
country around Broadway and Fifty-ninth Street. McAlmon reacted
against Frank; in his contributions to *Contact* he attacked what he
called "Semiticism," and later from France he wrote of "Jew-York."

This did not displease Williams. He was anti-Semitic himself—in
this, too, he was "ordinary." In Rutherford, as in the suburbs of
Philadelphia where Pound grew up, Jews were regarded with suspi-
cion. One of the teachings of Christianity was that Christ was killed
by the Jews. Jews were said to be moneylenders, and there was talk of
the Protocols of Zion, an international Jewish conspiracy. Williams
was no Christian, but he shared the prejudice of his neighbors.

Williams's *The Great American Novel,* published in 1923, concludes
with anti-Semitism, almost as though this were the whole point of
the novel—it is teetering on the edge. In the final paragraphs he
talks about the manufacture of "shoddy." Linda Welshimer Wagner,
in her discussion of the passage, praises the "Spanish irony" of the
writing. She fails to mention, however, that the person who is
described as making shoddy out of filthy rags and marketing it to
an unsuspecting public is a Jew. Other of Williams's admirers have
failed to notice his anti-Semitism.

His most offensive writing on the subject occurs in the novel *A
Voyage to Pagany,* published five years later when anti-Semitism had
become common, even chic, among intellectuals. The hero—like
most of Williams's heroes he is unavoidably recognizable as Williams

himself—is put off by the Jewishness of Michelangelo's statue of David, "The too big hand, the over-anxious Jewish eyes. The neurasthenic size of the thing. . . ." On a train he is unfortunate enough to meet with "a fat old Jew and his blubber wife." Later, ". . . the old Jew woman, having eaten too much, struggled over legs, flung open the door, and vomited full into the corridor—then came back, as she must have done, and slept again—perfectly unconcerned." There are other references of the kind: "the stinking Jews," "A Jew of the usual objectionable type."

Contact meant contact with experience. McAlmon was looking for writers who would "favor direct experience of life before intellectualism of any kind." This was right up Williams's alley.

With its anti-intellectualism and anti-Semitism *Contact* held seeds of the Fascism then spreading among European writers, but in the United States what writers say has little importance, either good or bad. Only four issues of *Contact* saw the light—"some fine poems by Marianne Moore, Hartley and a few others," "direct, uncompromised writing," but "Nobody bought—and there was much else in the wind."

Then McAlmon sailed for Europe. He had been planning to sail on a freighter to China, but something happened that changed his plans: H. D. arrived in New York on her way to California, "Same old Hilda, all over the place, looking as tall and as skinny as usual." She was traveling with a friend named Bryher, "a small, dark English girl with piercing eyes." Williams and McAlmon had tea with them at the Belmont Hotel. Then McAlmon had a card from Bryher in California—she was on her way back to England with H. D. and wanted to marry him.

Bryher turned out to be the daughter of Sir John Ellerman, "the heaviest taxpayer in England." "Bob," says Williams, "fell for it." Bob and Bryher were married and had a suite on the White Star liner *Celtic*, reserved by the father of the bride. The night before sailing there was an "intimate supper" in a small dining room at the Hotel Brevoort. Williams was divided between joy for his friend's good fortune and sadness at their parting. "Bryher was there, H. D. was there, not joining too excitedly in the ceremonies." Flossie was there, and Marianne Moore, "and good old Marsden, the most wonderful of party men."

Two days later Floss and Bill received a postcard representing a scene from a current play, men and women with their hands in a pot full of money. The card was signed D. H. Williams accused H. D. of being the sender—she denied it violently. He did not believe her.

So "Bob left and took his disastrous story with him." Presumably Williams means the story of Bryher's relations with H. D. The next time he saw the McAlmons, in Paris, H. D. was with them, looking silently on. It was like the Hemingway story, "The Sea Change."

As a result of his marrying Sir John's daughter McAlmon was able to start a publishing venture, Contact Editions, and bring out important writing in Paris: Gertrude Stein's *The Making of Americans*, the early Hemingway, Williams's *Spring and All*.

At that time, Williams says, writers and artists were full of energy—they had rediscovered a "primary impetus, the elementary principle of all art, in the local conditions." And he was hitting his stride. In September 1920 he published *Kora in Hell: Improvisations*. It was published by the Four Seas Company, Boston, the author contributing two hundred and fifty dollars to the cost of publication. He had tried writing something every day without planning—prose reflections—putting down anything that came into his head, writing at any hour of the day or night. He didn't revise, though he did tear up some of what he wrote. Some of the pieces could not be understood, so he wrote interpretations beneath the improvisations. He got the idea from a book, the poems of Pietro Metastasio, Pound left when he came on a visit.

Parts of *Kora* are Kandinsky's "direct impression of nature, expressed in purely pictorial form." There are the thoughts of the writer: "After thirty years staring at one true phrase he discovered that its opposite was true also." And the work of the doctor: "Stupidity couched in a dingy room beside the kitchen. One room stove-hot, the next the dead cold of a butcher's ice box. The man leaned and cut the baby from its stem. Slop in disinfectant, roar with derision at the insipid blood stench: hallucination comes to the rescue on the brink of seriousness: the gas-stove flame is starblue, violets back of L'Orloge at Lancy."

Kora has instances of the "poetic prose" that was fashionable at the time. The manner was carried over from the cult of beauty in the 1890's—in the hands of writers such as James Branch Cabell it would have a revival in the 1920's. The style was marked by archaic words, literary turns of phrase, and irony. It struck readers as very sophisticated. In *Kora* Williams tried to show that though he lived in New Jersey he could be as sophisticated as writers who lived in Greenwich Village. "There was a baroness lived in Hungary bathed twice monthly in virgins' blood." The sentence might have come from Cabell's *Jurgen*.

In 1921 Williams published, with the same publisher and on the same terms, a book of poems titled *Sour Grapes*. People jumped at the title—it showed that he was frustrated and disappointed. Instead of living like a poet he lived in the suburbs. "The young Frenchmen, yes, they really let go. But you, you are an American. You are afraid (this from the women and the men also) you are afraid. You live in the suburbs, you even *like* it. What are you anyway? And you pretend to be a poet, a POET! Ha, ha, ha, ha! A poet! You!"

"But," says Williams, "all I meant was that sour grapes are just the same shape as sweet ones:

Ha, ha, ha, ha!"

If this was what he intended he failed to take into account the plain meaning of the words. *Sour Grapes* means just what he says people took it to mean: frustration. In spite of his insistence on using the "American language," Williams can be surprisingly unaware of the effect words actually have. This is most evident when he writes expository prose and tries to reason—not so evident in the short stories, which approach poetry and are among the best of the kind. Prose allowed him to think loosely. On the other hand when he wrote poetry he wished to shape it "to perfection." He was driven by a need to be perfect, almost despair. It *had* to be right. "Most of my life," he said, "has been lived in hell—a hell of repression lit by flashes of inspiration, when a poem such as this or that would appear." His need to write a poem went back to the times he sought to please his father and mother by being perfect. The feeling of repression forced the poem into its necessary form as it escaped.

"To me at that time," Williams said, "a poem was an image, the picture was the important thing. As far as I could, with the materials I had, I was lyrical, but I was determined to use the material I knew and much of it did not lend itself to lyricism."

Besides their visual qualities the poems have a natural phrasing and movement of the line that give an impression of sincerity. In the poem, "To a Friend Concerning Several Ladies," Williams described his immediate surroundings:

> You know there is not much
> that I desire, a few chrysanthemums
> half lying on the grass . . .

But, he says:

> But there comes
> between me and these things
> a letter
> or even a look—well placed,
> you understand,
> so that I am confused, twisted
> four ways and—left flat,
> unable to lift the food to
> my own mouth:
> Here is what they say: Come!
> and come! and come! And if
> I do not go I remain stale to
> myself and if I go—

If he goes to the city which he can see at night blazing in the distance, perhaps he will get some good out of it. Out of the woman, that is. For there is "no good in the world except out of/a woman and certain women alone/for certain things." But "what if/I arrive like a turtle,/with my house on my back . . .?"

Here is the famous sincerity that distinguishes the style of Williams. The effect is got through natural-seeming sentences and right visual images: "like a turtle,/with my house on my back." It is not easy to find poems in English that give the appearance of sincerity. The English tradition is to embellish a thought, create a work that will be splendid, a poetry machine that will carry the writer out of himself and beyond the reach of criticism—the "great poem," suitable for anthologies. For poetry that seems to speak as men do we may go to Burns, Wordsworth and Whitman. There are specimens of sincerity here and there, and then there is William Carlos Williams. Sincerity was his style. For this he gave up nearly everything else and was obscure. When Williams was young he was over-shadowed by Eliot. Then Auden's style caught on; young poets imitated his catchy stanzas full of references to spies, nervous disorders, Kierkegaard, whatever was intellectually fashionable. Later, when fame still eluded him, Williams saw audiences flocking to readings by a young Welsh poet; they liked the stentorian voice on the platform though they could not have said what all the fuss was about.

He sacrificed fame for sincerity. He was like a monk who has taken a vow. A Buddhist monk—some of the poems are close in spirit to Buddhism. The intent to live here and now, to be conscious of everything he can see, hear, touch and taste, is reminiscent of Buddhist teaching. "Your ordinary life, that is the way," says the Buddhist Nansen. Williams's way was as ordinary as he could make it; at the same time he strove to lift things into perfection, the Nirvana of art.

> So much depends
> upon
>
> a red wheel
> barrow . . .

From where does vision proceed? From the life of the poet. Nancy Willard says, "For Neruda, Rilke, Williams and Ponge, the question of how to write is a question of how to live." To understand Williams's poems we must understand his life. This is not true of Pound and Eliot whose experiences passed through a process of dramatization before they issued as art.

Did Williams know anything about Buddhism? He had read *haiku*, the Japanese poems of seventeen syllables which suggest a scene and trigger a perception. All the Imagist poets read *haiku*. They did not know that *haiku* embody Buddhist teachings, but they learned something of the technique. Like a Buddhist monk giving a *koan* to his disciple, the Imagist poem presented, it did not explain. It was up to the recipient to make what he could of it. The truth must be experienced, not merely apprehended with the abstracting, reasoning mind.

Williams seems to have had a particular fondness for "The Great Figure," the poem he placed at the end of the book. Demuth did a painting based upon it. On a hot day in July Williams was walking to Marsden Hartley's studio on Fifteenth Street. There was a clatter of bells and a fire engine passed the end of the street. He turned just in time to see a golden figure 5 on a red background flash by. "The impression," he says, "was so sudden and forceful that I took a piece of paper out of my pocket and wrote a short poem about it."

> Among the rain
> and lights
> I saw the figure 5
> in gold
> on a red
> firetruck
> moving
> tense
> unheeded
> to gong clangs
> siren howls
> and wheels rumbling
> through the dark city.

He seems to feel this is the way poems should always be written—straight from experience.

Once he and Marsden were standing on the Erie platform in Rutherford, waiting for the train that was to take Marsden back to New York. An express train roared by, "right before our faces—crashing through making up time in a cloud of dust and sand so that we had to put up our hands to protect our faces.

"As it passed Marsden turned and said to me, 'That's what we all want to be, isn't it, Bill?'

"I said, 'Yes, I suppose so.' "

The drive and heat of the period were what made it great. Yes, and locality—that it was happening here and now, on the Erie platform in Rutherford, in the Village on Fifteenth Street.

Then, he says, their world caved in. "*The Dial* brought out *The Waste Land* and all our hilarity ended. It wiped out our world as if an atom bomb had been dropped upon it and our brave sallies into the unknown were turned to dust."

A sentence that follows is famous: "Critically Eliot returned us to the classroom."

This occurred just when Williams and his friends were "on the point of an escape to matters much closer to the essence of a new art form itself—rooted in the locality which should give it fruit. I knew at once that in certain ways I was most defeated."

Meaning, it seems, that of all the artists of the local who were defeated, he suffered the most. Presumably because he was the most committed to the theory.

It seems that it was Eliot's erudition, the allusiveness of *The Waste Land*, that had done so much harm. The poem was anything but local; it ranged in time from the Crucifixion to the Great War, in space from the Ganges to the Thames. It did not appear to have come out of experience—one or two of the early reviews had even suggested that it was a parody of literature of the past.

Syntax and grammar desert Williams when he thinks about Eliot: "Eliot had turned his back on the possibility of reviving my world. And being an accomplished craftsman, better skilled in some ways than I could ever hope to be, I had to watch him carry my world off with him, the fool, to the enemy." So it was merely Eliot's skill that made him successful—this from Williams, who in other places declares that technique is everything: "It is in the minutiae—in the minute organization of the words and their relationships in a composition that the seriousness and value of a work of writing exist—*not* in the sentiments, ideas, schemes portrayed."

Truly, when he tried to reason he was inconsistent, and when he talked about Eliot he hardly made sense. If only Eliot had stayed in America! "We needed him in the scheme I was half-consciously forming."

One is reminded of the cry of the Baroness Elsa von Freytag Loringhoven: "What are you in this town? Napoleon?"

It is possible that Williams did not enjoy Eliot's work, could not put aside his ideas of what poetry should be and experience the poetry of *The Waste Land*. But if he was unable to read Eliot it was because, in the first place, he did not want to. There is no getting around it—he was envious. He envied Eliot's success and growing reputation, he envied his friendship with Pound and the high opinion Pound had of Eliot's writing. Williams had already been wounded by this—the fame of *The Waste Land* rubbed salt into the wound.

> . . . inwardly he chawed his own maw
> At neighbor's wealth, that made him ever sad.

There was apprehension mixed with his envy. Writing to John Riordan in 1925 he said, "I must say Eliot inspires me with dread—since I see him finished and I do not find myself stepping beyond him. Since I cannot compete with him in knowledge of philosophy, nor even in technical knowledge of the conned examples of English poetry which he seems to know well—what is left for me but to fall back upon words? There they are just as they always were and the art of using them is no more dependent upon philosophic catastrophes or past examples of writing than are the words themselves . . .

"The words are there quite apart from any theory of arranging them. . . ."

What the soothsayer says to Mark Antony concerning Octavius might have been said to Williams concerning Eliot:

> Thy lustre thickens
> When he shines by. I say again, thy spirit
> Is all afraid to govern thee near him:
> But he away, 'tis noble.

But people did not fail to read Williams because they were reading Eliot—to paraphrase Bentley, no writer is ever put down by another writer, only by himself. Eliot succeeded because he had great talent and his poetry expressed what people were feeling at the time. Williams's poetry didn't. He would have to wait—he had always been a slow starter.

In the meantime it wasn't *The Waste Land* that did him harm; it was the feeling that he was in competition with Eliot. " 'History is England,' yodels Mr. Eliot. To us this is not so, not so *if* we prove it by writing a poem built to refute it—otherwise he wins!!" Williams said this after Eliot had published *Four Quartets.* Even by his own theory it doesn't make sense, for England was where Eliot lived, his "locality." Therefore, for Eliot history had to be English.

As long as Williams kept thinking that Eliot might "win" he kept losing, for if we fear a thing enough we come to believe that it is true. He felt that Eliot had won and he was out of the running. Williams didn't withdraw to the extent of giving up poetry, but in the thirties he concentrated on prose fiction. And when he did write a poem he set limits to it, leaving "philosophy" to Eliot and restricting himself to using just words—"The words are there quite apart from any theory of arranging them." He tried to use words as though they didn't have meanings and made dry work of it. He might have enjoyed himself more if he hadn't thought Eliot was watching.

Spring and All, published in 1923 by McAlmon's press in Paris, is a kind of watershed—after this Williams begins concentrating on prose. In *Spring and All* he achieves what he has set out to do; he is always a poet, even when he makes mistakes—what he says of Marianne Moore's writing is true of his own: "She writes sometimes good and sometimes bad poetry but always—with a single purpose out of a single fountain which is of the sort."

The book consists of a handful of poems and some short chapters of prose, thoughts about art and writing. He is especially concerned with the use of imagination. The artist uses what he has observed but out of this he makes a nature of his own.

"Crude symbolism" is empty—comparing anger with lightning, flowers with love. It is marked by the use of the word "like." Typing by association kills imagination. Evocation of images for their own sake also kills it. His object in the present book is to write about "the 'nature' which Shakespeare mentions and which Hartley speaks of so completely in his 'Adventures': it is the common thing which is anonymously about us."

This sounds as though he has suddenly reverted to naturalism. Not so. His writing will be "in the realm of the imagination as plain as the sky is to a fisherman. . . . The word must be put down for itself

not as a symbol of nature but a part, cognisant of the whole—
aware—civilized."

He is also concerned with form and the difference between
poetry and prose. The difference is not that poetry is written in a
pronounced rhythm. It is that poetry and prose have different
origins and a different purpose. "Poetry feeds the imagination and
prose the emotions, poetry liberates the words from their emotional
implications, prose confirms them in it."

In poetry the words have a direction that is separate from mean-
ing. "To understand the words as so liberated is to understand
poetry." Writing is not music and has nothing to gain by trying to be
like music—"the conditions of music are objects for the action of the
writer's imagination just as a table or—"

Having said this, Williams immediately contradicts himself—it
seems that writing should be like music after all. ". . . the writer of
imagination would attain closest to the conditions of music not
when his words are disassociated from natural objects and specified
meanings but when they are liberated from the usual quality of that
meaning by transposition into another medium, the imagination."

This is Surrealism, the doctrine being followed by André Breton,
Louis Aragon and other writers in Paris. Surrealism presented
objects in all their concrete reality—there was nothing symbolic
about Surrealist painting or poetry—but the objects were divorced
from their functions, the chair placed upside down. When Williams
speaks of "liberation from the usual quality of that meaning by
transposition into another medium, the imagination," he is recom-
mending Surrealism.

But there is nothing particularly Surrealist about his poems. For
all his talk of imagination and the need to transform the world, he
was fond of it as it was. "I can't write fiction," he told Pound. "All I do
is try to understand something in its natural colors and shapes." His
poems are a selection and rearrangement of things so that we can
look at them hard, but the things have not been divorced from their
usual qualities. Williams disliked the thought of divorce, either in
life or art.

Spring and All contains the poems with the famous beginnings,
"By the road to the contagious hospital," and "The pure products of
America/go crazy." The language of these poems is not particularly

American, but the content is: American landscape, American lives. There is something about this content that would not have sounded right in iambic pentameter. It goes better in irregular feet.

Sincerity becomes confession in the poem that begins "What about all this writing?" The poem is about love in the city—not any city, but Manhattan of the Wrigley's sign and warm summer nights.

> You lay relaxed on my knees—
> the starry night
> spread out warm and blind
> above the hospital—

Their lovemaking was watched by the chairs, the floor, the walls, "they which alone know everything/and snitched on us in the morning." The poem ends:

> but I merely
> caressed you curiously
> fifteen years ago and you still
> go about the city, they say
> patching up sick school children

How are we to describe the form of poetry such as this? Williams thought a great deal about the structure of his poems. "IT IS THE FORM . . . I have tried so hard to make this clear: it is the form which is the meaning." Yet, confronted with the broken shape of his writing on the page, we are tempted to say it is the shape of thought, and let it go at that.

James Breslin has done more. He speaks of the recurrence and "jagged, circling movement" of Williams's thinking, and undertakes to show how this "extends down into the most minute workings of the poem—the line itself." The lines end with "prepositions, adjectives, conjunctions, subjects, transitive verbs—all words we know will be followed by objects, modifiers, and so on." The effect is to prevent "quick movement through a conventional form." There is a "halting, disjunctive sequence of sharply defined images." The aim is to "break through the reader's protective shell, jar his relaxed euphoria," to force the reader's attention "down into an independent world of objects, solid and distinct in themselves yet fluid in their combinations."

Williams says, "By the brokenness of his composition the poet makes himself master of a certain weapon which he could possess himself of in no other way. The speed of the emotions is sometimes such that thrashing about in a thin exaltation of despair many matters are touched but not held. . . ." No wonder some readers have found his method unpalatable. There is an element of bullying about it. Readers, especially those whose idea of verse is the regular beat of iambic pentameter, dislike being hauled about so. They don't want poetry that, as Keats said of Wordsworth's poetry, "has a palpable design upon us." "Let us have the old Poets, and Robin Hood."

"The rhythmic unit," says Williams, "usually came to me in a lyrical outburst." The poem began to move in units of a few lines:

> Now the grass, tomorrow
> the stiff curl of wildcarrot leaf
> One by one objects are defined—
> It quickens: clarity, outline of leaf

The unit would expand, then again it would contract. Wagner speaks of Williams's "rationale of organic form, the art object as a machine made of words, searching for its own autonomous shape."

The origins of the forms his poetry took were as mysterious to him as they are to us.

Those were the days. "*Everyone* was in Paris . . . Sat at Dôme, saw Kiki, Mary Reynolds, etc. Sat at Dôme with Antheil. . . ."

"The next day it was raining but cleared, and the sun came out brightly. Rode a bus to the Louvre and walked thence, buying a few stamps at the outdoor market on the Champs Elysées for Bill. At the hotel neither trunk nor baggage had arrived; ate at Trianon, then to Dôme. Met Hemingway on the street, a young man with a boil on his seat, just back from a bicycle ride in Spain. . . ."

Bob McAlmon told Bill and Floss about an incident the year before when he was coming back from Spain with Hemingway. The train stopped and the passengers got off for a breath of air. There was a dead dog beside the track, belly swollen, "skin . . . iridescent with decay." McAlmon wanted to get away from the stink, but Hemingway got out his notebook and, to McAlmon's disgust, started taking notes in minute detail, "describing the carcass in all its beauty."

Bob showed them around. Williams had been nervous about seeing him again—the last time they had met had been at the Brevoort in New York. Bob was stouter, far less youthful and less discerning. But Bill got over his uneasiness—Bob and he still had a common need, the "desire to get down to some sort of sense about writing." He still loved Bob.

Bill and Floss had decided to risk everything. They left the kids at home—Bill aged nine and Paul aged six—and set out to see the world. McAlmon took them under his wing. He was at home in Paris. He was always doing something for someone—spending money like a prince. At one point he was giving the young American composer George Antheil a hundred dollars a month. He fed the Joyces. He gave big parties. "It was Sir John's money, but if Bob hadn't earned it, nobody ever earned a nickel." Bryher and H. D. were off somewhere together in Switzerland. McAlmon told them about "long train trips about the continent with the two women quarreling in the compartment driving him nearly insane, hard to go on like that."

McAlmon had a way of insulting people with his "blinkless and cold-eyed remarks," calling them liars to their faces. Then the bartender had to pull him over the counter—McAlmon weighed only 150 pounds—and keep him out of sight till he sobered up.

McAlmon took them to see Brancusi in his studio. Bill offended Brancusi by saying that Pound, whose opera *Villon* had just been performed at the Théâtre des Champs Elysées, didn't know one note from another.

They met Sylvia Beach, who had a bookshop on the Rue de l'Odeon, a sanctuary for writers. And Man Ray did some photographs of Bill Williams. But when he got the finished pictures he was furious—they made him look like a fool. And they were expensive—the six prints cost more than the hotel bill! There had been a beautiful girl present in the studio while Bill was having his picture taken, Man Ray's assistant. She gave him a penetrating look . . . he regretted not having got to know her better. He was infuriated when he saw the photographs. Man Ray had asked him to close his eyes a little—this gave him a sentimental, inexperienced appearance. He felt humiliated, especially when he thought of the "beautiful, courageous girl a thousand years off, experienced, unobtainable—in the background," laughing at him.

They had dinner at the Joyces', James and Nora (née Barnacle— he'd married her, Joyce said, because she'd stick). "Here's to sin!" said McAlmon, raising his glass. "I won't drink to that," said Joyce. McAlmon laughed and took it back, and they all sipped their wine in silence. The exchange seemed significant. Everything people say in Paris seems significant.

One night McAlmon gave a party for Floss and Bill at the Trianon. Tables were pushed together. "I was in the middle facing the wall, Floss next to me on the right with Joyce and Ford Madox Ford opposite, their wives and the others close about us; Harold Loeb with Kitty Cannell, Antheil, Marcel Duchamp. Bill Bird, Man Ray, Mina Loy and her daughter, Sylvia Beach, Louis Aragon; some were invited and some merely showed up (at Bob's expense)."

The reporter of dead dogs, however, was not in evidence. He was writing short stories. Some day he would put these people in a novel that would make him rich and famous.

Bill Williams had to make a speech. All eyes were upon him— what could an American say that would be significant? "I had nothing in common with them." Nevertheless he made his speech. He told them that in Paris he had observed that "when a corpse, in its hearse, plain or ornate, was passing in the streets, the women stopped, bowed their heads and that men generally stood at attention with their hats in their hands. What I meant was my own business, I did not explain, but sat down feeling like a fool."

It was a bad moment, he tells us. Indeed it must have been—the party had been subjected to some of his expository prose. What he meant exactly was known to him alone.

He did not shine in Paris. He felt himself "with ardors not released but beaten back in this centre of old-world culture where everyone was tearing his own meat, warily conscious of a newcomer but wholly without inquisitiveness." They weren't interested in his thoughts.

He had been thinking more and more about what it meant to be an American, and had brought with him drafts of chapters of a book he was writing on the subject. He was thinking of a chapter on Daniel Boone. To Boone the Indian was the best teacher. Boone didn't want to be like an Indian, though they wanted to adopt him into their tribe—he wanted to be himself in the new world. To possess the land as the Indian had possessed it. The Indian was not to be feared and exterminated—he was the natural expression of the place. It was up to the white man to discover the natural expression of his place.

On the other hand were those who brought their Old World habits and obsessions with them—men like Cotton Mather, who thought in abstractions. "Trustless of humane experience, not knowing what to think, they went mad, lost all direction. Mather defends the witchcraft persecutions."

The day after the party at which not only had Williams failed to shine, but with a foolish speech had brought upon himself incomprehension then gathering contempt in all their eyes, he went for a walk by himself, alone. He bought a pear and ate it. He discovered the Place François Ier by himself and admired the "French austerity of design, gray stone cleanly cut and put together in complementary masses . . ."

"I am lonely, lonely.
I was born to be lonely,
I am best so!"

Like Columbus, De Soto, and Daniel Boone. Explorers are always lonely.

"Paris," he wrote to Kenneth Burke, "would be wonderful if I could be French and *Vieux;* it would be still more wonderful if I could only want to forget everything on earth. Since I can't do that, only America remains where at least I was born."

Gertrude Stein felt as he did about locality. "After all," she wrote, "anybody is as their land and air is . . . It is that which makes them and the arts they make and the work they do and the way they eat and the way they drink and the way they learn and everything." But Gertrude Stein lived in Paris. So did Hemingway—an American author if ever there was one—and he would write about Americans who lived in Paris and went to bullfights in Spain. After this he would write a novel about the retreat from Caporetto.

Truly, as Henry James said, it is a complex fate being an American.

Bill and Floss traveled south to Carcassonne and the Riviera, to Rome and Vienna. On their return to Paris they found the pace quicker than before. They saw a good deal of Ezra and Dorothy Pound. The Pounds were living in a big studio with a courtyard. Ezra and Bill talked about Renaissance music, theory of notation, melody and time. A sense of time, Bill felt, was Ezra's chief asset as an appreciator of music. He could be listened to on the subject of melody, the musical phrase, and the early composers. But he knew nothing about tones, and his opinions of music in general were suspect.

Dorothy Pound disliked Paris, "as much because of its people as its winter weather, neither fish nor flesh." On the other hand she adored Italy. She showed them her paintings, linear and gray like herself, and gave them a painting of rocks on the Dartmouth moors, "cubistic in feeling, flat and cold." Pound made tea over the spirit lamp that seemed to be his specialty. Then they went to supper— Williamses, Pounds and Hemingways. Afterwards they went to a prize fight where Floss—to his horror and astonishment, Bill says— pounded on the back of the man in front of her, screaming "Kill him! Kill him!" The man the back belonged to was Ogden Nash.

They saw more of the Pounds and came to know Hemingway better. Bill played tennis with Hemingway and Harold Loeb, and he performed a small operation on the Hemingway baby, retracting the foreskin. "He naturally cried, to his parents' chagrin."

Then the Williamses sailed back to America where Bill understood things in their natural (native?) colors and shapes.

But Floss and Bill looked back on their time in Europe as a high point of their lives. "*Everyone* was in Paris—if you wanted to see them." Nancy Cunard and Iris Tree, for example . . . Bill thought Nancy was wonderful. "They were riding above the storm in Paris that we were witnessing. Nancy Cunard straight as any stick, emaciated, holding her head erect, not particularly animated, her blue eyes completely untroubled, inviolable in her virginity of pure act."

Épatante, as the French say.

Nancy and her mother, Lady Cunard, used to visit the Williamses in their pension at Villefranche. And there were the Birds, Bill and Sally. Bill could be wild—one night he wanted them all to go to Marseilles for bouillabaisse. "But I couldn't see it though Floss would have gone."

There was the time the innkeeper called Williams aside and asked him if either he or McAlmon would be willing to sleep with his, the innkeeper's wife, so that she could bear a child. He was impotent, having suffered a wound . . .

"You mean . . ." I began.

"Yes, precisely that."

"But you would shoot a man who would so presume."

Nothing came of it—neither Bill nor Bob being willing to oblige. Still, the incident was so typically French!

They heard that Eliot had appeared in Paris while they were there. He came to the Dôme and other bars in top hat, cutaway, and striped trousers. "It was intended as a gesture of contempt and received just that."

Not even T. S. Eliot could spoil "Their Trip Abroad."

The Split Lives of
W. H. Auden

Bringing together "all of the poems that W. H. Auden wished to preserve" is reason enough for a new *Collected Poems*. But readers who want all the poems, not just the ones Auden approved of at the end of his life, will have to wait. The editor promises that the excluded early poems will be published in a volume titled *The English Auden*. But poems will still be missing, and some of the approved versions will be different from the original. Auden was continually rewriting his poems and switching things around. He had an idea of his life as a construction into which the poems had to fit. If they didn't, out they went.

In the middle of Auden's life was a mystery, a secret he was trying to hide. It accounted for the splitting of his life in two—the first part in England, the second in America. In 1939 Auden left England and took up residence in the United States. He told Stephen Spender that he had done so because the future for writers lay in America; New York was the model of Cosmopolis, the city of the future. Auden's critics on the other hand were saying that he had

Reprinted from *A Company of Poets*. Ann Arbor: The University of Michigan Press, 1981. This review first appeared in *Ideas*, October 17, 1976.

fled England in her hour of need, on the eve of World War II, in order to be safe and to flourish in the lucrative pastures of the New World. Both his friends and critics were naive: they found intellectual reasons for everything he did, just as he wanted them to. The truth, however, was that as a homosexual Auden found life in England too confining. He was a public figure—he had even been awarded the George Medal—and when he thought of what would be expected of him in the years ahead, as a member of the literary establishment, it was a dreary prospect indeed. But in the States there would be plenty of room—no one paid much attention to writers. In the Village or on Fire Island he could be "cosy"—one of his favorite words. He could live with those he preferred, emerging only to teach, then again retiring into obscurity. Besides, he felt easier in his mind about being a homosexual in America. England was home, but what you did abroad didn't really count.

It is impossible to understand Auden's poetry, its style, the form it took, and the attitudes it expresses, without taking into account his homosexuality and his wish to conceal it. The wish is understandable; back in the 1940s people were not as tolerant of homosexuality as they are now. In order to conceal his feelings Auden wrote in pseudodramatic, "impersonal" forms. He wrote essays in verse, putting a distance between himself and the reader. He did not *present*—he was always careful to explain.

This was the later Auden. The young poet had been quite different, a poet of feelings—feelings that he himself could not explain. Influenced by Thomas Hardy, Edward Thomas, T. S. Eliot, and Icelandic sagas, the young Auden invented a compact, elliptical language that was strikingly original. He was obscure and prophetic. After leaving Oxford he went to Berlin; there he absorbed the ideas of Groddeck, Homer Lane, and Freud—as well as the homegrown theories of D. H. Lawrence, which he already knew. These men argued that people were sick because they willed to be, that nervous and physical disorders were symptoms of spiritual disease. When Auden returned to England he wrote poems that diagnosed English economic and cultural life from a Groddeckian point of view. He seemed gifted with double sight; the characters in his poems, lonely vicars, repressed spinsters, languishing esthetes, bluff and hearty types, each in his own way testified to the malaise of England as a whole. Auden's poems hinted at secret guilts and criminal wishes. As he saw it, the whole nation, in these years of economic depression, was suffering the effects of psychological repression. Readers felt that they were privy to the secret. *Poems* (1930) sold only a thousand copies in three years, but the copies were in the best hands at Oxford and Cambridge. When Auden's poems appeared in the anthologies *New Signatures* and *New Country* edited by Michael Roberts, they launched a movement. By the middle of the 1930s dozens of poets were trying to write like Auden.

He addressed himself to the public. He had always had a journalistic flair, a photographer's eye. His descriptions of modern landscapes were written with zest, though the view might be sinister:

> Smokeless chimneys, damaged bridges, rotting wharves
>   and choked canals,
> Tramlines buckled, smashed trucks lying on their side
>   across the rails . . .

He now wrote about history. It was widely assumed that he was a poet of the Left—in the thirties Marxism was fashionable among intellectuals. Auden did not deny it, though in fact he cared little for Marx and felt some contempt for the common man. He even made a brief journey to Spain. What he saw of the Civil War must have frightened him, and he was offended by the repression of the Church. He had been brought up in the Anglican faith, his mother was a stern Anglican; at any rate, the poet who had been urging his countrymen to some sort of revolution, overthrowing the Old Gang, after his return from Spain said no more on the subject of revolution.

In 1938 he traveled with Christopher Isherwood to China. On their way back they crossed the United States and met some congenial souls. This was why, as Auden told Cyril Connolly, he decided to live in the States. The decision had little to do with history and everything to do with his personal tastes.

It was a mistake as far as poetry was concerned. He had been at ease with England, he knew country and town like the back of his hand. His poems with their views of an industrial landscape anticipated the subject matter that would be explored by novelists after the war, the Angry Young Men. Auden knew the secrets of the

English vicarage and public school. But in the States he hardly knew anything. Unlike the American expatriates in Europe—Eliot or Hemingway—Auden had a reputation when he made his crossing. He was immediately accepted into the American literary establishment, and in a little while he was advising editors and sitting on prize committees. He never had to scrounge for a living, he never had to learn about America in his bones, and so he knew nothing of the way Americans thought and felt.

Auden's long poem, *The Age of Anxiety,* presents as American speech passages such as the following:

> After a dreadful
> Row with father, I ran with burning
> Cheeks to the pasture and chopped wood, my
> Stomach like a stone. I strode that night
> Through wicked dreams: waking, I skipped to
> The shower and sang, ashamed to recall
> With whom or how . . .

This is camp. And writing camp was Auden's solution for not being able to write American. As time passed the mannerisms became more precious until, as Jonson said of Spenser, he wrote no language at all. The distancing from American scene and character made the language of the poems distant from any kind of reality. Auden's later poems were full of ideas, but none of them had any urgency. They were not rooted in life.

In his later poems Auden played games with words, shifting from one level of usage to another. One critic, Justin Replogle, argues that Auden is a comic poet; all his inconsistencies are consistent with this. The comedy is created by "jamming together words that are ordinarily used only in very special environments, with widely varying degrees of solemnity," and by using dozens of highly technical terms and phrases. He quotes from Auden's poem, "Mundus et Infans":

> Kicking his mother until she let go of his soul
> Has given him a healthy appetite; clearly, her role

In the New Order must be
To supply and deliver his raw materials free . . .

Replogle comments: "The basic incongruity here is between the infant subject and the adult language used to describe him." And he proceeds to show "smaller incongruities" that "flourish endlessly in the diction." Most of Auden's later poems shift about and giggle in this manner. It isn't comic, except to readers whose idea of life is tea at the Faculty Club.

In later years Auden was opposed to experiment. The voice in the later poems is that of a querulous, aging man who is attached to his creature comforts and who fears that any rebellion of youth may take them away.

The message did not appeal to young people. They preferred Dylan Thomas, the roaring Welshman who seemed to be living passionately. From the day that Dylan Thomas came to America, Auden was a back number.

Auden hated biographical criticism—he would have hated this essay. Writing about a writer's life, he used to say, casts no light on the work. But in Auden's case it is not possible to see why he wrote as he did, in strict forms and in a language so far removed from the language of common speech, if we do not see the personal reason that lay behind it. Auden came to the United States in order to be a member of the sexual underground. It was a matter of personal freedom. And in order to preserve this freedom, he made his art less free. His poems were masques, eclogues, essays . . . anything but expressions of the poet's character. His habitual concealment of his deepest life led him to write in a trivial manner until—at an age when Hardy and Yeats wrote their greatest poems—he was writing light verse.

The Color of Saying

Dylan Marlais Thomas was born in 1914 in Swansea, South Wales. "Marlais" was the name of an uncle of his father who had been a poet and who took the bardic name "Marles" from a stream that ran near his birthplace. The name "Dylan" came from one of the medieval prose romances in the *Mabinogion*. As a noun the word means "sea" or "ocean." In the *Mabinogion* Dylan makes a brief appearance when Math the son of Mathonwy challenges Aranrhod, who claims to be a virgin, to step over his magic wand. "A fine boy-child with rich yellow hair" drops from her as she does so. Math son of Mathonwy calls him Dylan, and the child makes for the sea, his natural element.

Dylan Thomas's mother, Florence, came of a family named Williams in Carmarthenshire. They were farmers, but Anna Williams married George Williams who was employed by the railway. They moved to Swansea, and in the course of time George Williams rose to be an inspector. They had seven children, of whom Florence was the youngest.

Dylan's father was a schoolmaster. He, too, had come up in the world: his father had been a humble railway employee known as

Reprinted from Louis Simpson, *A Revolution in Taste: Studies of Dylan Thomas, Allen Ginsberg, Sylvia Plath and Robert Lowell.* New York: Macmillan Publishing Company, 1978.

"Thomas the Guard." But D. J. Thomas made the hard climb out of the working class into middle-class respectability. The poet's wife Caitlin speaks of his making the transition from "farmhouse and railwaymen standards, to schoolmaster in a semi-detached suburban matchbox." The Thomases had moved up to "penny-pricing gentility," and this required constantly keeping up appearances though they could scarcely afford to. "No blue-blooded gentleman," says Caitlin Thomas, "was a quarter as gentlemanly as Dylan's father." There was a strong streak of puritanism in Dylan himself that his friends never suspected but of which she got "the disapproving benefit."

Florence Thomas, however, was no puritan. Paul Ferris in his biography of the poet says that she liked "to kiss and cuddle," and suggests that all this physical contact made Dylan sexually precocious. His cot was placed in his parents' bedroom—a common enough practice among families with limited means, "though it can set a psychiatrist's teeth on edge." All his life, says Ferris, Dylan Thomas "hankered after the warm beds and mother-love of his childhood." He liked to be looked after, and he was very skillful at getting people to look after him. He would be disgusted with himself for doing it, but this did not stop him. He was particularly helpless when it came to food and drink. Psychiatrists would say that Dylan Thomas was a man with powerful "oral traits." He depended on being fed: by his mother, his wife, his friends, and the people he called "silly ravens," who had money they might be persuaded to part with.

Ferris suggests that Florence Thomas's doting on her son brought about the classic Oedipal situation in which the son competes with the father for the mother's love, and succeeds in ousting the father. But this brings guilt and a fear of punishment. Dylan Thomas's poems and stories contain references to mutilation of the sexual organs; references to tailors and scissors remind one of *Struwwelpeter*, especially the story of Little Suck-a-Thumb in which a child is punished by having his thumbs cut off by a tailor with flying hair and an enormous pair of scissors.

The fear of retribution may lead to impotence and the loss of other powers as well . . . for example, the ability to write. In later years Thomas showed a desperate need to assert his masculinity, drinking heavily and trying to get women to go to bed with him, and writing had become a difficult, almost impossible task.

However, Ferris observes that if Thomas's early experiences had bad effects, they were also "part of a process that helped produce a poet of Thomas' uniquely morbid self-interest."

"My horrible self," Thomas wrote to the poet Henry Treece, "would not be itself did it not possess the faults."

Attempts to psychoanalyze artists and their works are never quite satisfactory—there is a gap between life and the work of art. Knowing what a poet's childhood was like cannot explain why he turned to poetry or why he wrote in a particular form and style. On the other hand, psychoanalytic criticism can help us to understand the poet's attitudes, and these have a demonstrable relationship to the content of his work. It is only when we expect too much of psychoanalysis, when we try to make it take the place of aesthetic criticism, that it is plainly inadequate.

Dylan Thomas does appear to be a case of the Oedipus Complex. But it is not straightforward: one would expect Little Suck-a-Thumb to grow up hating his father, but Dylan respected his—in fact, had a great deal of affection for him. Daniel Jones, who went to school with him, says that Dylan avoided D. J. Thomas, who was one of the masters. But it can be embarrassing to be at a school where one's father teaches, and D. J. was very unpopular. According to Jones, Dylan stayed out of his father's way at home as well as at school. This, too, is understandable—D. J. was cranky and easily moved to anger. "However," Jones adds, "it was equally clear that he respected his father and was proud of him, and that any would-be detractor would be wise to remain silent about him in his presence."

When Dylan was a grown man his famous poetry-reading voice was patterned on his father's way of reading poetry aloud to his students. And he wrote poetry in praise of his father.

The young D. J. Thomas won a scholarship that took him to the University College of Wales at Aberystwyth. He graduated four years later with a first-class honors degree in English. But then something went wrong—instead of pursuing an academic career at one of the more prestigious English universities, he lapsed into a schoolmaster. According to Mrs. Thomas he was offered a traveling fellowship but did not take it because he was "tired." But there is no record at Aberystwyth of D. J. Thomas's having received a fellow-ship. It seems more likely that he got Florence Williams pregnant and had to marry her, and then found that he had to earn a living as best he could, by teaching English in a grammar school. It was commonly said that Florence Williams was pregnant before she was married. The child either was stillborn or died shortly after birth.

The Thomases started married life together in Sketty, a village to the west of Swansea. A girl child, Nancy, was born in 1906. Eight years later they moved to a bigger house in Swansea, in the Uplands. They were always short of money for they were living beyond their means. Mrs. Thomas used to pay the tradesmen in rotation, and D. J. did extra work, teaching Welsh in evening classes, a job he must have hated for he was never heard speaking Welsh at any other time.

When he was a boy D. J. Thomas had wanted to be a poet—Dylan Thomas told this to Ruthven Todd. But his efforts had been rejected, and his love of poetry found its only outlet in reading aloud. It is said that he read Shakespeare aloud to Dylan before the child could speak. Whether or not this is true, he did read Dylan nursery rhymes and some rhymes of his own making. Dylan Thomas once said that the first poems he knew were nursery rhymes: "I wanted to write poetry in the beginning because I had fallen in love with words. The first poems I knew were nursery rhymes, and before I could read them for myself I had come to love just the words of them, the words alone. What the words stood for, symbolised, or meant, was of very secondary importance; what mattered was the *sound* of them as I heard them for the first time on the lips of the remote and incomprehensible grown-ups who seemed, for some reason, to be living in my world. And these words were, to me, as the notes of bells, the sounds of musical instruments, the noises of wind, sea, and rain, the rattle of milkcarts, the clop-ping of hooves on cobbles, the fingering of branches on a window pane, might be to someone, deaf from birth, who has miraculously found his hearing. I did not care what the words said, overmuch, nor what happened to Jack & Jill & the Mother Goose rest of them; I cared for the shapes of sound that their names, and the words describing their actions, made in my ears; I cared for the colours the words cast on my eyes. . . ."

This was said in 1951 in answer to five questions asked by a student, and published ten years later in the *Texas Quarterly* under the heading, "Poetic Manifesto." Thomas made similar observations from time to time, insisting that sound, "the colour of saying," was of the first importance in his poetry, and that the meaning of words, and what the symbols might be said to stand for, had little importance. If Thomas's view of his poetry is correct, then much of the criticism of it has been mistaken. Critics have chosen to ignore his statements—perhaps on the assumption that what a writer thinks he is doing is not to be taken seriously—and have proceeded to show, line by line and symbol by symbol, the logic in his verse.

D. J. Thomas knew and quoted the Bible, and this may have helped to form the biblical phrases and images that are found in the works of his son. But D. J. was not religious—he had the same contempt for the Creator that he had for everyone else. There were moments when D. J.'s unwillingness to be pleased lifted him from the ruck of humanity to the sublime. Once the Thomases were staying at a house in the country. "Father," Dylan told Daniel Jones, "is still as bitter as ever. He got up the other morning and looked through the window to the left, to the right, and straight ahead. He sneered, and, putting every ounce of venom into the words, said, '*Grass! Grass!* everywhere—nothing but *grass!*' "

The Thomases lived at Number 5, Cwmdonkin Drive, a semi-detached villa like hundreds of others in Swansea, furnished for respectability with flowered wallpaper, a clock on the mantelpiece supported by horses of mock ebony, willow-pattern china, and tea cosies. No doubt there was also an aspidistra.

D. J. had a study lined with books to which he would often retire. Sometimes at the dining table Mrs. Thomas would be talking about the children, or clothes, or some other of the foolish things women talk about, whereupon D. J. would throw down his napkin, rise in a rage, and stalk off to his study.

The house was on a hill; from the upper windows you could look down a slope of slate roofs to the bay and harbor, with the Mumbles Head lighthouse to the west. There was a school across the way, with a playing field sloped so that the ball ran downhill . . . a crazy game, like something in *Alice*. Then there was the thick growth of trees that marked Cwmdonkin Park.

His nurse took him there almost daily in his pram to listen to the pigeons and feed the gulls that were blown over in windy weather. The nurse, Addie Elliott, remembers that the first word he spoke was "bird."

He grew up thin and active. A young woman who baby-sat for the Thomases when Dylan was five recalls that he was "an absolute tartar, an appalling boy. I remember him grabbing for oranges. He never asked."

At seven, wrapped in thick sweaters and layers of underclothes, he was sent trudging off to day school. There he soon was teacher's pet. He had shimmering curls and a cherubic face, and he was mischievous . . . an irresistible combination.

The discipline at the "dame school" was firm and kind. He would recollect a smell of galoshes . . . the sound of a piano drifting downstairs to the schoolroom where a small boy sat alone, doing penance for unfinished sums or for pulling a girl's hair or kicking a shin.

There was a lane behind the school where the oldest and boldest gathered to throw pebbles at the windows and to boast and tell fibs about their relations. As a grown man he would dream that he went from school into the lane and that he said to his classmates, "At last, I have a real secret." The secret was that he could fly, and when they did not believe him he flapped his arms and went flying over the school, the trees and chimneys, the docks, masts, and funnels, over the streets, the men and women, the children, idlers and cripples, "over the yellow seashore, and the stone-chasing dogs, and the old men, and the singing sea."

Dylan and his friends played in Cwmdonkin Park. It was approached by crawling under a wire for there was no entrance from the main road. Then they would be among the giant firs, palmettos, yuccas, and monkey puzzle trees. It was their African jungle. There was a lake which had formerly been a reservoir, and a fountain where Dylan sailed model boats. There was a rookery and "the loud zoo of the willow groves." It was the park where the Hunchback sat.

> Like the park birds he came early
> Like the water he sat down

And Mister they called Hey mister
The truant boys from the town
Running when he heard them clearly
On out of sound

Dylan was a town boy. But his mother's sister had married a farmer named Jones, and they had a farm in Carmarthenshire. Fernhill stood on a rise above a wooded valley shielded from the road by trees. The farm building made three sides of a square around a small courtyard. There Ann and Jim Jones kept a few cows and pigs and chickens. The place was dirty and run down—Jim Jones was shiftless, known throughout the district as "a terrible man." It was said that he drank. Ann Jones did most of the work, making the butter they sold. She has gained another kind of life as the Ann Jones of Dylan Thomas's "After the Funeral."

At Fernhill the town boy received his impressions of the country. "About the countryside in general," Ferris remarks, "Thomas always seemed in two minds. He needed to break away from urban life, but he soon tired of rural retreats. It was part of his inability ever to settle anywhere for long."

The countryside around Fernhill fed his sense of the macabre. As a child he dreamed of ghosts and vampires and he seems to have taken a perverse delight in frightening himself with them. "The Peaches," one of his autobiographical stories, includes a demon with "wings and hooks, who clung like a bat to my hair." When he arrived at the farm with his uncle, at night, he imagined that "nothing lived in the hollow house at the end of the yard but two sticks with faces scooped out of turnips."

In the autumn of 1925, shortly before his eleventh birthday, Dylan entered the Grammar School where his father was a master. According to Jones, while Dylan was at school his relationship with his father was "strained," and no wonder, for the boys feared D. J. Thomas. He was ironic and sarcastic—"The whip-lash of D. J.'s tongue," Jones says, "held us in terror." And he was capable of rage. Jones recalls an occasion when D. J. was reading aloud a poem by Wilfred Owen and one of the boys giggled. D. J. gave him a savage beating. Jones says, "We all thought he really was going to kill the boy. . . ."

D. J. despised his job—with his superior abilities he should have been holding a chair at Oxford or Cambridge. He had hoped for the chair in English at the new Swansea University College, but it went to a W. D. Thomas whom he thought less qualified than he. And a fellow student from Aberystwyth, T. J. Rees, had been made Director of Education at a higher salary than his. D. J. had nothing but contempt for his fellow masters who were satisfied with their humble place in life, chasing schoolboys to their tasks. He had been intended for better things, but Destiny had thrown an obstacle in his path, in the shape of Florence Williams, and chained him to Cwmdonkin Drive.

He was extremely fastidious. A coarse remark would make him angry; words that were sexually suggestive had an alarming effect. On the good side, he was an effective reader of poetry—Dylan said that it had been grand, all the boys thought so. It was D. J.'s reading that made them, for the first time, see that there *was*, after all, *something* in Shakespeare and all this poetry.

It has been said that D. J. had great hopes for Dylan—his son was to have the academic career that he had been denied. But in this, too, he was disappointed—Dylan had no inclination at all for study; he was absent from class as often as not. The surprising thing is that D. J. did nothing about it. One would have expected him to be enraged, but this was not the case: Dylan was allowed to do as he liked at the Grammar School, as he had done ever since he was a child.

It has been said that Mrs. Thomas stood between Dylan and his father's anger, pleading his poor health. But Dylan was not in poor health—he was "indecisively active, quick to get dirty." Here, from *Portrait of the Artist as a Young Dog,* are some of his activities.

> I let Edgar Reynolds be whipped because I had taken his homework; I stole from my mother's bag; I stole from Gwyneth's bag; I stole twelve books in three visits from the library, and threw them away in the park; I drank a cup of my water to see what it tasted like; I beat a dog with a stick so that it would roll over and lick my hand afterwards; I looked with Dan Jones through the keyhole while his maid had a bath; I cut my knee with a penknife, and put the blood on my handkerchief and said it had come out of my ears so that I could pretend I was ill and frighten my mother . . .

At Grammar School Dylan showed a surprising ability for long-distance running; on Sports Day in his first summer term he won the one-mile race for under-fifteens, and for years he competed successfully in school races and cross-country runs. Jones tells us that he could also fight like a wildcat, scratching and biting. Nevertheless, in the Thomas family it was understood that Dylan's health was not strong and that he had to be indulged—a belief he accepted willingly and traded on all his life.

But his poor record in the classroom cannot be attributed to Mrs. Thomas's coddling. After all, D. J. was on the spot and it was within his power to see that Dylan got an education. But he did not—on the contrary, he abetted his misbehavior. Dylan refused to observe discipline and was absent from classes as often as he pleased, and the masters did not dare to punish him because they feared a confrontation with his father. As a result Dylan, "if recorded at all," was listed at the bottom of the class in all subjects except English, and even in English he came close to the bottom. He did not pass any examination and left school as soon as possible. As Jones puts it, his appearances in class became more and more sporadic until they ceased altogether.

By bringing up his son in this way, D. J. Thomas showed his contempt for the world and, at the same time, bound Dylan to him for life. He encouraged him to be the rebel he himself could not be, permitting him to avoid all dull and dreary tasks; as a result Dylan knew nothing but poetry, which he got from his father, and only fine-sounding poetry at that. He would have to be a poet, and when the early lyric impulse was played out he would have no way of making a fresh start—lacking all discipline, he would not be able to submit himself to philosophy, religion, or any intellectual system. Like his father he despised all systems, or pretended to despise them—"He had," says Caitlin Thomas, "the . . . dislike, amounting to superstitious horror, of philosophy, psychology, analysis, criticism; all those vaguely ponderous tomes; but most of all, of the gentle art of discussing poetry. . . ." He was uncomfortable in the company of people who seemed to know about philosophy, psychology, and so on. These occasions would bring out his rudest behavior, and, of course, his drinking. D. J. Thomas, a tyrant to every other boy, was the most permissive of masters where his son was concerned, and the result—Dylan locked into the narrow round of his own immediate consciousness, his poetry restricted to a view of the world as an extension of himself, literally, his flesh and blood and bones—was disastrous.

When Dylan Thomas went to school "modern poetry" meant:

> When I was but thirteen or so
> I went into a golden land;
> Chimborazo, Cotopaxi
> Took me by the hand . . .

It meant:

> From troubles of the world
> I turn to ducks,
> Beautiful comical things
> Sleeping or curled
> Their heads beneath white wings . . .

It did *not* mean:

> "My nerves are bad tonight. Yes, bad. Stay with me.
> "Speak to me. Why do you never speak. Speak.
> "What are you thinking of? What thinking? What?
> "I never know what you are thinking. Think."

The poets whom Americans think of as the masters of twentieth-century verse in English—Yeats, Pound, and Eliot—were not taught in British classrooms. Yeats's "The Lake Isle of Innisfree" was taught, but not his later, more difficult poetry. A rare teacher might show his students one of Eliot's poems, but usually if Eliot were mentioned it was as an example of "this modern verse." Eliot was a hoax . . . the fellow was obviously pulling the public's leg.

The Georgian poets—Masefield, Drinkwater, Abercrombie, W. H. Davies, Walter De La Mare—were the fellows to read. Schoolboys were required to memorize and recite Robert Bridges's "London Snow," or:

> Lord Rameses of Egypt sighed
>   Because a summer evening passed;
> And little Ariadne cried
>   That summer fancy fell at last
> To dust; and young Verona died
>   When beauty's hour was overcast . . .

The Georgian poets wrote about a passing mood induced by the contemplation of nature. Sometimes they wished with James Elroy Flecker to be on a golden journey to Samarkand, or with W. J. Turner to be hunting velvet tigers in the jungle; usually, however, they were content to be in the Home Counties.

> God! I will pack, and take a train,
> And get me to England once again!
> For England's the one land, I know,
> Where men with Splendid Hearts may go;
> And Cambridgeshire, of all England,
> The shire for Men who Understand;
> And of *that* district I prefer
> The lovely hamlet Grantchester . . .

Recently there had been a disruption of the natural order, the Great War that had taken the best of the nation's youth, sixty thousand on the first day of the Somme alone. The names of battles in France and Flanders were sacred. Each name evoked the same landscape, acres of mud laced with barbed wire through which lines of men wound hopelessly. Photographs of the trenches showed white, strained faces with eyes that looked beyond the camera, beyond all observers, at some private vision of Hell.

English poetry had encouraged the nation's youth to go to war. In "The War Films" Henry Newbolt wrote:

> O living pictures of the dead,
>   O songs without a sound,
> O fellowship whose phantom tread
>   Hallows a phantom ground—
> How in a gleam have these revealed
>   The faith we had not found . . .

He wished that he could have taken the place of the "lads" whose death he was mourning. Other poets, however, who had seen active service, had a different view: they found nothing noble in a death by high explosive, machine gun, or gas. Siegfried Sassoon condemned the war in satirical lyrics, heaping sarcasm on the General Staff and patriots and war profiteers back in England. Wilfred Owen showed what it was like to be down in the mud with the troops.

> Our brains ache, in the merciless iced east winds that
>   knive us . . .
> Wearied we keep awake because the night is silent . . .
> Low, drooping flares confuse our memory of the salient . . .
> Worried by silence, sentries whisper, curious, nervous,
>   But nothing happens.

Wilfred Owen was one of the authors in D. J. Thomas's study, on the ground floor, behind a stained-glass door. There Dylan would read whatever struck his fancy. He read old ballads, and Henry Newbolt, and William Blake—not necessarily in that order. He read Keats and Shakespeare and D. H. Lawrence. He read Sir Thomas Browne and Thomas De Quincey. He read Traherne and other Metaphysical poets. And he read the Bible. Outside his father's study he read *Chums*, Baroness Orczy, and dozens of a schoolboy's favorite authors.

In the course of his reading he came upon poets who were not taught in the classroom. When he was fifteen he wrote an essay on "Modern Poetry" for the school magazine that started, as such essays usually do, with the claim that "Poetry has never been so wide and varied as it is today," and proceeded to describe "the modern artistic spirit."

The most important element of "poetical modernity" was freedom, "freedom of form, of structure, of imagery and idea." The roots of this freedom were to be found in Hopkins's compressed imagery and the "violation" of language this entailed. Then came the metrical experiments of Robert Bridges, "who introduced free rhythm into the confines of orthodox metre." Da La Mare continued Bridges's mixture of innovation and convention, and "at the present time Sacheverell Sitwell presents a great deal of his strange confusion of thought and beauty in the heroic couplet."

He mentions "neo-Romanticists" such as Eliot and James Joyce, who assume that no subject is unpoetical and write of sordid details, a damp despondent atmosphere, their attraction for the gutter. And W. B. Yeats, "At the head of the twilight poets," who writes of "a fragile, unsubstantial world, covered with mysticism and mythological shadows" . . . Yeats's entire poetic creation is "brittle." He praises the simple beauty and charm of W. H. Davies's lyrics.

He speaks of the Imagists, "founded by John Gould Fletcher." Richard Aldington is the best known of the group; he accentuates the image, but "has modified it and made it more intelligible." Then there are the Sitwells, who are said to be obscure but whose writings, examined closely, reveal images and thoughts "of a new and astonishing clarity."

There has been a revolution in English poetry as a result of the Great War. The war caused some of the bitterest and loveliest poetry in the language to be written, by Siegfried Sassoon, Rupert Brooke, Robert Nichols, Wilfred Owen, Robert Graves, Julian Grenfell, "and the other heroes who built towers of beauty upon the ashes of their lives."

But it is the poetry of today that shows the clearest influence of the war. "The incoherence caused by anguish and animal horror, and the shrill crudity which is inevitable in poetry produced by such war, are discarded. Instead, we have a more contemplative confusion, a spiritual riot. No poet can find sure ground; he is hunting for it . . . Today is a transitional period."

He concludes with thumbnail definitions of some contemporaries: "D. H. Lawrence, the body-worshipper who fears the soul; Edmund Blunden, who has immersed himself in the English countryside; Richard Church, the poet of detached contemplation; Ezra Pound, the experimental mystic. . . ." These men are only laying the foundations of a new art. The poetry that will be built on these foundations promises to be "a high and novel achievement."

No need to show how mistaken Dylan was about the state of contemporary verse, how ridiculous it was to call Eliot and Joyce "neo-Romantic," to think of Yeats as a writer of merely "fragile" verse, to list Richard Church with Lawrence and Pound, "the experimental mystic." However, the essay shows that he has been reading

and educating himself at a furious rate within the narrow area of
his special interest.

He started writing early. The poem from which the following
lines are taken is said to have been written before his tenth birthday.

> She stooped to grief's remembered tears,
> Yearned to undawned delight.
> Ah, beauty—passionate from the years!
> Oh, body—wise and white!

Sound is everything, meaning practically nil. A hand, presumably
his father's, has made corrections in the margin. It is possible that
D. J. did more than correct, that he also made suggestions—though
Dylan was precocious this seems too good for a nine-year-old.

At the end of the first term at the Grammar School he published a
humorous poem in the school magazine. It was titled, "The Song of
the mischievous Dog."

> There are many who say that a dog has its day,
>   And a cat has a number of lives;
> There are others who think that a lobster is pink,
>   And that bees never work in their hives . . .

The anapests go trotting along so that the absence of logic is hardly
felt. At the end there is a surprise:

> But my greatest delight is to take a good bite
>   At a calf that is plump and delicious;
> And if I indulge in a bite at a bulge,
>   Let's hope you won't think me too vicious.

This is sex, but as the author is supposed to be a dog the lines were
able to get by the eagle eye of his father, who was in charge of the
magazine. That Dylan liked to think of himself as a young dog, we
know—it is the title of one of his books. On other occasions he
would use other disguises. In the poems of his late adolescence
there are references to masturbation and copulation, but the mean-
ing is concealed in a welter of images. In this way he avoids being
understood by his father, always on the *qui vive* for pornography.

A year later "D. M. Thomas" had a poem, "His Requiem," published in the Cardiff *Western Mail*. Many years later it was discovered that this was plagiarism: he had taken a poem by Lillian Gard in the *Boy's Own Paper* and submitted it as his own. Ferris remarks that he must have felt a great need to prove that he was a poet—to his friends, to his father, to himself. The incident brings Dylan's motives into question: he may have wanted the name of a poet more than he loved poetry. And Ferris adds that his poems were "thick with the affectations of poetry." But this is true of most beginners: they want to succeed long before they know how to go about it.

He became one of the editors of the school magazine. P. E. Smart, a co-editor, admired his light verse—it was delightful, "sparkling, bright and clear." But he was aware that Dylan was also writing verse of the kind that people could not understand. When he asked him what was the use of writing "privately" in this way, Dylan couldn't really understand the question—"he wrote," he said, "what was in him, and it was really quite irrelevant whether anyone else ever read it."

By the time he wrote the essay on modern poetry he had become modern. "The Elm," written in 1929, is an imitation of Imagist poems, especially Aldington's. He was becoming ethereal.

> They are all goddesses;
> Nodding like flowers,
> They are further and more delicate
> Than the years that dwindle;
> They are deeper in darkness
> Than the hours.
>
> Celestial,
> Slenderly lethal things,
> Beautifully little like clouds:
> Leaf driftwood that has blown.

A year later he was entering his poems in an exercise book under the heading "Mainly Free Verse Poems." The first poem in the 1930 notebook, "Osiris, Come to Isis," is a serious imitation of Yeats—at the same time that, in the school magazine, he is parodying Yeats with "In Borrowed Plumes." There are two Thomases, one for his private notebook, the other for school—but this is not unusual, as any writer who has been to school will testify. "Cast not your pearls before swine, lest they turn and rend you."

The notebooks show his discovery of a style. It appears as early as 1930:

> Now I may watch
> The wings of the bird snap
> Under the air which raises flowers
> Over the walls of the brass town . . .

Four years later it has been perfected:

> The force that drives the water through the rocks
> Drives my red blood; that dries the mouthing streams
> Turns mine to wax.
> And I am dumb to mouth unto my veins
> How at the mountain spring the same mouth sucks.

The essential quality of this writing is its concreteness. Sound first of all, a linking of vowel and consonantal sounds from line to line.

Then images—objects in nature being compared to parts of the human body. "All thoughts and actions," Thomas wrote Pamela Hansford Johnson, "emanate from the body. Therefore the description of a thought or action—however abstruse it may be—can be beaten home by bringing it on to a physical level. Every idea, intuitive or intellectual, can be imaged and translated in terms of the body, its flesh, skin, blood, sinews, veins, glands, organs, cells, or senses."

A man once asked Thomas to explain his "theory of poetry." "Really," he said, "I haven't got one. I like things that are difficult to write and difficult to understand; I like 'redeeming the contraries' with secretive images; I like contradicting my images, saying two things at once in one word, four in two and one in six."

Then he made the point that is essential for an understanding of his work: "Poetry should work from words, from the substance of words and the rhythm of substantial words set together, not towards words."

He began with words, not ideas. Some critics have ignored this, perhaps not being able to accept it. Elder Olson explains that

Thomas's "Altarwise by owl-light" sonnets refer to six levels of meaning "which the poet intricately interrelates."

1. a level based on the analogy of human life to the span of a year, which permits the use of phenomena of the seasons to represent events of human life, and vice versa;
2. a level based on an analogy between sun and man, permitting the attributes of each to stand for those of the other;
3. a level of Thomas' "private" symbolism;
4. a level based on ancient myth, principally Greek, representing the fortunes of the sun in terms of the adventures of the sun-hero Hercules;
5. a level based on relations of the *constellation* Hercules to other constellations and astronomical phenomena; and
6. a level derived from the Christian interpretation of levels 4 and 5.

This is God's plenty! But how are we to reconcile Olson's explanation with Thomas's view of his work? In answer to a man who asked what one of his poems was "about," he said, "I can give you a very rough idea of the 'plot.' But of course it's bound to be a most superficial, and perhaps misleading, idea because the 'plot' is told in images, and the images *are* what they say, not what they stand for."

Moreover, images were not as important as sounds. To someone who asked whether he wrote for the eye or the ear, he said, for the ear.

However, words do mean something, and while one may not want to go as far as Olson it is not possible to read a poem by Dylan Thomas without perceiving that an argument of some sort is going on—though it may be hard to disentangle and no two critics are likely to agree what it is.

But sound came first. From the time he was a child, being read to by his father, it was the *sound* of poetry he was after.

> Young Mr. Thomas was at the moment without employment, but it was understood that he would soon be leaving for London to make a career in Chelsea as a free-lance journalist; he was penniless, and hoped, in a vague way, to live on women.
> —*Portrait of the Artist as a Young Dog*

Dylan was dropping out of school long before he quit. Outside the classroom he was busy: he had an interest in theatricals and took the part of Cromwell in the school play. Together with Daniel Jones he composed poetry and plays, giving comical concerts, and projected or actually carried out elaborate practical jokes. Jones was clever—in later life a composer and doctor of music—and he appears to have filled the role of Dylan's intellectual friend and mentor. Dylan would listen to his opinion as to no one else's. In later years he would read his poems to Jones at whatever stage they happened to be and whenever opportunity arose—in Swansea, Laugharne, London, and Oxford.

Jones lived at Warmley, and Dylan was a regular guest in the house. The Joneses were everything that Dylan's own family was not—"unconventional and easy-going in the extreme, and unselfconsciously so. . . . Our games," says Daniel Jones, "literary or musical, were approved, and sometimes even the older members of the family took part." Jones's father composed vocal church music and was a great storyteller in the bargain. Jones's brother also composed a little, and his mother played Beethoven energetically, but her specialty was needlework—her tapestries had been exhibited in London. And there was an Aunt Alice who was a gifted teacher of music. They were, as Pound says of another artistic family, "a darn'd clever bunch."

Daniel and Dylan tried their hand at various arts. They tried sculpting heads out of rocks, but after a week Dylan put down the chisel and said, "I'm fed up with sculpture." They tried composing music, and as Dylan had no knowledge of music or musical skill the result was never conventional. They invented a mythology of composers, singers, and instrumentalists, "above all, the Rev. Percy, who dominated the musical scene with his innumerable piano pieces for four hands." They wrote the libretto for an opera; it consisted of a repetition of the word "Heinrich," "sung with every possible shade of emotion." And they collaborated in writing poetry, Daniel writing the odd lines, Dylan the even. These were attributed to one Walter Bram. Here is a specimen:

> They followed for seven days
> The youngest shepherd with exotic praise,
> Seeking grass unshepherded,

Worship-laden where the magic led.
They followed the shepherd through diverting ways,
Watching his satyr footsteps as he fled.

Though most of this, Jones says, was insignificant, they were playing seriously with words. "We had word obsessions: everything at one time was 'little' or 'white'; and sometimes an adjective became irresistibly funny in almost any connection: 'innumerable bananas,' 'wilful moccasin,' 'a certain Mrs. Prothero.' . . . these word games, and even the most facetious of our collaborations, had a serious experimental purpose."

Dylan failed his examination for the school-leaving certificate, and spent his last year in the Lower Sixth marking time. One of the stories in *Portrait* evokes this in-between period of adolescence. He is "a lonely night-walker and a steady stander-at-corners." He walks through the wet town after midnight, "when the streets were deserted and the window lights out, alone and alive on the glistening tram-lines in dead and empty High Street under the moon. . . ."

In his solitary walks he feels that the world is "remote and overpressing," but that he is very much a part of it. He is full of love and arrogance and pity and humility, "not for myself alone, but for the living earth I suffered on and for the unfeeling systems in the upper air. . . ." Full of cosmic yearning, he stands under a railway arch with two young men named Tom and Walter. They stand there for a long time, while trains pass overhead and the citizens of Swansea are sitting down to their evening meal in warm, comfortable surroundings. Tom and Walter tell the narrator—we may as well call him Dylan—the story of their relations with two young women named Doris and Norma. The upshot was that the women brought paternity suits against them, whereupon Walter married Norma and Tom married Doris. But Tom doesn't love Doris— Norma was the one he loved—and Walter doesn't love either Norma or Doris. "We've two nice little boys," Tom tells Dylan. "I call mine Norman." The young men, it turns out, are brothers.

The story takes its title, "Just Like Little Dogs," from the remark made by the magistrate who heard the paternity suit. Thomas seems to feel that marriage is a miserable business—at least, as he has seen it. His own parents in their way were just as mismated as

Tom and Doris. From standing on street corners he has a depressed view of Swansea—"scorning girls and ready girls, soldiers and bullies and policemen and sharp, suspicious buyers of second-hand books, bad, ragged women who'd pretend against the museum wall for a cup of tea. . . ." It is sordid, but he prefers to stand in the street rather than go home—as much of an outcast as Tom and Walter, though for a different reason. It is better standing under the railway arch, or leaning against the wall of a derelict house, or wandering in the empty rooms, "gazing through the smashed windows at the sea or at nothing. . . ."

Dylan left school at seventeen and his father got him a job on the *South Wales Daily,* later *Evening, Post.* He worked there for eighteen months, beginning in the "reader's room" where he read copy aloud while someone else checked the proof for mistakes. Then he moved on to the reporters' room and did the usual rounds of hospitals, police stations, concerts, and bazaars. Ferris tells us that an older newspaperman who sub-edited Dylan's copy said that it was "appalling, with many lacunae," and that there are a lot of funny stories about his reporting events that never took place, or not reporting events that did. These stories, Ferris observes, "are unlikely to have been funny at the time, assuming they ever happened." Dylan did not take pleasure in the stories—"My selfish carelessness and unpunctuality," he wrote to Henry Treece in 1938, "I do not try to excuse as poet's properties. They are a bugbear and a humbug." Nevertheless, he was beginning to have a reputation for irresponsible behavior—it would soar after he became famous.

In December of 1932 he was fired from his job on the *Evening Post.* This brought no real hardship for he was living at home where his mother saw to it that he was properly fed. He had no income, however, so he cadged money from acquaintances and sometimes he would steal. He stole shillings from his sister Nancy's handbag, and when one of her friends came to tea robbed her of a pound note.

In letters to her fiancé, Haydn Taylor, Nancy describes life on Cwmdonkin Drive. Her father has been using foul language and accusing her of being a parasite—"All you and your beautiful brother do is to take my money from me." To be classed with Dylan, she says, is ghastly. She wishes she were dead. "Last night Dylan said one day he'd strangle me."

Dylan is very difficult to live with.

> Dylan has just risen (11:30) & is in the most foul temper—
> rushing and raving like a tormented thing. He stays in bed most
> mornings & then gets up and writes. In the evening he visits
> Danny. *Unless* he gets any sum of money—then he goes and
> drinks. What will become of him Heaven knows. . . .

Nancy escaped through marriage. Dylan stayed home and wrote.
"Poets live and walk with their poems; a man with visions needs no
other company. . . . I must go home and sit in my bedroom by the
boiler."

It was the most prolific period of his life. He wrote drafts of many
poems . . . for years he would turn to the notebooks and rework
these early drafts. An early version of "The hunchback in the park"
is dated May 9, 1932. "After the funeral" first say light on February
10, 1933, though the draft is rudimentary. It was written on the
occasion of the death of Ann Jones, his aunt at Fernhill. The draft
trails off with a remark about the uselessness of things—"one more
joke has lost its point." The finished version, published five years
later, is different—it speaks of the quality of the individual life. The
difference is that Thomas now has a point of view, a way of organiz-
ing the material so that it appears to say something.

He had another interest, the theater. While still a reporter he had
joined the Little Theatre (so did Nancy—it is said that she out-acted
Dylan and there was talk of her going on the stage professionally).
He appeared in Noël Coward's *Hay Fever,* taking the part of Simon,
and in the next two or three years he appeared regularly in Little
Theatre plays. Ferris tells us that Dylan's idea of acting was to
overact, and that "His voice was already strong; soon it would
thicken and begin to acquire the boom that made him as famous as
his poetry." It is curious that in later years when he reminisced
about his life in Swansea he would never refer to his acting. "An
actor in so many things he did, he preferred not to remember
himself as one."

He became interested in politics through Bert Trick, an older
man who was a grocer and had been an income-tax clerk. Bert was a
Communist; he undertook to educate Dylan, explaining the com-

ing demise of Capitalism and the triumph of Communism. For a while Dylan mouthed the platitudes of the Left though it is doubtful that he understood them. His political sophistication may be measured by a statement he made to Daniel Jones: ". . . the only politics for a conscientious artist . . . must be left-wing under a right-wing government, communist *under* capitalism."

He was for revolution—without bloodshed: "All that we ask for is that the present Disorder . . . shall be broken in two, and that all there is in us of godliness and strength, of happiness and genius, shall be allowed to exult in the sun." Everything was wrong that forbade the freedom of the individual.

This was in a letter to Pamela Hansford Johnson. She lived with her mother in London, and when a poem by Dylan, "That sanity be kept I sit at open windows," was published in Victor Neuberg's "The Poets' Corner" in the *Sunday Referee*, she wrote him saying how much she liked it. Dylan wrote back, thanking her for her praise and for letting him see her own poetry. "It shows a tremendous passion for words," he told her. "Your grasp of form and your handling of metre is among the best I know today. And—the main thing—your thoughts are worth expressing. Have you written a great deal? . . ."

He knew how to lay it on thick—with a shovel if need be. Their correspondence, begun with mutual compliments, continued full spate. He preened himself before her as an intellectual and beautiful soul. At times he played the devil-may-care bohemian who smoked too much and drank more than was good for him and was subject to temptations of the flesh—but he hastened to assure her that his ideas about sex were serious. He believed that boys and girls in puberty should be allowed to know their bodies and that their sexual expression should be encouraged. ". . . both would grow up physically and mentally uncontaminated and refreshened."

He was repelled by the sordidness around him, "hideously pretty young girls with cheap berets on their heads and paint smudged over their cheeks; thin youths with caps and stained fingers holding their cigarettes; women, all breast and bottom, hugging their purses to them and staring in at the shop windows; little colliers, diseased in mind and body as only the Welsh can be, standing in groups outside the Welfare Hall."

His opinions were less original than his poems. He thought that marriage was a "dead institution"—no doubt the thought of women "all breast and bottom," staring in shop windows, inclined him to think so. He had an aversion for homosexuals, denouncing them as "willing-buttocked, celluloid-trousered degenerates."

His opinions bring with them the atmosphere of a pub shortly before closing time when talk is loud and the foaming tankards pass swiftly across the counter. Dylan talked with the best and emptied his glass.

He had a romantic view of himself and gave it out that he had consumption. The *poète maudit*—like Chatterton and Keats.

He worked in his bedroom. It smelled of tobacco, for he was a chain smoker. To save money he had bought a machine with which he could roll his own. He would write a line of words, change a word or two, and write the line again. When the sheet was covered he would start on another. Absorbed like a child at play, he scarcely noticed the passing of hours, the changing light outside.

He told Pamela Johnson that the labor of writing was becoming more and more difficult, and that he was becoming more obscure: "It gives me now a physical pain to write poetry." He would work all day on a few lines, but when he had picked them over and cleaned them nothing remained but their "barbaric sounds." The words he used did not mean what he wanted them to, they only came near to expressing the half.

In August 1933, D. J. Thomas's dentist discovered an ulcer on the floor of his mouth, below the tongue. A specialist was called in; he diagnosed the growth as cancer and D. J. was given five years to live. He was taken up to London and admitted to University College where, for a week, he was treated with radium needles. In the following months he made several journeys to London. In October he was again treated with radium, this time for two weeks. For a while his voice was affected. The treatment, however, was a success; by early in 1934 the ulcer had begun to heal, and the adjoining glands were not affected. D. J. was to live for another twenty years.

As Ferris shows, D. J. Thomas's cancer of the mouth had an important effect on Dylan Thomas's poetry. There are direct references to it in the notebook: "Take the needles and the knives" (September 12, 1933) and "The root of tongues ends in a spentout cancer" (October 17). But, "More significant is the fact that the first complete, full-blooded 'anatomical' poem is also the first poem to follow the news of his father's cancer. . . ." This is the poem beginning "Before I knocked," in which Thomas sees himself as an unborn child:

> Before I knocked and flesh let enter,
> With liquid hands tapped on the womb . . .

There is a reference to D. J.'s ulcer (in a letter Dylan would call it "cancer of the throat"):

> My throat knew thirst before the structure
> Of skin and vein around the well
> Where words and water make a mixture
> Unfailing till the blood runs foul . . .

"The stage is set for Thomas' distinctive organic imagery," and, indeed, it appears that we can date the beginning of his "real" poetry from this incident.

He identified himself with his father, especially his father's voice. The ulcer was located in the mouth, at the base of the tongue—it was poetry, his identity, that was threatened. Therefore he began to write in earnest, drawing images from the physical body.

Ever since he was a child he had lived in his body almost to the exclusion of thought. At Fernhill when he went to sleep the world went away, and it came back the next morning with a cock on its shoulder. The self, the ear that hears, the eye that sees, is the center of everything. Impelled by the dread of not hearing and not seeing he began to write, making poems that were solid, made of bone, flesh, sinew, blood.

The imagery of these poems is "almost totally anatomical."

"But," he says, "I defend the diction, the perhaps wearisome succession of blood and bones, the never-ending similes of the streams in the veins and the lights in the eyes, by saying that, for the time at least, I realise that it is impossible for me to raise myself to the altitude of the stars, and that I am forced, therefore, to bring down the stars to my own level and to incorporate them in my own physical universe."

As Maud says, Thomas uses the word "stars" to mean beliefs. He is presenting himself as a mystical poet, "in the path of Blake." His poems echo the language and imagery of the Bible, and the central Christian mystery of Incarnation figures in his thinking.

How seriously are we to take him as a religious poet? The answer is, not at all, unless we are to expand the word "religion" to mean any writing that uses the properties of religion. The error of readers who take Thomas to be religious comes of their not understanding that in Britain, and especially Wales, chapel-going is part of people's ordinary lives, and that it is possible for a man to be familiar with the Bible—as Dylan's father was—without real conviction. In America, as Church and State are separate, if a man chooses to use the trappings of religion there must be a reason. But this is not the case in Britain; for hundreds of years people have been going to church as they go to the club—it is something to do on Sunday.

The poems of Dylan Thomas are romantic and "cosmic," exactly the kind of thing T. E. Hulme and Ezra Pound had warned poets against twenty years earlier.

He would pack images together without explanatory links so that the poem had the sound and appearance of a concrete thing. At times his poetry appears surrealistic, especially in this early period—that is, it appears to make no sense, to be pure invention of sounds and images. However, it does not fit André Breton's definition of surrealism: "the actual functioning of thought . . . in the absence of any control exercised by reason, exempt from any aesthetic or moral concern."

There is plenty of aesthetic concern in Thomas's arrangement of sounds and images, and even morality of a kind, in order to make an argument and bring the poem to a conclusion. A poem by Dylan Thomas is like the country visited by Alice: once you accept being there, everything that happens is perfectly logical.

Breton's definition, however, is not final, and if we can extend the label of surrealism to cover works with some control by reason and some aesthetic or moral concern—as the Surrealists themselves did, when they honored Lautréamont's *Maldoror* and Walpole's *Castle of Otranto,* and narratives in prose by Aragon and Breton—then some of Thomas's poems are surrealistic. The poetry is a new thing with its own internal organization and does not take its meaning from reference to the world. It can be explained, but we are aware that to explain is to miss the point, the experience of the thing itself.

There has been very little surrealist writing in English. The English-speaking mind has been trained over the centuries to think of literature in moral terms, as an appendage to "life." It resists the idea of imagination as a different and valid kind of life—of works of art making their own reality. For this reason the poems of Dylan Thomas have been hacked over in order to make them conform to a "meaning." The enterprise is, at best, of secondary importance, and may do more harm than good, substituting "meaning," paraphrasable content, for the experience of listening and seeing.

The way to read a poem by Dylan Thomas is to allow oneself to visualize the things in the poem as they are described.

> Light breaks where no sun shines;
> Where no sea runs, the waters of the heart
> Push in their tides;
> And, broken ghosts with glow-worms in their heads,
> The things of light
> File through the flesh where no flesh decks the bones.
>
> A candle in the thighs
> Warms youth and seed and burns the seeds of age;
> Where no seed stirs
> The fruit of man unwrinkles in the stars,
> Bright as a fig;
> Where no wax is, the candle shows its hairs.

Candles are candles, thighs are thighs, and figs are figs. As Thomas said, ". . . images *are* what they say, not what they stand for."

> Dawn breaks behind the eyes;
> From poles of skull and toe the windy blood
> Slides like a sea;
> Nor fenced, nor staked, the gushers of the sky
> Spout to the rod
> Divining in a smile the oil of tears.

In this writing Thomas is like Rimbaud, especially Rimbaud's "Bateau Ivre," and, in fact, Thomas would poke fun at himself as "the Rimbaud of Cwmdonkin Drive." In "Bateau Ivre" Rimbaud undertakes to make visible a world of waterspouts, sea-monsters, and tropical jungle. He is a visionary, not a symbolist. The same is true of Thomas: in "Light breaks where no sun shines" he is envisioning a world that appears to be an extension of the human body. It begins inside the body, with our consciousness.

> Night in the sockets rounds,
> Like some pitch moon, the limit of the globes:
> Day lights the bone;
> Where no cold is, the skinning gales unpin
> The winter's robes;
> The film of spring is hanging from the lids.

What is the purpose of this "anatomical" imagery? Does Thomas believe in the Microcosm and the Macrocosm? Are we, when we read him, deep in Gnostic lore? Or is there a Christian interpretation?

Others have asked another question: is it a hoax?

The way to read these lines is to visualize what they say. We are inside the body, and from this viewpoint we see night, "like some pitch moon," traveling across the sockets. I visualize these as eye sockets, but I could be wrong. The seasons are changing within the body, and Spring hangs on the eyelids.

> Light breaks on secret lots,
> On tips of thought where thoughts smell in the rain;
> When logics die,
> The secret of the soil grows through the eye,
> And blood jumps in the sun;
> Above the waste allotments the dawn halts.

We spin the world out from our consciousness of it. We are the Creators of the universe—just as, in fact, we are poets.

Thomas says, "It is my aim as an artist . . . to prove beyond doubt to myself that the flesh that covers me is the flesh that covers the sun, that the blood in my lungs is the blood that goes up and down in a tree. It is the simplicity of religion."

Reading "Light breaks where no sun shines" I find myself falling into the error of interpreting I have warned against. But this is unavoidable to some extent; words have a meaning, and though the poet may want his poem to be a pure invention, there is always a statement of some kind. It is not wrong to interpret the meaning of a poem—it is only wrong to interpret too much. This is where critics go wrong, and the end of it is that the critic sets himself up in the place of the poet.

We must not let the possible meanings of the poem overwhelm the experience of listening and seeing. To read poetry is to be aware of the impression the poem makes, not to try to have the lines fit an argument in every particular. I would go so far as to say that a meaning that does not contribute to the effect a poem makes does not exist.

Before he was twenty Thomas had published poems in the *Adelphi*, the *New English Weekly*, the *Listener*, and other journals. *The Criterion* and *New Verse* had accepted poems for publication, and one of his poems had been read over the BBC. Stephen Spender wrote asking if he would like to do reviews and suggesting that they dine together when Dylan came up to London. Best of all, T. S. Eliot, having read "Light breaks where no sun shines," wrote from Faber and Faber where he was an editor, inviting Dylan to call on him. It would be like having an audience with the Pope.

In June 1934 he was in London. One evening he and Pamela Hansford Johnson decided to get married, but the next day she changed her mind, and at the end of the month he went back to Swansea. He returned to London in August and lived in the house of his fiancée's mother. "The strain of such propinquity in platonic circumstances," says Constantine Fitzgibbon, editor of the *Letters*, "began to tell on the two young people." Thomas took to drinking and staying out late and they quarreled. In mid-September they all went to stay with Thomas's parents in Wales; Mrs. Johnson found Mrs. Thomas boring and it rained for two weeks. Then, says Fitzgibbon, "Pamela discovered Dylan's true age, nineteen, and realized that marriage was out of the question." Why marrying a man younger than herself—she was the older by two years—should have appeared like a breach of nature, is not evident. It was probably an excuse for not marrying, and served as well as any.

In November Thomas came to London with the painter Alfred

Janes, and they roomed together off the Fulham Road, near Chelsea, an area of writers, artists, and bohemians. Thomas was in full spate of publishing: his first book, *18 Poems*, was to be published by a small press around Christmas, and he hoped to find a publisher for his stories. He was meeting "notabilities," among them the sculptor Henry Moore, the poet Edwin Muir and his wife Willa, and the painter and novelist Wyndham Lewis.

Dylan was now a professional literary man, his opinions of people determined by what they thought of his work. He disliked Geoffrey Grigson, editor of *New Verse*, until Grigson wrote asking him to submit poems—then he found him tolerable. When Grigson accepted two poems, he wrote him: "New Verse is awfully good this month, and I was pleased to see William Carlos Williams given one in the eye." When Edith Sitwell included a parody of Thomas's poems in her new book, he called it her "latest piece of virgin dung." Two years later she wrote an enthusiastic review of his *Twenty-five Poems*, whereupon he wrote her: "I hope you aren't cross with me really [He had failed to keep an appointment] . . . Will you meet me again, in spite of things? You're still a great encouragement to me—and always will be."

18 Poems caused a sensation—among poets, that is. It was something new, radically different from the poetry of Auden, Spender, MacNeice, and C. Day Lewis, the currently fashionable poets of the left. They were nothing if not rational; their poems began with ideas, not words. Spender had romantic attitudes, but these played second fiddle to his leftish views, and, like Auden, Lewis, and MacNeice, he wrote the language taught in public schools.

Thomas's poems were also very different from the poems of Eliot. There was nothing diffident about the voice coming out of Wales. People were not sure what Thomas's poetry meant, but they got a definite impression that sex was involved, and some kind of prophecy. On the whole they welcomed the poet who spoke of sensual life in riddling terms.

His second book, *Twenty-five Poems* (1936), was not so well received—in fact, an air of disappointment hangs about the reviews. Many of the poems had actually been written before *18 Poems;* they were less startling in their imagery and easier to understand—with an exception, the "Altarwise by owl-light" sonnet sequence. If readers found some of the poems disappointingly simple, the sonnet sequence was altogether too obscure. The *Times Literary Supplement* complained about the obscurity, and the *New Statesman* said that it preferred *18 Poems,* "the record of a volcanic adolescence." The new book showed a split between fairly simple poetry and "eerie bombast." The reviewer gave his opinion that Thomas was a really original poet who for the time being seemed to have lost his way.

Whatever the reason, after *Twenty-five Poems* Thomas wrote hardly any poetry for two years. The spate that began at the Swansea Grammar School had come to a stop. The years from sixteen to twenty were the most productive of his life; in this short time he developed his own original style. He never again was so visited. And though his writing would pick up again, and poems he wrote in later years would be acclaimed, there are readers who prefer the inchoate gropings in the notebooks to the finished poems, and would rather have "Light breaks where no sun shines," with all its obscurities, than the clear sentences and argument of a poem such as "Fern Hill," written long after the time it describes. Or the descriptiveness of "Over Sir John's Hill":

> Over Sir John's hill
> The hawk on fire hangs still;
> In a hoisted cloud, at drop of dusk, he pulls to
>   his claws
> And gallows, up the rays of his eyes the small birds
>   of the bay
> And the shrill child's play
> Wars
> Of the sparrows and such who swansing, dusk, in
>   wrangling hedges . . .

This can be easily understood, but it lacks the excitement of creation that we feel in the early poems; it is reporting the world rather than creating a world of its own. In the later poetry when there is some complexity it appears to have been put in; the difficulty is only skin deep, a matter of style, and if this is stripped away the underlying ideas are trite. But in the early poems it is impossible to separate the surface from the thought: sound, image, and idea are fused together in one solid mass.

In a sense, the rest of Thomas's life was an anticlimax. And he was aware of it—feeling that the best was past contributed to his drinking and self-destructive behavior.

In July 1937 Dylan Thomas married Caitlin Macnamara in a registry office in Penzance, "with no money, no prospect of money, no attendant friends or relatives, and," Thomas said, "in complete happiness." He thought that she looked like the princess on the top of a Christmas tree, or Wendy in *Peter Pan*—but, he cautioned Vernon Watkins, "for God's sake, don't tell her that." The caution was necessary because Caitlin was not sentimental—anything but.

She came of a Protestant Irish family in County Clare, people of property with a mansion that looked down on the surrounding countryside. Her father, Francis, was a great talker who expected that one day he would come into a fortune or write a great book. Shortly after the birth of Caitlin, his third daughter and fourth child, he went away with a married woman and never came back.

Mrs. Macnamara moved from place to place with the children. She had very little money but maintained the standards of a gentlewoman, holding that it was vulgar to pay bills or to worry about paying them at all. Caitlin grew up doing much as she pleased. She had good looks, her father's blue eyes and curly, golden hair, and she is said to have been witty.

She had a passion for dancing and when she was seventeen or eighteen worked as a chorus girl at the Palladium. A talent scout offered her a job in Paris, but her mother would not let her take it. Then she took up "eurhythmic" dancing and, together with an older woman, gave performances in Dublin and Paris, "striking dramatic poses to Bach and Mozart." At one of these performances T. S. Eliot was seen in the audience, looking at his shoes. No wonder, his wife had had a passion for dancing before she became a mental case.

Caitlin sat for the painter Augustus John and went to bed with him, but not, she says, with any enthusiasm: "It was merely a question of a brief dutiful performance for him to keep up his reputation as a Casanova ogre." She may have met Dylan in the Spring of 1936 in a London pub. One account has John introducing her to Dylan. We do know that in July she went with John to the home of the novelist Richard Hughes in Laugharne. Thomas arrived with

Fred Janes. They all drove over to Pembrokeshire to see an exhibition of paintings; on the way back there was a scene—John punched Dylan and drove off with Caitlin. "Painter and poet," Ferris remarks, "had fought for her." This was probably the beginning of Dylan and Caitlin's affair.

From the letters he wrote it appears that Dylan was very much in love with her. As he saw it, they were two innocents—"our discreditable secret is that we don't know anything at all, and our horrid *inner* secret is that we don't care that we don't."

So they were married, and began that life together which has become legendary. They would fight and make up. In the view of John Malcolm Brinnin "their marriage was essentially a state of rivalry." The quarreling was worse after Dylan began his American tours. Caitlin thought that the adulation turned his head.

In the book she wrote after her husband's death she has many acerb things to say. She describes Dylan's father as a small-minded man obsessed with keeping up appearances, and she accuses Dylan of being as puritanical as his Welsh forebears. In spite of his own outrageous behavior he expected her to be turned out prim and proper, "black from head to foot, relieved with a touch of white, as a concession." He had other shortcomings: "He read interminable Dickens novels, to which he was loyally devoted . . . he categorically refused to look at Proust, Jane Austen, Tolstoy, Dostoyevski, and a lot of the obvious classics."

There is no doubt that she had a great deal to put up with. In her book she says that children kill the "holy fire" of marriage—and they had three. While her husband was off meeting editors and doing the rounds of the pubs, she was banging pots and pans or changing nappies. The tasks of parenthood can be hard under the best of circumstances, and their circumstances, always short of cash, were not the best—though, as Brinnin points out, Dylan made enough money for them to have lived comfortably, if they had not been wildly extravagant. It comes down, then, to the people in the case: neither Dylan nor Caitlin Thomas was temperamentally suited for domesticity.

He labored like a man bailing water with a sieve—and the sea kept rushing in. "I must have some money, and have it immediately," he wrote to James Laughlin in America, editor of New Directions. "I am forced to do away with dignity and formality. . . . Can you, at once, give me money for which, in return, I promise you all the work I have done and will do?"

His wish was to sit at his table in Laugharne covering sheets of paper with lines of poetry. Yet for weeks, sometimes months on end, he couldn't find the time to write poetry at all, but had to write prose instead. For prose has a market, poetry none.

When war threatened—"What are you doing for your country?" he wrote Henry Treece. "I'm letting mine rot." He had the feelings of a liberal who had grown up in the shadow of the Great War. He knew the poems of Wilfred Owen and the preface to the poems: "This book is not about heroes . . . My subject is War, and the pity of War. The Poetry is in the pity." Owen's poems and his death spoke to a generation of younger brothers: they could imagine the horrors of trench warfare. Moreover, they were wise, they knew that all wars were a swindle brought about by a conspiracy of the rich.

When England declared war on Germany, Dylan busied himself collecting "statements of objection to War" from young writers. He was not banging a drum, he said, for a Right, "right, left or wrong." He was opposed to the evil of war, "the evil of which is the war itself and not the things it is supposed, wrongly, to be attempting to exterminate." He appears to have thought that the worst possible fate would be to kill or to be killed.

He found his antiwar views supported by the pacifism of the Left. Since Nazi Germany and Communist Russia had come to terms, dividing Poland between them, the Communists in Britain had taken the line that it was a "phoney war." "You are right," Dylan told Henry Treece, "when you suggest that I think a squirrel stumbling at least of equal importance as Hitler's invasions."

He went to the Ministry of Information—along with the half-poets, boiled newspapermen, dismissed advertisers, and other Grub Street scroungers. A job with the Ministry might keep him out of the war; he was determined to stay out, and he foresaw being hauled as an objector before a military tribunal and assigned to stretcher-bearing or jail or potato peeling or the Boys' Fire League. Whereas all he wanted was the time to write poems. He humbled himself and wrote to Sir Edward Marsh who, a war ago, had been a friend of Rupert Brooke, and had put out the anthologies of Georgian Poets. Thomas addressed Sir Edward in his best groveling

manner: "I am writing to you, a patron of letters, to ask for any help
that you may be able to give me. You may have read some of my
work, or heard it spoken of. If not, I can refer you to Miss Edith
Sitwell and Mr. T. S. Eliot, who will tell you that I am a poet of some
worth and deserving help. I have a wife and child and am without
private means. . . ." Sir Edward sent him a small sum of money, ten
or twenty pounds.

Dylan did not have to be tried as a conscientious objector—the
doctors found him asthmatic and unfit for military service. He and
Caitlin went on living in Laugharne on some money that had been
raised through the magazine *Horizon* on their behalf. When this
came to an end they went to stay with a friend in Gloucestershire. In
the autumn of 1940 he went to London and found work with a film
documentary company, and then he began doing programs on the
BBC. He would travel between jobs in London and his family in
Wales. A second son, Aeron, was born in 1943.

After the war he conceived the idea of emigrating to the United
States. His books were being published there by James Laughlin at
New Directions, and he had other friends. An American poet and
anthologist, Oscar Williams, was most eager to be of service; he sent
Dylan a copy of his poems and a few of his anthologies, "all of
them," Dylan remarked, "so heavy and in large lovely type, so dear,
and with such lovely ladies and gentlemen to be seen out at the back:
all portentously smoking (the pipes of bedpan), prinking, profiling,
horizon-eyeing, open-collared and wild-haired in the photogra-
pher's wind, facing America and posterity and the music. . . ." How
Dylan could run on, especially in prose and especially when he was
biting a hand that had fed or was about to feed him! A nip such as
might be delivered by a large, playful dog. It left you eyeing your
hand, nevertheless.

He would salve the wound, however, on this occasion by praising
Oscar's poems. He told him that they were pieces that flew "hot and
violent and exuberantly unhappy, off a poem in the making." He
told him, "The rules, the form, spring up urgently as the temper of
making needs them." He avoided saying anything in particular, and
the recipient, bathed in the flood of this gab, may have felt that he
was a great poet after all.

Then Dylan got down to business: "I have been trying to find out what legal etc. complications I will have to go through before leaving this country for America." He asked Oscar what his first step should be. If he got the forms from the American Embassy that had to be filled out by a prospective employer in the States, could Oscar "do anything about them?" Meaning, in plain Welsh, could Oscar get him a job? Could he approach *Time* "and get some definite promise, however small, from them?"

Dylan had the artist-and-actor's gift of being able to get people to put aside their own petty concerns and devote themselves to his. This requires an unswerving conviction that one's needs are more urgent than anyone else's, one's work more important. In such cases it helps a great deal if the artist-actor has charm. Dylan had it in abundance—very few could resist his gift of the gab.

Some did, however. In 1956 when Robert Conquest put together an anthology, *New Lines,* he said that a "sort of corruption" had affected the general attitude to poetry, "the debilitating theory that poetry *must* be metaphorical." Obviously the chief offender was Dylan Thomas. Among the contributors, and presumably in agreement, were Elizabeth Jennings, John Holloway, Philip Larkin, Kingsley Amis, John Wain, and Conquest himself, sober, rational workmen all.

Amis appears to have had an extraordinary dislike of Thomas. He wrote an insulting "epitaph" for him.

> They call you "drunk with words"; but when we drink
> And fetch it up, we sluice it down the sink.
> You should have stuck to spewing beer, not ink.

In his novel, *That Uncertain Feeling,* he would portray Thomas as a drunkard, a lecher, and a professional Welshman.

It took more than a quarrel over metaphor to produce so much aversion. Kingsley Amis and other postwar English writers were called the Angry Young Men, but they were not angry about the social order, only their place in it. With hard work and a sense of the fitness of things, in time they were sure to arrive. English writers, even poets, were learning to be modest, to write with irony about their marriages and their jobs. It was as though Shakespeare and Milton, Blake and Shelley and Lawrence, had never existed—in any case they were not applicable to postwar Britain. Life was drab and austere, and English writers were withdrawing from Modernism, the kinds of experimental writing that had been imported into Britain in the early decades of the century. The opinion was heard, among novelists and poets, that the whole Modernist enterprise had been a mistake, un-English. Once more Englishmen were putting on their bicycle clips. Truth was to be found in small things and mean streets.

Some people regarded Thomas as a charlatan, and John Wain spoke for others who conceded that he was a poet but were not sure how much. "It is perfectly possible," said Wain, "to furnish even his wildest pieces with a 'meaning' (*i.e.* a paraphrasable content or set of alternative paraphrasable contents), but the gnawing doubt remains as to whether the writer really *cared* whether it meant anything precise or not."

As he approached middle age, Thomas himself was unsure of his meaning. Most of his hard thinking about poetry had been done before he was twenty; then he had produced a stock of images and a distinctive voice. Since that time he had been practicing his craft assiduously and publishing books, but he had not developed intellectually—he still hoped that words, and the passion with which they were uttered, would make a poem. The obscurities that Wain speaks of must have appeared obscure to him too, and no doubt he frequently asked himself if there were really anything there, or only a noise. Poets are very liable to doubt, especially in the modern world where few people care about poetry; all poets have is their own feelings to go on, and suppose these are merely personal, with no support in an objective reality? The poet may attempt to create some sort of reality outside his feelings by writing about ideas, as Pound did in his *Cantos;* or he may choose a material object, as Hart Crane did in *The Bridge,* in the hope that by sheer ingenuity he will elevate it into a myth. But the ideas may be rejected by others, or they may seem inadequate, the object carefully constructed may collapse. It may have no significance really, and then he will think that all his work is rubbish, as Pound did at the end of his life, or he may kill himself, like Crane. Feeling is the only reality poets have, but as they usually live, the world being what it is, outside a community, they have no way to be sure of the value of their feelings or to sustain them over a long period.

As Brinnin remarks, Thomas suspected that his creative powers were failing. He could no longer be the "roaring boy, the daemonic poet"; on the other hand he would never be able to undergo intellectual and moral discipline. "It was my sense," says Brinnin, "that the term of the roaring boy was over, and that the means by which Dylan might continue to grow were no longer in his possession. I was convinced that Dylan knew this and, whether or not he comprehended the meaning of his actions, that the violence of his life was a way of forgetting or avoiding the self-judgment that spelled his doom."

At the point where Crane jumped overboard, Thomas traveled to the States. Brinnin, then director of the Poetry Center in New York, made the arrangements for a poetry-reading tour and, with growing excitement, like a boy about to be let out of school, Dylan interested himself in the business. He would like very much to go to California. He would prefer to fly, "not liking the big dull sea to look at." He presumed that the five hundred dollars to be paid by the Poetry Center included his traveling expenses—hoping, of course, that it didn't. He had ideas about poetry readings: he hoped he would not have to read only his own poems—"An hour of me aloud is hell, & produces large burning spots in front of the mind. "—but he would like to mix in poems by some British contemporaries.

Caitlin would not be coming with him. Their third child, Colm, had been born in the summer of 1949 and she had not been well since. New York in February would not be suitable—he was thinking of her going to Italy instead for three months. Money, as usual, was the difficulty. "I'm having a tough time here at the moment," he wrote James Laughlin. "I want to write only poems, but that can't be. Never have I wanted to more. But debts are battering at me. I cannot sleep for them." He wanted to know if Laughlin would advance money on half a novel he had written—"Well, nearly half."

He arrived at Idlewild Airport on February 21, 1950, and was met by Brinnin, who drove him through Queens in the direction of Manhattan. Thomas stared out at the dismal streets with their junkyards and lots full of weeds and debris. "I *knew* America would be just like this," he said.

He was installed at the Beekman Tower Hotel. Then Brinnin showed him Third Avenue, and he took to it immediately. In the

following days he spent much of his time in the bars of Third
Avenue and Greenwich Village. People sought him out and he held
court behind a table, filling himself with beer. He was not a prepos-
sessing sight: "His hair a matted aureole, his crooked teeth brown
with tobacco stains, his paunchy flesh bunched into fuzzy tweeds, he
was not even a memory of the seraphic young artist Augustus John
had painted some fifteen years before." Among those who de-
scended upon him was a woman who had not seen him for ten years.
"Oh, Dylan," she said, "the last time I saw you you were an *angel.*"
Brinnin remarks that Dylan winced—he would be wincing often in
the days to come.

He enjoyed himself, however, being interviewed and asked his
opinions of this and that. And he conducted imaginary interviews.
"Mr. Thomas, why have you come to America?" "To continue my
lifelong search for naked women in wet mackintoshes."

He was extremely nervous before his performances at the Poetry
Center. But they went splendidly. As much could not be said for his
behavior at parties. Brinnin had been forewarned: a few weeks
before, he had met Auden on the subway, and Auden said that he
doubted it was wise to invite Thomas to the United States "in view of
his London reputation for roaring behavior." Brinnin soon had an
opportunity to see for himself. He took Dylan to a literary gather-
ing in New York. The very best people were there.

"We went up into a room buzzing with writers and editors, some
of whom were old friends of mine. Wystan Auden was there, James
Agee, Louis Kronenberger and the Trillings, Lionel and Diana, and
James and Tania Stern and Charles Rolo, Katherine Anne Porter
and many others. As Dylan, by a loud and awkward entrance,
seemed to demand considerably more attention than the party was
disposed to grant him, becoming again the very figure of the wine-
soaked poet, I looked at Auden and winced inwardly. I could not
help feeling that his eyes showed more than a hint of accusation,
that before the evening was out he would somehow say, 'I told you
so.' "

At the end of the party Dylan lifted Katherine Anne Porter up to
the ceiling and held her there. She was a lady, says Brinnin, and did
not seem distressed, but other of the guests were "half amused, half
appalled."

Auden's dislike of Thomas had complex roots. Auden was an Englishman of the professional middle class, Anglican in religion, educated at public schools and Oxford or Cambridge. Thomas's people were Welsh dissenters, and anyone who does not know the suspicion with which most Englishmen regard the Welsh, Scots, and Irish, knows little of England. Celts are dreamers—they even believe in magic. They are music hall turns, entertaining there perhaps, but nowhere else. Moreover, not only was Thomas a Welshman, he came of a lower class—his father had raised himself by his bootstraps. Finally he was in bad taste: he cadged money, he drank too much, his behavior was a disgrace.

When it came to poetry, Auden and Thomas stood at opposite poles. Auden was rational, Thomas "demonic." "Insofar as poetry," said Auden, "can be said to have an ulterior purpose, it is, by telling the truth, to disenchant and disintoxicate." Thomas's whole purpose, on the other hand, was to enchant. Auden wrote with irony and in many voices—Thomas had a distinctive voice; he seemed to be standing personally behind every line he uttered. "He can create worlds," said a critic, "but he creates worlds in his own image, and remains the centre of his own thought and feeling."

Auden was a reasoner, harking back to a time when poets explained their ideas—a theory of psychology, their belief in Marxism or Existentialism. Thomas was a poet of "the most exalted emotions, the most exalted grief or joy." At times he spoke like a prophet, another Blake:

> Hear the voice of the Bard!
> Who present, past, and future, sees;
> Whose ears have heard
> The Holy Word
> That walk'd among the ancient trees.

Thomas looked forward to a new generation of poets who would express their emotions and adopt a prophetic stance. It was the voice of Dylan, speaking with an authority that was entirely personal, that woke the sleeping poets of America. Before Dylan, poetry readings had been tame, academic gatherings—one has only to listen to a recording by Auden or Elizabeth Bishop to get the

tone—dry, impersonal discourse. Dylan's readings changed all
that: he showed that a poetry reading could be a highly dramatic
performance. For better or worse he brought back personality, and
the audience loved it. Offstage he was gregarious, a hard drinker,
and a bedder of women—at least he gave that impression. He
appeared to be enjoying life passionately and on a large scale.

Kenneth Rexroth testifies to the transformation wrought in San
Francisco by Thomas's public readings. Ginsberg, however, dis-
claims the influence—"I like 'Fern Hill,'" said Ginsberg, speaking
to students at Berkeley in the sixties, "it's something like 'Intima-
tions of Immortality'—but on the whole I don't really dig Thomas.
He's too romantic. With his kind of gift, the way to groove was to
begin with bricks and build a starry tower, but Thomas *began* in a
starry tower." Ginsberg went on to speculate about the psychology
of Thomas and Hart Crane. They had tried to recreate the uncon-
scious through rational, conscious means, "so maybe they had to
drink to get at it. They didn't follow what Stein said—that like the
mind is goofy enough itself if you only listen to it." He said that
Thomas and Crane were too influenced by people like Keats and
Yeats and Bridges—whereat, says Ginsberg's biographer, his audi-
ence groaned. Ginsberg said that he himself, in contrast to Thomas,
had been influenced by Stein, Pound, Whitman, and Williams.

Ginsberg had a point: Thomas's obscure writings were very dif-
ferent from the direct expression of thought that would be the
Beats' stock in trade. Thomas began as a young man by imitating
the Imagist poets, and he still wrote in images, making his thoughts
as concrete as possible:

> Especially when the October wind
> With frosty fingers punishes my hair,
> Caught by the crabbing sun I walk on fire
> And cast a shadow crab upon the land . . .

The Beats, on the other hand, would express their thoughts in plain
words. They had no time for imagining—they were in a hurry to
live, and writing was merely one means to this end. For the Beat
poets, words were not realities as they were for Thomas, they were
an extension of life.

316 • LIVES AND WORKS

His influence, however, was considerable, and though Ginsberg would write in a different way, he found the way a great deal easier because Thomas had been before him. Thomas was the ice-breaker—he ended the Age of Auden.

The change can be seen if we look, for example, at the poems of Theodore Roethke. Roethke was always very conscious of what was in and what was out, and trimmed his sails accordingly. His early poems contain Audenesque passages.

> Though the devouring mother cry, " 'Escape me? Never—' "
> And the honeymoon be spoiled by a father's ghost,
> Chill depths of the spirit are flushed to a fever,
> The nightmare silence is spoken. We are not lost.

When Thomas appeared, Roethke forgot about Auden and learned to write like Thomas.

> And I acknowledge my foolishness with God,
> My desire for the peaks, the black ravines, the rolling
>   mists
> Changing with every twist of wind,
> The unsinging fields where no lungs breathe,
> Where light is stone.
> I return where fire has been,
> To the charred edge of the sea . . .

Thomas made a second visit to America in 1952, this time bringing Caitlin. According to John Malcolm Brinnin, she was thoroughly suspicious, and with reason: Dylan had become seriously involved with two American women on his first tour and had been quite willing to go to bed with others. Caitlin hated these women: they "hunted singly, in pairs, and more often in packs . . . they were candidly, if not prepossessingly, spreadeagled, from the first tom-tomed rumour of a famous name." She found American charm cloying, especially when it met Dylan's "professional" charm. She disliked the intelligence of Americans, who had all been to college and received such a thorough grounding in so many subjects.

Standing in the wings at the Poetry Center as Dylan was about to go on, she told him, "Just remember, they're all dirt!"

A whispered, high-pitched argument ensued, but then he was on stage, being greeted by an ovation that lasted two minutes. He read a selection of his own new poems, and poems by other British poets, including a hilarious imitation of T. S. Eliot's voice in a parody by Henry Reed.

The Thomases departed on a cross-country tour, quarreling as they went. When they returned to New York things had reached the breaking point. Dylan had neglected to pay his son Llewelyn's school fees back in England—he did not get around to mailing the check, so that Llewelyn had been dismissed from school. When Caitlin was informed of this she announced that she was leaving America and leaving Dylan—he could make his own plans for the future. Dylan went out to a bar with Brinnin. "Nothing," Brinnin says, "would help Dylan now, neither liquor nor my words of comfort that attempted to convince him that Caitlin was but justifiably upset, and that I at least did not take seriously her threat of leaving him. 'She knows just how to hurt me most,' was all he said."

This passed, however. Caitlin did not leave, Llewelyn was readmitted to school, and "the air was cleared and the way opened for the next still nameless but inevitable crisis."

Thomas made a third trip to America between April and July of 1953. When in New York he would frequent the White Horse Tavern on Hudson Street. Business there doubled, the customers standing two deep to catch a glimpse of him.

A winter sun gleamed outside and the oil stove shone. On the facing wall hung his own drawing of the Two Brothers of Death, one a Christ that looked syphilitic, the other Moses with a green beard. Their skins were the color of figs, their feet were set on a ladder of moons. He could hear the hot water hissing in the pipes, but his hands were frozen.

He used to sit for hours covering sheets of paper with lines, crossing out words, rocking his head for a better word, smoking the while, filling the room with a reek of tobacco. In those days the only relief he had had was acting—the part of a madman or one of the nasty "modern" young men, or low comedy. He had been a roaring boy, a foursquare stander-up for life, taking no guff from the arty types, the amateur hobos and homos of Bloomsbury.

Over a pint he had been willing and able to give anyone the hard facts of Communism and a reasoned program for Revolution.

He caught the eye of the stewardess as she came down the aisle, a pretty woman with ash-blonde hair and marble-bright eyes. "Another, if you please," holding up his glass. "Sir, there is a limit of two to a customer," she said. "Ah, but I'm Welsh," he answered, quick as a flash. "Your rule doesn't apply to us." He gave her his cupid smile. "Well," she said, "I'll see what I can do."

So that when he arrived at the airport he was walking six inches above the tarmac, and bubbly when the welcoming committee met him at the gate: two young men who looked like overgrown puppies, and herself, the rich woman who gathers visiting artists to her talcumed breast and hurries them into a limousine, and through the outskirts of the city, the crowd of dead souls going home at twilight from their dreary jobs, up a driveway to her mullion-windowed house, Tudor.

You enter, preceded by the puppy-men, one carrying your bag, the other your coat, a big room where people sit in chairs and sofas pretending not to have been kept waiting. How well you know them: the rich woman's husband, smirking and offering the hand that decides men's fate down at the office, but here lies dead as wax. And Grandmother, blue hair and white cheeks, a hectic spot the size of a sixpence in each. And, may Heaven preserve a poet, their daughter who has come all the way home from Wellesley College in the East, just for the occasion. "We have just been studying your *Portrait of the Artist as a Young Dog,*" she whimpers, shoving her tits in your face. She has auburn hair and legs made for long hours afield and abed. This is temptation, and a man needs a drink or two to deal with it.

And a drink or two at dinner, the faces now growing steamy above the white cloth and shining crystal. They are cracking the claws of lobsters and lifting salad on forks. They are slicing thick, black-crusted steaks and stuffing their mouths with floury baked potatoes. The wine glasses are filled again and again.

At some point in the evening's proceedings he found himself telling the story about Oscar Wilde and the jockey. This was after someone asked if he had ever met Mr. Warwick Deeping the novelist, and he realized that authors were all alike to them, the living and the dead. That there was no difference between a Deeping and a

Dickens, a Thomas and a Tambimuttu. So then he told the story about Wilde and the jockey—to make a definite impression.

An hour later he was in a hall big enough to house a dirigible and he played the part, stumbling over chairs on his way to the platform. He sat slumped forward during the introduction, trying not to slide off sideways like a ton of coal. The introduction was delivered by one of the professors at the university—which university, for Christ's sake? Minnesota? Michigan? He had lost track. The professor made some references to the bardic schools of Wales and Ireland. But at last he had finished.

Whereupon drunken Thomas, rude Thomas, Thomas the unspeakable, rose straight up and advanced to the lectern and, seizing it with both hands, spoke to the people gathered there in a voice that sounded like deep music, a voice from the beginning of creation, when hills and valleys were new and the beasts came forth to be named.

He said that he would first read a handful of poems by other men, beginning with a quiet poem by Thomas Hardy of which he was fond, perhaps because it was not like his own. He read the poem, "Lizbie Brown," and indeed it was very quiet and still in the room—when he finished you could have heard a pin drop. He read a poem by Yeats and one by Ransom. Then he began to read his own poetry, his voice booming out, a sound to melt the marrow in men's bones, and women's too.

> Do not go gentle into that good night,
> Old age should burn and rave at close of day;
> Rage, rage against the dying of the light. . . .

He then read aloud the poem "Fern Hill," about his childhood:

> . . . honoured among wagons I was prince of the apple towns
> And once below a time I lordly had the trees and leaves
>   Trail with daisies and barley
> Down the rivers of the windfall light . . . .

There was a poem, he said, about the life and death of one particular human being he had known—and not about the very many lives and deaths whether seen, as in his first poems, in the "tumultuous world of his own being," or, in his later poems, in war, grief, and the "great holes and corners of universal love." The ending of the poem was strange—perhaps all original images in poetry are strange, and it still appears so now that I have the book in front of me. It speaks of something I have seen for myself, the concentration of feeling that certain lives collect about them.

> . . . this monumental
> Argument of the hewn voice, gesture and palm,
> Storm me forever over her grave until
> The stuffed lung of the fox twitch and cry Love
> And the strutting fern lay seeds on the black sill.

Within three years of his coming to America, Thomas would be dead. He killed himself with drink. At the end he had *delirium tremens,* and the doctors spoke of "insult to the brain." The curious phrase was repeated—it stuck in people's minds.

While he lasted he put on a terrific show. The writing of verse had been becoming an exercise in reason—he reminded people of what they had forgotten: that poetry can be passionate speech, and that this proceeds from the life of an individual.

Honoring Whitman

He most honors my style who learns under it how to destroy the teacher.
"Song of Myself"

I began reading Whitman seriously around 1959. I had read him before that out of curiosity, but in 1959 I was changing from writing in regular meters and forms to writing in irregular meters and forms, and Whitman was one of the poets I read to see how they did it.

I liked the pictures in Whitman's poems: cavalry crossing a ford, a tree standing by itself. I liked his idea of a "Muse install'd amid the kitchenware," i.e., making poetry out of common things. This seemed useful in view of the part played by machinery in our lives a hundred years later.

On the other hand, his whooping it up over the chest-expansion of the United States didn't do a thing for me. His wish for young men to throw their arms about his neck struck me as incomprehensible. I was put off by his use of big-sounding words or French words. He was capable of writing long passages naming countries he'd read about or heard about, the names of mountains and rivers, the races of men, et cetera.

> I see the Brazilian vaquero,
> I see the Bolivian ascending mount Sorata. . . .

This essay first appeared in *Walt Whitman: The Measure of His Song,* ed. by Jim Perlman, Ed Folsom, and Dan Campion. Minneapolis: Holy Cow! Press, 1981. Reprinted in *The Character of the Poet.* Ann Arbor: The University of Michigan Press, 1986.

I don't see how anyone could ever have read these passages in Whitman with pleasure.

At times, however, he was capable of a surprising compression of thought and style—he was almost epigrammatic: "The nearest gnat is an explanation," "Trippers and askers surround me."

On the whole I found Whitman exhilarating. His freedom of line and style, and his interest in pots and pans, bringing them over into poetry, were what I needed at the time.

So far I haven't mentioned Whitman's "philosophy." It consists of two or three ideas. One, it is possible to merge in your feelings with others, and it is possible for others to merge in their feelings with you. Two, if this occurs over a distance, or over a span of time, it seems to annihilate space and time. This is a kind of immortality. Three, in order to convey your feelings to others you must, by a process of empathic observation, using all your senses, take things into yourself and express them again. The senses are "dumb ministers" of feeling . . . through them we know one another. The poet is the manager of this process—he puts what we feel and see into words.

These ideas, which can be found in "There Was a Child Went Forth" and "Crossing Brooklyn Ferry," are the substratum of Whitman's thinking. This is quite enough for a poet to go on. Poets don't have to be philosophers on the scale of Kant—they need only have ideas that enable them to make sense out of their experience and make it seem worthwhile to go on writing. They don't need to be original—the first ambition of those who are profoundly unoriginal. It isn't so hard to be original—it's a sight harder to say something true and useful.

It may appear that I've overlooked Whitman's mystical, visionary side. I haven't overlooked it, but Whitman doesn't strike me as mystical or visionary—he is a naturalist first and last. He wills to see things—even "The Sleeper" is laid out and proceeds according to plan. His most ecstatic passages are descriptions of sexual intercourse or frottation.

> I mind how once we lay such a transparent summer
>   morning,
> How you settled your head athwart my hips and gently
>   turn'd over upon me . . . .

These lines are addressed to his soul, but can there be any doubt as to what is actually happening? Sex may be the link with a mystery, but at least let us see that it is sex and not rush to find an alternative explanation. There is the kind of reader who, having no knowledge of religion, is always looking in books for the secret of the universe. For such a one, Whitman will be mystic, together with Kahlil Gibran and the authors of pamphlets on astrology.

Insofar as Whitman enthuses over "a great round wonder rolling in space" he is a rudimentary poet, the eternal sophomore enthusing over "the great ideas" and neglecting his physics lesson and his French. Insofar as Whitman talks about the universe he is not worth the attention of a grown person.

On the other hand, when he looks at what he sees, he is certainly a great American poet (though he cannot stand comparison with Dante, Chaucer, or a dozen others). These are the passages to look for:

> The little one sleeps in its cradle,
> I lift the gauze and look a long time, and silently brush away
>   flies with my hand.

> The youngster and the red-faced girl turn aside up the
>   bushy hill,
> I peeringly view them from the top . . . .
>
> "Song of Myself"

> Through the ample open door of the peaceful country barn,
> A sunlit pasture field with cattle and horses feeding,
> And haze and vista, and the far horizon fading away.
>
> "A Farm Picture"

I don't want to suggest that Whitman is only a picture-artist. "When Lilacs Last in the Dooryard Bloom'd" and "Out of the Cradle Endlessly Rocking" hold our attention through rhythm and sound as well as imagery. But as rhythm and sound are operating just as audibly in his empty, monotonous, forgettable poems, I do not think that Whitman's impressiveness depends on rhythm and sound. It is what he describes that makes him a poet. Rhythm and sound are only an aid to this.

Critics who wish to pore over a phrase in Whitman, or the structure of a line, and show how perfectly suited it is to his purpose, should choose a banality and show why the meter and phrasing are perfect. This is the trouble with criticism that concentrates on technique—it is an *arrière-pensée*. We know that the poetry is fine, and set about finding reasons why the meter and the syntax had to be just so. But these things in themselves do not make fine poetry. If nothing worthwhile is being said, meter, syntax and the rest of the prosodist's and the grammarian's bag of tricks are so much useless baggage.

There are ranges of poetry that lie beyond Whitman. Of situations such as occur in people's lives he appears to have known very little, and these are our main concern. He is good at describing shipwrecks, which are infrequent, but does not show affections, attachments, anxieties, shades of feeling, passions . . . the life we actually have. The human appears in his poems as a crowd or as a solitary figure . . . himself, looking at others.

In recent years there has been talk by American poets of developing new kinds of consciousness which would, presumably, enable us to advance beyond the merely human. But it is self-evident that if we are to continue to exist it will be as human beings, not some other species. Our poets are trying to be like stones . . . another way of saying that they would rather be dead. Paul Breslin made the point clearly in an article ("How to Read the New Contemporary Poem," *The American Scholar*, Summer 1978) but the thought had occurred to me independently. According to Breslin, our poets of darkness and stones are trying to escape the consequences of being human. They are trying to cast out the ego and live in a Jungian universe of archetypes.

Readers of this kind will find Whitman reassuring—he never becomes involved. "I am the man," he states, "I suffer'd, I was there." The passage may be so well known because it is so refreshing, in the wasteland of his usual detachment. He is a stroller, an onlooker, a gazer, and has nothing to say about what goes on in the houses he is passing, or behind office or factory windows, or in the life of the man turning a plough. He does not seem to know what people say to each other—especially what men say to women, or women to men. Reading Whitman's poetry one would think that the human race is dumb—and indeed, as he tells us, he would rather turn and live with animals.

His poetry is about a spectacle . . . a crowd on the ferry, "the fine centrifugal spokes of light round the shape of my head in the sunlit water." But the actualities of human society are a closed book to him. It isn't the "proud libraries" that are closed to him—indeed, at times we could wish they were. What is closed is the life of the individual, and the lives of two, and three.

Whitman has plenty to say about man *"En-Masse."* His optimism about the common man reflects the optimism of the bankers and railroad builders in the Gilded Age. Man *"En-Masse"* provided them with labor and then with a mass market. But optimism about the masses seems out of place in our century. The masses elect mass murderers—if we survive it will not be due to the good nature of the common man. Whitman's view of mankind is of no use at all—it doesn't help when it comes to understanding one another and building a community.

As he has so little to say about actual circumstances, Whitman is not among the very great, realized poets. There is hardly any drama or narration in his poetry—ideas aren't realized in action. We rise from reading Whitman with the feeling that he has talked about life rather than created it.

Building on his achievement we may hope to do much better, as he himself, in one of his generous moods, said that we would.

Disorder and Escape in the Fiction of V. S. Naipaul

To be born on an island like Isabella . . . was to be born to disorder.
The Mimic Men

The greater part of the fiction of V. S. Naipaul is set in the newly independent states of Africa and the Caribbean, and the view is pessimistic: the natives have taken the government into their own hands but are unable to establish order. As Robert Boyers has observed, "Naipaul is our primary novelist of disorder and breakdown."[1]

But though the novels offer controversial views of life in the new states this is not why they are compelling. In art it is the mind of the artist that makes the difference, his own interest in the work he is creating. Boyers remarks that Naipaul "seems more interested in a spiritual or psychological state than in the machinery of action," and I would add that the spiritual or psychological state he is most interested in is his own.

As a child Vidyadha Naipaul grew up in a big house in Chaguanas, a community of East Indians whose forebears had immigrated to Trinidad as indentured laborers. They perpetuated Indian rituals and marriage customs, and had little contact with the

[1] Robert Boyers, "V. S. Naipaul." *The American Scholar,* Summer 1981: 118, 366.

Reprinted from *The Character of the Poet.* Ann Arbor: The University of Michigan Press, 1986. This essay first appeared in *The Hudson Review* 37, No. 4. Winter 1984–85.

world outside—with the Negroes, for example. But Vidyadha's father, Seepersad Naipaul, was different—he was a writer of newspaper articles. And he was exceedingly troubled—he did not get along with his wife's family. His son tells us that these in-laws were a "totalitarian organization. Decisions—about politics, about religious matters, and, most important, about other families—were taken to a closed circle at the top—my grandmother and her two eldest sons-in-law."[2]

The recurring theme of Naipaul's fiction, the need to escape from a "totalitarian" environment, was the obsession of his father, and of course Naipaul has shown it to be so in *A House for Mr. Biswas*. For house read a separate life.

Seepersad Naipaul challenged Hindu beliefs and superstitions. He informed his readers that native farmers were practicing rites of Kali in order to cure their diseased cattle. Thereupon he received an anonymous letter in Hindi warning him that he would develop poisoning, "die on Sunday and be buried on Monday," unless he offered the sacrifice of a goat to Kali. He made the sacrifice. This, his son observes, was a great humiliation. "It had occurred just when my father was winning through to a kind of independence."

When Vidyadha was six his father moved his family into Port of Spain. This was "in the nature of a migration from the Hindu and Indian countryside to the white-Negro-mulatto town." The child was delighted with the sights and sounds and characters—men like Bogart, who had shaken off Hindu family conventions and taken a new name from the movies.

But Seepersad Naipaul's bid for independence was aborted. His mother-in-law bought a cocoa estate in the hills to the northwest of Port of Spain, and "it was decided—by the people in the family who decided on such matters—that the whole family . . . should move there." So the freedoms of the town were suspended and made way again for family quarrels.

After two years of this Seepersad Naipaul moved his family back to Port of Spain where he managed to have a job with the government. But they were living crowded into rooms and the street was changing. There was an American military base at the end of the

[2] V. S. Naipaul, "Prologue to an Autobiography." *Vanity Fair* 46, No. 2. April 1983.

street—one of the houses or yards had become a brothel. "Disorder within," says the novelist, "disorder without. Only my school life was ordered; anything that had happened there I could date at once. But my family life—my life at home or my life in the house, in the street—was jumbled, without sequence."

There must have been much in the street to appall him. He had been brought up by people who were scrupulously clean and who disapproved strongly of sexual relations with non-Hindus. The characters in Naipaul's fiction echo these attitudes. In *The Mimic Men* Singh tells how as a boy he used a girl's toothbrush by mistake—"I felt," he says, "dreadfully unclean." In *An Area of Darkness* Naipaul remembers that once in a science class he would not suck on a length of tube that had been touched by other mouths, and another Indian boy in the class remarked approvingly, "Real brahmin." As for habits that are obviously unsanitary, such as defecating in the streets, Naipaul's revulsion is memorable. Everything else he has to say about life in India pales in comparison with the strength of his feelings on this subject.

One can imagine the mingled fear and fascination of the young Hindu when confronted with the sexual disorder of Port of Spain, the "brothel ground" at the end of the street.

"Only my school life was ordered." The school was Queen's Royal College, which appears in *The Mimic Men* as Isabella Imperial. The headmaster was an Englishman; the curriculum would have been that of a public school in England. Discipline would have been firm, with "lines" for lesser derelictions and caning for more serious offenses.

A colonial education such as this offered a good deal of security. In Naipaul's *Guerillas* the writer Roche says that he is not usually afraid, and attributes this to his having been educated at a British school. "It's the way I am. It probably has to do with the school I went to. I suppose if you accept authority and believe in the rules, you aren't afraid of any particular individual."

Queen's Royal College offered Naipaul a refuge from the disorder at home and in the streets. And his education taught him the value of order. If he was like other young men and women who were educated in the colonies, he came to think that the Mother Country was the pattern of a good society. And it would follow that other

places were inferior. The more he studied English history and litera-
ture, the more he would feel that the culture of the Caribbean—if it
could be called a culture at all—was inferior. Such was the inevitable
result of an education in a British colony. England was the real
world to which colonials might aspire, but they could never hope to
be included. The history of the West Indies was not real history, the
English they spoke was not as correct as that spoken in England.
The grass was greener in Sussex and the birds sang more sweetly.

Naipaul traveled to England on a government scholarship and
studied at Oxford. The descriptions of the immigrant's life in *The
Mimic Men* shows how disillusioning that life could be. Nothing
would have prepared the West Indian for the English climate or the
dreariness of living in a boarding house. Confronted with greasy
wallpaper and a gas meter into which you had to feed shillings to
keep warm, he would have had long thoughts.

Outside you were overwhelmed by the monuments and public
buildings that seemed to be saying that you had no part in the
centuries. It takes more than a public school education to make you
English—you have to have been born in England.

Some of the immigrants, in order to keep their self-respect,
withdrew from the life around them. The narrator of *A Bend in the
River* observes: "Indar had said about people like me that when we
came to a great city we closed our eyes; we were concerned only to
show that we were not amazed."

At this point Naipaul became a writer. Going to Queen's Royal
College was his first escape from disorder—writing was his second.
Ever since he was a child he had wanted to be a writer like his father,
who wrote articles for the *Trinidad Guardian* about "village feuds,
family vendettas, murders, bitter election battles." He wrote about
strange characters such as a Negro hermit who had once been rich
and pleasure-seeking but now lived alone with a dog in a hut in the
swamplands. "I read the stories as stories," Naipaul remarks—a
hint, perhaps, to those who would read his own fiction as something
else.

Naipaul's first novels, *The Mystic Masseur* and *The Suffrage of
Elvira,* are about people and events such as his father described.
The Mystic Masseur was not farfetched: there was a Camār from
Janglī Tolā—that is, an East Indian of lower caste—who "set him-

self up as a Brahman pundit." In writing about the Mystic Masseur, also, Naipaul was reenacting his own escape by way of an education. "This reading," says one of the characters in *The Mystic Masseur*, "is a great great thing."

Naipaul's *Mr. Stone and the Knights Companion,* which might have been written by J. B. Priestley—it seems like an exercise in writing a perfectly English novel in order to prove that he could do it—has one lively passage in which Mr. Stone discovers the joy of writing. This it is that gives meaning to his existence—he is never so happy again as when composing the plan for the Knights Companion. "He wrote, he corrected, he re-wrote; and fatigue never came to him." Afterwards "He felt exhausted, sad and empty."

This was how it felt to escape from life into writing. And the following sentences about Mr. Stone's writing strike me as Naipaul's own thoughts about the art he practices: "The only pure moments, the only true moments were those he had spent in the study, writing out of a feeling whose depths he realized only as he wrote." Then Naipaul observes: "What he had written was a faint and artificial rendering of that emotion, and the scheme as the Unit had practiced it was but a shadow of that shadow. All passion had disappeared. . . . All action, all creation was a betrayal of feeling and truth."

But unlike other writers without a cause, Naipaul does not make a religion of his art. Eugene Goodheart surmises that Naipaul would scorn "the Flaubertian dream of a perfect work of art, which is all form and no content."[3] I would put it another way: while Naipaul appears to find the act of writing completely satisfying, he is not attached to the results.

Naipaul has told how he hit on a subject. He had left Oxford and was working for the BBC Caribbean service in London, presenting a weekly literary program for the Caribbean. One day when he was sitting in the dimly lighted "freelances' room" his thoughts reverted to Port of Spain and he typed the sentence: "Every morning when he got up Hat would sit on the banister of his back verandah and shout across, 'What happening there, Bogart?' " The story thus

[3] Eugene Goodheart, "Naipaul and the Voices of Negation," *Salmagundi* no. 54, Fall 1981 : 56.

begun led to other stories. *Miguel Street* was written quickly. He was putting a part of his life behind him, an area of darkness.

This is what gives Naipaul's fiction its compelling power. He is always putting darkness behind him. As he has made his escape from disorder, first through his education, then through writing, in his novels and stories people struggle to escape. Sometimes they do escape and sometimes they don't. In the novel titled *In a Free State* the Africans have taken over from the white people. Bobby and Linda, who are white, are driving toward the safety of the European compound. "Somewhere up there," says Linda, "they've taken off their nice new clothes and they're dancing naked and holding hands and eating dung." Bobby and Linda meet up with a group of native soldiers who humiliate and beat the white man, but they manage to reach the compound. In *Guerillas* the woman Jane becomes involved sexually with the leader of the guerillas—that is, they call themselves guerillas, but the writer Roche calls them a gang. Jane is leaving the island, but she makes a detour to say goodbye to her lover and is murdered. Her annihilation is total—her body will never be found.

The narrator of *A Bend in the River* manages to escape from the new state, but many do not. As the steamer travels into the sunset he sees dugouts full of people who are desperately trying to tie up to the steamer. "They were in flight from the riverbanks. They jammed and jostled against the sides of the steamer and the barge, and many were swamped. Water hyacinths pushed up in the narrow space between the steamer and the barge. We went on. Darkness fell."

The plot I have described is that of a nightmare. As Nazruddin says in *A Bend in the River,* "You can always get into those places. What is hard is to get out." He makes the further observation: "That is a private fight. Everybody has to find his own way." Naipaul has found his own way—the characters in his fiction sometimes do not. In any case, we share their anxiety, the pressure to escape. We hurry to the end of a novel by Naipaul as we hurry to the end of a nightmare. Anything, even confrontation with the worst, is better than being in suspense.

We are between two worlds, the old order that has ended, the new order that has not begun. Naipaul is the novelist of the state in between—a state that is psychological as well as political. I have tried to describe the psychology because I think it more likely to last.

The characters in Naipaul's fiction may be planning for a future state, but the writer is not to be identified with his characters. He resists absorption by any place or nation. In *An Area of Darkness* Naipaul speaks of an Indian "philosophy of despair, leading to passivity, detachment, acceptance. It is only now," he remarks, "as the impatience of the observer is dissipated in the processes of writing and self-inquiry, that I see how much this philosophy had also been mine. It had enabled me through the stresses of a long residence in England, to withdraw completely from nationality and loyalties except to persons; it had made me content to be myself alone, my work, my name (the last two so different from the first); it had convinced me that every man was an island, and taught me to shield all that I knew to be good and pure within myself from the corruption of causes."

The protagonist in a novel by Naipaul is escaping but does not hope to arrive—he knows there is no great, good place. I am reminded of the writing of another novelist, Joseph Conrad. Conrad grew up in Poland under Russian occupation; his father was enlisted in the hopeless cause of revolution. G. Jean-Aubry says of Conrad in his early years, "Unconsciously he was being trained in a secret and inflexible fidelity to ideals disassociated from hope." The same might be said of Naipaul. In his writing there is a conflict between intellectual curiosity, a first-rate reporter's interest in the way people live, and a tremendous passivity, a conviction of the futility of intelligence . . . its weakness when confronted with brute force.

Like Conrad, Naipaul has chosen to live in England where people leave you alone and you need have no loyalty except to persons. In this neutral environment he is able to write novels that reenact his escape from disorder and his father's struggle to escape. The novels tell us how corrupt and violent life can be, and that it is necessary to fly from others in order to preserve all that is "good and pure" within oneself.

Flowers and weeds cling to the boat, and a thousand hands reach out to hold it back.

5

ON THE ART OF POETRY

Walt Whitman at Bear Mountain

. . . life which does not give the preference to any other life, of any previous period, which therefore prefers its own existence . . .

Ortega y Gasset

Neither on horseback nor seated,
But like himself, squarely on two feet,
The poet of death and lilacs
Loafs by the footpath. Even the bronze looks alive
Where it is folded like cloth. And he seems friendly.

"Where is the Mississippi panorama
And the girl who played the piano?
Where are you, Walt?
The Open Road goes to the used-car lot.

"Where is the nation you promised?
These houses built of wood sustain
Colossal snows,
And the light above the street is sick to death.

"As for the people—see how they neglect you!
Only a poet pauses to read the inscription."

Reprinted from *A Company of Poets*. Ann Arbor: The University of Michigan Press, 1981. This essay first appeared in *Poet's Choice*, ed. Paul Engle and Joseph Langland. New York: Dial Press, 1962.

"I am here," he answered.
"It seems you have found me out.
Yet, did I not warn you that it was Myself
I advertised? Were my words not sufficiently plain?

"I gave no prescriptions,
And those who have taken my moods for prophecies
Mistake the matter."
Then, vastly amused—"Why do you reproach me?
I freely confess I am wholly disreputable.
Yet I am happy, because you have found me out."

A crocodile in wrinkled metal loafing . . .

Then all the realtors,
Pickpockets, salesmen, and the actors performing
Official scenarios,
Turned a deaf ear, for they had contracted
American dreams.

But the man who keeps a store on a lonely road,
And the housewife who knows she's dumb,
And the earth, are relieved.

All that grave weight of America
Cancelled! Like Greece and Rome.
The future in ruins!
The castles, the prisons, the cathedrals
Unbuilding, and roses
Blossoming from the stones that are not there . . .

The clouds are lifting from the high Sierras,
The Bay mists clearing;
And the angel in the gate, the flowering plum,
Dances like Italy, imagining red.

I have chosen to be represented by "Walt Whitman at Bear Mountain"—not because I think it the best poem I have written, but because it marked a turning point in my work. I had recently published a book of poems, *A Dream of Governors,* in which I had solved to my satisfaction certain difficulties of writing "in form"— that is, in regular meter and rhyme. But now I felt that my skill was a straitjacket. Also, inevitably, the adoption of traditional forms led me into a certain way of ending a poem, polishing it off, so to speak, that sometimes distorted my real meaning. It was time, I felt, to write a new kind of poem. I wanted to write a poem that would be less "willed." I would let images speak for themselves. The poem would be a statement, of course—there really is no such thing as a poem of pure metaphor or image—but I wanted the statement to be determined by the poem itself, to let my original feeling develop, without confining it in any strict fashion.

Of course, this was a matter of degree. Even the poem that seems most free is confined in some way—if by nothing more evident than the limitations of the poet's subconscious. What I did manage to arrive at in "Walt Whitman" was a poem that presented certain images and ideas in an almost colloquial manner, in lines whose rhythm was determined by my own habits of speech. This was not absolute freedom, but the result was more satisfying to me than recent poems in which I had presented ideas in neat rhymes. In fact, whatever theory about the writing of verse enables a poet to speak the truth and fills him with energy, is good. My groping toward a poetry of significant images and spoken lines enabled me to say certain things that I had not been able to say before. This poem was followed by others in which I was able to deal with material that interested me—poems about history, my own personal life, America.

"Walt Whitman at Bear Mountain" springs from an actual experience, as do most of my poems. About three years ago I traveled up the Hudson River to Bear Mountain with my wife and the poet Robert Bly and his wife. We came upon the Jo Davidson (I believe that's the right spelling) statue of Walt Whitman. The statue was very impressive under the leaves. A few days later I started this poem. I didn't finish it for months, not until I had moved to California. The fragments of what I had attempted then cohered all at once—this is the way it happens with me, if I'm lucky.

Whitman means a great deal to me. When I came to America, at the age of seventeen, an intelligent cousin gave me a copy of *Leaves of Grass*. I recognized immediately that Whitman was a great, original poet. I now think that he is the greatest poet we have had in America. But I think that most of his prophecies have been proved wrong. It is a strange fact, when you think about it—that a poet can be great and yet be mistaken in his ideas. The Whitman who heralds an inevitable march of democracy, who praises the intelligence of the masses, is nearly always mistaken. At least, if there ever was an America like that, it no longer exists. But the Whitman who uses his own eyes and ears, who describes things, who expresses his own sly humor or pathos, is unbeatable. I tried to show the two Whitmans in my poem. I used my ideas about Whitman as a way of getting at my own ideas about America. And I think a great deal about the country I live in; indeed, it seems an inexhaustible subject, one that has hardly been tapped. By America, I mean the infinitely complex life we have. Sometimes when I look at Main Street, I feel like a stranger looking at the Via Aurelia, or the Pyramids. But our monuments are ephemeral. Poetry is the art of the ephemeral.

It is hard to talk about a poem, for talking about poetry leads you out in every direction. I do not see the art of poetry as separated from life.

The Terms of Life Itself: Writing "Quiet Desperation"

Quiet Desperation

At the post office he sees Joe McInnes.
Joe says, "We're having some people over.
It'll be informal. Come as you are."

She is in the middle
of preparing dinner. Tonight
she is trying an experiment:
Hal Burgonyaual—Fish-Potato Casserole.
She has cooked and drained the potatoes
and cut the fish in pieces.
Now she has to "mash potatoes,
add butter and hot milk," et cetera.

He relays Joe's invitation.
"No," she says, "not on your life.
Muriel McInnes is no friend of mine."

Reprinted from *The Character of the Poet*. Ann Arbor: The University of Michigan Press, 1986. The poem "Quiet Desperation" was originally published in *The Best Hour of the Night*. New York: Ticknor and Fields, 1983. "The Terms of Life Itself: Writing 'Quiet Desperation'" originally appeared in *Singular Voices*, ed. Stephen Berg. New York: Avon Books, 1985.

339

It appears that she told Muriel
that the Goldins live above their means,
and Muriel told Mary Goldin.

He listens carefully, to get things right.
The feud between the Andersons and the Kellys
began with Ruth Anderson calling Mike Kelly
a reckless driver. Finally
the Andersons had to sell their house and move.

Social life is no joke.
It can be the only life there is.

*

In the living room the battle of Iwo Jima
is in progress, watched by his son.
Men are dying on the beach,
pinned down by a machine gun.

The marine carrying the satchel charge
falls. Then Sergeant Stryker
picks up the charge and starts running.

Now you are with the enemy machine gun
firing out of the pillbox
as Stryker comes running,
bullets at his heels kicking up dust.
He makes it to the base of the pillbox,
lights the charge, raises up,
and heaves it through the opening.
The pillbox explodes . . .
the NCO's wave, "Move out!"

And he rises to his feet.
He's seen the movie. Stryker gets killed
just as they're raising the flag.

*

A feeling of pressure . . .
There is something that needs to be done
immediately.

But there is nothing,
only himself. His life is passing,
and afterwards there will be eternity,
silence, and infinite space.

He thinks, "Firewood!"—
and goes to the basement,
takes the Swede-saw off the wall,
and goes outside, to the woodpile.

He carries an armful to the sawhorse
and saws the logs into smaller pieces.
In twenty minutes he has a pile of firewood
cut just the right length.
He carries the cut logs into the house
and arranges them in a neat pile
next to the fireplace.

Then looks around for something else to do,
to relieve the feeling of pressure.

The dog!
He will take the dog for a walk.

*

They make a futile procession . . .
he commanding her to "Heel!"—
she dragging back or straining ahead.

The leaves are turning yellow.
Between the trunks of the trees
the cove is blue, with ripples.
The swans—this year there are seven—
are sailing line astern.

But when you come closer
the rocks above the shore are littered
with daggers of broken glass
where the boys sat on summer nights
and broke beer bottles afterwards.

And the beach is littered, with cans,
containers, heaps of garbage,
newspaper wadded against the sea-wall.
Someone has even dumped a mattress . . .
a definite success!
Some daring guy, some Stryker
in the pickup speeding away.

He cannot bear the sun
going over and going down . . .
the trees and houses vanishing
in quiet every day.

The ideas that make a poem present themselves as images. Their significance may not immediately be apparent and indeed may never be. But poetry does not wait on meaning, and certain things insist on being noticed, at times with the power of hallucinations. When I wrote "Quiet Desperation" the scenery was already in place, the situations familiar: a woman looking at a recipe as she prepared dinner; television going in the living room; sawing some wood for the fireplace; walking down to the water. There were houses overlooking the road, a screen of trees, and everything seemed to drowse in a sea light.

But poetry is more than description, just as a living creature is more than the sum of its parts. Poetry is a drama in which objects are cut loose from their moorings and sent flying to make their own connections. The first step, therefore, was to get my controlling mind out of the poem and treat the subject impersonally. So I embodied my ideas in a narrative—there would be a character to do the observing, and one or two others. The method isn't infallible—a particularly obstreperous ego will struggle not to let go, but writing about people in a narrative turns the poem away from the self and compels it to face the world.

I sent the man in the poem to the post office where he met a man named McInnes who invited him to his house. I brought my character home and gave him a wife. They had a conversation in which she rejected McInnes's invitation, and this gave me an opportunity to express my own feelings about the narrowness of small-town life.

Not only in small towns . . . the problem of how to get along with people sociably is universal. I write about a small town because in order to write with conviction I must have a place in mind, and this is a setting I know—it is where I live.

I had the man go into the living room, and gave him a son who was watching John Wayne on television capture the island of Iwo Jima. I enjoyed putting in the details, especially "bullets at his heels kicking up dust." This is what machine-gun bullets do in movies. I like putting into a poem things people accept as true—it is the pleasure Flaubert got from quoting "received ideas." If you want to write poetry about people you must put in what they think, not just your own feelings and opinions. Novelists know this, but these days few poets seem to—they have little interest in the thoughts and feelings of others. This makes for poetry with no observed life in it and, of course, no humor.

When I put in John Wayne on Iwo Jima I had no idea how this would tie in, but you have to let things happen and trust there will be a connection. The more the poem seems to be writing itself, the more joy you take in it. And if you can bring it off, if the connections are there, you have a real poem, one that lives and breathes by itself.

This is writing by impulse, and I know no other way in which good poetry can be written. But you must be able to trust the poem and withstand frustration. For the impulse may flag and the poem cease to move. When this happens the writer may try to forge ahead by sheer will, to think of something, to invent. . . . Many poems are written in this way, and the results are not good. They may look like poems but they are only exercises—they don't make you feel that they had to be written.

I had come to such a place—could not see where the poem was going. But instead of trying to make up something I put what I was feeling into the poem—my frustration.

Wordsworth said that poetry takes its origin from emotion recollected in tranquility. Readers have concentrated on the recollecting but the phrase "takes its origin" is just as important. The act of writing begins with memory but is different from mere recollection—it is a reconstruction of experience with something added, the plus being the emotion of the poet as he writes. The emotion that creates a poem is not the emotion you had when you were having the experience, but the emotion you are having now, as you write.

If you write out of impulse, as I have said, it may leave you suddenly. Then,

> As high as we have mounted in delight
> In our dejection do we sink as low . . .

And now I was dejected and the poem was sinking. And still there was a pressure to write. I felt a kind of desperation.

This was what I put into the poem—I made the character feel my own desperation. Putting this feeling into the poem made it more than a description and gave it such depth and meaning as it has. It brought the character to life and made him interesting—to myself and, it has seemed, to others.

Many have known the dread that can come upon you suddenly, a cloud blotting out the sun. You are aware that life is passing, "and afterwards there will be eternity,/silence, and infinite space." Your pulse is racing and you feel a need to act, to stave off some disaster.

I once remarked in a poem that I could never think of anything to make my characters do. I meant this as irony, but a critic took it to be an admission of failure. When you are writing out of feeling you don't have to make anything happen—the writing is interesting and the characters are alive, like Hamlet, though they are standing still. On the other hand, if feeling is absent no amount of plotting helps. The writing and incidents will not move.

In "Quiet Desperation" form follows feeling. The third part begins with "A feeling of pressure. . . ." The sentence fragment and short line suggest that the pressure is overwhelming. A longer line follows:

> There is something that needs to be done

The next line consists of one word, "immediately." This is urgent and peremptory. Then there is a step down, the poem continuing to the right of the page. The form sags as the feeling sags:

But there is nothing,
only himself.

There follows the reflection about eternity with its echo of Pascal.
Then the thinker pulls himself together and acts, the short brisk
lines evoking decisive action:

He thinks, "Firewood!"
and goes to the basement . . .

Having given my own anxiety to the character I knew what he
would do . . . saw firewood, walk the dog . . . things I had done
myself on such occasions. Anything to relieve the pressure.

He is walking past the slopes and woods of the landscape cele-
brated by William Sidney Mount a hundred years ago in his paint-
ings of Long Island. As he walks he looks at the trees and grass and
the cove glimpsed through the trees. Nature is beautiful.

But when he gets down to the shore he finds that garbage has
been dumped on the natural scene. There are daggers of broken
glass on the rocks. At this point I discover the relevance of the battle
of Iwo Jima. In a time of war the young men who smash bottles and
strew garbage would be heroes. They have no education to speak
of—our public schools have seen to that. They cannot sit still and
think. But they are full of energy, so they get drunk and smash
bottles. Or perhaps try a bit of burglary . . . anything to break the
monotony of their lives. If there was a war they would go to it.

Not only in the States . . . millions of people all over the world are
suffering from boredom and what Baudelaire called "spleen," a
feeling of frustration, a rage at conditions, at the terms of life itself.

Deprived of the opportunity to lead a company of marines, Ser-
geant Stryker dumps a mattress on the beach and speeds away in his
pickup. It is a small victory over the forces of law and boredom.
Sergeant Stryker needs a war to keep him going. He cannot stand
the monotony of peace and the feeling that his life is being spent to
no purpose. But this is what life is—it is banal, and the rewards are
fleeting. If we wish to live we must learn to withstand the banality.

My own solution is to write a poem—others will have other
solutions.

What there is to say about the form and style of the poem may be said in a few words. The stresses within the lines are so variable that I would not call them feet. I do observe, however, a preponderance of lines with three or four stresses. The lines vary in length, and I pause at the end of the line or run on as I would if I were speaking. This kind of verse isn't entirely free and it isn't written in meter. The term I think best describes it is "free form."

Writing in 1844, Emerson said, "It is not metres, but a metre-making argument that makes a poem—a thought so passionate and alive that like the spirit of a plant or an animal it has an architecture of its own, and adorns nature with a new thing."

"Quiet Desperation" has "architecture," to use Emerson's word. The lines have marked rhythms and a form, not predetermined but rising from the matter in hand. The term "free form" describes this kind of writing more accurately than "free verse," which suggests an absence of form of any kind.

The voice of poetry is not the voice in which you say good morning or talk to the man who fills your gas tank—still, there is a connection. I agree with Wordsworth that poetry should be a selection—with the word *selection* emphasized—of the language people actually use. I listen as I write for the sounds of speech.

There are readers who want the images in a poem to be far-fetched, things we have not seen or heard. Others want a style that draws attention to itself. And there are those who estimate the value of a poet in direct proportion to his unwillingness or failure to make sense. For such readers my writing can hold little interest—I write about feelings people share, in language that can be understood.

"Chocolates"

Chocolates

Once some people were visiting Chekhov.
While they made remarks about his genius
the Master fidgeted. Finally
he said, "Do you like chocolates?"

They were astonished, and silent.
He repeated the question,
whereupon one lady plucked up her courage
and murmured shyly, "Yes."

"Tell me," he said, leaning forward,
light glinting from his spectacles,
"what kind? The light, sweet chocolate
or the dark, bitter kind?"

The conversation became general.
They spoke of cherry centers,
of almonds and Brazil nuts.
Losing their inhibitions

Reprinted from *The Character of the Poet.* Ann Arbor: The University of Michigan Press, 1986. The poem "Chocolates" was originally published in *Caviare at the Funeral.* New York: Franklin Watts, 1980. The essay that follows was written at the request of Alberta Turner for *Forty-Five Contemporary Poets: The Creative Process,* ed. Alberta T. Turner. New York: Longman, 1985. Copyright © 1985 by Longman Inc.

they interrupted one another.
For people may not know what they think
about politics in the Balkans,
or the vexed question of men and women,
but everyone has a definite opinion
about the flavor of shredded coconut.
Finally someone spoke of chocolates filled with liqueur,
and everyone, even the author of *Uncle Vanya,*
was at a loss for words.

As they were leaving he stood by the door
and took their hands.
                   In the coach returning to Petersburg
they agreed that it had been a most
unusual conversation.

The poem is based on an actual incident. Some women who admired Chekhov paid him a visit. They wanted to talk about his writing, but Chekhov, who probably welcomed the interruption of his work, said to one of them, "Do you like chocolates?" What followed was pretty much as I have it, though I don't know if Chekhov stood by the door and took their hands as they left—I have imagined his doing so, like a character in one of his plays.

The reader will have noticed a difference between this account and my poem. Chekhov's visitors were women—in the poem they are "some people." I had to make this change, for if I had said they were women it might have appeared that Chekhov was condescending to women, talking about a frivolous subject, chocolates, because he thought women were not to be taken seriously. Nothing, of course, could have been further from Chekhov's mind—no one who has read Chekhov could accuse him of holding women in contempt. But there are always those who misunderstand, so I protected Chekhov, and myself, against the charge by changing "women" to "some people." Of course, if a reader wishes to be aggrieved he, or she, can always find a reason.

Reactions to the poem have been very favorable. I recall a letter in the London *Times* praising "Chocolates" because, the letter-writer said, it showed that poetry could be understood. And audiences at poetry readings seem to understand: they laugh at the line, "They spoke of cherry centers"—from relief—this is not going to be a

serious poem—and laugh again at the lines about shredded coco-
nut and chocolates filled with liqueur. Audiences at poetry readings
are grateful for poetry that is at all entertaining—most poetry is
deadly dull. They make appreciative noises at the words *"unusual
conversation,"* right at the end.

"Chocolates" is more serious than some of these listeners think.
Superficially it may appear that I am poking fun at the kind of
people who would go to see a famous author, but readers who feel
superior to these visitors are missing the point. In real life I might
find such people absurd but I would not hold them up to ridicule in
a poem—I am more intelligent when I write than I am in person.
The desire to see and speak to a great man or woman is not
something to poke fun at. Only snobs, who are usually people of no
talent, look down at those who have a sincere wish to better them-
selves.

Then what is the poem about? It is about happiness . . . the things
that make people happy, and the delight we feel when we are able to
express our happiness to another person. This may be the closest we
get to heaven. Chekhov knew that people have preferences, though
they may not be aware that they have them and may think that they
should talk about philosophy instead. As Schopenhauer pointed
out, we live according to our instincts and fashion our ideas accord-
ingly—not the other way round, as Plato has it. A taste for choco-
lates may run deep—deeper than the wish to discuss *The Cherry
Orchard* or politics in the Balkans.

And yet, though they like chocolates, people will talk about the
things they think are expected. How boring for everyone!

This was why Chekhov brought up the subject of chocolates. It
didn't have to be chocolates—anything they liked would have done
. . . birthdays, for instance, or picnics . . . but chocolates were a
happy choice. The visitors were relieved—like the audience at a
poetry reading when the solemnity is broken. The visitors gave their
opinions, tentatively at first, then in a torrent, "interrupting one
another." This was what Chekhov wanted, to have them express
their enthusiasm. It is the conversation that matters, not the subject.

What happened that day was nothing grand—nothing as holy as
what might have taken place in Tolstoy's house, but far more enjoy-
able all around.

Chekhov's poems and stories are about people who are prevented

by character or circumstance from being happy. "My holy of holies,"
Chekhov said, "is the human body, health, intelligence, talent, inspi-
ration, love and the most absolute freedom—freedom from violence
and lying, whatever forms they may take."

So he asked his visitors to tell him if they liked chocolates, and
when they said they did, the barriers were broken down. What
followed was a communion of souls, and as they were talking about
something they liked it was a happy communion.

Writers like Chekhov—but is there any writer like Chekhov?—
through their sympathy and humor show that it is possible to live in
the world. There is poverty, sickness, and old age. There is bureau-
cracy. . . . Still, we can understand and love one another. Since the
world will never be any different from what it is—not as long as it is
inhabited by human beings—Chekhov's is the ultimate wisdom.

About the writing of "Chocolates"* . . .

I had heard this story about Chekhov some years before I wrote
the poem.

I was staying at a friend's house in the country. On Sunday he and
his wife went to church, and I didn't feel like going. I was left
behind with *The New York Times* and the *Boston Globe*. Perhaps
"Chocolates" was triggered by something he and I had been talking
about, some remark about poetry . . . I don't recall. I picked up my
notebook and started writing. The poem was written in a few
minutes. I may have changed one or two words afterwards, or
changed a line break, but nothing important.

"This poem," one reader observes, "generally uses the rhythms,
syntax, and diction of prose fiction." I don't think so—to my ear the
poem moves in lines of verse. If "Chocolates" were printed not in
lines but as prose, the reader would soon be aware that lines of verse
were struggling to break free.

(Incidentally, I have a low opinion of prose poems, unless they are
written by Baudelaire. They don't have the absolute rhythm that
you get from lines of verse; the rhythms are arbitrary, and so the
work as a whole falls short of poetry. Poetry is absolute—it could not
be other than it is. The "prose poem" could be written several

*The editor (Alberta Turner) had mentioned certain aspects of the writing of "Chocolates"
that I might wish to discuss. The following remarks were an attempt to answer her questions.

different ways and the effect would be more or less the same. Prose may be very well written, of course, but it can never have the power of poetry written in lines.)

Are the syntax and diction of verse different from the syntax and diction of prose? I don't think so. A long time ago Ezra Pound remarked that poetry must be as well written as prose. That is to say, verse must sound as though the writer meant it. Verse is not a convention of style but an expression of mind. If the language of verse differs from prose it is not because the style was fetched from a distance but because verse is more highly charged with meaning, requiring more complex expression.

All good writing is experimental, but readers are listening for the rhythms and diction of poems they already know, so a new kind of poetry is said to be "antipoetic." Wordsworth in his time was said to be writing prose. So were Whitman, Frost, Eliot, and, of course, William Carlos Williams.

For twenty years I have been developing a kind of writing in verse that would accommodate my thoughts as easily as prose yet have a lyric flow. Coleridge said that the poet "diffuses a tone and spirit of unity, that blends, and (as it were) *fuses*, each into each, by that synthetic and magical power, to which we have exclusively appropriated the name of imagination." In poems such as "Chocolates" I have attempted to enter into a situation and imagine it strongly so that everything—words, phrases, and sentences—would fall into place with no seeming effort on my part.

Rhythm

When we have understood the social and psychological conditions that affect an artist's life and form his ideas, we still have not understood the impulse and nature of art itself. After all, many people have unusual lives, but very few are artists. Why does a man choose to be a writer? And why poetry?

He doesn't choose—he is moved by the rhythms of speech. Certain people have a physical, visceral way of feeling that expresses itself in rhythm. Some people play music, others dance, and others—who are attracted to words—utter lines of verse. These are the poets.

The rhythms of poetry rise from the unconscious. This is not generally understood, even by critics who write about poetry. Before a poet writes a poem, he hears it. He knows how the lines will move before he knows what the words are.

Descriptions of poetry by men who are not poets are usually ridiculous, for they describe rational thought processes. For example, in the novel *Keep the Aspidistra Flying*, George Orwell describes a poet at work—putting one idea logically after another, choosing the next word, image, and rhyme. This is completely false; prose may be written in this way, but not poetry. A poet begins by losing

Reprinted from Louis Simpson, *North of Jamaica*. New York: Harper and Row, 1972.

control; he does not choose his thoughts, they seem to be choosing him. Rhythms rise to the surface; a fraction of a moment later the necessary words fall into place.

Poets agree that rhythm is of the first importance. Paul Valéry, for example, describes the physical state of a man on the threshold of poetry:

> I had left my house to find, in walking and looking about me, relaxation from some tedious work. As I went along my street, which mounts steeply, I was *gripped* by a rhythm which took possession of me and soon gave me the impression of some force outside myself. Another rhythm overtook and combined with the first, and certain *strange transverse* relations were set up between them.

This was more strange, Valéry says, than anything he could have expected of his "rhythmic faculties"—meaning his will, his rational mind. The rhythms rising from the unconscious seem to arrive from outside. In former ages poets were often "visited" in this manner, and their utterances were regarded as divine truths. But the world has grown rational, and no head of state would consult a poet—except as a prop under the spotlights on a public occasion. Instead, it is the physicists who hand down our oracles.

When we try to explain poetry and defend it, we forget that it needs no defense, for poetry is a form of reality with certain definite powers. There is no substitute for the form and sound of a true poem. The poem is unique, therefore it exists. And the more powerfully it exists the less possible it is to explain it—that is, to replace it with prose.

Poetry is essentially mysterious. No one has ever been able to define it. Therefore we always find ourselves coming back to the poet. As Stevens said, "Poetry is a process of the personality of the poet." This personality is never finished. While he is writing the poet has in mind another self, more intelligent than he. The poet is reaching out to the person that he would be, and this is the poet's style—a sense of reaching, that can never be satisfied.

To Make Words Disappear

Emotional intensity—this, as far as I can tell, is what poetry consists of. A poem will move from one moment of intensity to another, and there will be a connection. This, I suppose, is where I part company with surrealism and with some of my contemporaries—they don't care about the connection, don't feel a need to get a narrative line into their work. They seem to think that it is enough to say that they are having a feeling—but they do not try to convey it in an image or a narrative line. I'd rather not read such poetry—I don't care about writing that merely tells me that the writer is having a feeling. I want to be able to experience the feeling—I want lyric or narrative poetry.

As for poetry that preaches, I can do without it entirely. I don't want to listen to a poet berating people for their shortcomings—for example, for not being as "politically aware" as he is. It would be better to give them some pleasure rather than make them feel inferior. The most pleasurable poetry I know is lyric or narrative, and sometimes it's a poetry of ideas, but the ideas are transformed into emotion, as images, so that the reader can experience them.

None of this is new, but it seems to have been forgotten in recent

This essay first appeared in *American Poetry Review 3*, No. 1. 1974. Reprinted in *A Company of Poets*. Ann Arbor: The University of Michigan Press, 1981.

years. There is a lot of hard breathing going on—you see the poet straining to say something important, and you may feel sympathetic, but it doesn't do a thing for your life. It would be better if he were less self-absorbed and told you something that was interesting. To be interesting is an act of love—it may be the best thing we can do for each other.

I would like to write poems that made people laugh or made them want to cry, without their thinking that they were reading poetry. The poem would be an experience—not just talking about life, but life itself.

I think that the object of writing is to make words disappear.

Rolling Up

For some time American poets have been writing almost exclusively about their personal lives. We have become accustomed to poets telling us what they are doing and thinking at the moment. The present moment is everything—there is no sense of the past. Nor is there any sense of a community. If poetry is the language of a tribe, it seems there is no longer a tribe, only a number of individuals who are writing a personal diary or trying to "expand their consciousness." But the stress on the individual does not seem to stimulate imagination; we have almost forgotten what it is like to read lyric or narrative poems.

It seems, however, that we are coming to an end of a period. After the life studies, the case histories ... We are tired of looking in mirrors. Every year there is a new style in personalities. Everyone exhibits himself, we try to draw attention to ourselves ... and soon, what does it matter? No one is listening.

In order to feel anything at all, we exaggerate. And then we don't take pleasure in anything, because we don't believe it.

In order to break out of the prison of the self, poets have tried

This essay first appeared in *American Poets in 1976*, ed. William Heyen. Indianapolis: Bobbs-Merrill, 1976. Reprinted in *A Company of Poets*. Ann Arbor: The University of Michigan Press, 1981.

meditating. Some poets have used drugs. Others have studied the ways of the Indian. It is clear that meditating can make a difference. Fifty years ago in Paris the Surrealists used the technique of free association. This released images from the unconscious, or wherever images come from, and enabled them to write more freely. Meditation can have a similar effect. I suspect, however, that poets who rely on drugs for inspiration will exhaust their ability to write. Images may be released, but the desire to arrange them will be weakened. As for images and sounds without an arrangement ... there is nothing more monotonous than the material produced by chance, if thought and feeling are not brought to bear upon it.

There is much to admire in the life and poetry of the American Indian. But it is not easy for an American of the white middle class to think like an Indian. I would go so far as to say that you can write convincingly only about things that you have been compelled to feel. It is easy to put on the costume of a nation other than your own ... to share the emotional life of that nation is another thing entirely. Americans like to dress up and play at being what they are not. This has a good side—the social mobility of Americans, which is envied throughout the world, stems from the same impulse. But in poetry the results are not convincing. A hundred years ago Longfellow wrote about the Indian. In some ways "Hiawatha" is an impressive performance, but it remains a performance. Under the feathers and paint there is an American tourist. Ugh.

To read some American poets you would think they lived far away from roads and supermarkets, that they never had the thoughts of the people you meet, that they looked with the eyes of the crow and listened with the ears of the beaver. That their habitation was darkness and their house made of earth and stones. That they were pure in thought and deed.

But the Indian must have lived as a man. I would not be surprised if the Indian had an equivalent for television. He could not always have been thinking about animals and gods and having significant dreams.

Why is it that magical events are always happening in faraway places where we cannot see them?

The reader may think, What harm does it do? If an American poet wishes to think he is a shaman, or imagine he is a moose, what's wrong with it? Shouldn't we welcome the chance to expand our consciousness? Besides, what do we really know about the mind? Why try to set limits to it?

To the contrary, I believe that a great deal is known about the mind and that there is no shortage of consciousness. We have more consciousness than we know how to use. There is, however, a shortage of wisdom. We seem unable to live together without maiming one another. And we are running out of space; we have to learn to live with one another. This goes for people everywhere, not just in the United States. What we need is not to expand consciousness but to increase understanding. And there is no mystery about it—the tools are at hand if we wish to use them. But this would require work, while going on a trip does not. Americans like to go on trips. To the Virgin Islands, the moon, or an Indian reservation, it is all the same—an attempt to escape from necessity, the need to live an intelligent, useful life.

My objection to the pursuit of esoteric knowledge, shamanism and so on, is that it neglects the life right under your nose. While you are playing children's games you cannot think like a man. While the American poet is imitating the language of a tribe to which he does not belong, he is not learning to speak for the tribe to which he does belong. And this, like it or not, is the tribe that uses supermarkets and roads.

Here I must make a confession—but it has a point, it isn't just the expression of a personal grievance. I don't like the tribe that uses supermarkets and roads. These days I find that when I am in the company of Americans, the people down the street, I feel as if I were living in Germany after the gas ovens. With this difference— the Americans got away with it.

I am referring to the recent war. We still haven't paid that bill. The refusal or inability of Americans to atone for their war crimes has brutalized American society. If we can't admit our guilt, what can we admit? It is necessary not to think seriously about anything at all. Consequently, Americans have become callous, violent, and inwardly disgraced. This is not a society that inspires you to write; these are not people who understand poetry.

I seem to have painted myself into a corner: it is necessary for the American poet to write about his tribe, the nation of roads and supermarkets. At the same time, I don't want to.

Here Confucius comes to my aid. Speaking of the philosopher, he says, "When the government is rotten, he rolls up and keeps the true process inside him."

I've been rolling up. But this isn't, as some may think, a refusal to face life. To the contrary, it is the real work that has to be done if poetry, or any feeling life, is to survive. If the nation is to survive we have to recreate a sense of the spiritual, imaginative life that we have lost. My disagreement with the cultists is that what they are talking about has no connection with the life of the nation. There is not the slightest chance that Americans will become Indians. There is not the slightest chance that Americans will cease using household appliances and, instead, attempt to sustain themselves by magic. Therefore poetry written out of these ideas has no reality.

But poets are needed to recreate the image man has of himself and in this way reconstitute the nation. There have been precedents for this. Wordsworth, for example . . . He was for the French Revolution. Then he was frightened by the bloodshed and went back to England. Subsequently, England declared war on France, on the revolutionary ideals that Wordsworth still cherished. This was a profound shock. He tells us how, during church services when everyone was praying for the success of British arms, he hoped for their disappointment. He felt like a traitor; at any rate, he was cut off in his affections from the people around him. It is hard to imagine a more desolate situation for a poet, and it is the situation American poets have found themselves in for some time. It would be bad enough if poets alone felt so, but what poets feel many other people are feeling too. The United States contains a large number of people who no longer like it.

Wordsworth removed himself from the centers of English culture and went to live in the mountains. In effect, he left England. Then, among the mountains and lakes, he set about creating imaginary men, a race of people in his mind. He imagined men and women who were full of feeling, who communed silently with nature and loved one another. He gave them heartfelt words and high sentences. These people are not found in nature but in the imagination of a poet. Wordsworth's aim was to hold up models for human behavior. He created the nation that he could not find.

In his broodings on human character he perceived new states of feeling. He became a psychologist in poetry and enlarged our sympathies. The political revolution failed—therefore he attempted to replace it with a revolution of feeling. He wished to reveal the deep springs that join one man to another and constitute a real nation. Indeed, if this nation does not exist, there is no other.

Blake was a poet for the sixties—I mean, in America. He was for people who wished to blow their minds. Wordsworth is the poet of life—he shows the way to the future, a community built on human feeling and sympathy.

There was never as great a need for the poetry of feeling as there is in the United States at the present time. By this I mean poetry that addresses itself to the human condition, a poetry of truth, not dreams. The poetry I am speaking about depicts human actions and the way we live. I do not mean poetry that merely talks about the obvious, automobiles and washing machines. Poetry must express the reality behind appearances. The poetry I mean can be subtle and mysterious, but it is related to the way we live. There is as much poetry in a suburb as by a lake, if we have a mind to see it.

As it deals with life, this poetry will frequently be in the form of a narrative. Not a mere relation of external events, but a narrative of significant actions. The poet will aim to convey states of feeling. In our time poets have stayed away from narrative because it has often been merely descriptive—there has been too much dead tissue. But this can be avoided if the poet reveals a situation with no more than a few words, and concentrates on the feeling.

In my attempts to write narrative poetry I have used the rhythms of speech. I bear in mind what it would be like to say the poem aloud to someone else. This helps me to form the lines. At the same time it eliminates confusion—I have to make my ideas clear. I eliminate words out of books, affected language, jargon of any kind.

I have tried to bring into poetry the sense of life, the gestures that Chekhov got in prose. And I have tried to bring in humor. I do not believe that this is common; there is plenty of satire, but this is not what I mean by humor. I have mixed humorous and sad thoughts in my poems, because this is the way life is. People want the sights and sounds of life; they ask for life in poetry. They ask for bread, but instead they have been given stones.

The poem "The Foggy Lane" states my ideas about poetry and its relation to life. By "the uneven, muddy surface" I mean human life. There is no end to the material—the question is what to make of it.

This kind of poetry requires a sacrifice of the individual, his peculiar fantasies. On the other hand, it is an on-going process.

The Foggy Lane

The houses seem to be floating
in the fog, like lights at sea.

Last summer I came here with a man
who spoke of the ancient Scottish poets—
how they would lie blindfolded
with a stone placed on the belly,
and so compose their panegyrics . . .
while we, being comfortable, find nothing to praise.

Then I came here with a radical
who said that everything is corrupt;
he wanted to live in a pure world.

And a man from an insurance company
who said that I needed "more protection."

Walking in the foggy lane
I try to keep my attention fixed
on the uneven, muddy surface . . .
the pools made by the rain,
and wheel ruts, and wet leaves,
and the rustling of small animals.

Images

The discussion of images that began in American poetry around 1910 may be a reflection of twentieth-century man's inability to make general statements in the face of a world that is increasingly unsure. We don't know what to believe, so we make an image.

Which is a sin, according to Scripture: "You shall not make graven images."

But the image according to Pound isn't graven—it is "that which presents an intellectual and emotional complex in an instant of time." Also, "One is trying to record the precise instant when a thing outward and objective transforms itself, or darts into a thing inward and subjective."

The image of the Imagists is a moment of perception, a movement of some sort. It is not just a sensation, a thing perceived by the senses. "Images in verse," said Hulme, "are not mere decoration, but the very essence of an intuitive language."

How does it work? The image as we have it from the Imagists and, ten years later, the Surrealists, is composed by bringing two entities together. Or three, or a dozen. The mind flies from one to the other.

In metaphor we are made to see the similarity between one thing

This essay first appeared in *Field*, No. 23, Fall 1980. Reprinted in Louis Simpson, *The Character of the Poet*. Ann Arbor: The University of Michigan Press, 1986.

and another: "My love is like a red, red rose." Metaphor suggests that things are really the same.

The image of the Imagists also brings different things together, but it doesn't merge them. Instead, a third thing is created ... something unexpected. In Pound's famous poem about faces in a Metro station, the third thing is a black bough with petals. The faces of the people in the station have vanished, the station has vanished, to be replaced by a wet, black bough.

Surrealism uses the same technique, with this difference. The third thing is not like anything that we have seen or heard—it is not in nature, but purely invented.

> The sphere, colored orange, floating in space
> has a face with fixed brown eyes.
> Below the sphere a shirt with a tie
> in a dark, formal suit
> stands facing you, close to the parapet
> on the edge of the canyon.[1]

Moreover, the aim of Surrealism is to surprise, and the further apart things are, the more astonishing the effect when you juxtapose them. André Breton said, "To compare two subjects as distant as possible one from the other, or, by any other method, to bring them face to face, remains the highest task to which poetry can aspire."

Bringing together objects that appear to have nothing in common ... this is the main Surrealist technique. It can be used mechanically, like every other poetic device, until it has lost its power to surprise. In the hands of a gifted poet, however, the technique can still produce the "intuition" of which Hulme spoke, Pound's "intellectual and emotional complex in an instant of time."

Juxtaposition of far-removed entities compels us to recognize that the mind is capable of anything and is its own master. "Man is the creator of values, which have their sense only from him and relative to him."[2]

[1] Louis Simpson, "Magritte Shaving," *Caviare at the Funeral.* New York: Franklin Watts, 1980. p. 39.
[2] Ferdinand Alquié, *The Philosophy of Surrealism.* Ann Arbor: The University of Michigan Press, 1969. p. 102.

But here we are confronted with a difficulty. If the mind is absolute master, aren't all images equally good? All poets equally interesting? But anyone who reads Surrealist poems, or poetry of any kind, soon realizes that some poets are more interesting than others: their images arouse more feeling, yield more pleasure, a keener surprise.

The painter Magritte said, "There exists a secret affinity between certain images; it holds equally for the objects represented by these images." I would put it another way: There is a secret affinity between objects, and if you perceive it your images will be alive.

But doesn't this talk of affinities bring us back to metaphor, a way of showing a likeness between things? Yes, the aim in creating metaphors or creating Symbolist, Imagist, or Surrealist images is the same: to show a meaning behind the veil of appearances. What difference is there between Baudelaire's forest, beloved of Symbolist poets, full of symbols that watch him with knowing eyes, and Breton's "facts which . . . present all the appearances of a signal"? In each case the poet is the receiver of signals from Beyond.

The images, however, are different. The image of the Symbolist, taken from the world perceived by the senses, is composed so as to evoke a trancelike state in the reader. The Symbolist image takes you away from the world, to the Over-Soul. The Symbolist poet would evade the world entirely, if he could.

The Imagist poet on the other hand believes with Hulme in a clear separation of earth and heaven. The image is a quick opening into another order of reality. Then it closes again. But, again, the principle is to show you something. Not just the sea and the pines . . . it is to be an "intuition."

The Surrealists went one better. The image would be entirely original, like nothing ever seen on earth. Again, however, the aim was the same: to reveal "a kind of absolute reality."

Whether we are speaking of Symbolist, Imagist, or Surrealist poets, it is their perception of affinities that is important. This is why some poets' images are alive. The poet has seen something happening between objects. Or the movement may be between ideas, as in Pound's *Cantos*.

In Williams's and Olson's theory of the poem as "a field of action," the poet himself is seen as an object in the field, interacting with other objects. I don't see why human beings have to be thought of as objects . . . I would think it fairly obvious that they aren't . . . but, in any case, in field theory also you are perceiving affinities. This is what the field looks like: juxtaposition of objects and a movement between them. A significance.

The poet's ability to see and feel affinities counts for much—some would say, for everything. In the hands of a poet such as Wordsworth, writing about the "spots of time," or Pound in some of the *Cantos,* images may evoke the supernatural.

> . . . juxtaposition will be used to show metamorphosis, the changing of one thing into another, the breaking of solid surfaces that allows a permanent idea or god to emerge. ("A god is an eternal state of mind.") . . . Pound's image, composed of parts in an active relationship, allows the supernatural to be seen. The image is an opening, "a 'magic moment' or moment of metamorphosis, bust thru from quotidien into 'divine' or 'permanent world.' Gods, etc." The eyes of a sea beast become the eyes of a girl, and these are the eyes of Helen, "destroyer of men and cities."[3]

American poets are still walking in the paths trodden by the Symbolists, Imagists, and Surrealists. They have found new names . . . the "deep image," for example, to describe images with a certain psychological resonance or dreamlike quality. But only the name is new . . . "deep images" were created by poets writing many years ago.

[3] Louis Simpson, *Three on the Tower.* New York: William Morrow and Company, 1975. p. 35.

English Poetry
1900–1950:
An Assessment

The author of this assessment declares at the start that
literary history is "very rarely what contemporaries imagine it to
be," and he proceeds to allot praise or blame with little regard for
established opinions. There is a principle behind his views—he is
interested in innovation; he believes that the "indubitable rhythm of
the twentieth century" is "a language free from pretension as from
any effort to be 'poetical,' words that follow speech so closely that
the reader is hardly aware that he has not merely overheard the
sentence." "But," he adds, "any rubbish will not do; the lines have
the weight of long experience and digested thought."

C. H. Sisson's view of modern poetry in English is entirely per-
sonal; he makes no pretense of objectivity. English poetry, he says,
includes any poetry written in English. He therefore admits the
Scottish, Irish, and Welsh, as well as two Americans, Ezra Pound
and T. S. Eliot. But there are surprising exclusions. Dylan Thomas is
discussed, but not David Jones. Louis MacNeice and Austin Clarke
are excluded. One could go on listing names. Edith Sitwell is dis-
missed—fair enough; her poetry was inferior to her publicity. But

Robert Frost lived in England, and Mr. Sisson could scarcely be unaware of his existence—Frost may be said to have turned Edward Thomas into a poet.

Mr. Sisson is providing an assessment, not a survey. If we take the book this way it has a great deal to offer—the discovery of good poets who have been neglected and new views of those who are well known. He begins with A. H. Bullen who wrote at the turn of the century, a "lover of hedgerows," free, says Mr. Sisson, from "any suspicion of fashion," who wrote without pretensions to the poetic. "It could not be said that he did not speak out before he died, and that is all that anybody can do." Speaking out is another of Mr. Sisson's touchstones. The verse by Bullen that elicits his praise was of this kind: "Be wary; practice incredulity/Which makes the soul subtle and sinewy."

Thomas Hardy and W. B. Yeats began writing in the late nineteenth century and continued well into the twentieth. It is instructive to compare Mr. Sisson's treatment of these figures. Hardy's achievement, "the sheer bulk of closely-felt impressions, covering sixty years or more of his writing life, is without parallel in our literature." Hardy's very awkwardnesses are a virtue, "like a particular lurch or other movement which is habitual to some bodies." The rhythm of Hardy's verse is the rhythm of thought. Mr. Sisson even finds good things to say about *The Dynasts,* Hardy's magnum opus about the Napoleonic wars which few readers, certainly on this side the Atlantic, can have plowed through. The blank verse in *The Dynasts,* Mr. Sisson thinks, is "saved by its very flatness, for he is pretending to nothing that he does not mean to say." Hardy's lack of pretension is his profoundest contribution to the literature of the twentieth century.

Yeats, on the other hand, is pretentious. Though many have taken him at his own evaluation, Mr. Sisson has a different view. He thinks Yeats's "moralism" makes him Victorian rather than modern, and he gives Yeats's egotism short shrift. Yeats is "cut off from any fruitful tradition—from Swift, Berkeley and Burke . . . by the frivolous attitude to Christianity exhibited in 'The Mother of God' and in the references to von Hügel." There is worse. At moments Yeats "seems to approximate rather to the Marquis de Sade, whose not very profound, and perhaps insane, view was that the first duty of women was to lay themselves open to whatever lusts he chose to exercise upon them." Mr. Sisson's admiration of Yeats, such as it is, rests on the early poems, which have a languid charm, and those later poems in which Yeats casts aside pretense and conveys an impression of experience. The accent of truth is in the lines, "O who could have foretold/That the heart grows old?" Too often Yeats is cutting a figure, or there is a "parade of conventional conceptions," as in "Meditations in Time of Civil War" where he broods on the great houses that "helped him to build up his grandiose conception of himself" or which serve as a symbol for his "isolation from inferior persons."

There is a great deal of value, I believe, in reassessments such as this. In the United States we are exposed to much academic criticism—sometimes one wonders if there is any other—in which a few large figures are praised to the skies, their least writings tediously explained until the authors and their works seem unapproachable, the criticism standing between ourselves and any fresh reading of the material. We need very much to have critics such as Mr. Sisson, with his fearless views, if so-called "major" authors are to be read with enjoyment and understanding.

Mr. Sisson brings forward some poets of whom one has never heard—Edgell Rickword, for example, who wrote in the mid-1920s. He wrote about the Great War, "a few necrophilous poems, which are like nobody else's and which combine recollections of the trenches with a rather sinister eroticism." He wrote, for example, about the moon rising over the battlefield:

> Then I thought, standing in the ruined trench,
> (all round, dead Boche white-shirted lay like sheep),
> "Why does this damned entrancing bitch
> seek lovers only among them that sleep?"

Rickword also wrote in a Baudelairean manner about the "crowded, lust-ridden streets of London." It is not possible, of course, to claim that Rickword deserves as much attention for his war poetry as Wilfred Owen for his, or that Rickword's London is as memorable as the city in Eliot's *The Waste Land*. But the writings of "minor" authors are not dispensable. Poetry is valuable wherever it is found, and Rickword's pint is poetry as well as Eliot's gallon. Moreover, by concentrating exclusively on "major" authors, American critics exaggerate the originality of those authors and have no understanding of their place in a culture.

Once when I was driving toward the Welsh border the name Wenlock appeared on the road map. I quoted some lines by A. E. Housman to an American friend who was driving with me. He had never heard of Housman. And this was a professor of English in an American university! Many of our scholars know very little outside the figures they have been blinkered toward. They are not educated in any real sense.

Mr. Sisson's reassessments of major figures are as useful as his inclusions of neglected names. He considers Eliot's "Sweeney Agonistes" original and unique—in the poem Eliot dealt with common life as nowhere else in his verse—"the very rhythms show an openness to the draughts of the great world." On the other hand, Mr. Sisson does not share the general admiration for *Four Quartets.* The poetry is concocted, he thinks; the style of discourse "does not convince us as poetic apprehension of something hitherto undiscovered. It is *not* a raid on the 'inarticulate' but the articulation of an idea consciously accepted." Yes, that is the difference between *The Waste Land* and *Four Quartets,* and I think ability to see the difference is a measure of one's ability to appreciate poetry.

Mr. Sisson considers Pound's "Hugh Selwyn Mauberley" one of the essential poems of the century, and the *Cantos* are a "great treasure-trove," though the treasures are not equally valuable on every page. Pound's usury is a "noble subject" and perhaps the only possible one for a long poem in our age. Mr. Sisson is one of the critics who don't think Pound's support of Hitler and Mussolini worth discussing; he merely remarks that in Pisa "the United States military authorities incarcerated the sixty-year-old poet in a cage on a suspicion of treason." Some suspicion!

Mr. Sisson is a Wyndham Lewis enthusiast. There couldn't be many. Even if we concede that Lewis's "One-Way Song" is "the most subtle piece of argumentation put into English verse in the twentieth century," arguing in verse seems a bit foolish. Whom are you hoping to convince? In any case, when the occasion fades, so does the argument. Moreover, rhyming couplets and fourteen-syllable lines do not strike me as the "contribution to literary innovation" Mr. Sisson is looking for.

His opinion of W. H. Auden is likely to distress Auden's followers. According to Mr. Sisson Auden began with an explosion, and settled into a public voice with *Look, Stranger!*, but after Auden came to the United States, "those interested simply in his contribution to literary innovation may stop."

No American critic would write a book as quirky and interesting as this. Mr. Sisson isn't afraid to say what he thinks. He isn't looking over his shoulder at an establishment as he writes. He isn't using the most recently approved critical method, just the intelligence that Eliot said was the only method.

On finishing the book one would like to have a satisfying quarrel with the author, then buy him a drink. If Pound and Eliot are admitted, where is William Carlos Williams, master of the kind of verse closely related to speech and based in experience that Mr. Sisson wants? But rather than complain about what is missing in Mr. Sisson's view of poetry in the twentieth century, I shall be grateful for what he has given us: an assessment of Edward Thomas as "one of the most profound poets of the century"; praise of Patrick Kavanagh's "The Great Hunger" that could induce readers to discover this remarkable narrative poem; praise of Hugh MacDiarmid, one of the great, neglected poets. Surely there have been enough books about Yeats, Pound, Eliot and even Williams. It is time to put aside the views of the establishment, as this critic has done, and read poetry wherever it is found, flourishing in the byways.

6

MOTIONS OF
THE WINDS

Visionary power
Attends the motions of the viewless winds,
Embodied in the mystery of words . . .
                              Wordsworth, The Prelude

The Poet's Theme [1]

I. THE POET'S THEME

Proust said that poetry originates in a room "shuttered and sealed against all traffic with the outer world, the poet's soul." I think this is true and that the poet who invites the world into the room of the private self soon ceases to have any self to speak of. The world, being ungrateful, will turn to some other whose writing has the power of solitary thought, so that it may barge into that room too and send thought flying.

But we are not the world—we love poetry and wish to understand it. Our being here to speak of poetry shows that the need to understand is as strong as the need to create, and it seems to be so with poets, even those who are skeptical of literary criticism. Poets are critics in spite of themselves. Wordsworth was a critic; every good writer is necessarily a critic, otherwise he or she would write bathos instead of tragedy, instead of comedy bad jokes. To read the odes of Keats, for example, is to be aware that with every line he had to be a critic; there are gulfs of poor logic and bad taste to each side of

[1] Reprinted from *The Hudson Review*, Vol. XLI, No. 1. Spring 1988. This essay was originally given as a series of lectures called the Dancy Lectures, delivered at the University of Montevallo, Montevallo, Alabama, on March 18, 19, and 20, 1986.

every step he takes. (Some readers have fallen into those gulfs on his behalf. I recall one who quoted the famous lines from the "Ode on a Grecian Urn":

> Thou shalt remain, in midst of other woe
> Than ours, a friend to man, to whom thou say'st,
> 'Beauty is truth, truth beauty,'—that is all
> Ye know on earth, and all ye need to know.

He said these lines were to be interpreted as the poet's saying to the urn, "That is all you need to know because you're only an urn." The important difference is not between the mind that creates and the mind that criticizes, but between intelligence and stupidity.)

If poets are critics, readers are justified in being critics too and venturing into the shuttered room. But once we are in, what can we expect to find and what are we to do?

"In the first place," a poet once remarked, "it is necessary to be a poet." This is what we are given: the poet, a man or woman with a peculiar constitution. Poets are born, as the saying has it, and it is no use asking why. They are born with a talent that will issue as writing, and this writing will be of a special kind, in the heightened rhythm of verse. (I am using the word "poet" in the sense the world uses it, meaning a writer of verse, rather than in the general, Shelleyan sense of one who "expresses imagination.")

The act of creation cannot be explained, but we would like to understand, and so we approach as close as we can. A common approach is to find out all one can about the life of the poet. In recent years there has been a vogue of biographies dealing with the lives of poets—Robert Lowell, Delmore Schwartz, John Berryman. Proust had something to say about the genre:

> Sainte-Beuve came to set up that celebrated Method which, according to Taine, Bourget, and the rest of them, is his title to fame, and which consists, if you would understand a poet or a writer, in greedily catechising those who knew him, who saw quite a lot of him, who can tell us how he conducted himself in regard to women, etc.
>
> "The Method of Sainte-Beuve"

Proust remarks that this kind of biographical writing touches on every point where the poet's "true self" is not involved.

But the "true self"—these are my words, not his—is the product of a life lived in a certain way. The mind that creates is the mind of a temperament with a personal history. "Fiction," Joseph Conrad observed, "appeals to temperament," and that which appeals is the temperament of the writer: "The artist descends within himself, and in that lonely region of stress and strife, if he be deserving and fortunate, he finds the terms of his appeal." If Proust is right, poetry is not an expression of the everyday, shoelace-tying life of the poet. On the other hand, if Conrad is right, poetry is an expression of temperament. Therefore it appears that poetry has to be both personal and impersonal, both an expression of the individual and of a community.

Wordsworth describes the poet as one who has extraordinary imagination and power of expressing what he or she imagines. "But," he adds, "these passions and thoughts are the general passions and thoughts and feelings of men." But this does not explain how the imagination of the poet is translated into general passions, thoughts, and feelings. This is what I wish to consider: how the life of the poet becomes imagination and is turned into poetry—how fact is changed into fiction.

The mind that writes is not the ordinary mind—the "I" of the poem, as Rimbaud said, "is another." And the life that appears in the poem is not the ordinary life of the poet—it has been changed so that it connects with other lives. Yeats speaks of this in "Sailing to Byzantium." The speaker of the poem has grown old in a place where "Fish, flesh, or fowl, commend all summer long/Whatever is begotten, born, and dies," and he wishes to escape his mortality. So he has set sail for Byzantium, the city of art.

> Once out of nature I shall never take
> My bodily form from any natural thing,
> But such a form as Grecian goldsmiths make
> Of hammered gold and gold enamelling
> To keep a drowsy Emperor awake;
> Or set upon a golden bough to sing

To lords and ladies of Byzantium
Of what is past, or passing, or to come.

Yeats deliberately gathered ideas that would enable him to write. Out of occult lore and magic of various sorts he gathered a philosophy, and he envisioned himself as the descendant of hard-riding, independent-minded country gentlemen. These views of himself gave him the confidence and the authority, the voice, that is distinctively his—gave him his style. It can be a grand style, rather too grand for some tastes, but the point is that it bridged the gap between the merely personal life and the poetry—it enabled him to write. He found the terms that would appeal to the passions, thoughts and feelings of an audience. Or that at least would be clear and recognizable . . . for we do not have to agree with the terms of a poet's thought—we have only to understand them. We don't read Dante because we are Catholics but because he is a poet. It is possible to disagree with the ideas in a poem and yet feel its force as drama.

Poets may not be as deliberate as Yeats in gathering ideas and adopting an attitude that will enable them to write—his is an extraordinary case. But even a poet as natural and unaffected as Keats is quite aware that he is, or is going to be, a poet, and must shape his thinking to this end. Keats imagines himself as one having "negative capability, that is, when a man is capable of being in uncertainties, mysteries, doubts, without any irritable reaching after fact and reason." The idea Keats has of his character as a poet enables him to write the odes. The odes show us a character that is capable of being in uncertainties, mysteries and doubts without grasping at philosophy or, on the other hand, losing itself in confusion, though at times it comes pretty close.

The style is the man. Yes, and woman too—but not directly. Style reflects the thought of the man or woman. Poets put their thought into imagery that appeals to the senses, into engaging sounds and rhythms. In this way their thought is conveyed. "Nothing can be perceived by the mind," said John Locke, "unless it has first been perceived by the senses." Sense-perception is the bridge between the thought of the poet and the mind of the reader. Through *poema*, a made thing, the imagination of the poet appeals to the "general passions and thoughts and feelings" of the audience.

Let us return to the shuttered room. It is not all darkness within. We can see certain outlines of themes being formed . . . by experience, everything the mind has received from childhood to maturity. The poet discovers a theme through a process of living and thinking. The theme is expressed in writing and so becomes a part of our lives. Literature is the folklore of the educated.

The poetry of Yeats, for example, has several themes. There is the theme of love for a beautiful and unattainable woman, and the theme of a country torn by civil war—a condition that has, nevertheless, a sanctity about it, gained by blood-sacrifice. There is the theme of growing old and how one can fight against it by creating "monuments of unaging intellect." These themes in which the private man speaks to a public audience are what give Yeats's poetry its force.

In order to understand poetry we must read closely—we must understand what the words mean. But it is not possible to understand unless we grasp the ideas lying behind the words, the themes underlying all. We may grope forever from line to line without grasping the real meaning or having a true impression of the whole, not seeing the wood for the trees.

It is a legitimate use of biography to give us the facts we need in order to understand a writer's thought—not in the act of writing, for that cannot be explained, but the steps leading up to it. In the hands of an intelligent author, "critical biography" can be literary criticism of the most persuasive kind, for it is based in fact, not in speculation. Jackson Bate's biography of Samuel Johnson is a model of such writing. Here is Bate on Johnson's "The Vanity of Human Wishes."

> Though *The Vanity of Human Wishes* is a deeply personal utterance, it also embraces tradition and convention, so much so that it might at first seem almost anonymous to readers habituated to Romantic and post-Romantic modes. Loosely based on a satire of Juvenal's, it adopts the closed heroic couplet of Dryden and Pope. The argument itself is a traditional one in religious apologetics, put unforgettably in the Biblical book of Ecclesiastes, and in such works, among others, as Augustine's *Confessions,* Jeremy Taylor's *Holy Living* and *Holy Dying,* and William Law's *Serious Call:* the complete inability of the world and of worldly life to offer genuine or permanent satisfaction, and our

need to turn from this world in order to seek safety and joy in religious faith and in another world.

So Bate explains the theme not only of "The Vanity of Human Wishes," but *Rasselas,* and places it in a great tradition. It is not Johnson's theme only, but one that has been expressed through the ages. Bate makes some further observations:

> His poem is formally a satire, but his irony differs essentially from that in most classical or Augustan satiric writing, for it articulates a vision more essentially tragic than comic. In most satire, that is, the irony is in the author, who thus stands above his subject. Frequently in the poem Johnson also adopts this stance. But pervasively through *The Vanity of Human Wishes,* the irony is in the world, in the way of things, and the author is as helpless before it as the persons he writes about. In this respect Johnson is closer to Hardy than to Pope.

This is literary criticism of a high order. The distinction between merely satirical writing and writing that tells an unpalatable truth is one that many readers are unable to grasp. Bate understands Johnson's temperament: Johnson has "less playfulness and wit than Dryden and Pope, but far more meditative weight and power of direct emotion." The observation does not proceed from the critic's fancy but from his knowledge of Johnson's life and thinking up to this point.

Literary criticism may make use of the methods of biography to show how a poet's life shaped a theme. Thomas Crawford's study of the poems of Robert Burns, for example, describes Burns's background, especially his exposure to Calvinism, in order to explain Burns's attitudes to religion. His attitudes are complex, and without some understanding of the man we may misunderstand the poems.

A case in point . . . I have a friend who is a very competent reader of poetry, one on whose judgment I rely. But in reading Burns's "Holy Willie's Prayer" she took the words "Holy Willie" literally to mean that Willie was a saintly man—she had no knowledge of Scottish Calvinism and the doctrine of predestination, with its division of humankind into the elect and the damned. She did not know about a consequence of the doctrine: the tendency of the elect to forgive themselves for their own trespasses while coming down like a ton of bricks on other people's. Burns's Willie is no saint—he has lifted a "lawless leg" upon more than one woman, he has been drunk on occasion, and he is spiteful and vindictive. All this went clean by my reader, and she took Willie to be a good man beleaguered by reprobates. With some knowledge of Burns and his culture she would have read the poem the other, right way—as the portrait of a hypocrite. Willie's posture of a holy man would have appeared ridiculous in the light of the facts about himself that he himself lets slip. But she was not looking for the slips, for she did not know that Burns detested the type.

You may think that the irony in "Holy Willie's Prayer" would be apparent to most readers. What kind of man would say, as Willie does:

> Besides I farther maun allow,
> Wi' Lizzie's lass, three times I trow—
> But, Lord, that Friday I was fou,
>> When I cam near her,
> Or else Thou kens Thy servant true
>> Wad never steer her.

and follow this with the self-justification:

> May be Thou lets this fleshly thorn
> Beset thy servant e'en and morn
> Lest he owre high and proud should turn
>> That he's sae gifted;
> If sae, Thy hand maun e'en be borne,
>> Until Thou lift it.

Is this not the peak of humility, the perfect logic of fanaticism—is this not mad? But, admitting that many readers who have not studied Burns and Scotland will seize upon the irony—and I am still surprised that this reader did not—would these readers suspect that Burns himself was not entirely unlike Willie? There is a division in Burns's attitude to sin; he will do it, and he will be sorry. If Holy Willie is a comic rather than a detestable character it is because Burns has committed Willie's sins, and is not above hoping that God will be lenient to himself. Burns understands and enjoys Holy Willie for reasons that have to do with his own religious upbringing, his revolt against it, and his arguments with his own conscience—none of which can be deduced from the poem.

The reader who thinks that Willie is just a hypocrite and a figure of fun will not appreciate what is happening in the penultimate stanza when Willie, speaking of his enemy, says:

> Lord, in the day o' vengeance try him;
> Lord, visit them wha did employ him,
> And pass not in Thy mercy by them,
>   Nor hear their pray'r:
> But, for Thy people's sake, destroy them,
>   An' dinna spare.

This is the voice of John Calvin, a thunder heard on the Sabbath in churches throughout Scotland. If one thinks that Burns is laughing at Willie here, one is wrong; this is Burns listening to the voice of conscience magnified in the voice of Calvin's *Institutes*. It is not a force to be trifled with, especially if it seems to be aimed at one-self—as in Burns's thinking it frequently was. But to get the full flavor of this one would have to read more than the single poem—one would have to read other poems by Burns, and it would certainly help to know something about Burns's life and the history of Scotland.

It is necessary to read at a distance as well as up close. The microscope is not the only instrument for viewing—there is also the telescope. My criticism of the New Criticism with its faith in close reading is that it tended to forget the telescope. The New Critics have denied, some of them vociferously, that this was their intent—they say that they assumed knowledge of history on the part of the reader. But this is not the way close reading was taught, and in universities all over the country we still see literary criticism that crawls over the text, from comma to comma, without lifting its head to see where it is going and whether it really matters.

In great poetry—writing that moves us to feel and think deeply—there is a theme or pattern of thought expressing a general truth that appears to have been arrived at through experience. And it appears to be involuntary—inspired, poets of an earlier age would have said. "Poetry," Shelley says, "is not like reasoning, a power to be exerted according to the determination of the will. A man cannot say, 'I will compose poetry.'" Two thousand years before Shelley, Plato said that "All good poets, epic as well as lyric, compose their beautiful poems not by art, but because they are inspired and possessed."

What they are possessed by is a theme, an idea that expresses the passion of the poet and, at the same time, speaks to our passions. It is for lack of this that much writing in verse fails to move—the idea is expressed without passion. Or if it is expressed with passion, the writer has forgotten the other part of the equation: it must be expressed in such a way as to appeal to our passions, as a thing we ourselves might have seen or heard. That is, it does not appeal to the senses.

Discovering the theme is the nearest we can come to the central mystery of the poem—all other parts depend on this. It would seem best, therefore, in reading to go straight for the theme, to see the most important thing about the poem before we become engrossed in the details. Indeed, unless we see the most important thing we are likely to be bogged down in the details and perhaps to misread them. To understand poetry we must understand the mind of the poet. We must have a feeling for the style—know when the words mean what they say and when the poet is being ironic.

If one grasps basic patterns of the poet's thought, textual difficulties will appear less difficult and in many instances to be of no real importance. To take a notorious case, the *Cantos* of Ezra Pound . . . If one sets out to read them through with a *Guide to the Cantos* at one's elbow, looking up every reference, the experience ceases to be poetry and becomes an exercise in looking things up. If, on the other hand, one grasps the themes of Pound's writing: his belief that there are certain gods or permanent ideas that reappear throughout the ages, destroying society and building it again—if one grasps, above all, the desire of a personality to flaunt itself and assume the posture of a talented, reckless, incorrigible bohemian, a latter-day Villon—if one grasps what it is to be Ezra Pound, then it is not necessary to look up every reference to the banking system in an Italian city some centuries ago or the behavior of an emperor in ancient China—matters, in any case, of which Pound was spottily and unreliably informed. One may treat such references as notes of music, as sounds . . . . The themes, as I have described them, are the meaning of the *Cantos*—they are what give the poem such coherence as it has: the coherence of a personality that expresses itself in a few patterns or themes that are always the same. These patterns are not produced by Pound's will—they arise from the sources of his being, sources that, it is apparent, were mostly hidden from himself. One theme, that of usury, was so far from being voluntary that it turned on its maker, took over his personal life, and made him, to his everlasting ignominy, the advocate of Fascism.

One does not choose a theme, it chooses one—hence its power. Hence, also, the bad poems great poets write, along with the poems that appear to have been, in Plato's word, inspired. At the risk of seeming frivolous, I would say that the mark of a great poet is a kind of bad writing that he or she does when aesthetic considerations or social prudence would urge taking a more pleasing route. The bad writing of a great poet is compelled by the same theme or themes that produced the good—it is all of a piece. Consider this by Keats, from *Endymion:*

> O magic sleep! O comfortable bird,
> That broodest o'er the troubled sea of the mind
> Till it is hush'd and smooth!

This is a ridiculous metaphor, for birds do not smooth the waves by brooding on them. Fancy here has taken leave of sense. Nevertheless, sleep, the wish to sleep, the comfort sleep may give, in other words, a playing with the idea of death, is a major theme of Keats's writing. Within two years of writing the lines I have quoted, he was able to write these:

> Darkling I listen; and, for many a time
> I have been half in love with easeful Death,
> Call'd him soft names in many a mused rhyme,
> To take into the air my quiet breath . . .

The second passage is so much better poetry than the first, not merely because the words are better but the thought behind the words. In the first passage the poet is satisfied to express his theme—the wish to be unconscious. In the second passage he has meditated on his theme, and developed it so as to engage the world. He speaks of wishing for a drink that would enable him to fade away and forget, "The weariness, the fever, and the fret/Here where men sit and hear each other groan." This is vastly more interesting. In both passages, however, the weak writing and the strong, the theme is consistent.

Theme is an expression of consistent thinking, an expression of character. And character is different from personality, the external man Proust said Saint-Beuve aimed to show. To speak of the poet's theme is to speak of the character of the poet—the quality that enables us to tell at a glance that a few lines of writing are by Robert Frost, or by Whitman, or by Donne. If you wish to call it style, I have only this objection—the word "style" tends to turn attention to the writer's choice and use of language, while I want to concentrate attention on the theme, the underlying, urgent thing.

Why is it so urgent? Isn't the choice and use of language just as important? Poems, followers of Mallarmé like to remind us, are made of words. Indeed they are, just as men and women are made of flesh and blood. But the flesh and blood are draped on a skeleton—and the poem must have a structure, a form dictated by the theme.

In the poetry-writing workshops that have proliferated all over the United States, I think if one were to ask the instructor what is the most difficult thing about teaching writing—if it can be taught at all—he or she would say that it is to discover a theme in a student's writing. For the most part it does not exist. Writing may come easily to young people, but very few have written great poetry. They do not have a theme, a pattern of thought that expresses the deepest self and also a truth external to the self. They find it easy to express moods and opinions, but the other part eludes them.

Without a theme writing is what Paul said of words without charity: they are sounding brass and a tinkling cymbal. One arrives at a theme by living—there is no other way. To be a poet is to be open to experience; it is the feeling and sound of experience that gives writing its authority.

My dictionary defines theme as "a subject or topic of discourse, a written exercise." I have wished to show that it is something more than that. The poet's theme is an expression of his deepest, unalterable self. Some poets, the greatest, seem to have more than one theme, more than one self that compels expression. I have mentioned Yeats, but Shakespeare is the most flagrant example of the species. It is this in Shakespeare that aroused Tolstoy's antipathy. Himself divided, and unhappily so—though he did his most appealing work when divided—Tolstoy strove toward a monolithic theme, an expression of Christianity that would be perfectly simple and straightforward. It came down finally to this: "Sell all you have and give to the poor."

Whether a writer have one theme or several, it is his development of a theme that makes him effective and memorable.[2] By development I do not mean deliberate manipulation, for, as I have said, the theme is involuntary. Though the poet will meditate on the ideas that concern him most, and may consciously refine them, the reason these ideas are urgent will always elude him. Fortunately, when it comes to understanding themselves poets are no wiser than other people. They are not able to analyze themselves successfully—I think that if they could they would no longer be driven to write.

A poet should wish for enough unhappiness to keep him writing. His happiness will lie in the expression of a theme—a pattern of thought that is peculiar to him and, at the same time, of interest to the world.

Robert Frost is a case in point, and I would like to consider him at some length. Frost's poetry has been read by people who do not usually read poetry, and adopted as a rallying point for those who find modern poetry obscure. He has not, however, had nearly as much attention from the critics as Eliot, Pound, Williams, and Stevens, and much of the criticism of Frost that does exist seems amateurish. It seems not to know how to go about discussing the poetry. I think this is because the reader of Frost's poetry feels that he is being confronted with the life of the poet at every turn, but he knows that it is wrong to take a work of art as autobiography. Yet a

[2] I have occasionally used the pronoun "he" or "his" to stand for both masculine and feminine. E.g., "The world the poet moves about in, the materials of his art . . ." There are times when to say "he or she" or "his or hers" would be distracting. My use of the masculine pronouns is not intended to exclude women or deny their stature as poets.

poem by Frost seems to be hovering around a secret, some real event—the passion in the poem seems personal. How is one to deal with this and not fall into the trap of reading the poem as a window into the life of the poet?

In reading Frost I am struck by a polarization of feelings between two characters, a husband and a wife. It occurs in "The Death of the Hired Man," "Home Burial," and "The Hill Wife." In every instance the male figure is rather hard-headed, and even dense. It is a willed denseness—he does not want to see and feel too much. The tension between those figures, so different and yet joined by marriage, is what makes the poem move.

One notices the isolation of the two. There seems to be no one else in the world—the drama is to be played out between them. I have said that the life shown in poems is different from the life of the poet, and these poems are evidence of it. In the real-life household of Robert and Elinor Frost there were several children who must have moved about or sat still, spoken or been silent. There are no children in these poems—the drama is between husband and wife alone.

What title for this theme? Robert Poirier has said that "home" is a major theme in Frost's poetry. Home is "a place, a form, a mode of discourse in which unmanageably extreme states of feeling occur." But the word "home" does not describe the drama I have in mind. The word "marriage" comes closer. And it is a marriage of poets: each of the participants is a poet, she in her way, he in his. Of the two, the woman seems to have the more poetic character—she feels deeply and speaks out of her feelings, or is feelingly silent. He, on the other hand, tends to be practical; he doesn't want to look into things too deeply—whether it be the life of a hired man or the death of a child. His motto would be, "Life must go on." In his denseness he allows the other, more feeling partner to slip away, and he learns of finalities besides the grave.

Being a poet—that is, having the temperament—may demand all one's intelligence and energy, so that one may not actually write anything. To write poetry, on the other hand, one has to be at a distance from one's feelings and be able to play with the facts. In this "marriage of two poets" a struggle is going on between the one who feels more keenly, and fears more, and the other, more worldly poet.

It is the poet of grief—and passionate love—who will lose the struggle and slip away. The poet of wisdom will survive; he has promises to keep and miles to go before he sleeps.

This is the theme, the central drama, of Frost's poems; other poems are footnotes to this.

I have not attempted to psychoanalyze Robert Frost—I have arrived at my ideas by reading his poems. I think that any author can be understood in this way, and that what we arrive at is what Proust called the "true self," that part of the author which thinks and creates, rather than the ordinary self which sits down to dinner and has all sorts of opinions, none of which have any direct bearing on the works he has written. The written work springs from depths of the psyche: it is written at the dictates of the character of the poet, a different self from the one who, having lit a cigar, is about to deliver an opinion on politics.

In order to discover the poet's true self one immerses oneself in the poet's works. The pattern can hardly be discovered from a single work, for poetry is dramatic, and what the poet says in one place he may not say in another—or he may contradict himself. The theme will have its variations. But when all the works are considered a basic pattern of thought will emerge.

If the single work is read in the light of this, it will have deeper resonance. The reader who grasps the thought of a poet in its entirety is able to approach the text with confidence. He knows what the poet must be thinking. In a sense, he has become the poet.

To be a poet one must discover the themes that are proper to oneself. There can be no formulas for such discoveries—there has to be an openness to experience such as Keats describes: "If a Sparrow come before my Window I take part in its existence and pick about the Gravel." Or Whitman:

> There was a child went forth every day,
> And the first object he look'd upon, that object he became . . .

This is the first step. Then the matter must be transformed into poetry.

If we look into the lives of poets we shall find there was a time of withdrawal from the world, of silence and meditation. We tend to think of poetry as trying to write, as having original ideas and fetching images from afar. But does poetry have no power in itself? No reality? What would happen if instead of trying to write one allowed silence to speak?

Dante has told us how he became a poet. For nine years love had ruled his soul—the image of Beatrice was always present in his mind. Then one day he saw her walking in the street between two older women of distinguished bearing. She greeted him—he experienced the height of bliss and his senses reeled.

He returned to his lonely room where, thinking of Beatrice, he fell asleep and had a vision of a lordly figure, "frightening to behold," says the poet, "yet in himself, it seemed to me, he was filled with a marvellous joy." The figure said many things of which he understood only a few, among them the words, *"Ego dominus tuus,"* "I am your master." The figure held Beatrice in his arms; she was asleep, naked, and he seemed to say, *"Vide cor tuum,"* "Behold your heart." It seemed that he wakened the sleeping Beatrice and prevailed upon her to eat the glowing object in his hand. Reluctantly and hesitantly she did so. A few moments later his happiness turned to bitter grief and, weeping, he gathered Beatrice in his arms and together they seemed to ascend into the heavens.

The poet felt such anguish at their departure that he woke. It was, he tells us, the first of the last nine hours of the night. Pondering what he had seen in his dream, he decided to make it known to a number of poets who were famous at the time. "As I had already tried my hand at composing in rhyme, I decided to write a sonnet in which I would greet all Love's faithful servants; and so, requesting them to interpret my dream, I described what I had seen. This was the sonnet beginning, 'To every captive soul.' "

With the passing of the old religious world poets no longer thought of themselves as inspired by a god, but still they felt prompted to write by a power outside themselves. For Wordsworth this power spoke through nature. He tells how he first became aware that he was to be a poet. He was returning home at dawn from a night spent in "dancing, gaiety, and mirth," with "Slight shocks of young love-liking interspersed," when

> Magnificent
> The morning rose, in memorable pomp,

> Glorious as e'er I had beheld—in front,
> The sea lay laughing at a distance; near,
> The solid mountains shone . . .

The scene before him included laborers going out to till the fields. "Ah! need I say, dear Friend," he says, addressing Coleridge,

> that to the brim
> My heart was full; I made no vows, but vows
> Were then made for me; bond unknown to me
> Was given, that I should be, else sinning greatly,
> A dedicated Spirit. On I walked
> In thankful blessedness, which yet survives.

I believe that all true poets feel a sense of dedication, and that this comes to them in solitude and silence. The silence of which Pascal spoke, the silence of infinite spaces, is terrifying, and most avoid it, but poetry feeds on silence. To apprehend the silence of the universe is to wish to break it, to speak to those who are in the same boat with ourselves.

The measure of a man, said Ortega, is the amount of solitude he can stand, and great poets are those who have listened greatly. Rilke speaks of this.

> Voices. Voices. Listen, my heart, as only
> saints have listened: until the gigantic call lifted them
> off the ground; yet they kept on, impossibly,
> kneeling and didn't notice at all:
> so complete was their listening. Not that you could endure
> *God's* voice—far from it. But listen to the voice of the wind
> and the ceaseless message that forms itself out of silence.
> Trans. by Stephen Mitchell

The task of the poet is to put into words the message that formed itself out of silence.

II. ENGAGING THE WORLD

"The earliest of all nations generally wrote from passion excited by real events." From this beginning Wordsworth developed an idea of the degeneration of poetic language. At first daring and figurative, it came to be used mechanically—figures of speech were applied to "feelings and thoughts with which they had no natural connection whatsoever. A language was thus insensibly produced, differing materially from the real language of men in *any situation*." (Appendix to the *Lyrical Ballads,* 1802)

What Wordsworth considered degenerate others have regarded as the best language of poetry. In his 1848 essay on "The Poetic Principle," Edgar Allan Poe said that the aim of art was to give pleasure, not to instruct. The poet should aim at creating "supernal beauty," and to be beautiful poetry must be unified and brief. Poe's ideas were introduced into France by Baudelaire, and became the doctrine of the Symbolist school that flourished in the 1880s. Mallarmé, leader of the school, said that poetry should "approach the condition of music." It should not state explicitly but suggest— "suggestion makes the dream." He spoke of a special language of poetry that would be different from the language of everyday, which he likened to coins that passed from hand to hand. For Mallarmé and his followers there was only one kind of poetry, the hermetic; narrative and discursive poetry were mixed with "impure" elements.

Fifty years later the Surrealists would divorce poetry from life altogether. The images in Symbolist poetry are recognizable—they are taken from the world perceived through the senses. But the images in Surrealist poems are invented—the further removed from anything one might actually see the better. Surrealist art breaks with logic and the tyranny of nature. As Ferdinand Alquié observes, in Surrealism "man is the creator of values, which have their sense only from him and relative to him." (*The Philosophy of Surrealism*)

The poetry of "real events" has not fared well at the hands of theorists such as these, and present critical theory finds little in such poetry that it can use. Those who study literature for the purpose of linguistic analysis do not find what they are seeking in poetry that is an "imitation of life." They want a "sub-text" that lends itself to the tools of analysis.

And, of course, the poetry of "real events" has lost some of its functions. It is no longer news and information. In ancient times one could learn from poetry the history of the tribe and something about the gods, or about the art of war, or when to sow seed and when to harvest. From Ovid one could learn the art of love, from Virgil how to be a good citizen. But poetry no longer relays the news—we have newspapers and television. Government manuals will tell you how to farm, and television will tell you how to have sex.

The poetry of real events could survive these losses well enough, but its main *raison d'être* appears to have been lost—why should we read narratives in verse when there are narratives in prose? If we want characters and situations, aren't they to be found in thousands of novels? There are narratives of every kind in prose that ranges from the complexity of James Joyce to the simplicity of the latest bestseller. What need, then, for characters and situations in verse?

Because they *are* in verse. Verse performs a unique function—the rhythm of measured language gives a pleasure prose does not give. Therefore it cannot be displaced by prose. It may seem to have been displaced if we go just by numbers: there are a thousand readers for a book of verse, a million for the latest blockbuster novel. But wait and see: if the verse is good it will continue to be read by someone, and read carefully, long after the prose has been forgotten.

Here is a hypothetical situation. A ship sailing on the Pacific Ocean is becalmed. It seems as motionless as a ship in a painting. This is a prose description and I think it is fair to say that none of you will remember it five minutes from now: you may remember the situation but not the sentences, because they had no definite shape and sound. There was no measure to evoke a response from that part of our being that responds to measured speech. Suppose, on the other hand, that I had said:

> Day after day, day after day,
> We stuck, nor breath nor motion;
> As idle as a painted ship
> Upon a painted ocean.

I think we are likely to remember this description because it is in rhyme and meter. The sound and the beat compel us to remember. With free verse the point is harder to make. It is not the measure of free verse that makes an impression—though some lines of free verse do have a striking rhythm. In free verse other elements play the part that used to be played by rhyme and meter: in free verse a great deal depends on the images. And free verse is more concentrated than prose.

Poe began his essay with a disclaimer: he had no intention of being thorough or profound, but wished to discuss some minor poems that he liked—that is, "poems of little length." He then proceeded to give *Paradise Lost* and *The Iliad* the back of his hand for being uneven—poetic passages being followed by platitudinous passages. The day of these artistic anomalies, he said, was over. "If, at any time, any very long poems *were* popular in reality—which I doubt—it is at least clear that no very long poem will ever be popular again."

In Poe's time some mediocre long poems were being written—he wished to knock the classics off their pedestals in order to put a stop to the rubbish being committed in their name. I would not object to Poe's expression of his taste were it not for the effect these statements have had on the writing of *all* narrative poetry, no matter what the length. In the hands of Mallarmé and his followers, Poe's dicta were made to apply to all poetry that deals with real events—it was all considered to be inferior to hermetic poetry.

As I have said, this prejudice is common at the present time—it is in line with structuralist theory. If one regards language as a reality in itself that does not derive its importance from the things it refers to, then Mallarmé's kind of poetry, with its complex sentences and obscure symbolism, will be more interesting than a poetry that presents dramatic or narrative situations. Among American poets Wallace Stevens will be ranked high, and Robert Frost low. Nor will T. S. Eliot and William Carlos Williams be ranked high, for though their writings are experimental in form and style, they draw images from life and frequently present a human situation. "The Waste Land" is good drama, and in poem after poem Williams presents a character sketch or a passage of narrative.

At this point, encouraged by the example of Poe, I shall state a preference. Pleasant as the verse of Mallarmé or Wallace Stevens may be to listen to—I say "listen to" rather than read, for it is primarily a poetry of sound: it is impossible to grasp the sense immediately—I prefer another kind of poetry, the kind that deals with situations we recognize and ideas that seem true. And I prefer it to be written in a style that is familiar. The first of the great English poets wrote this kind of poetry, and it is still as fresh as a daisy:

> Whan that Aprille with his shoures soote
> The droghte of March hath perced to the roote,
> And bathed every veyne in swich licour
> Of which vertu engendred is the flour;
> Whan Zephirus eek with his sweete breeth
> Inspired hath in every holt and heeth
> The tendre croppes, and the yonge sonne
> Hath in the Ram his halve cours yronne,
> And smale foweles maken melodye,
> That slepen al the nyght with open ye
> (So priketh hem nature in hir corages);
> Thanne longen folk to goon on pilgrimages,
> And palmeres for to seken straunge strondes,
> To ferne halwes kowthe in sondry londes;
> And specially from every shires ende
> Of Engelond to Canterbury they wende,
> The hooly blissful martir for to seke,
> That hem hath holpen whan that they were seeke.
> —Geoffrey Chaucer, *The Canterbury Tales*

The liveliness and color of Chaucer's descriptions have not been surpassed. But this is not all: he is a storyteller of considerable subtlety—see, for example, his rendering of character in *Troilus and Cressida*—and considerable power—see "The Pardoner's Tale." The background of the tale is such as we see depicted on the walls of medieval churches: the world of the Black Death in which people of every kind are snatched suddenly from the midst of their pleasures and hurled into Hell. The narrative has the evocative power of the old allegorical writing—people are not just what they appear to be, but supernatural powers in disguise:

> Whan they han goon nat fully half a mile,
> Right as they wolde han troden over a stile,
> An oold man and a povre with hem mette.

This olde man ful mekely hem grette,
And seyde thus, "Now, lordes, God yow see!"

One of the three dice-players and swearers of oaths greets the old
man roughly and asks him why he has lived so long. To which he
replies that he has not been able to find anyone who will exchange
his youth for age, and that Death will not take his life.

"Thus walke I, lyk a restelees kaityf,
And on the ground, which is my moodres gate,
I knokke with my staf, bothe erly and late,
And seye 'Leeve mooder, leet me in!' . . ."

The three demand to know where they can find this Death he
appears to know, and he tells them: he has left Death in a grove,
under a tree. Whereupon they run off and find a treasure of money
lying under the tree. The plot advances to its inevitable outcome.
The interest is no less because the outcome is inevitable—it is grati-
fying to see how the nature of the actors, their drunkenness, gam-
bling and swearing leads to their murdering one another. The tale,
through its allegorical method, evokes levels of meaning and a sense
of mystery one does not usually find in prose fiction. Who is the old
man the gamblers meet? He may be Death itself, or he may be Old
Age—certainly he is unforgettable, this child of earth who goes
wandering and knocking with a stick on his mother's breast.

At the same time the tale is realistic, evoking in a few lines the
atmosphere of the plague:

Thise riotoures thre of whiche I telle,
Longe erst er prime rong of any belle,
Were set hem in a taverne for to drynke,
And as they sat, they herde a belle clynke
Biforn a cors, was caried to his grave.

The "pure poetry" of Mallarmé seems trivial if we compare it with
Chaucer's—so much intelligence has been omitted!

What was said of one poet might be said of many: "The moment
he thinks, he is a child." But how different it is when the poet
presents his ideas in real situations! Following the laws of character

and action, he discovers what is true in his ideas and what is false. The poets the world considers great are not those who have had fantastic ideas but whose ideas have been tested, as Keats said, on our pulses.

Wordsworth is a philosopher, but who would pay attention to his philosophy if it had not been drawn from real situations? In the lines that follow he tells how, when he was a schoolboy, in his ramblings he would come upon a shepherd of the hills, and from this came his idea of human nature.

> When up the lonely brooks on rainy days
> Angling I went, or trod the trackless hills
> By mists bewildered, suddenly mine eyes
> Have glanced upon him distant a few steps,
> In size a giant, stalking through thick fog,
> His sheep like Greenland bears; or, as he stepped
> Beyond the boundary line of some hill-shadow,
> His form hath flashed upon me, glorified
> By the deep radiance of the setting sun:
> Or him have I descried in distant sky,
> A solitary object and sublime,
> Above all height! like an aerial cross
> Stationed alone upon a spiry rock
> Of the Chartreuse, for worship. Thus was man
> Ennobled outwardly before my sight,
> And thus my heart was early introduced
> To an unconscious love and reverence
> Of human nature . . .
>
> *The Prelude,* VIII

William Carlos Williams has been our Wordsworth. Williams said, "I go back to people. They are the origin of every bit of life that can possibly inhabit any structure, house, poem or novel of conceivable human interest . . . . If we don't cling to the warmth which breathes into a house or a poem alike from human need ... the whole matter has nothing to hold it together and becomes structurally weak so that it falls to pieces." ("The Basis of Faith in Art")

Williams's own poems are located in "real events," or at least a recognizable scene. In many a poem by Williams his curiosity about people is enough to carry the day. But poems that have no human characters, that seem to be simply describing a landscape or some common object, hold our interest for another reason. Williams is obsessed with the need to make poetry out of the most seemingly antipoetic materials; it is a challenge he has set himself. He said, "the thing that stands eternally in the way of really good writing is always one: the initial impossibility of lifting to the imagination those things which lie under the direct scrutiny of the senses, close to the nose. It is this difficulty that sets a value upon all works of art and makes them a necessity." ("Prologue to Kora in Hell")

This side of Williams has had considerable influence on the poets who came after. I don't think it is an exaggeration to say that Williams's theory of poetry is the basic text of most poetry-writing workshops in this country. It seems that one can do no wrong if one begins from Williams, describing things exactly as they are, close to one's nose. But objects and images are only half the battle. Poetry consists of two parts, an object and an idea, and though aspiring poets can usually manage to describe an object, they are not so able to have an idea. The objects in a poem by Williams, and the arrangement of objects, reflect his mind developed over a lifetime of thinking as a poet, a doctor, and a man. This is what gives his writing a vibrancy and a sense of leading somewhere. Actually the writing is leading back into the mind, pouring back into it. A young poet who adopts Williams's method of "objectivist" description without having the mind to give it coherence is likely to make poems that are pointlessly dull.

The circulatory system failed Williams when he wrote his long poem, *Paterson*. A state of mind is a good enough basis for writing a short poem, but for a long poem one needs a theme, a compelling idea, and as one ploughs through *Paterson* it is evident that Williams did not have one. Williams himself says:

> There is no direction. Whither? I
> cannot say. I cannot say
> more than how.
> *Paterson,* II

There are admirers of Williams who admire this—he is writing aimlessly on principle. But I think most readers will agree that *Paterson* is heavy going.

To engage the world one has to stand at a distance from the

subject. "Give me where to stand," says Archimedes, "and I will move the earth." The poet's lever is his idea—with this he can move the object. As I have said, poetry consists of the object and an idea. If one or the other is lacking it is not poetry but a gas, or an unmoving lump.

In spite of the low estate to which narrative has fallen in the past hundred years, there are many who read it eagerly when they get it. Robert Frost is still a popular poet—critics may not have enjoyed his work but thousands of readers have. Eliot's "The Waste Land" is a narrative poem, though the narrative is disjointed, and it is the most prestigious poem in English written in this century. The *Cantos* of Ezra Pound deal with real events.

These poets are well known, but there have been others, not known, who have written notable works in a form of narrative. I am using the word to mean writing that is an imitation of life.

Patrick Kavanagh, for example . . . I discovered his poems ten years ago. Before this I had not thought it necessary to read them. No critic had written about Kavanagh's poems. Besides, I had met the man at a cocktail party in Manhattan. There was a young girl— I think no older than seventeen—who had been brought by her mother, a literary agent, to breathe the air of Parnassus. The poet was talking to this girl—then she turned to move away. He raked his fingernails down her back. The girl uttered a scream and disappeared. For some time Kavanagh walked around looking for her, saying "Where's my Baby Doll?"

When I thought about Kavanagh I saw black-rimmed fingernails. But one day in the West of Ireland I took his *Collected Poems* with me in a boat, and read them while I fished. The poetry is accompanied in my mind by the lapping of water, sighing of reeds, and crying of birds. I wonder how much of our liking for the arts depends on circumstances—a good breakfast, interesting company, or some fine bit of natural scenery. And I wonder if much literary criticism is not oppressively grim because it was written in a study.

This is a poem by Kavanagh. The title . . . "Memory of My Father."

> Every old man I see
> Reminds me of my father

When he had fallen in love with death
One time when sheaves were gathered.

That man I saw in Gardner Street
Stumble on the kerb was one,
He stared at me half-eyed,
I might have been his son.

And I remember the musician
Faltering over his fiddle
In Bayswater, London,
He too set me the riddle.

Every old man I see
In October-coloured weather
Seems to say to me:
"I was once your father."

This poem has always affected me strongly. There is pathos in the descriptions of the old man stumbling on a curb and the old fiddler. In the final stanza the writing takes on the power of myth; the old men appear ancient and larger than life.

Kavanagh's most sustained poetry is "The Great Hunger." He said that he did not like the poem himself, because it was not detached—it was polemical in a way a policeman might understand, and "There is something wrong with a work of art, some kinetic vulgarity in it when it is visible to a policeman." But we cannot take as definitive what poets say about their works. They are no longer the self that wrote, and their understanding may be no better than anyone else's. Indeed, it is possible for a reader to have better insight into the meaning of a poem than the author.

The poem's title is ironic: it appears to refer to the famine in the nineteenth century that swept Ireland, killing thousands and driving other thousands into exile. But the "great hunger" of Kavanagh's poem is sexual hunger. It is not the potato that is blighted but human life. Patrick Maguire's mother "praised the man who made a field his bride," and he has done just this, passing up the women he might have married, so that in old age his life is married wretchedly to the soil.

He lives that his little fields may stay fertile when
   his own body
Is spread in the bottom of a ditch under two coulters
   crossed in Christ's Name.

Kavanagh is speaking of the perversion of sex but not as D. H. Lawrence speaks. Lawrence found solace in the beauty of nature and the instinctual life of the peasant. Kavanagh has something to say about this:

The world looks on
And talks of the peasant:
The peasant has no worries;
In his little lyrical fields
He ploughs and sows;
He eats fresh food,
He loves fresh women,
He is his own master
As it was in the Beginning
The simpleness of peasant life.

To this idealization Kavanagh contrasts the reality:

   the peasant in his little acres is tied
To a mother's womb by the wind-toughened navel-cord
Like a goat tethered to the stump of a tree—
He circles around and around wondering why it should be.
No crash,
No drama.
That was how his life happened.
No mad hooves galloping in the sky,
But the weak, washy way of true tragedy—
A sick horse nosing around the meadow for a clean
   place to die.

Kavanagh develops his theme in hundreds of strong lines. The phrase "strong poet" has been used by Harold Bloom to mean the poet who replaces the poetry of the past with his own vision of things. But, as William Blake said, there is no competition among poets. Strength comes of speaking the truth, and "The Great Hunger" carries a truth in every line. Kavanagh wants us not merely to see but to share the peasant's life:

> O let us kneel where the blind ploughman kneels
> And learn to live without despairing
> In a mud-walled space—
> Illiterate, unknown and unknowing.
> Let us kneel where he kneels
> And feel what he feels.

So we walk with Maguire behind the traces, or stand in the evening at the crossroads listening to the talk of the men—"words as wise/As the ruminations of cows after milking." We have a rare moment of self-generated pleasure:

> Sitting on a wooden gate,
> Sitting on a wooden gate,
> Sitting on a wooden gate,
> He didn't care a damn.
> Said whatever came into his head,
> Said whatever came into his head,
> Said whatever came into his head
> And inconsequently sang.

But the direction is downward, into the clay. Maguire, denying life—that is, the love of a woman—plods to an old age without joy or meaning. And this we are told, and the poetry makes us believe, is not just the story of Patrick Maguire.

> October creaks the rotted mattress,
> The bedposts fall. No hope, No lust.
> The hungry fiend
> Screams the apocalypse of clay
> In every corner of this land.

They take poetry seriously in Ireland, as they seem to do in every country but this, and one can see why a policeman called on Kavanagh, as he tells us, with a copy of the poem in his hand, and asked, "Did you write that?" The lines that offended the policeman may have been those that describe Maguire's autoeroticism. Or the lines showing the denseness of a priest:

> "You were a good woman," said the priest,
> "And your children will miss you when you're gone.
> The likes of you this parish never knew" . . .

and the mindlessness of the peasant's religion:

> She reached five bony crooks under the tick—
> "Five pounds for Masses—won't you say them quick."

"The Great Hunger" is effective social criticism because the poet shares the life he is writing about, kneels where the blind plough-man kneels.

A poetry of social criticism is convincing only insofar as the poet seems to know the people he is writing about and to feel with them, sharing their hardships and pleasures. Especially their pleasures . . . It is not enough to want to help people—you have to like them too, and for what they are, not what you want them to be.

It is instructive to compare "The Great Hunger" with the Leftish poems written by W. H. Auden, Stephen Spender, and their friends in the 1930s. The "Oxford Poets" preened and congratulated them-selves on their social awareness and moral superiority to those who had no such awareness. But the poetry they wrote shows no famil-iarity with the common man and woman—they are merely figures in a landscape. This is how Spender describes a worker's funeral in the socialist state he envisages. The workers, it seems, are delighted with technology—this is what they like.

> Death is another milestone on their way.
> With laughter on their lips and with winds blowing
>   round them
> They record simply
> How this one excelled all others in making driving
>   belts.
>
> "The Funeral"

Has anyone ever known workers like these? Not even in the states of Eastern Europe. Even under socialism the workers are not devoted to their labor as these English poets, themselves children of the middle class, think workers should be.

Wordsworth said that poetry is written by a person "of more than usual organic sensibility" who has also "thought long and deeply." This applies to writing for a cause as much as to writing about daffodils—perhaps more, for the subject is not so attractive.

The poems that move one to feel some social injustice keenly may not be overtly political. The most useful writer, from the point of view of a reformer, is not the one who proclaims that his heart is in the right place and produces stereotypes of vice and virtue, but the one who renders things as they are in a manner that convinces people to change them. This is why Marxist thinkers, from Marx and Engels to Lukacs, have placed a high estimate on the novels of Balzac. Engels, in a letter to a novelist, says that Balzac gives us a wonderfully realistic history of French society, describing the pressure of the rising bourgeoisie upon the society of nobles that established itself after 1815. Though Balzac's sympathies are with the class that is doomed to extinction ". . . his satire is never keener, his irony never more bitter, than when he sets in motion the very men and women with whom he sympathizes most deeply—the nobles. And the only men of whom he speaks with undisguised admiration are his bitterest political antagonists, the republican heroes of the Cloître Saint Méry, the men who at that time (1830–36) were indeed representatives of the popular masses." (Friedrich Engels to Margaret Harkness, 1887)

This is what is meant by "sincerity" in writing—an adherence to truth that compels the writer to render things accurately though they may be against his or her own prejudices. The sincere poet will turn satire against himself, if need be. The insincere poet, on the other hand, is the censor of his own works, wishing to show himself in the best possible light.

There was a poet—let us call him X. In his poems he himself appeared as a paragon of virtue, while others were corrupt. Once I showed him some lines of verse in which I expressed a passing mood. In my poems I express such moods; they are to be taken as part of the drama in which I—the one who is speaking—am an actor. My poems are works of imagination, not tracts or sermons: on this occasion I was showing X a poem in which the speaker saw a spirit who told him that everything his, the speaker's, senses rejected sprang up in the spiritual world. Conversely, from the spirit's point of view, matter appeared mysterious:

> Things which to us in the pure state are mysterious,
> Are your simplest articles of household use . . .

Encouraged by this, the speaker, the "I" of the poem, confesses a thought:

> . . . I have suspected
> The Mixmaster knows more than I do,
> The air conditioner is the better poet.

At this point X protested strongly—it was wrong of me to say such a thing, self-denigrating to say that the air conditioner was a better poet than I was. My dramatizing the idea, placing it in the mouth of a fictional self in a dramatic situation, went for nothing. My showing the fictional self to be something less than confident went by X entirely—there was no humor in his view of the poet's role. When X appeared in one of his poems it was in his own person; he aimed to speak at all times with the accent of sincerity and be regarded as a person of serious views.

I do not think, however, that sincerity is achieved by aiming at it. I think it is achieved by being frank and admitting one's weaknesses as well as one's strengths. X's idea of poetry has been held by many American poets, especially when they have written in aid of one cause or another. This kind of earnestness exhibits the superior moral position of the writer—I doubt that it convinces anyone. I suppose it may give its readers or listeners the sense of belonging to a group that thinks as they do. It has never reassured me, however, to think that my ideas were those of a group. When I thought that they were, I suspected they were wrong.

The poet is formed as the individual is, by contact with the world, and the poets who seem original are those in whom we find life keenly observed. Hugh Kenner remarks that Ezra Pound is "fanatic" about facts and dates because he believes in "the inexhaustibility of the actual, and so in imitation—reflection—rather than fabrication."—" 'Originality' consists in being able to *see* something, often to see that it has been done before." ("The Broken Mirror and the Mirror of Memory") This idea must be anathema in places where originality—that is, thinking something no one seems to have thought of before, is regarded as the be-all and end-all. This is what people are educated to think art is, and art dealers make a pretty penny out of the belief, proclaiming a new movement every few months. But originality of this kind, having no substance, blows away like a feather in the wind.

The poet who would be original must steep himself in experience. Not drown, of course—he is, after all, a poet, different from other people because he desires to write poetry, though why he so desires it is useless to ask. The poet is like the speaker in Whitman's poem, "both in and out of the game." It is the being in I want to talk about, for I cannot say anything about the thought processes of the poet—they are unpredictable. The world the poet moves about in, however, the materials of his art, will bear some looking into.

It can be, at the first glance, a dreary scene, repellent and anti-poetic. I am speaking of the city and the suburbs. There are, of course, pleasant walks, well-designed apartments, and commodious houses. But millions of people have no access to these. If poetry is to say anything important it must deal with modern life in its less attractive aspects, "those things which lie under the direct scrutiny of the senses, close to the nose." And these do not attach our affections—on the contrary. It is not only the slums that are repellent—buildings erected at great expense appear to have been designed to amaze the individual, disappoint his expectations, and deny him comfort. These labyrinths of metal and glass are more forbidding to the wish to create than a slum would be.

The answer is to consider people—they, not things, are the proper subject. One American poet went wrong on this point and, through an error in his thinking, was brought to despair. In "The Bridge" Hart Crane set out to write "an epic of the modern consciousness"—his own phrase—but the poem has no real idea. He concentrates on describing things, hoping to wring a meaning from them. So he apostrophizes the Brooklyn Bridge:

> Unto us lowliest sometime sweep, descend
> And of the curveship lend a myth to God.

This is a puerile hope—matter has no ideas to impart, least of all to God. The poet, in order to hide his lack of direction, makes his language as gorgeous as he can, and the result is bombast:

> Of stars Thou art the stitch and stallion glow
> And like an organ, Thou, with sound of doom—
> Sight, sound and flesh Thou leadest from time's realm
> As love strikes clear direction for the helm.

"The Bridge" is like those modern buildings I have spoken about—uninhabitable.

The thing can be done, however—a poetry of "real events" is being written in our time. Seamus Heaney, for one, is writing it. Consider this poem from the sequence titled "Singing School":

A Constable Calls

> His bicycle stood at the window-sill,
> The rubber cowl of a mud-splasher
> Skirting the front mudguard,
> Its fat black handlegrips
>
> Heating in sunlight, the "spud"
> Of the dynamo gleaming and cocked back,
> The pedal treads hanging relieved
> Of the boot of the law.
>
> His cap was upside down
> On the floor, next his chair.
> The line of its pressure ran like a bevel
> In his slightly sweating hair.
>
> He had unstrapped
> The heavy ledger, and my father
> Was making tillage returns
> In acres, roods, and perches.
>
> Arithmetic and fear.
> I sat staring at the polished holster
> With its buttoned flap, the braid cord
> Looped into the revolver butt.

"Any other root crops?
Mangolds? Marrowstems? Anything like that?"
"No." But was there not a line
Of turnips where the seed ran out

In the potato field? I assumed
Small guilts and sat
Imagining the black hole in the barracks.
He stood up, shifted the baton-case

Further round on his belt,
Closed the domesday book,
Fitted his cap back with two hands,
And looked at me as he said goodbye.

A shadow bobbed in the window.
He was snapping the carrier spring
Over the ledger. His boot pushed off
And the bicycle ticked, ticked, ticked.

This is a drama . . . "Arithmetic and fear." But more is involved than the inquisition of one farmer by a constable. What is going on here is going on all over the land, and the words "domesday book" remind us that it has been going on for a long time. If one wishes to create a mythology it is in writing such as this that it may be accomplished. Truth is never far away, nor poetry that has the ring of truth.

III. THE DRAMA OF THE POEM

"What is poetry?" Coleridge observes, "is so nearly the same question with, what is a poet? that the answer to the one is involved in the solution of the other." (*Biographia Literaria*, XIV) If Coleridge is right, and I think he is—I do not see how anyone can deny that poetry originates in the mind of the poet—then to understand poetry we must understand the poet. But not the man or woman who eats, sleeps, and goes about the business we all have in common . . . it is the creative mind that concerns us. This reveals itself in patterns of thought and appears as the themes of the poet's writing.

In the poetry of Keats, for example, a theme appears repeatedly. He is tempted to "die a death/of luxury" ("Sleep and Poetry"); "to hear her tender-taken breath,/And so live ever—or else swoon to death" ("Bright Star"); to "leave the world unseen,/And ... fade away into the forest dim." ("Ode to a Nightingale") The theme itself is rather depressing, that pleasure brings on death, but the life of poetry is not in the subject, it is in the poet. Whenever Keats expresses this idea he is energized; his writing takes on a power of authority, a distinctive tone. He appears to have thought long and feelingly on the subject. We are moved by his sincerity, if not by the idea, and are moved to feel as he does.

"Sincerity" is a vague word, but if we are to discuss poetry we must use such words. We might use more technical words, but as poetry has to do with feelings they would miss the mark. We might find that we had invented a language of literary criticism that was an end in itself, one word relating to another but not relating to experience, having nothing to do with the effect of the poem on the reader—nothing to do with poetry at all.

The word "sincerity" is not as impractical as it seems. When we are familiar with an author we recognize his or her true self in a turn of phrase, a tone, or a rhythm. And recognition is not ours alone—poetry evokes a fairly consistent response. The response may be pleasure for some readers and dislike for others, but that is another matter. The feelings in the poetry affect the readers' feelings, and reactions are fairly predictable. A reader may not care for the poetry of Keats but he will admit that Keats is a poet. If pressed, he would admit that the poetry of Keats has certain definite virtues. Pressed further, he would quote stanza and line to explain why he feels as he does.

In speaking of readers I do not mean the public at large. The public at large does not read poetry. It may read books of verse by Rod McKuen, for example, but these are not poetry. In the discussion of poetry, as with the weather, or automobiles, or any other subject, only the opinions of those who are well-informed matter. They need not have studied poetry at a university, may have read it for themselves, but in any case they must have read widely and thoughtfully.

Such readers are capable of judging whether or not the feeling in poetry is sincere. They are clear in their own minds about what they feel. It is only a certain kind of literary theorist, caught in the thickets of his profession, who finds no meaning in words such as "sincerity" when they are applied to literature. Readers have to deal with situations every day that demand a feeling response; they know the words and gestures that denote love and hate, sincerity and insincerity. How can they, and why should they, have a different set of responses when they read? To the reader the words of poetry have the same meaning as they do in life. Poetry is an imitation of life, and he is moved by the poem as he would be by a real event.

When reading plays or narrative poems we see clearly that poetry is an imitation of life. Life is action, it is drama, and this is what engages our interest. Not in plays and narrative poems only, but any kind of poetry. In poetry that does not have characters and a plot there is an action of ideas.

Nothing could be wider of the mark than Mallarmé's saying that "poetry is not written with ideas, but with words." If this is true we cannot admit that Homer, Dante, and Shakespeare are poets. In our time this saying of Mallarmé has given rise to the kind of literary theory I have already mentioned, that holds that literature has no meaning, it is only a series of metaphors. One cannot argue with thinking such as this—but there is no need to argue. For literature to have meaning all that is necessary is to think that it does.

There is a struggle of ideas in poetry and our response is in direct proportion to the intensity of the struggle. There is a greater pleasure in reading *Macbeth* than some simple song or ballad because in *Macbeth* more is involved.

There may be poetry that shows no struggling—indeed, no ideas. I am speaking of poetry that is felt to be good, not the usual published poetry which, indeed, has no ideas. There are poems that approach the condition of objects—the Imagist poets, and the Objectivists who came after them, attempted to write poetry that would show no trace of thought. If one examines their writings, however, one finds a tension of syntax, rhythm, and ideas. What is the image in this poem by H.D. but a juxtaposition and tension of different ideas—the idea of the sea and the idea of the forest, merging to become one thing?

> Whirl up, sea—
> Whirl your pointed pines.
> Splash your great pines
> On our rocks.
> Hurl your green over us—
> Cover us with your pools of fir.
>   "Oread"

William Carlos Williams's poems appear to be plain descriptions of things as they are:

> All along the road the reddish
> purplish, forked, upstanding, twiggy
> stuff of bushes and small trees
> with dead, brown leaves under them
> leafless vines—
>   "Spring and All"

The writings of the Objectivists are not as impersonal as they seem. In "Spring and All" the words "reddish, purplish, forked, upstanding" evoke human figures.

> But now the stark dignity of
> entrance—Still, the profound change
> has come upon them: rooted, they
> grip down and begin to awaken.

What appeared to be a description of Spring is actually an extended metaphor or allegory of childbirth.

Keats's ode, "To Autumn," is famous for its description of calm and quiet, its sculptural immobility. Nothing could be less agitated than the personification of Autumn:

> Who hath not seen thee oft amid thy store?
>   Sometimes whoever seeks abroad may find
> Thee sitting careless on a granary floor,
>   Thy hair soft-lifted by the winnowing wind;
> Or on a half-reap'd furrow sound asleep,
>   Drows'd with the fume of poppies . . .

Could anything be less dramatic? What struggle can there be in this description? Not only is there no drama, ideas seem to be entirely absent. Keats once exclaimed, "O for a Life of Sensations rather than of Thoughts!" In the ode "To Autumn" he seems to have attained his wish—at least, on paper.

But let us look again. This picture of Autumn as a harvester is the center of the poem. We see him at rest on the granary floor, sleeping beside a furrow, "And sometimes like a gleaner thou dost keep/ Steady thy laden head across a brook." Finally he sits by the cider-press as it yields "the last oozings hours by hours." This is the very picture of fulfillment.

The following stanza, however, is full of sound and activity.

> Then in a wailful choir the small gnats mourn
> Among the river sallows, borne aloft
> Or sinking as the light wind lives or dies;
> And full-grown lambs loud bleat from hilly bourne;
> Hedge-crickets sing . . .

We feel the contrast between this murmuring life and the sleep or drowsy watch of the harvester. We are finding beneath the surface what I have described as Keats's theme, a wish to "Fade far away, dissolve and quite forget." We may remember, too, that in another place he describes the poet as a harvester:

> When I have fears that I may cease to be
> Before my pen has glean'd my teeming brain,
> Before high-piled books, in charactery,
> Hold like rich garners the full ripen'd grain . . .

Keats has always been attracted to easeful sleep and oblivion. On the other hand, he is keenly appreciative of sensuous life—no poet more so. Therefore in the "Ode to a Nightingale" he argues himself out of the temptation to fade and dissolve. Listening to the nightingale's song is a pleasure so keen that he almost swoons. He would like to remain in this condition—but if he did, he would be unable to feel anything at all.

> Still wouldst thou sing, and I have ears in vain—
> To thy high requiem become a sod.

Excess of pleasure brings on death. Therefore he pulls back and finds himself, like the Knight in "La Belle Dame Sans Merci," on the

cold hillside of life. But the argument has only been suspended—
the dilemma is not solved. How do I know that the "I" that thinks
is the real self? "Do I wake or sleep?" Perhaps the real self is the one
that fades and sleeps.

In "To Autumn" the argument is still continuing. The figure of
the harvester at the center of the poem is so richly conceived that it
looms larger than life—the sleeping or motionlessly watching fig-
ure appears giant-like in comparison with the busy, noise-making
gnats, lambs, hedge-crickets, redbreast, and swallows of the final
stanza. In this poem the ease and oblivion Keats has been courting
overwhelm the arguments of life. Beneath the apparently calm,
untroubled surface a struggle is drawing to a close. The poet is
reconciled to dying—more than reconciled, he appears to welcome
it—the figure of the harvester contains a power greater than life.
"Ode to Autumn" is an ode to oblivion, and in fact Keats would be
dead in a year.

Aristotle in the *Poetics* confines his observations to tragedy—that is,
in the theater—and epic poetry, and gives the palm to tragedy as the
superior form of art. It might seem that a better title for the *Poetics*
would be *How to Write a Play*. But in writing about the theater
Aristotle was also writing about poetry. On the stage the drama is
plain to see, in the actions of the characters. In written poetry the
same actions take place in words and the stage is in the mind of the
reader. Whether it be on the stage or in writing, poetry is drama—it
consists of ideas in action.

Aristotle's description of poetry as an imitation of life explains
why some writing moves the reader while other writing does not.
The poet and the reader have an interest in common—they are
human beings and subject to the same passions. The reader is
engaged by ideas that speak to his hopes and fears. Writing that
does not do this—that expresses feelings the reader does not
share—cannot concern him much. Wordsworth described poetry as
"the spontaneous overflow of powerful feelings," and since the
Romantics we have seen a great deal of poetry of this kind. But
much of the feeling expressed has been private to the author, with a
consequent diminution of the reader's interest. In his own poetry,
however, Wordsworth did not apply the formula—his best poems,

"Tintern Abbey," "Resolution and Independence," "Michael," the "Immortality" ode—are dramatic. There is a drama of ideas and frequently these are embodied in character and scene.

Anyone can overflow with feeling—not everyone is a poet. The poet is a "maker," embodying feeling in a form that appeals to the reader's sympathy. I think it was Randall Jarrell who told the story of a monk who was visited by an angel who told him to take up his pen and write. The angel dictated a poem; it went on for days; word of this spread through the monastery and there was a reverent hush. But when the angel vanished and the poem was read it turned out to be doggerel. So much for a spontaneous overflow of feeling unaccompanied by a sense of drama—that which speaks to the audience.

Verse that is not dramatic makes no impression. As Robert Frost said, "No tears in the writer, no tears in the reader." Much of the verse we see in books and magazines is pointlessly descriptive— there is no investment of emotion on the part of the author and no play of ideas.

Poems are made with ideas, and the greatest poets, those who have given their name to an age, are those who express the most profound and far-reaching ideas. Their ideas may not have been original with them—on the contrary, the ideas we find in great poets appear to have been shared with the majority. Insistence on originality is symptomatic of a decline in the importance of poetry. The wish to write a poem that in its form and style is unlike any other poem, to express an idea no one has ever thought of, leads to writing poetry no one wants to read. And the wish of poets to be original is complemented by the wish of readers not to appear unfashionable. So they honor the writing they do not understand.

But the "state of poetry" is not our concern. Nothing could be less to the point than newspaper and magazine articles about how many books of poetry are sold, or poetry readings given, or who has won the prizes. Lovers of poetry need not concern themselves about such matters.

I discussed Keats's "To Autumn" because it seemed untroubled by ideas. The play of ideas is usually more obvious. Consider the most influential poem written in this century, Eliot's "The Waste Land." It is obviously dramatic—it is spoken in different voices and there is much shifting of scene. We may not grasp the meaning of the poem as a whole—and many have taken Eliot to be saying something he did not mean to say—but in line after line our interest is engaged, by an image or fragment of conversation. We felt the drama though we missed the meaning.

Eliot was particularly aware of the dramatic nature of poetry. His description of the "objective correlative" is well known:

> The only way of expressing emotion in the form of art is by finding an "objective correlative"; in other words, a set of objects, a situation, a chain of events which shall be the formula of that *particular* emotion; such that when the external facts, which must terminate in sensory experience, are given, the emotion is immediately evoked.

In other words, ideas in poetry are to be embodied in objects and actions, for, as Locke remarked, "Nothing can be perceived by the mind that was not first in the senses."

Eliot's poetry is intensely dramatic. "An idea to Donne," he wrote, "was an experience," and the same might be said of his own writing. Ideas appear as images. There are dramatic situations, and the lines have complex meanings—the writing is dramatic in detail. Coleridge observes that poetry "is discriminated by proposing to itself such delight from the *whole* as is compatible with a distinct gratification from each component part." In the writings of an Eliot or Donne the poetry is in the play of words and phrases as well as in the whole. Every word contributes to the effect of the whole, and this is what compels us to read. Prose, on the other hand, does not have this interest. There are exceptions—the prose of Flaubert, or Conrad, or Joyce—but in general prose sentences do not have the complexity of meaning and therefore compelling force of poetry. The words and phrases are not dramatic in themselves, there is not a play of ideas in every sentence. Prose may be translated into another language without losing anything essential, because the choice of words doesn't really matter, the rhythm doesn't really matter. But these things are essential and provide the delight of poetry.

Consider the following lines:

"On Margate Sands.
I can connect
Nothing with nothing.
The broken fingernails of dirty hands.
My people humble people who expect
Nothing" . . .

The speaker is one of the women in "The Waste Land" telling how she was seduced. Her words seem straightforward, their meaning plain: she is unable to connect, to make sense of the event. But, she seems to be saying, that is the way life is for people of her class—humble people "who expect nothing." The passage reads like a statement of disillusionment—but then, she has had hardly any illusions. (Early readers of Eliot read "The Waste Land" as the statement of the disillusionment of a generation. He said that it might be their disillusionment, but it was not his.)

This is the obvious reading of the passage, but there is another and opposite meaning that lies hidden beneath the surface. At this point the reader may object that a meaning that cannot be seen may as well not exist—and I have sometimes felt that way myself when reading the exegesis of an obscure text. But what is obscure to me may be clear to another. If the critic is finding meanings we have not found for ourselves, we should not dismiss them—rather, we should ask if they are true.

As I have said, the words "I can connect/Nothing with nothing" appear to mean that the woman cannot make sense of the event. On another level, however, they can mean something entirely different, and this contrast of meanings is dramatic. The word "nothing" has appeared before in "The Waste Land." The lady in the bedroom is speaking to someone, presumably her husband or lover—

"What is that noise now? What is the wind doing?"
          Nothing again nothing.
                              "Do
"You know nothing? Do you see nothing? Do you remember
"Nothing?"

This emphasis on nothing gives it a positive rather than a negative value—it is darkness visible. Nothingness is a state of being, and one is reminded of the writing of Saint John of the Cross, with which Eliot is familiar, to the effect that one must have arrived at a feeling of nothingness—one must be convinced that experience is meaningless, and that there is no happiness in the world, in order to find the path of the spirit. In "The Waste Land" the word "nothing" evokes this dark stage in a spiritual journey. To ask "Do you know nothing?" is not just to be insulting, though it is that too—it is to pose a serious question about the spiritual condition of the person one is talking to.

The woman who says, "I can connect/Nothing with nothing," though she seems to be saying, "I can make no sense of anything," may actually be saying something quite different: "I am the connection—that is, I could be, if you would let me. I could connect nothing with nothing." That this is a possible interpretation of the passage appears toward the end of the poem:

> The sea was calm, your heart would have responded
> Gaily, when invited, beating obedient
> To controlling hands

The "I" of "I can connect/Nothing with nothing" is not a negligible person—she holds the key to happiness. Her people are humble people—but so, we have been told, are those who will inherit the earth. The denseness of the seducer prevented him from seeing this.

There is a complex play of ideas in these lines, and it is this kind of activity that makes the language of poetry different from the language of prose. The language of poetry is more dramatic.

What of verse that seems to have no play of meaning? I would say that it may be verse but it is not poetry, unless some other kind of activity is occurring—through imagery, for example. Images and metaphors can provide the action in a poem as effectively as complex meanings—in a song by Burns, for example:

> O, my luve is like a red, red rose
>   That's newly sprung in June:
> O, my luve is like the melodie
>   That's sweetly play'd in tune.

I have been reading the poems of Juan Ramón Jiménez. One would look in vain to the poems of Jiménez for characters and scenes such as "The Waste Land" provides. There are no voices but the poet's own, and no ambiguous remarks, unless with my poor understanding of Spanish I have failed to see them. Here is a poem by Jiménez in its entirety. The translator is Antonio T. de Nicolás.

I Am Measuring Myself With God

In the middle of the sea, a ship, this one,
places, measures, cuts up, fixes, relates to
your consciousness, mine, god.
We are not crossing the sea (I alone with the ship
while all the others sleep)
we are crossing your consciousness, which now is
round, gray, rainy, welcoming,
as I am myself, god, now.

This night is identical to the one
of my departure, the one
with the pure sea, sea of even waves,
night of the gate of the moon
that one could reach climbing its trail,
moon today covered with a curtain of rain.

We are crossing, god, a consciousness
of total water in harp strings of high music,
with the accompaniment of a deep moral density.

But in the middle of the sea suddenly
your geometry appears, it places you,
it measures you, it cuts up, fixes, relates
to me and your ship I keep watch over;
this ship breaks my life in three:
one life to the east,
one to the south, another to the north,
and I in the middle, calm in the sea of the west,
filled with love,
the center of a rose made of rains of love.

Full of love, my own, a ship
and I, love in the center of love,
of so much love as the sea needs
to measure you, god.

In the middle of the sea I am measuring you,
in the middle of the sea and of this ship, this one;
I am measuring you with me, god.

This is a kind of poetry for which there are hardly any precedents in English. The writings of Donne, Herbert, and other Metaphysical Poets express religious ecstasy and an eagerness to leave the world for heaven. In Whitman's "Song of Myself" there are passages that suggest an unearthly state of consciousness. But Whitman is usually earthbound, and though the Metaphysical Poets use far-fetched conceits, their arguments are perfectly rational.

As I one ev'ning sat before my cell,
Me thoughts a starre did shoot into my lap.
I rose, and shook my clothes, as knowing well,
That from small fires comes oft no small mishap.
When suddenly I heard one say,
"Do as thou usest, disobey,
Expell good motions from thy breast,
Which have the face of fire, but end in rest."

This conceit by George Herbert is typical—a shooting star compared to artillery fire. The speaker brushes the star from his clothes, and a voice tells him that, as usual, he is rejecting "good motions." The comparison is far-fetched—as Doctor Johnson said, the Metaphysical Poets "ransacked art and nature for comparisons"—but the argument is logical. But images in the poetry of Juan Ramón Jiménez are not used for comparison—they are not metaphors to illustrate an argument. They are what he feels and sees.

Jiménez's kind of poetry is an answer to Johnson's objection to devotional poetry on the ground that it could only belittle the subject. If the poet is not concerned with glorifying God, if he is expressing his sense of God, then the question of whether the poetry is "effective" is irrelevant—he is expressing his feelings. A poem by Jiménez is like a prayer.

An image in Jiménez is not intended to start a train of thought—
it is the thought. As I have said, this writing is not metaphorical. A
metaphor or simile is a comparison of one thing with another, the
thing one is concerned about with some other thing that has the
quality one wishes to emphasize: "my luve is like a red, red rose."
But suppose one actually sees one's love as a red rose? This is not
comparing one thing with another, it is seeing a new thing. It is a
vision.

When Rimbaud said that the poet should transform himself into
a visionary, it was poetry such as this he had in mind:

> we are crossing your consciousness, which now is
> round, gray, rainy, welcoming
> as I am myself, god, now.

Jiménez means that he is crossing a gray, rainy sea that is God—he
does not mean that God is like a sea. Moreover, there is no separa-
tion of the "I" that is seeing and the thing perceived. The "I" is the
sea that is God.

This visionary writing is not what Aristotle called an "imitation of
life." The drama is between the poet and God, directly.

The words of Diotima to Socrates point the direction this poetry
is taking: ". . . the true order of going, or being led by another to the
things of love, is to begin from the beauties of earth and mount
upwards for the sake of that other beauty, using these as steps only,
and from one going on to two, and from two to all fair forms, and
from fair forms to fair practices, and from fair practices to fair
notions, until from fair notions he arrives at the notion of absolute
beauty, and at last knowns what the essence of beauty is."

AFTERWORD

The ideas I have put forward in these essays are not in favor at the
present time. The poetry of "real events" is out of favor, especially in
our universities. The most prestigious critics prefer writing that
does not imitate life but offers a text that may be construed as the
critic wishes. For these critics, ideas in poetry do not relate to life.

Indeed, it is absurd to speak of life, for no one knows what it is. Poetry is only an arrangement of words, and its meaning is what the critic says it is.

There is no way to prove that such thinking is wrong. You cannot prove any thinking wrong, you can only hope people will see that another way of thinking leads to something better. "By their fruits you shall know them." The ideas about poetry I hold have been held by poets. They have written about "real events" and hoped that their words, written with feeling, would seem true. The attitude I have described as being held by critics has not helped anyone to write poetry anyone would want to read.

In the beginning people had visions of the supernatural, they saw things we no longer see, and from these visions came the need to speak of what they had seen. From the age of Homer to that of Dante poets would refer to the gods as though their existing could be taken for granted. When Dante has his dream or vision of the god of love, he writes a poem and sends it to other poets as though it were news. He does not expect them to think, "This is a pretty figure of speech." He expects them to think that the vision was of a real thing. The task of the poet is to make language measure up to the reality.

We no longer see in this way. We have not seen an absolute truth or beauty, and therefore our writing has no authority, and anyone can interpret it any way he or she pleases.

When I think of the men and women in my time who are generally felt to be poets, they are individuals who have seen something the rest have not seen, and as it is not possible to argue against a wisdom one does not possess, they have been recognized as having some authority. Their names have a ring—they are poets. On the other hand, most published verse has no ideas and no passion, because the writer has nothing to report.

To argue for a poetry of "real events," and to use words like "soul," "truth," and "beauty," is not merely to be against the grain of present critical theory but to be completely outside it. But I think there are readers of poetry who feel as I do a revulsion from the jargon of criticism. That is a dead end as far as poetry is concerned—it has led, and can lead, to nothing good. It would be better never to speak of poetry at all, and instead just read it to one another, than to approach it with a theory, straining to find some phrase that may be blown up into an interpretation that will reflect credit on the ingenuity of the critic, while the poetry is lost.

In these essays I have, with one or two exceptions, avoided speaking of living poets. This may be disappointing to readers who have their favorites, but I have wanted to avoid the appearance of trying to advance the reputation of this poet or that. If you wish, you may apply my remarks yourself. It will be clear that I may think highly of the writings of Denise Levertov. It is not likely that I will appreciate the writings of an Amy Clampitt.

But I shall leave ranking poets to the kind of person who likes to do it, and there are some sentences I would like to pass on to you against the next time you read an article praising or blaming a poet. The author, C. H. Sisson, is a poet. The passage is taken from his lively, perceptive, quirky book on the poetry of the first half of the twentieth century. He has this to say about listening to other people's opinions:

> In the case of either the reader or the writer of poetry, a direct relationship with the work is a *sine qua non,* and the prestiges of fashion, reputation, prizes, publications, anthologies, and public praisings and blamings are all irrelevant. The discipline is a very hard one, so that anyone who thinks literature is an easy option does not know what he is talking about and is certainly not talking about literature. On the other hand, it is also a release, for no pressure of examinations or of a desire to say what is acceptable to the people around one can alter the fact that the reader and writer have to find their own ways and that the satisfactions of literature, which are as real as anything in this world, in the end come only to those who do so.
>
> *English Poetry 1900–1959: An Assessment*

"The Man Freed from the Order of Time": Poetic Theory in Wordsworth and Proust

One can hardly imagine two writers who seem less alike than William Wordsworth and Marcel Proust—one a poet living in the Lake District of England at the beginning of the nineteenth century, the other a Parisian of the twentieth, essayist and novelist, habitué of salons. But they had the same theory of literary creation: they believed that it originates in certain experiences that give the mind a sense of its own independent power. I wish to consider the theory, for it was realized in poems and novels that have influenced and continue to influence our thinking. If faith can be justified by works, the ideas of these writers have been justified.

Wordsworth states his belief in a passage that will be familiar to many. But though it is familiar the questions it raises have not been settled. It occurs in Book Twelve of *The Prelude*:

> There are in our existence spots of time
> That with distinct pre-eminence retain
> A renovating virtue, whence—depressed
> By false opinion and contentious thought,
> Or aught of heavier or more deadly weight,
> In trivial occupations, and the round
> Of ordinary intercourse—our minds
> Are nourished and invisibly repaired;

A virtue, by which pleasure is enhanced,
That penetrates, enables us to mount,
When high, more high, and lifts us up when fallen.
This efficacious spirit chiefly lurks
Among those passages of life that give
Profoundest knowledge to what point, and how,
The mind is lord and master—outward sense
The obedient servant of her will. Such moments
Are scattered everywhere, taking their date
From our first childhood.

Here, as in "Lines Composed a Few Miles above Tintern Abbey,"
Wordsworth says that memory has a power to nourish and repair the
mind. He speaks of extraordinary experiences, "spots of time"
when we perceive the workings of a supreme intelligence and know
that we are like it, and that the mind makes use of the senses for a
purpose of its own. The passage is followed by a description of two
incidents in the early life of the author. I shall consider the first of
these—the second repeats the impression made by the first and is
less striking.

Once, he tells us, when he was a small boy, he was riding toward
the hills accompanied by a servant, and they became separated. As
he was afraid, he dismounted and led his horse across the moor. At
the foot of a slope he came to a place where a murderer's body had
been hung in chains. The gibbet and bones were gone, but the
murderer's name was cut in the turf, and out of superstition people
had kept the grass cut and name visible. He fled from the place,
then, as he climbed again, he came upon a pool beneath the hills, a
beacon on the summit, and

A girl who bore a pitcher on her head,
And seemed with difficult steps to force her way
Against the blowing wind.

It was, he says, an ordinary sight, but he would need

Colours and words that are unknown to man,
To paint the visionary dreariness
Which, while I looked all round for my lost guide,

Invested moorland waste, and naked pool,
The beacon crowning the lone eminence,
The female and her garments vexed and tossed
By the strong wind.

Note that the impression made by the scene is described as "visionary," and that this vision lies beyond the reach of language to describe. In view of some current theories of literature, the point needs to be made. A witty remark by Mallarmé to Degas, "Poems are made with words, not ideas," has been the cornerstone of a theory that separates language from meaning and, in effect, denies that there is any reality outside language—words relate to other words, not to objects. But Wordsworth's theory of imagination posits a set of sense impressions that cannot be done justice to by words. Poetry is an attempt to reproduce the effect of a powerful experience, one so strong that it seizes upon the senses and stamps them with a configuration of objects. Poetry such as this is not made with words alone—it is made by a force acting through nature to impress the mind with a sense of power. The mind so impressed retains the power. Poems are made not with words but feelings and ideas.

The description of the scene on the moor is followed by reflections of a kind that readers of "Tintern Abbey" will recognize. On returning to the scene years later, with his lover at his side, every day roaming the same dreary scene, the poet felt "A spirit of pleasure and youth's golden gleam." The pleasure was greater because he could look back upon the experience of childhood and recollect the strong impression, "the power/They had left behind."

This is not all—it is only part of the explanation. There follows a description that goes beyond anything the poet might actually have seen or heard and shows the difference between memory and imagination. Wordsworth is often quoted as having said that poetry is "emotion recollected in tranquillity"—the *Everyman History of English Literature* tells us that he said so. But he said nothing of the kind—he said that "poetry . . . takes its origin from emotion recollected in tranquillity," which is a different thing altogether.[1] The emotion that creates a poem is not the emotion you had when you

[1] Preface to *Lyrical Ballads*, 1800.

were having the experience, but the emotion you are having now, as you write. The poem is *poema,* a made thing.

Imagination is already at work in the description of the moor, the pool, the beacon, the girl whose garments are tossed by the wind. These objects have been arranged by the poet to produce a certain effect, and the thoughts we have as we read the passage will be different from the thoughts of the child on the moor. As we read about the child's being frightened we are not frightened but take pleasure in the sight and arrangement of objects and the language and movement of verse. This is the "tranquillity" Wordsworth meant. If he had done no more than describe what was actually there, in this order of seeing and these words, he would have done much. He would have shown, as he says in "Ode: Intimations of Immortality," that though the man has lost the habit of losing himself in sense impressions he has gained a "philosophic," that is, poetic mind. The complex of sensations and thoughts that arise from our reading the poem is more interesting than anything memory itself could have produced.

If Wordsworth had only done this he would have shown the mind's power to make poetry out of experience, but he did more: he passed beyond the selection and arrangement of received images to make a new thing:

> I am lost, but see
> In simple childhood something of the base
> On which thy greatness stands; but this I feel,
> That from thyself it comes, that thou must give,
> Else never canst receive. The days gone by
> Return upon me almost from the dawn
> Of life: the hiding-places of man's power
> Open; I would approach them, but they close.

"the hiding-places of man's power/Open . . . ." This image is a pure invention. In this writing the mind appears to be "lord and master—outward sense/The obedient servant of her will."

I am reminded of Ferdinand Alquié's observation about the Surrealists: "If surrealism wishes to bring together in images the most distant realities, is it not because of its unlimited confidence in the powers of the spirit? . . . Surrealism would justify the axiology of

Raymond Polin, for whom man is the creator of values, which have their sense only from him and relative to him."[2]

The memory of the moor, the pool, the beacon, and the girl in the wind, through a process of meditation, have made a sudden opening into an order of reality that does not depend on memory: a surreal vision of "the hiding-places of man's power." What I have called "pure invention" is a product of mind and seems to reflect an order that lies beyond human experience. On this point we shall divide into separate parties. Those who believe that invention reflects a reality beyond this world will take their leave, waving to the majority who stay on shore. There have been poets who did not venture beyond the first stage of imagining, making aesthetically pleasing objects out of their experiences. Keats, I would say, was one. Blake comes to mind as an example of the other kind; he would have preferred to break all ties with nature and inhabit a world of his invention.

Some works of art, like some lives, are unlike anything in experience. Are these intimations of immortality? We shall surely disagree about this. But I think we can agree that certain works of art seem to display an absolute power of mind. The image of "the hiding-places of man's power" has this effect. I am not surprised that the poet who created the image would feel that the mind is "lord and master—outward sense/The obedient servant of her will"—that he would feel, in a word, immortal.

I am suspicious of influences. As Coleridge remarked, there are those who think that everyone draws water from the same well—they don't conceive of its being in streams and fountains. Besides, when you have established that a poem or novel has been influenced by someone else's ideas, are you better able to read it? I am not so much concerned to show that Wordsworth influenced Proust as to show that they had similar ideas. Indeed, I could wish there were no trace of influence, that ideas could be shown to rise by their own force, like water in a fountain.

[2] Ferdinand Alquié, *The Philosophy of Surrealism.* Ann Arbor: The University of Michigan Press, 1969. pp. 101–102.

But Wordsworth did influence Proust, indirectly. In 1899 Proust ended work on his novel, *Jean Santeuil,* feeling that the attempt was a failure. His mother encouraged him to read Ruskin, and in October he was reading *The Seven Lamps of Architecture.* In the following year he published some pieces on Ruskin in periodicals. "I admire him," Proust wrote, "listen to him, and make a greater effort to understand him than I do a good many of the living."[3] He continued to read Ruskin, and in 1904 published a translation of *The Bible of Amiens.* In a long preface to his translation he explains his ideas, not only about Ruskin but literary criticism. The first task of the critic is to familiarize himself with the works of the author and so seize upon the salient traits of his genius. The next task is "to reconstitute what could have been the singular spiritual life of a writer haunted by realities of such a special kind, his inspiration being the measure in which he had the vision of those realities, his talent the measure in which he could recreate them in his work."[4]

Proust's "realities of such a special kind" that haunt the author are Wordsworth's "spots of time." And his remark about inspiration, that it is strong or weak according to the impression made by a "vision of those realities," evokes Wordsworth's theory of poetic composition.

John Ruskin, whose works Proust studied so carefully, was a devoted reader of Wordsworth and shared Wordsworth's enthusiasm for nature. In *Praetitita,* the account of his early years, Ruskin says, "A snowdrop was to me, as to Wordsworth, part of the Sermon on the Mount."[5] Kenneth Clark, in his comments on Ruskin, observes that he "approached art through nature . . ." Nature could be read like a holy book, which it was his privilege to interpret. He often spoke of himself as nature's priest. In this he was to some extent the successor of Wordsworth, and a quotation from *The Excursion* was printed on the title page of each of the five volumes of *Modern Painters.*

---

[3] *Marcel Proust: Selected Letters 1880–1903,* ed. Philip Kolb. Garden City, N.Y.: Doubleday, 1983. p. 212.
[4] *La Bible d'Amiens,* trans. Marcel Proust. "Préface du Traducteur." Paris: Mercure de France, MCMXLVII. pp. 10–11. The translation into English is mine.
[5] *Ruskin Today,* ed. Kenneth Clark. Harmondsworth, England: Penguin, 1982. p. 22.

Accuse me not
Of arrogance
If, having walked with Nature,
And offered, far as frailty would allow,
My heart a daily sacrifice to Truth,
I now affirm of Nature and of Truth,
Whom I have served, that their divinity
Revolts, offended at the ways of men.

Clark observes that "Wordsworth is not often as Ruskinian as this," by which he means that Wordsworth is not so given to telling us what Nature thinks or Truth is. Clark draws a distinction between the poet and the factotum: "Ruskin's encyclopedic intelligence was not satisfied by Wordsworth's immediate delight, and his strict religious upbringing made it impossible for him to accept the pantheism of the Immortality ode, which he refers to as 'absurd.' As a child, however, he had responded to nature with almost Wordsworthian intensity."

The child is father of the man, and Ruskin continued to respond to nature with an almost Wordsworthian intensity. As Proust read Ruskin he encountered this, his Wordsworthian side. But, as I have said, I am not so much concerned to show the influence of Wordsworth on Proust as to show that Proust developed a theory of imagination that is remarkably similar to Wordsworth's. To read Proust's *A la Recherche du Temps Perdu* is to encounter Wordsworth's "spots of time," moments of contact with "realities of a special kind" in which Proust finds, as did Wordsworth, the meaning of existence and the organizing principle of his work.

Proust, like the mature, "philosophic" Wordsworth, was no simple lover of nature—he was always looking for the principle it embodied. "There is no particular form in nature," he observes, "however beautiful it may be, that has value other than by the share of infinite beauty that has been able to embody itself in that form."[6]

At this point we had better drop the word "nature," for it has a meaning in Wordsworth it does not have in Proust. Or if we do refer to nature, the word must have its widest meaning, as the whole visible world. It may refer to nature in the Wordsworthian sense,

---

[6] "Préface," *La Bible d'Amiens*. p. 88.

but it may also mean human society: it includes the Guermantes' drawing room as well as the hawthorns of Combray. It applies to a fashionable courtesan as well as a peasant girl, and to the searchlights over Paris seeking out the raiding Gothas.

For Wordsworth nature is the mask of a power that manifests itself in terror and beauty. The decaying woods of the Alps, the waterfalls, winds, torrents, and rocks, are

> all like workings of one mind, the features
> Of the same face, blossoms upon one tree;
> Characters of the great Apocalypse,
> The types and symbols of Eternity,
> Of first, and last, and midst, and without end.[7]

In "Tintern Abbey" nature is a power that rolls through all things and through the mind that observes them. In Proust, also, nature is the mask of a power that we glimpse at certain moments, but not in winds and torrents; it is manifest in the rapid walk of one man, the wandering speech of another. Inexorable laws are working themselves out in these characters. It is the task of the novelist to grasp the reality and show how it manifests itself in speech and gesture, as the sculptor shows it in stone. The characters of fiction are a Bible, just as much as the figures of Vices and Virtues: of Courage, Cowardice, Patience, Anger, Gentleness, Rudeness, and Love, that one sees in the central porch of the Cathedral at Amiens.

Proust, like Wordsworth, placed his most deeply revolved ideas about art in the artwork itself. It is to *A la Recherche* that we must turn if we wish to discover Proust's aesthetics, especially the concluding volume, *Time Regained* (*Le Temps Retrouvé*). "There was in me," says the narrator, "a personage who knew more or less how to look, but it was an interrupted personage, coming to life only in the presence of some general essence common to a number of things, these essences being its nourishment and its joy."[8] In *Time Regained* the intermittent personage is brought to the front and given a

---

[7] *The Prelude*, VI., 636–640.

[8] Marcel Proust, *Remembrance of Things Past*. Vol. 3: *The Captive, The Fugitive, Time Regained*. London: Chatto and Windus, 1981. pp. 737–738.

thorough examination. Proust, like Flaubert, had a medical man for a father.

The narrator of *Time Regained* returns from a second sojourn in a sanatorium where he has been confined for a nervous disorder. He is disillusioned, especially with nature. " 'Trees,' I thought, 'you no longer have anything to say to me. My heart has grown cold and no longer hears you. I am in the midst of nature. Well, it is with indifference, with boredom that my eyes register the line which separates the luminous from the shadowy side of your trunks. If ever I thought of myself as a poet, I know now that I am not one.' "

The day following these reflections the narrator is on his way to an afternoon party at the house of the Princesse de Guermantes, and is looking forward to it, for, as he can hope for nothing better, why deprive himself of such frivolous pleasures? He reflects on his situation, that he has given up all hope of being a writer. But, he tells us, it is just at the moment when we think that everything is lost that "the intimation arrives which may save us." And so it happens now. (I do not wish to delay the appearance of the "intermittent personage," but there is a striking resemblance between this train of thought and that of Wordsworth in "Resolution and Independence.") In the courtyard outside the Guermantes mansion the narrator fails to see a car approaching . . . the chauffeur shouts a warning and as the narrator moves out of the way he trips on a paving stone. Recovering his balance he steps on a stone that is lower than its neighbors, whereupon, he says, "All my discouragement vanished and in its place was that same happiness which at various epochs of my life had been given to me by the sight of trees which I had thought that I recognized in the course of a drive near Balbec, by the sight of the twin steeples of Martinville, by the flavour of a madeleine dipped in tea, and by all those other sensations of which I have spoken and of which the last works of Vinteuil had seemed to me to combine the quintessential character. Just as, at the moment when I tasted the madeleine, all anxiety about the future, all intellectual doubts had disappeared, so now those that a few seconds ago had assailed me on the subject of the reality of my literary gifts, the reality even of literature, were removed as if by magic. . . . The emotion was the same; the difference, purely material, lay in the images evoked . . . a profound azure," says the narrator, "intoxicated my eyes, impressions of coolness, of dazzling light, swirled around me." As he repeats the motion of staggering in order to recapture his feeling of happiness, to the amusement of the chauffeurs, he recognizes the source of his vision of "profound azure." It is Venice, where, in St. Mark's, he once stood on two uneven paving stones. This sensation is restored to him now "complete with all the other sensations linked on that day to that particular sensation, all of which had been waiting in their place—from which with imperious suddenness a chance happening had caused them to emerge—in the series of forgotten days. In the same way the taste of the little madeleine had recalled Combray to me. But why," the narrator asks, and it is the important question, "why had the images of Combray and of Venice, at these two different moments, given me a joy which was like a certainty and which sufficed, without any other proof, to make death a matter of indifference to me?"

This question is left unanswered while the narrative continues. The narrator is in the Guermantes' sitting room waiting for a piece of music to finish when a servant knocks a spoon against a plate. This evokes the train journey on which he saw the trees that failed to arouse his interest. While the train was stopped near a wood a railway workman struck one of the wheels with a hammer. Returning to the present ... the narrator drinks some orangeade and wipes his mouth with a napkin. The rough texture of the cloth evokes the sea—it has the same stiff texture as a towel he used to dry his face at Balbec. It evokes "the plumage of an ocean green and blue like the tail of a peacock." The happiness he feels is caused not by the colors but by an instant of his life at Balbec that had "aspired" towards happiness but had been prevented by some fatigue or sadness. But now, freed from the sensations of the moment, the instant has caused him to be happy.

Happiness is enclosed within our sensations and perceptions, a thousand "sealed vessels" that are separated by time and space, "a colour, a scent, a temperature." When two such identical moments are brought together by some physical accident—uneven paving stones, a napkin, the sound of a spoon on a plate, the taste of a madeleine—the time between is removed and one sees that, concealed by temporal circumstances, there lives a being whose nature it is to be happy. This is the "intermittent personage" or true self, perceived only outside time and therefore existing outside time. "This being made its appearance only when, through one of these identifications of the present with the past, it was likely to find itself in the only medium in which it could exist and enjoy the essence of things, that is to say: outside time."

The "true self" cannot be captured by an effort of the will. "In the observation of the present, where the senses cannot feed it with this food, it languishes, as it does in the consideration of a past made arid by the intellect or in the anticipation of a future which the will constructs with fragments of the present and the past . . . But let a noise or a scent, once heard or once smelt, be heard or smelt again in the present, and at the same time in the past, real without being actual, ideal without being abstract," then the true self is revealed. "A minute freed from the order of time has re-created in us, to feel it, the man freed from the order of time."[9]

We have arrived with Proust at the point we have reached before with Wordsworth:

> This efficacious spirit chiefly lurks
> Among those passages of life that give
> Profoundest knowledge to what point, and how,
> The mind is lord and master . . .

Wordsworth says that the mind, having realized its own independent existence, can make use of the senses—"outward sense" being "The obedient servant of her will." The narrator of *A la Recherche* will take this step too by writing a novel. He decides to find the fragments of real time, his true happiness, that are dispersed among the scenes and acts of his life. If he succeeds in his task he will have recovered his immortal part, "the man freed from the order of time."

Both Wordsworth and Proust argue that there is a reality outside the world that is perceived at certain moments and that it is the task of the poet to capture and make visible. The argument stands on sensations and feelings and therefore, from one point of view, is no

[9] *Ibid,* p. 906.

argument at all. All theories of art rest on sensations and feelings. It is only science that claims to operate in a realm of pure logic . . . and perhaps it no longer does, not since Werner Heisenberg and his Principle of Uncertainty. There is no longer, we are told, any such thing as a "scientific fact."

The proof of an artistic theory is in the results. Wordsworth follows his statement about the "efficacious spirit" by composing two incidents in which the spirit showed itself—to him as a child and to the present reader. Proust's explanation of the true self comes toward the end of a novel that has already shown, in numerous passages, the happiness of this "intermittent personage." How has it been shown? In the writing, the style of the passages.

The argument for immortality is in those passages of literature that seem immortal. This is what the poet and novelist seem to say. And this is the argument for reading their works. But how? Should we practice "close reading"? Analyze the choice and use of words? The structure of sentences? Should we search for symbols and see what they mean? The method is certainly tempting. I might, for example, choose these lines by Wordsworth and attempt to explain the symbolism:

> the hiding-places of man's power
> Open; I would approach them, but they close.

Think what a Freudian analyst might make of this! But to do so would be to destroy the larger effect of the image. As it stands it radiates outward to the furthest reaches of imagining. Explained by the analyst it is immediately reduced to a symptom of the author's personality.

To dissect, Wordsworth tells us, is to murder, and this is no mere figure of speech. Though we may gain information when we dissect, it is certain that the subject must be dead. The style of a writer does not consist of logic but a felt reality. What Proust says of nature is true of style: "There is no particular form in nature, however beautiful it may be, that has value other than by the share of infinite beauty that has been able to embody itself in that form."

It is for want of contact with the infinity Proust speaks of that the theory of literature is, at the present time, in such a confused and dreary state. Theoretical critics have attempted to bring logic to bear on literature, whereas they are two quite different things. The theorists have had no experience of the "special realities" of which Proust speaks—they have had no visions, and spin their ideas out of themselves. One theorist tells us that institutions are only verbal agreements; another, that words have no real meanings—they only relate to other words. Theorists such as these have never experienced the "spots of time" of which Wordsworth writes, nor Proust's moments of intuition into a reality that is more enduring than the life of the individual. For such theorists the only reality is society, and its voice is rhetoric, a way of manipulating language so that it means what one wants it to mean.

How then, if we do not read like surgeons dissecting a cadaver, are we to read? I think we should drop all pretense to a scientific objectivity, which is not objective anyway. I am not asking for a suspension of intelligence: there is a way of reading intelligently but not analytically. Proust, in a passage I have quoted, gives us the method: it is to grasp the salient ideas and reconstitute "what could have been the singular spiritual life of a writer haunted by realities of . . . a special kind." In short, one surrenders to the writer's vision of things. Unfortunately, surrendering is quite beyond the ability of most theorists, attached as they are to their theories.

To reconstitute the spiritual life of a writer one would have to read the works widely and in depth—one would have, in a sense, to become the writer. Then one would be able to see the truth, the amount of "infinite beauty," contained in a passage of the text. One would be able to read as the author wrote, feeling that one has done justice, or failed to do justice, to the subject. This is close reading, not the mechanical exercise that frequently passes by that name in graduate schools. Reading requires the same intuitive intelligence that is used in writing. Everything depends, as Proust says, on the amount of "infinite beauty" that has been able to embody itself in the particular form, and on the reader's ability to perceive it.

But, does an "infinite beauty" exist or is this only a manner of speaking? Wordsworth refers to

> all the mighty world
> Of eye, and ear,—both what they half create,
> And what perceive . . .[10]

[10] "Lines Composed a Few Miles Above Tintern Abbey," 105–107.

Consciousness, then, is an amalgam of ideas and sense percep-
tions. Here the analyst rushes in to say that sense perceptions are
just that: there's no intelligence behind them. The external world
does not stamp the mind, as I have said it does, with a "config-
uration of objects." The mind alone can do this: out of some psy-
chic need the poet fastens on certain objects and so composes his
poem.

The same argument could be made about Proust. If, jarred by a
paving stone, his mind flashed back to Venice, this was no more than
an association of ideas, and the ideas can be accounted for. The rest
of it . . . a reality "aspiring" to make itself known, a "pure and
disembodied" reality . . . was only a fantasy born of some inner
need. Indeed, one could discover the writer's "true self"—this is
what psychoanalysis does. But it is nothing that cannot be explained
by science.

We cannot disprove this way of thinking. We can only say that the
writers had a different idea; they believed there were powers exter-
nal to the mind that acted upon it at certain moments to bring it to a
higher level of consciousness. They would not have denied that
writers are peculiarly constituted—as Wordsworth says, the poet is
"finding everywhere objects that immediately excite in him sympa-
thies which, from the necessities of his nature, are accompanied by
an overbalance of enjoyment." But they also believed that nature
acts upon the poet—it is sending him messages. The poet "con-
siders man and nature as essentially adapted to each other, and the
mind of man as naturally the mirror of the fairest and most interest-
ing properties of nature."[11]

There was a time when the belief I have been describing was the
common belief of all peoples. Homer and Dante assumed that it was
so. By the time of Wordsworth the idea had to be argued on the
basis of the poet's experience—it was no longer held by a commu-
nity. Proust represents perhaps the last stage of the great tradition.
And now, so far have we come from having experiences of the kind
that we are inclined to think that poets never had them and their
testimony is merely figurative. We think that when Homer de-
scribed the acts and speeches of the gods, and Dante related the
appearance of Eros in a dream, they did not believe in the reality of

[11] Preface to *Lyrical Ballads*, 1800.

the things they were saying. The balance of belief in our time has swung overwhelmingly towards scientism and away from any line of thought that could be called "spiritual."

I do not think, however, that the prejudice will continue to have things all its own way. I think that the rapid advances in technology in our time do not entail a surrender of the imaginative to the calculating side of life, but a reification of scientific beliefs so that we shall see, once and for all, what their limits are, and that poetry and the arts proceed from

> those passages of life that give
> Profoundest knowledge to what point, and how,
> The mind is lord and master—outward sense
> The obedient servant of her will.

WORDSWORTH, PROUST, AND "THE NEW HISTORY"

At the present moment in English studies there is talk of "the new history" and an "interdisciplinary approach" to the teaching of literature. William E. Cain—I choose his book because it appears to be an accurate account of trends in literary criticism—recommends an interdisciplinary approach. "I am not," he says, "recommending simply that the literary critic and teacher become more 'historical' in attitude and orientation. Nor am I proposing (as might be suspected) that critics should transform themselves into historians." (From his treatment of Booker T. Washington's *Up from Slavery* one might indeed have the suspicion.) He hastens to reassure us that the literary critic will be retained, for "The literary critic . . . possesses skills that the historian does not." What are these skills? The ability "to grasp the workings of figurative language in texts as his colleagues in other disciplines cannot." The *raison d'être* of the critic is to "elucidate texts and probe inter-textual configurations."[12]

It seems that the literary critic is a sort of mechanic. It does not seem to have occurred to this author that literary criticism may be something more than finding hidden meanings and pointing out

[12] William E. Cain, *The Crisis in Criticism*. Baltimore and London: The Johns Hopkins University Press, 1984, p. 270.

figures of speech, that it may be based in a belief that is just as real as his belief in history. If the thought occurred to him he must have rejected it as not being to his purpose. The "interdisciplinary" study of literature is based on the assumption that literature is produced by conditions. But many writers have believed something quite different: that their thoughts are original and do not merely report conditions, that which is already known.

Though he disclaims any intention of trying to replace the study of literature with the study of history, Cain says, "Whether we are studying the canonical texts, counter-traditions, children's novels, translations of the Bible, or some other grouping, we should direct discussion towards history, society, and culture." What is this but substituting the study of history, society, and culture for the study of literature? Directing the discussion towards history means discussing history, especially when those who direct the discussion have no bias in favor of literature. Indeed, some of them are positively eager to deny that "the canon" has any particular merit. The kind of literary criticism we may expect from those who are oriented toward history is shown in Cain's discussion of a passage from *Up from Slavery*. He says that he is explicating the language but all his discussion brings forth is Washington's ideas about culture and society. This is the historical approach to literature—it has everything to do with history and little to do with literature.

I would have no objection to relating English studies to the other disciplines if it were understood that there is an essential difference between literature and the other disciplines. But whenever the attempt is made to study the other relations of literature we see that the interest is in those other relations and in making literature serve them. From the point of view of the historian, a sentimental novel of the year 1850 is as rewarding to study as *The Scarlet Letter*— indeed, more rewarding, for the ideas are simpler and set forth more plainly. What is omitted from such considerations is the power of the writing of great authors. In "interdisciplinary" studies of literature the only discipline that seems to be missing is the discipline of literature.

The more sentimental and clumsy the writing, the more it lends itself to be studied as something else. But when we are dealing with imaginative writing of the quality of Proust's fiction or Wordsworth's poetry, what does history have to tell us? The better the writing the more clearly we see that it proceeds from the mind of an individual and not from social conditions. The works of Wordsworth and Proust do have something to say about society and do cast a light on history, but to make that the focus of our study would surely be a mistake. The message of such writing is set forth in images of a reality that has been perceived by the mind at moments of extraordinary experience. The mind that creates such works is not the handmaid of history. With Joyce's Stephen Dedalus it says, "Non serviam."

A long time ago Thomas De Quincey explained the difference between the "Literature of Knowledge" and the "Literature of Power." The kind of interdisciplinary study that is being recommended would deny that there is an original power in literature. The approach of the historian would make literature the servant of economics, of sociology, or anything that might be called knowledge. But poetry is the expression of power, and power is always original. The only reason for literary criticism is to show the workings of this power and show, if it can, from where the power proceeds.

7

ENTRIES

1962–1980

November 18, 1962

> I write, write, write as the Wandering Jew walks, walks, walks.
> Madame Blavatsky

> If you prefer not to exaggerate you must remain silent.
> Ortega y Gasset

From the Autobiography *of William Butler Yeats*

The most fundamental of divisions is that between the intellect, which can only do its work by saying continually "thou fool," and the religious genius which makes all equal.

Emotion is always justified by time, thought hardly ever.

Whatever happens I must go on that there may be a man behind the lines already written.

George Moore got under Yeats's skin. In the *Autobiography* Yeats has this lofty saying:

One should not—above all in books, which sigh for immortality—argue at all if not ready to leave to another apparent victory. In daily life one becomes rude the moment one grudges to the clown his perpetual triumph.

Nevertheless, he attacks Moore at length—perhaps because Moore would not take him seriously when he was being the great man. Moore thought that Yeats' manner of chanting poetry, in accordance with an idea he had of the ancient, heroic way of reciting, was hilarious.

So Yeats in his *Autobiography* tried to even the score. Today no one reads George Moore, and all that effort was wasted. Don't waste your time on literary politics!

Percolation of Literature

On a poster for Progresso Espresso Coffee in the IRT subway, 168th Street Station: "Joe wants to perne in Alice's gyre."

The Roman name for Paris: Lutetia, "the muddy town." Mudville!

Les son et lumière . . . "The sound and light people." What the younger generation in France call their elders. From the government program for lighting the national monuments and playing martial airs.

Seen From the Café de la Paix[1]

Académie Nationale de Musique

La Grande Maison de Blanc

Chocolats Lindt

Montres Kody

Coryse Salome Parfums

Quinquina DUBONNET

Flaminaire   Tabac   café   bar   Coryse   Salome

---

[1] From this, five lines of a poem, "With Memory. And With Love." written twenty years later.

Lancel

Chocolat Suchard Milka

Clerc

Tourisme en Allemagne

From The Life and Work of Sigmund Freud *by Ernest Jones*

". . . the moderate amount of discomfort necessary for intensive work . . ."

"Happiness is the subsequent fulfillment of a pre-historic wish. That is why wealth brings so little happiness: money was not a wish in childhood."

Description of Freud's "tides" and recessions of creativity . . . exactly those of a poet.

"The whole matter resolves itself into a platitude. Dreams all seek to fulfill *one* wish, which has got transformed into many others. It is the wish to sleep. One dreams so as not to have to wake, because one wants to sleep. *Tant de bruit.*" [c.f. *The Tempest:* "when I waked I cried to sleep again."]

Kennst du das Land wo die Citronen blühen?[2]

Goethe

Vedere Napoli e poi morire.

. . . Freud's ancient and passionate identification of himself with the Semitic Hannibal. Hannibal's attempt to gain possession of Rome, the "Mother of Cities," was thwarted by some nameless inhibition when he was on the point of success. For years Freud could get little nearer to Rome than Trasimeno, the place where Hannibal finally halted.

---

[2] I used this as the epigraph of "The Beaded Pear," 1978.

Der Hass sieht scharf . . . Hate has a keen eye.

"We Jews have an easier time, having no mystical element."
[Freud in a letter to Karl Abraham, speaking of Jung.]

When the Nazis entered Vienna we tried to save whatever
was possible and they decreed that only an "Aryan" should be
allowed to conduct the Psychoanalytical Clinic. Unfortunately
the only member of the Vienna Society answering to this
description had just fled over the mountains to Italy. On hear-
ing this I cried out *"O weh; unser einzigger Sabbat-Goy ist fort,"* a
remark that dispelled for a moment the gloom of the gather-
ing.[3]

He also dealt with certain fears or criticisms concerning
psychoanalysis: for instance, the fear that forbidden impulses
if admitted to consciousness might run riot. He explained the
reasons why such impulses necessarily lose strength in con-
sciousness and why, through coming under better control, they
have less power to create disturbances than when in their disso-
ciated state inaccessible to any influence.
[Speaking of the last of Freud's *Five Lectures on Psychoanalysis*]

Psychoanalysis and Art

Art is a special form of the attempt to gratify otherwise
unsatisfied wishes, both for the artist and his audience. "Art
constitutes an intermediate territory between the wish-denying
reality and the wish-fulfilling world of phantasy." Psycho-
analysis is able as a rule to trace the source of those wishes from
the manifest content of the art form to their origins, but,
according to Freud, it can throw no light on the nature of the
artistic talent itself. "Whence the artist derives his creative
capacities is not a question for psychology."

The triple blow to man's narcissism: Copernicus, Darwin, Freud.

[3] *Sabbat-Goy:* a gentile hired by Jews to carry out the household tasks on the Sabbath which
their religion forbids them to carry out themselves.

Dante: "In the middle of my life's journey I found myself in a wood."

Freud's interpretation: The landscape, sex. The hill, female. The wood, pubic hair.

He is attacked by wild animals—"evil impulses."

Idea for an Essay on Hamlet

Why does Hamlet think so much about dying? And why is the "To be or not to be" speech so effective on the stage, though it is not called for by the plot?

After all, dying is not Hamlet's problem. His problem is revenge—killing the "damned, incestuous Dane."

Claudius has usurped Hamlet's place—the throne, his mother's love. Therefore Claudius to all intents and purposes *is* Hamlet, and killing Claudius presents itself to Hamlet's mind as "self-slaughter."

The thought of dying is uppermost in his thoughts. Though irrelevant to his task, it expresses what is most important to him as a man. And this strikes the audience as dramatically right, for character is drama.

Hamlet hesitates to kill Claudius because this amounts to killing himself—the incestuous Hamlet who would have killed his father and married his mother. And, in fact, when Hamlet kills Claudius, Hamlet dies.

Lessons of the Master

Observed in London last summer: Be Taught Ladies' Hairdressing at the Henry James Institute. 25 Years Teaching at Your Disposal. 104 Wardour St., W. 1.

Hugh Macdiarmid

I have seen violence, I have seen violence—
Give thy heart after letters.

He attributes this to "a forgotten poet of Egypt."

A fig for most of your pretexts! But my soul
   for the results.

"Speaking fine," as the Scots say—i.e., like an Englishman.

... rhythm is an animal function, whereas
   poetry and music,
Involving no bodily activity of the artist
   in their making,
Can exist in a purely psychological relation
   to society
And would be equally "true" in a world of
   disembodied spirits ...

False. Rhythm is essential to poetry and music.

August, 1965

I shall say "I", because that is the way to be natural.
                                        Henry de Montherlant

U. S. Grant's Personal Memoirs

Experience proves that the man who obstructs a war in which
his nation is engaged, no matter whether right or wrong, occu-
pies no enviable place in life or history.

Grant's sentences are clear and hard, like the general who pushed
the army through the Wilderness.

He was "bitterly opposed" to the war with Mexico—he saw that it
had been sought by the Tyler administration in order to annex
Texas. To this day, Grant says, he regards the war "as one of the most
unjust ever waged by a stronger against a weaker nation."

He went to it all the same. "The man who obstructs a war ..." et
cetera.

At San Cosme he had his men carry a howitzer up to a church
belfry. "The shots from our little gun dropped in upon the enemy
and created great confusion." For this action he was promoted to
first lieutenant.

The most feeling passage in the *Memoirs* is about a colt he was fond of when he was eight. The colt went blind and he had to sell it; he came upon it six years later, working the tread-wheel of the ferry.

Remarks to Make Your Blood Run Cold

> You have heard that I am cruel. Well, I am more cruel than you can imagine.
>
> Galliffet

Galliffet ordered executions of the defeated workers during the Commune (1871). They would be brought before him—men, women, even children, roped together—and he would pick out individuals to be shot, and for the most frivolous reasons—he didn't like the cut of a man's beard or the expression on a woman's face. His words have been preserved by the Left for a hundred years to fuel their hatred of the ruling class.

It is said that the young ladies of Paris looked on, laughing and twirling their umbrellas, while the workers were being executed.

In revenge the Communists hauled out some priests, officials, and other, innocent people whom they had been holding hostage, and massacred them.

When the Bolsheviks came to power in Russia in 1919, the Commune was much in their thoughts. They had a score to settle.

I once thought of keeping a record of words and phrases that were in vogue. Nothing came of the idea—I had other, more urgent things to do. It's a pity, for such a list, if it were kept carefully, would show more about the way we live than most "creative" writing.

In 1953 people spoke of "coping." You didn't cope with anything in particular, you just coped. Before this they spoke of being "mature." Or have I got it the wrong way round? This is the trouble with not writing things down at the time.

Later on there was "adjustment."

I don't mean words and phrases that are merely slang, but that issue from and preserve the beliefs of the moment, Flaubert's *idées reçues.*

1969: "Right on!," "relevant," "meaningful," "life style."

1980: "I can relate to that." "Do you know where I'm coming from?" "counter-productive," "parameters," "viable alternative," "feasible," "the bottom line."

In Italy

The pain of living is like a cloud stretched over the earth which each must support in his own way. The rich also . . . It may seem they are free to do as they please, but they have to dress for dinner.

They have to lock up the house in town and move to the country. The many things they have to do—*molto da fare*—require the management of a staff of servants, secretaries, gardeners and chauffeurs. The rich reject out of hand any suggestion that they are enjoying a greater share of the pleasures of this world than falls to others. "What? Just try finding a cook who knows her business and is willing to work. As for wages, you have no idea what these people are asking these days."

Lucca

The most notable sight in Lucca is the wall that surrounds it. Completed in 1645, it incorporates fragments of a Roman wall built two centuries B.C. It is four kilometers in circumference and so wide that a road has been made around the top, lined with trees and shady bays where the traveller may rest.

Lucca is provincial, dominated by Genoa and Pisa to the West and Florence to the East. The people of Lucca have specialized in minting currency and building churches. There are a hundred churches in Lucca, now empty most of the time.

The Church of San Fabriano exhibits the mummy of a local holy woman who has been dead these hundred years. The cadaver, no bigger than a child, is displayed like a pheasant, under glass. The hide has turned black and the bones are pushing through. People kneel and pray to this.

In the fourteenth century an army from Lucca led by Castruccio was on its way to lay siege to Florence, but Castruccio fell sick and died. There was a possibility, say the Lucchesi, that they would have conquered Florence. If they had, there would have been no *Pri-*

mavera—instead, Tuscany would have been filled with religious gloom.

Piazza dei Mercanti

Gran Miscela Colombo (where you sit outdoors)

Gelateria

Moradei (shirts)

Profumeria Venus (speaks for itself)

Musetti (clothes)

P. Mennucci

Writers say they want justice. But did a writer ever write to a newspaper complaining that his book had been unjustly praised? I suspect the sense of justice of writers.

Two things constantly cry out in creation—the sea and man's soul.

Apollon Grigoryev[4]

Reading the Times[5]

January 22, 1969
Lane High School Closed
Principals decry violence

SVARE OF GIANTS RESIGNS AS COACH
Knicks Conquer Sonics Here,
But Russell Fractures His Ankle

LSD, opium, codeine, heroin
and methedrine, known as "speed"

---

[4] Quoted in a poem, "Why Do You Write about Russia." *Caviare at the Funeral*, 1980.
[5] These lines in the *New York Times* gave me lines for poems written years later: "The Beaded Pear" (1978) and "Copyboy" (1986).

CHEMICAL NEW YORK

You'd expect to pay more
for these 3-piece Italian knits

$85,000,000
Virginia Electric and Power Company

the next generation
radar and
display
challenges

Voyage to the Enchanted Isles

MUSIC HALL: "Sound of the 60's"
Bobby Darin is host, with
Buddy Rich, Laura Nyro, Judy
Collins, Stevie Wonder

The British in Old India

Delightful family fare
Excellent melodrama of the Mafia

President Resigns from Eastern Air Lines

Student's Death Stirs Demonstration in Madrid

January 23
U.S. SINKS 45 SMALL WICKER BOATS NEAR
DANANG

Prophecy is too great a thing for Baruch.

Jewish saying[6]

[6] See the poem, "Baruch," *Searching for the Ox*, 1976

On the Other Hand

Flippancy builds up around a man the finest armor plating
. . . that I know . . . It is a thousand times away from joy; it
deadens, instead of sharpening the intellect, and it excites no
affection between those who practise it.

C.S. Lewis

New York poets please copy.

Singing

The final word on the marvelous, mysterious art of singing
was undoubtedly that of the tenor Angelo Masini: "*Quando la
voce c'è, c'è; e quando non c'è, non c'è;* you can drink, smoke, swim,
make love, do anything you like, and still, when the voice is
there, it's there, and when it isn't there, it isn't."

John Briggs

[Larry Williams on Rock] . . . "In truth it has no beginning
and no end, for it is the very pulse of life itself."
Uh huh.

"No, my dear fellow, this is not the work of a homicidal
maniac. It is something infinitely more sinister."

Sherlock Holmes and the Woman in Green

People who love the earth—the hills and lakes, trees, and ani-
mals—will also love one another. But if they don't love the earth they
will steal from one another, and murder and rape.

December 1970
London

From the Meditations of Marcus Aurelius

Love the art which you were taught, set up your rest in this.
Nothing befalls anything which that thing is not naturally
made to bear.

This remark seems very foolish. Does it come of being an aristo-crat and not having suffered calamities?[7]

Remember that to change your course and to follow someone who puts you right is not to be less free. For the change is your own action, proceeding according to your own impulse and decision, and indeed according to your mind.

. . . man's proper work is . . . disdain of the movements of the senses.

This goes with his contempt for poetry and accounts for the arid impression of his ideas.

Men have come into the world for the sake of one another.

The Gospel of Interpersonal Relations.

Wipe out imagination: check impulse: quench desire: keep the governing self in its own control.

And then tell me why life is worth living.

Vladimir Ilyich at a Loss Before Art

. . . the matter concerned a monument to Karl Marx. The well-known sculptor M. was especially insistent in his claims. He presented his design of a large monument entitled "Karl Marx supported by Four Elephants." This unexpected motif struck all of us, and Vladimir Ilyich too, as most peculiar.

Anatoly Lunacharsky

Not so funny, all the same . . .

I however make bold to declare myself a "barbarian." It is beyond me to consider the products of expressionism, futur-ism, cubism and other "isms" the highest manifestation of artis-tic genius. I do not understand them. I experience no joy from them.

V. I. Lenin

---

[7] Aurelius's life could hardly be described as without "calamities." He saw the plague and died on a campaign.

Who said, "When I hear the word culture . . ."? According to Carl Zuckmayer, Hans Johst said it, in his play *Schlagter* (Germany, the early thirties). "When I hear the word culture I reach for my revolver." The remark is often attributed to Goebbels.

No, no, I don't want to be a writer like the others, an inventor of more or less agreeable stories. I want to talk only of that which has touched me, taken hold of me, of that which I have loved or from which I have suffered.

. . . as I liked writing and was incapable of inventing anything, I had to write about what had actually happened, and . . . in any case I only liked true stories.

Paul Léautaud

Ordinary Mind

Your ordinary mind, that is the way.

Nansen

May 2, 1971
London

Arrest of the ice cream man.

June 29, 1971

"Laziness is the mother of invention."—D.

From The Anatomy of Melancholy

What a company of poets hath this year brought out! as Pliny complains to Sosius Senecio. This April, every day some or other have recited.[8]

Eyes and Ears

. . . whatsoever pleaseth our eyes and ears, we call beautifull [sic] and fair. Pleasure belongeth to the rest of the senses, but grace and beauty to these two alone.

[8] I used this for the title of a book about poets and poetry: *A Company of Poets,* 1981.

Venus, Aspects of

Venus omitted.
Intemperate Venus.
. . . a young wife in a hot summer . . .

A Poet

. . . a poet? esurit, an hungry jack . . .
. . . what's matrimony but a matter of mony [sic] . . .

Cleft Houses

For, behold, the Lord commandeth, and he will smite the great house with breaches, and the little house with clefts.

Holy Bible

Living well is the best revenge.

Spanish saying

On the other hand

If you go out and amuse yourself when you can't write, your art and life will waste to nothingness.

George Moore

December 1971
London

Papa Hemingway has become Colonel Pannu of the Indian army . . .

Television news, Pakistan-India war.

From the Diary of Julian Green

Happiness is a story that cannot be told. Love is a story that cannot be told.

Words form a sort of current that one must constantly swim against . . .

With talent, you do what you like. With genius, you do what you can.

In a world that goes too fast, I have decided to live slowly.

A scrupulous man will never produce a great novel. For fear of offending God, he will write prudent platitudes and who knows if God does not wish a risk to be taken? Who knows if this is not the way to please Him and to fulfill one's vocation?

"A good translation is not a glove turned inside out; it is another glove." [He is quoting "Robert"]

[On Byron] . . . "All this is strangely melancholy. Nothing so much resembles a life that fails as certain successful ones."

But the sentence cries out to be completed with "certain lives that succeed." Translation with a tin ear.

. . . what Montherlant calls *biophages* (or people who devour the lives of others) . . .

The Child of the World

Propheten rechts, Propheten links, das Weltkind in der Mitte.
Prophets to the right, prophets to the left, the child of the world in the middle.

Goethe

A great man is one who acts and speaks from a vision of himself. It is not that he is always right and everyone else is wrong—often it is the other way round—but that even when he is wrong he is speaking from "the foul rag-and-bone shop of the heart," the central volcano from which all creation comes.

Frank O'Connor

The Thirty-Six Hidden Saints[9]

. . . the thirty-six hidden saints—the simple Jews, the tailors, shoemakers, and water carriers upon whom depends the continued existence of the world. Father spoke of their poverty, their humility, their appearance of ignorance so that none would recognize their true greatness.

There are in this world some very strange individuals whose thoughts are even stranger than they are.

Isaac Bashevis Singer

Names

I am unable to make up names, and have to search them out. It's not enough for a name to be common—on the contrary, a common name may seem out of place, while a far-fetched name is accepted by the reader—"It's too peculiar to have been made up. It must be true."

Aphasia (for a female character. Meaning inability or unwillingness to speak).

Anorexia (from "anorexia nervosa," the compulsive urge to starve oneself).

Voigt

Venable

Voss

Dawson or Lawson (first name Harry?)

Bowrey (from an old word meaning "bowmaker." First name Gordon?)

Humfres Onagar

Stroud (for a villain, D. says).

Mlle. Passavant

Peter (I can't find a surname for Peter. Thorne? Corie? Lindsay or Lindsey?)

"Ringlets" Donavan (woman who put wine in nail-polish bottles)

Evatt

Max Brule

[9] See "The Daled," *Searching for the Ox*, 1976.

Supernaturalism

The Confucian verdict that the superior man never talks about miracles, wonders, and supernaturalism, is the true expression of Chinese psychology.

D. T. Suzuki

Morality

Morality, which should concern itself with our own duties and rights but which instead instructs us in what we are to expect of our neighbours . . .

August Strindberg

Every way of a man is right in his own eyes: but the Lord pondereth the hearts.

Holy Bible

Private truths, arrived at with much doubt, are always shared by others. Thus, having written in "The Anti-Theorist" about the importance of a patch of wall in Rome, I find in Valéry's *Analects,* "every spectacular experience can be whittled down to gazing at the corner of a table, a bit of a wall . . ."

Not only the same thought but the same image out of all possible images.

From Valéry's Analects

When a single note struck on a piano at a certain distance, under certain circumstances, at a certain psychological latitude and longitude, is enough to cause such strange effects, reaching down to the utmost depths of the soul, paralyzing our powers, veiling the sunlight, and calling up undreamt-of overtones, need we be surprised if quite trivial words, coincidences, daydreams, casual expression of a face should sometimes come to act as *signs* charged with a momentous import and forcing us to regard them as revelations or commands, more valid or more imperative than any positive, well-authenticated form of knowledge?

Such is the tyranny of the feelings, those arch-deceivers.

A man's public life degrades his personal life. Fame is hard on anyone who wants to *be himself*.

I find myself agreeing with much that he says, on important questions, yet do not like the impression of his mind as a whole, especially his preference for traditions, rhymes, etc., and his insistence on the superiority of "the man of intellect," i.e., himself.

Again:

There is only one thing to be done—and that's to remake oneself. And it's no easy task.

And this is too much!

A leader is a man who needs others. [I once wrote: A politician is a sick man—he has to be supported.]

A State is all the stronger the more it can preserve within itself what lives and acts against it.

An intelligent woman is a woman with whom a man can be as stupid as he pleases.

An American author could not have written the last two sentences. Not because American authors are inferior to French, but because they do not have the training to say things in this way: briefly, perfectly, and with the appearance of absolute truth.

Since making the above remark about French style, I have come across a striking example of the importance to a Frenchman of writing epigrams.

You would think that Zola, being a "naturalist," would avoid flourishes of style. But in *Germinal,* speaking of a woman who is sleeping with her nephew, and her husband who tolerates the situation because he is afraid that, if he doesn't, she will draw her lovers from lower on the social scale, Zola says: "He tolerated his nephew for fear of his coachman."

You can positively see him smacking his lips and rubbing his hands together when he had written this sentence. He could visualize it going the rounds of the cafés, among the wits whose approbation means more to an author of the race of Molière than the consciousness of having written moving passages, scenes in which the human heart is plumbed to its depths, et cetera.

With this epigram Zola felt that he had *arrived*.

From *Chekhov's* Notebooks

The University brings out all abilities, including stupidity.

A woman is fascinated not by art, but by the noise made by those who have to do with art.

"Why are your songs so short?" a bird was once asked. "Is it because you are short of breath?"
"I have very many songs, and I should like to sing them all."

Chekhov attributes this saying to Alphonse Daudet. I have rewritten the translator's English, which reads, "Why are thy songs so short? . . . Is it because thou art . . ." etc.

The public really loves in art that which is banal and long familiar, that to which they have grown accustomed.

If you are afraid of loneliness, do not marry.

Simenon agrees with this appalling observation. He says, "I have no real friends. I have a wife. I think you have to choose."

Radda in Chianti

Eight or nine hill-crests receding. A few cypresses. Olive trees growing close to the house. Groves of trees. Terraces on a hill to the left, and a vineyard sloping down to the valley floor, each plant distinct, a green stud in the brown earth. Chirping of birds. Noise of a plane going over. Basco the hound puts his paws on the parapet, looking over the valley as if trying to see what I am seeing. He seems to be listening to the sounds.

At night Basco gets loose and chases hares through the woods, stirring up every dog within a mile. The night is filled with the barking of envious dogs who are tied up. But this is breaking the law—it is out of the hunting season. When the season starts it will be all right if Basco runs after hares, but not now. G. has been threatened by the police that the next time it happens he will be deported to America. The police in Italy are once more taking on a Fascistic tone, as they are everywhere (I find it sinister when, upon entering an Italian town, above the name of the town I see the word *Carabinieri*).

A. says, if they try to deport G. she'll hire the best lawyers in Italy. The cause of our anxiety finally returns wagging his tail, his tongue hanging out. G. congratulates him. After all, this is what Basco was born to do, and he has a feeling of a job well done. Is G. supposed to punish him?

At night, the moon seen through a telescope . . . The craters are visible and there are crust-like irregularities on the circumference. Also Jupiter, with two moons on one side, one moon on the other.

The Road From Siena to Lucca

Rows of vines, lines of cypresses. The road screened with small trees and bushes. On the tops of hills, farmhouses with yellow and reddish walls. Red tiled roofs. From time to time a ruin, or a building with crenellations to give it an antique appearance. There are rectangular factories of concrete and brick in the valleys and, in the approach to a town, new apartment buildings.

As Their Land and Air Is

After all anybody is as their land and air is . . . It is that which makes them and the arts they make and the work they do and the way they eat and the way they drink and the way they learn and everything.

Gertrude Stein

Private Property, Private Emotions

Nowhere more than in the kibbutz did I realize the degree to which private property, in the deep layers of the mind, relates to private emotions. If one is absent, the other tends to be absent as well.

Bruno Bettelheim

Jack's

Close to the *Tribune* newspaper building on West Fortieth Street there was Jack Bleeck's Artists and Writers Club, catering to the newspaper crowd.

John Keats

I used to drop in at Jack's now and then, when I worked on the *Trib*. But I'd forgotten the name.

I have to look up things I took no note of at the time. I knew there was someone who would fill in the details. I am the someone.

For When You Write Your Novel

John Bell & Croyden (Chemist) 50 Wigmore Street, London.

Phenomenology

. . . phenomenological description is "the attempt to tell not what a thought is, so much as what it feels like."

Frederic Jameson

T. S. Eliot on Poetry

The changing poet:

We ourselves are not the same person that we were a year ago. This is obvious; but what is not so obvious is that this is the reason why we cannot afford to stop writing poetry.

. . . the delicate relation of the Eternal to the transient.

Verse is actual (prose is not):

... I should say that in one's prose reflections, one may be legitimately concerned with ideas, whereas in the writing of verse one can only deal with actuality.

Everyone has a natural cadence of his own from which in the end he cannot escape.

Ford Madox Ford

That is, everyone who has it.

The most beautiful, the liveliest, the most striking images are enclosed in everyday words.

Remy de Gourmont

beni-girai-e (Japanese): "red-avoiding picture."[10]

Edward's

Plumbing and Heating Co. . . .

Inv. No. 710356   February 15, 1971
S.R. . . .
. . . Eagle Ave.
West Hempstead, N.Y. 11552

Feb. 8, 1971
Shortened bathtub spout connection. Caulked spout and spindle openings in tile wall.

Labor and material	$13.14
5% sales tax	.66
Total	$13.80

---

[10] Idea for a poem, "Red-Avoiding Pictures" (1983).

1. Write a poem as objective as this bill.
2. Make an arrangement of consonants and vowels as musical as the lines beginning: "Shortened bathtub spout connection . . ."
3. "Caulked spout and . . ." Is this the right place for the line break?
4. Write an essay on the differences between English poetry and poetry in the United States.

Narrative

Dante, in taking up narrative, chucked out a number of MINOR criteria, as any writer of a long poem must in favor of a main virtue.

Ezra Pound

The Poet as Normal Man

I cry continually against my life. I have sleepless nights, thinking of the time that I must take from poetry—last night I could not sleep—and yet, perhaps, I must do all these things that I may set myself into a life of action and express not the traditional poet but that forgotten thing, the normal active man.

William Butler Yeats

But to be serious one should have a hernia . . .

In the modern era, serious writing seems to require some rupture of faith and connection.

Irving Howe

not try to make sense . . .

Prophète de la "ténébreuse et profonde unité," il aura le tort de vouloir par la savante critique de son esprit donner forme à ce qui n'en a pas.

Durozoi et Lecherbonnier

and, finally, shut up.

Le poète est enfin celui qui assumera la fabuleuse liberté de ne plus ecrire . . .

Durozoi et Lecherbonnier

Few of these poets are much bothered by anything that is in them.

Robert Frost

True. You don't have to have a demon to write for *The New Yorker.*

Gnats[11]

"Suppose I did sing! What about gnats? They sing all their lives, but it's not for joy."

Nikolai Leskov

Prophecy, Madness, and the Muse

. . . For prophecy is a madness, and the prophetess at Delphi, and the priestesses at Dodona when out of their senses have conferred great benefits on Hellas, both in public and private life, but when in their senses few or none.

. . . he who, having no touch of the Muses' madness in his soul, comes to the door and thinks that he will get into the temple by the help of art—he, I say, and his poetry are not admitted; the sane man disappears and is nowhere when he enters into rivalry with the madman.

Socrates, according to Plato

It is a pity that these statements, intended to show that inspiration—or as we might say, intuition—is essential in writing poetry, so eloquently confirm the popular idea of the poet as a lunatic.

It is one of the ideas that enable the middle class to think well of itself.

---

[11] From this, some lines of a poem, "Why Do You Write about Russia?" *Caviare at the Funeral,* 1980.

Flaubert himself laid it down as a principle that "hatred of the middle classes is the beginning of wisdom."

Frank O'Connor

Solicitations From Beyond

. . . those perpetual solicitations which seem to come from beyond, which momentarily possess us before one of those chance arrangements, of a more or less unfamiliar character, whose secret we feel might be learned merely by questioning ourselves closely enough.

André Breton

A Feeling of Mystery

Inventiveness and creativity depend on the individual's ability to let himself sink deeper into a feeling of mystery, to be overcome later by proportional efforts at mastery. Imitation of others and reliance on accepted authorities are time-honored and popular because they make possible a wholly "active," self-controlled intellectual performance.

Thomas Szasz

An idea is only a worn-out image.

Remy de Gourmont

Perhaps a symbol is nothing but an image with a reputation.
Richard H. Simon (student . . . Spring, 1973)

In The Dark and Cold

The things of a man for which we visit him were done in the dark and cold.

Emerson

This is an honorable saying, but from another point of view I'm not sure that I like it. The implication is that things done in the dark and cold are better than things done in the light. It smacks of the mean, pleasure-hating Puritanism of New England. One may have to go through a period, God forbid, of darkness and cold, but only a fool would recommend it.

How often, in fact, does anything good come out of suffering and privation? For every Dostoyevski or Solshenitsyn who survived, there have been thousands who were never heard from again.

The human being needs to hear the human voice. And writers need to draw their poems and stories from life—the more various the better. Even the Surrealist composes his unearthly works out of familiar objects. It is only the arrangement that is strange.

The Way It Works

. . . the processes of imagination are carried on either by conferring additional properties upon an object, or by abstracting from it some of those which it actually possesses, and thus enabling it to react upon the mind which hath performed the process, like a new existence.

Wordsworth

Beauty appears only from the moment when the unproductive begin to miss it.

Arnold Schoenberg

I don't understand this. I must have thought I did when I wrote it down.

Genius Is Patient

. . . cette longue patience qui est la marque du génie.

And Serene

Vers le ciel, où son oeil voit un trône splendide,
Le Poète serein lève ses bras pieux,
Et les vastes éclairs de son esprit lucide
Lui derobent l'aspect des peuples furieux . . .

Baudelaire

The First New Critic

> I hold that no work of art can be tried otherwise than by laws deduced from itself.
>
> Thomas Griffiths Wainewright

There is something wonderfully appropriate about Wainewright's metaphor for the process of criticism. He himself was tried, convicted, and transported to Van Diemen's Land.

Wainewright was both a painter and a writer. In London in the 1820s he was well known as a contributor to *The London Magazine,* for which he wrote under the pseudonym Janus Weathercock. Two-faced Wainewright certainly was, but he did not veer with the wind—under his frivolous appearance and way of life lay a purpose from which he did not swerve. He intended to collect Helen Abercrombie's life insurance. But there were preliminaries. First he poisoned his uncle in order to obtain his house and live at ease. Then he had to poison his wife's mother, because she might be suspicious. Then he was free to poison Miss Abercrombie.

As I have said, Wainewright wrote for *The London Magazine.* He belonged to what was called the Dandy School, anticipating Oscar Wilde by sixty years in his views and deportment. The above quotation is a specimen of his aesthetics. William Hazlitt and Thomas De Quincey knew Wainewright and dined at his table. Charles and Mary Lamb were his friends.

Wainewright lived on a lavish scale. He dressed like a dandy—his lemon-colored gloves caused a sensation. His house was furnished with a Brussels carpet, a cast of the Venus de Medicis, a piano "by Tomkisson," and other expensive articles. After dinner there would be fine conversation, Wainewright playing the genial host and speaking of truth and beauty, on which he was considered an authority.

In order to afford this luxury he had committed a crime for which the penalty in those days was hanging. Wainewright's father on his decease left £5000 in trust for his son. Wainewright forged the signatures of the trustees on a power of attorney, and conveyed nearly half of the sum from the bank to himself. This swindle passing undetected, he conveyed £3000 more.

These funds, however, were exhausted. Having got rid of his uncle and his mother-in-law, he set about insuring the life of his wife's sister, Helen Abercrombie, with several insurance companies, for a sum of £16,000. He then poisoned her with antimony and strychinine. But when he tried to collect the life insurance, the companies refused to pay.

His wife and a remaining sister grew afraid and fled the house. Wainewright saw that he was suspected, and sailed to France. He returned six years later, no one knows why, and was arrested and charged with forgery with intent to defraud the Bank of England. The Bank charitably allowed him to plead guilty to two of the minor indictments, on the understanding that they would not press the more serious charges. So Wainewright cheated the gallows. He was never tried for murder.

Transported to Van Diemen's Land—the present Tasmania—Wainewright managed to make his lot as a convict somewhat easier by drawing portraits of the notables of Hobart, their wives and female relations. There were some who thought that Wainewright was a gentleman who had had a run of bad luck—the point of view Wainewright himself appears to have held. There exists a self-portrait by Wainewright under which he has written, "Head of a Convict, very characteristic of low cunning & revenge." This was meant to be ironic.

The flattering state did not last. Bulwer-Lytton published a novel, *Lucretia; or the Children of Night,* in which Wainewright and his deeds were set forth. The novel was read in the antipodes, and even there it was perceived that Wainewright was wicked.

Wainewright was a New Critic, a hundred years before the breed appeared in America. "I hold that no work of art can be tried otherwise than by laws deduced from itself" puts the case in a nutshell—whole books have been written that have not expressed the aesthetics so clearly.

The New Criticism began to appear in the United States in the 1930s, when many writers were concerned with the need for social reform and literature was becoming the handmaid of economics. In reaction some critics strove to maintain the autonomy of art. The text was to be judged for its style and structure. Consideration of the writer's intention, or circumstances that might have influenced the making of the work, or the effect it might have upon the reader, was irrelevant. The value of a piece of writing did not lie in its content, what it "said," but in itself . . . the experience you had when you read it.

The New Critics had a point. The poem or story or play does create its own sense of reality. How can anyone who writes not agree with this? But there is a point the New Critics did not make—indeed tended to deny by their concentration on style and structure: the intensity and importance of the work is derived from the extent and intensity of the writer's experience.

To live is to be involved with content and meaning. It would have been fortunate for Wainewright if he had been tried by laws deduced solely from himself—but life does not permit it.

Morality gets into the work somehow, though it may not be obvious—and indeed, for the sake of surprise, which is half the pleasure of reading, it is better if the morality is not stated but allowed to show itself by its consequences, as it does in real life.

The Uncertainty Principle

The result of [Werner] Heisenberg's reflections, announced later in 1927, was the celebrated Principle of Indeterminacy (or Uncertainty). It abolished, to state it simply, the whole idea of exact observation. There was no longer any such thing as a "scientific fact." The most that one could determine, according to Heisenberg, was that a certain observer, at a certain point in space and time, had seen certain phenomena which he believed to represent the possibility of thus-and-such. The implications of Heisenberg's Indeterminacy Principle were as fundamental and as radical as those of Einstein's Relativity Theory. If, basically, Einstein taught that all facts are relative, Heisenberg taught that all facts are momentary perceptions of possibilities. There was no real difference between what we think of as laws of cause and effect and what we think of as random events or pure chance. Or, to put it another way, Karl Barth was right in arguing that all we can know about God is our own lack of knowledge. Or, to put it still another way, Hans Arp was indeed recreating reality when he dropped some pieces of paper to the floor and glued them where they fell, for the whole universe is a Dada universe.

The most passionate opponent of Heisenberg's theory was, oddly enough, Albert Einstein, who clung to the belief that the scientist's purpose was to discover the laws of God's creation. In answer to the idea that any such laws were unknowable, Einstein repeatedly said, "God does not play at dice."

Otto Friedrich

Most of the stories I wrote were the stories I told myself just before I went to sleep.

Edgar Rice Burroughs

And the stories I write are the stories I tell myself when I have woken up.

A Fiction Writer

"I was born in Peking at the time that my father was military adviser to the Empress of China and lived there, in the Forbidden City, until I was ten years old." So Burroughs once began a short autobiography accurately titled, *Edgar Rice Burroughs, Fiction Writer.*

Actually, Burroughs was born in Chicago, 1875, and his father was a distiller of fluids for car batteries.

Anthony Haden-Guest

Best-Sellers

The Splendid Legacy, by Eleanor Farnes
Cage of Gold, by Rachel Lindsay
Lovely is the Rose, by Belinda Dell
The Golden Madonna, by Rebecca Stratton
Storm Over Mandargi, by Margaret Way
Cinderella in Mink, by Roberta Leigh

These were in the book racks in Woolworth's next to the soda fountain. The books are published in a series ... "A Harlequin Romance, Harlequin Books, Toronto and Winnipeg."

Special $1.88[12]

do-it-yourself

Beaded Pear

No glueing [sic] or sewing required. Beautifully beaded fruit is easily assembled using enclosed pins, beads and decorative material. Easy-to-follow instructions included.

Another exciting craft kit from WALCO.

Collect the Complete Series of Walco Beaded Fruit Kits: Apple, Pear, Peach, Banana, Lemon, Orange, Grapes, Strawberry, Plum, Lime.

[In Woolworth's, Middletown, Connecticut]

Sunrise Highway[13]

Fabric Gardens
Discount Dog Food
Scelfo Realty
Amoco
Exit 42 Howells Rd.
  Bay Shore

I am making these notes holding the pad on the steering wheel

Buick Opel Raymond
Color TV
Washers
Dryers

Cold Beer
Hot Heroes Cold
Clams 'n Stuff

Candi's
X-Rated
Dancers

[12] See my poem, "The Beaded Pear," *Caviare at the Funeral,* 1980.
[13] I used the signs in two poems: "An Affair in the Country," *Caviare at the Funeral,* 1980, and "Waiting in the Service Station," 1987.

Hecksher Pky.
State Park

Speed
Zone
Ahead

Signal
Ahead

Jung's Symbol of the Sacred

Jung describes the "quaternity symbol"—a circle divided in four parts, a square room, a clock, the four seasons, et cetera—as "the formula of the unconscious mind" and "an archetypical image of the Deity." He traces the history of the symbol in mythology, philosophy and religion. The quaternity is "an abstract and almost mathematical representation of some of the main problems abundantly discussed in medieval Christian philosophy."

This history doesn't explain the origin and meaning of the symbol. Jung attempts to explain it, however: "The unconscious is often personified by the anima, a female figure. Apparently the symbol of the quaternity issues from her."

He goes on to say that, in a world that has lost belief in God, the symbol "denotes and supports an exclusive concentration upon oneself," for man has replaced the Deity.

"Apparently" is weak—there is nothing apparent about either of these ideas. Jung needs to think of human consciousness as reducible to a formula, an "almost mathematical representation."

To Jung the individual life is not very important—what is important is the archetypical image, the encoded memory of the race, of which the unconscious affords us glimpses.

The opposite of this way of thinking would be Chekhov's. Chekhov sees the individual life as irreducible. He cares about men and women as they are, as they live and have their being. Life is not the reflection of an image but bears within itself a truth that is striving to be fulfilled.

"My holy of holies is the human body, health, intelligence, talent, inspiration, love and the most absolute freedom—freedom from violence and lying, whatever forms they may take."—Anton Chekhov

At the Bazuft River[14]

Iran's Bakhtiari tribe. Nomads. Sheep and goats and herd dogs. They bake bread in the Biblical manner: unleavened bread on hot stones. Life centers on the flock; they milk the herd and make yoghurt. They spin wool "to make the repairs that are essential on the journey, and no more." They obtain metal pots, etc., by barter. There is no room for innovation, no time . . . for a new device or thought or tune. A life without features. Can the flocks be got over the next high pass? They must find new pastures every day.

Crossing the Bazuft River: "What happens to the old when they can't cross the last river?" They stay to die.

> Jacob Bronowski, "Ascent of Man"—
> documentary on TV, Sunday,
> October 5, 1975

Old people who can't fill out the forms . . . can't do their own shopping . . . what happens to them? This is our Bazuft River.

Same World, Different People

> . . . each man hopes and believes he is better than the world which is his, but the man who is better merely expresses this same world better than the others.
>
> Hegel

Saul's Gang[15]

Poochie
Nori (pronounced Nawry)
Red Ann
Nick d'Amato
Murray Chubinsky

[14] A poem, "The Bazuft," was written ten years later.
[15] That is, Saul Galin's. I used some of the names in poems: "Boots and Saddles," *Searching for the Ox*, 1976, and " 'Mad' Murray," 1987.

Lefty Looie
Chink the Knife (after a real gangster)
Mad Murray Kadish
Alfred Dubitch

They frequented the Hotel Diplomat on 43rd Street, between Seventh and Eighth Avenue.

Forty-Second Street

At the Avenue of the Americas . . .

Eton's Luggage Gifts, Cambridge Hosiery, Barricini Candy, Health Foods, Locksmith, Restaurant . . . Bickford's Coffee Shop, American Savings Bank.

Fateful Compulsion

All my writings may be considered tasks imposed
from within; their source was a fateful compulsion.

C. G. Jung

The World As It Is

You wish the world better than it is, more poetical. You are that kind of poet. I would rate as the other kind. I wouldn't give a cent to see the world, the United States or even New York, made better. I want them left just as they are for me to make—poetical on paper.

Robert Frost

Try this saying on one of your friends. He will turn either red or blue, like litmus paper.

Bad Poets and Misguided Men

He pointed out as worthy of the severest reprehension, the conduct of those writers who seem to estimate their power of exciting sorrow for suffering humanity by the quantity of hatred and revenge which they are able to pour into the hearts of their Readers. . . . They are bad poets and misguided men.

Wordsworth

. . . it is necessary for you to use all the intelligence you have to get rid of those who are decaying, who have lost their youth. Regard them as enemies and beasts: do not be influenced by them, do not associate with them.

Ch'en Tu-hsiu (teacher of Mao Tse-tung)

Do not act the part of a madman, for the night is thickening fast.

Kabir

For Your Novel, Mr. Fitzgerald

"Oh Me, Oh My, Oh You." From *Two Little Girls in Blue,* 1922.
"Glad Rag Doll."
"In Araby With You." From *Criss Cross,* 1926.
"Do, Do, Do." From *Oh Kay!* (George Gershwin) 1926.
"Thinking of You." From *Five O'Clock Girl,* 1927.
"Rio Rita." 1927.

Anorexia

The good girls, the over-achievers, who starve themselves. They can't relax . . . exercise continually . . . live in a small, controlled world. Do deep knee bends while brushing their teeth.

Her parents avoided fighting at any cost.

TV—"20 Minutes"

Names

Ron and Audrey (black cafeteria workers behind the counter at LaGuardia)
Charles E. Music—Building Products of Metal (sign in Houston, Texas)
Johnny Ramora (fish that attaches itself to a shark)

The Women Passing By

Instead of weighing the behavior of men, look over the women passing by.

Louis Aragon

. . . to belong to the Left in France seems to be, above all, to affirm that one is more purely Left than other men of the Left, to prove that one's fellows on the Left are hardly more than rightists. What saves the Right, in the final analysis, is the paralyzing fear of the Left that it may be suspected of being reactionary.

Jean-François Revel, Without Marx or Jesus

The same may be said of the avant-garde in art and literature. There are writers who are so afraid to be thought "traditional" that they write in a style no one can understand.

The Philosopher and the Moose

I had been invited to speak at a conference that was being held near Montreal.

I was met at the airport by a woman with a chauffeur-driven limousine. She spoke to me in French and I remarked that it was fortunate that I understood the language. She said that my talk the next day would be given in French, of course. "Bien entendu," I said.

The conférenciers were staying the night in Montreal. It was well past midnight when I finished translating my talk from English into French, approximately. The next morning as soon as shops were open I went looking for a French and English dictionary. I found a bookstore and, in addition to the dictionary, bought *501 French Verbs*. "Are you sure you don't want 1001?" the clerk asked slyly. I returned to my room and began revising my translation. At eleven the conférenciers assembled and we traveled on a bus into the country. I revised all the way, oblivious to the scenery. When the conference began I was still revising.

A group of Frenchmen had come from Paris. The one sitting on my left bore a striking resemblance to the actor Jacques Tati. He spoke looking at the ceiling and moving his hands in undulant gestures. He spoke of "text," "signifier," and "différance." His thoughts seemed to be floating visibly between himself and the ceiling . . . a hand would rise languidly and coax one down. It seemed that he was performing in a comedy and that in a moment the audience would break into laughter. But it didn't.

The subject of the conference was, "Is Writing Recoverable (Récuperable)?" No one seemed to know what was meant by this exactly. When my turn came I read my sentences carefully, enunciating. I said that certain individuals would continue to write in any event. The next speaker was a bald Frenchman with black-rimmed glasses who looked as though he would brook no nonsense. He said that the only remarks worth listening to were those of the French delegation.

Next day there was a panel discussion. Some writers from Quebec attempted to discuss the situation of French-speaking citizens of an English-speaking nation. This was quashed by the gentlemen from Paris who continued to speak in terms to which only Molière could have done justice. I decided to leave.

The conference was scheduled to run for three days and transportation would not be provided for drop-outs. But there was a bus that would connect with a bus to Montreal. I took it and it let me off in the middle of Canada. The air was cold and the scene desolate, bare fields extending to the horizon.

A car drew up and paused at a stop sign. Tied to the fender was the head of a moose. It was about six feet long . . . I don't think I am exaggerating. Its eyes were open and as large as billiard balls. Then the car with its awful burden drove away and the bus came.

I have thought about the conference and the scene on the road. The philosopher is looking at the ceiling and spinning one sentence out of another, with accompanying motions of his hands. I hear sentences that lead to other sentences, with clauses and parentheses. Then I see the head of the moose. It exists, it is real, and stranger than anything I could have imagined.

What a universe, that has such extremes: language divorced from fact and fact divorced from language! I am standing between them. Why? Am I supposed to reconcile such opposites? But that is impossible.

It seems that I am here to ask questions to which there are no answers.

The Siren

Ne l'ora che non può 'l calor diurno
   intepidar più 'l freddo de la luna,
   vinto da terra, e talor da Saturno
—quando i geomanti lor Maggior Fortuna
   veggiono in orïente, innanzi a l'alba,
   surger per via che poco le sta bruna—
mi venne in sogno una femmina balba,
   ne li occhi guercia, e sovra i piè distorta,
   con le man monche, e di colore scialba.
Io la mirava; e come 'l sol conforta
   le fredde membra che la notte aggrava,
   così lo sguardo mio le facea scorta
la lungua, e poscia tutta la drizzava
   in poco d'ora, e lo smarrito volto,
   com' amor vuol, così le colorava.
Poi ch'ell' avea 'l parlar cosi disciolto,
   cominciava a cantar sì, che con pena
   da lei avrei mio intento rivolto.

Dante

The passage is translated by Charles S. Singleton as follows.

At the hour when the day's heat, over-
come by Earth and at times by Saturn, can
no more warm the cold of the moon—when
the geomancers see their *Fortuna Major* rise
in the East before dawn by a path which
does not long stay dark for it—there came
to me in a dream a woman, stammering,
with eyes asquint and crooked on her feet,
with maimed hands, and of sallow hue. I
gazed upon her: and even as the sun revives
cold limbs benumbed by night, so my look
made ready her tongue, and then in but lit-
tle time set her full straight, and colored her
pallid face even as love requires. When she
had her speech thus unloosed, she began to
sing so that it would have been hard for me
to turn my attention from her.

Tender Comrade

Une femme qu'on aime, c'est un petit camarade de lutte, tendre et silencieux.

Jean Anouilh

Jealousy

It frequently happens that women who do not really love their husbands are jealous and destroy their friendships. They want the husband to belong entirely to them because they themselves do not belong to him. The kernel of all jealousy is lack of love.

C. G. Jung

A Frightened Pleasure

Yes. The degradation of the soul, a frightened pleasure, the danger of the law, the path of hell. Considering these four, let not a man go after another man's wife.

Dhammapada

Robert Burns, who had reason to know, wrote the following:

> I waive the quantum o' the sin,
> The hazard o' concealing,
> But och, it hardens a' within
> And petrifies the feeling.

I don't have the text with me, so the wording may be slightly different.

Every Contact

Every contact leaves a trace.

Dr. Edmund Locard, "French criminologist"

... whoever walks a furlong without sympathy walks to his own funeral drest in his shroud.

Walt Whitman

Wandering

As I left my native land when I was seventeen, and have never been back, remarks about exile and wandering have always struck me as having a personal application.

Dante . . . on eating the bread of exile. How bitter it is.

Shakespeare . . . A traveller is one who has sold his land in order to look at other men's. On the other hand, "home-keeping youth have ever homely wits." Impossible to pin him down, as usual.

Emerson . . . "Travelling is a fool's paradise."

Kipling . . .

> For to admire an' for to see,
>> For to be'old this world so wide—
> It never done no good to me,
>> But I can't drop it if I tried.

Apollinaire . . . "Il faut voyager loin en aimant sa maison."

Ezra Pound . . . "Much conversation is as good as a home."

Walter Scott . . . His remarks are perhaps the most famous of all. He speaks of the expatriate "whose heart hath ne'er within him burned/As home his footsteps he hath turned." Scott curses him soundly; the wretch, "concenter'd all in self," will come to a bad end.[16]

The passage by Scott has always made me uneasy, but to offset it there is this saying by Hugh of St. Victor: "The best is to consider that we have a home nowhere, and only then does one really love the world."

Preservation Hall Jazz Band, New Orleans

A set:

> "Sweet Lorraine"
> "Alabama Jubilee"
> "Walking with Jesus"
> "La Marseillaise"
> "A Shanty in Old Shanty Town"

Traditional requests $1.00
Others $2.00
"The Saints" $5.00

---

[16] See the poem, "Silence" (1987).

The instruments were: trombone, trumpet, banjo, bass fiddle, snares, big drum, piano.

Fort Worth[17]

Seen through a picture window:

Trees: Flowering Judas (or Redbird), Hackberry, Cherry Laurel, Sycamore, Golden Rain Tree, Magnolia.

Flowers: Peony, Pyracantha (waxwings eat the berries and get drunk), Bougainvillea, Calaucho (I can't find it in the dictionary), Ceniza ("very Texan" says my hostess).

In the room behind me, Isaac Bashevis Singer, talking about golems and other supernatural creatures in Russia long ago . . .

On a Train

Clutching a paper cup . . . blonde, gray eyes, blouse with a brown and black pattern (modernistic), black skirt . . .

Seems drunk or deranged. I'd say, drunk.

She takes out a ball-point pen and writes, staring at the newspaper held open by the man sitting opposite, as though trying to read the headlines.

Now and then her lips move.

In The Graveyard at Hauppauge[18]

Erikson
Kratochwill
Blydenburgh
Payne
Joshua and Jerusha Wheeler (Joshua d. 1854, Jerusha d. 1866)
Wesley Wheeler (d. 1840)
Woolley, MacCrone, Nichols, Hubes, Smith, Davis
Aletta
Augusta Brunce
Phebe Almira
Temperance A. Wheeler

[17] See my poem, "Numbers and Dust" (1985).
[18] See "The Old Graveyard at Hauppauge," *Caviare at the Funeral.*

First names: William, Sarah, Caroline, Elizabeth, Jacob,
Jonas, Isaac, Nathaniel

London

Looking across the Thames from the south side, toward Big
Ben—the clock reads 4:25—and the Houses of Parliament. Golden
color of the stone. Westminster Bridge. People strolling on the
embankment. Plane trees lining the walk. Also, along the embank-
ment, lamps with big globes on iron pillars with big fish (carp?)
wound around them. Sound of a train crossing a bridge over the
river, to my right. Sun shining through gray clouds.

Massive building on opposite bank. One directly opposite is
ornate . . . 19th Century? One to the right—my right as I look—is
white concrete 30s type. Skyscraper to far left. Post Office tower in
the distance.

White pleasure boats with blue superstructures in the Thames:
Greenwich Belle, Chay Blyth, Princess Rose, London Belle. Directly
opposite on other bank, a gold metal bird on a pedestal, wings
spread.

Just Like Berlitz

A deux pas de la Place Pigalle . . . Chez Georgette
BAR
Hotel Confort
English spoken. Man Spricht Deutsch. Se habla Espanol. Si parla
Italiano.

rue Blondel, rue St.-Apolline

Man: "You're beautiful."
Whore: "You have to be." ("Il faut l'être.")

Viareggio[19]

The window of my room looks across the via Carducci on which
an unbroken stream of automobiles, motorbikes, mopeds, and bicy-

[19] See the poem, "In a Time of Peace," *The Best Hour of the Night,* 1983.

cles passes day and night. There is an open space where, last night, there was an exhibition "per la pubblicita," i.e., advertising a shampoo . . . a fountain of colored water leaping to the rhythm of music blaring from a loudspeaker.

There is a car park; then the bathing establishments with their red-tiled roofs: Lidino, Antaura, Principe, Europa. Blue umbrellas, now folded, standing upright in the brown sand, in parallel lines going down to the sea . . . Last night there was a heavy rainstorm, and today the red flag is up. No swimming.

Signs to my left across the street . . . Stock, Coca-Cola, Principe di Piemonte . . . "tutte le Sera DISCOTECA."

The effect of all the superb, almost naked bodies . . . long, well-shaped legs, heavy, curved breasts . . . is anti-aphrodisiac. Those who wish to propel man into heaven or into space could do no better than satisfy his sexual curiosity.

> Principe di Piemonte
> Turitalia
> Odeon Cinema
> Bar Olimpic
> Ristorante Foscolo
> Sala Giochi (pinball machines)
> Pensione Dolfi

Only George Grosz could do justice to the people you see in restaurants and cafés along the waterfront. Sheer piggishness. R. says that it's because they remember the war, when you couldn't find a potato. But the war has been over for thirty-four years.

> Foto Gioattoli. Sviluppo e Stampe (developing and prints)
> Galletti (for handbags)
> Diana Interiors
> Pelliceria le Gemelli—Casa di Mode
> prodotti Motta
> Caffé Segafredo
> Gelateria Prati
> Bagno Bulena
> Seiko
> Bar—sali e tabacchi

Sauna Finlandese
Salvatore—coiffeur pour dames
Galleria del Libro
Timpano (handbags, cigarette lighters,
    etc. . . . an expensive smell of leather)
and
Ristorante Tito del Molo

Typing these notes a year later, in Hawaii, I remember the at-mosphere of Italy, the street and the crowd, the search for diversion.

I am working at a window with a view of Diamond Head. Two miles down Kalakaua Avenue there's the same crowd, pricing hand-bags, bowls carved out of monkeypod wood, swim-suits . . . the same search for things to buy that will change one's life. It is going on all over the world . . . in Zagreb, Tokyo, Sydney, Miami.

And why not? What else would you have them do? People are seldom so innocently employed as when they are spending money, to borrow from Dr. Johnson.

All the same, it's pathetic.

Translation

Let's face it, the poems of Basho, in the translation by Nobuyuki Yuasa, are banal. Everything must reside in the original. Is this, by any stretch of the imagination, a poem?

> It is a bit too cold
> To be naked
> In this stormy wind
> Of February

Not for the first time I think that translating poetry is a waste of time. In poetry everything depends on the sound. I don't say this lightly: the sound of poetry is the perfect wedding of thought and emotion. But this essential element is lost in translation. All that remains is an image perhaps, or an idea. You lose the sound of the original poem, and as you have to keep to the meaning of the original you are prevented from creating the sound of poetry in your own language.

> . . . novels will give way, by and by, to diaries or autobiographies—captivating books, if only a man knew how to choose among his experiences that which is really his experience, and how to record truth truly.
>
> Ralph Waldo Emerson

Baudelaire hated the United States—Americans had vilified his beloved Edgar Poe. There would come a day, he prophesied, when there would be poets in the United States who could not spell.

He would be pleased to know that I have just received a book-length manuscript of poems by a woman who spells rehearse, "rehurse." In the accompanying letter she informs me that she has six other manuscripts of the same length which she is hoping to publish.

American Prose

Each of these sacramental things are important for all humans by the very fact that they are humans.

Thus, attempts to persuade us to perceive a thing as symbol results in necessarily odd, unusual, and apparently bizarre language.

Andrew W. Greeley, *The Mary Myth*

The State of Learning

L. E. was teaching a course in Henry James to a class of graduate students. He mentioned Balzac and discovered that there was not one student in the class who had heard of Balzac, much less read one of his novels. He tried Turgenev . . . with the same result.

Realists[20]

July 23, 1980

Have finished *He Knew He Was Right* and begun *The Claverings* . . .

When one considers the novel, its special province, "life," Trollope is unbeatable. He has a broad knowledge of men and manners. Other novelists have this—Trollope's peculiar strength is his moderation.

Consider Captain Boodle's conversation with Archie in which he advises him how to go about wooing Lady Ongar. The advice is proffered in terms having to do with horses, Captain Boodle's trade: "When I've got to do with a trained mare, I always choose that she shall know that I'm there." Think what Dickens might have made of Captain Boodle! But Trollope is content to tickle our funnybone and get on with the story.

In the *Autobiography* he tells how, before beginning each day's work, he read some pages from the day before. In this way he maintained an even tone, like the rising of the sun every day.

Trollope is not Zola: blood is not shed in front of us, but lives are at stake all the same. The scene in which Harry Clavering confesses to Cecelia Burton that he has been seeing Julia Ongar, and being "false" to Cecelia's sister, is painful . . . so painful that, like Harry, we wish it were over. Harry forfeits the affection Cecelia has had for him up to now. In her eyes he sees himself clearly for the first time: he is not a fine fellow, but very ordinary. This is all, yet it is everything—in a sense Harry dies.

In *The Claverings* Trollope is writing about a young man who has no character, as does Flaubert in *L'Education Sentimentale*. I'm not sure but that Trollope does a better job.

July 27

Well, *The Claverings* fell apart, and it's clear why Trollope isn't ranked with the great novelists. From the moment that Harry Clavering decides to break with Julia Ongar and go back to his

---

[20] This part of "Entries" first appeared in *The Hudson Review*, No. 4. Winter 1981–82. It was reprinted in *The Character of the Poet*. Ann Arbor: The University of Michigan Press, 1986.

insipid fiancée, not because he wants to but because it is the conventionally "right" thing to do, we cease to care one way or the other. Yet Trollope goes on turning out his eight pages a day, tying up loose ends. As though it mattered!

In his autobiography Trollope attributes the comparative failure of this novel to the "weakness" of Harry Clavering, by which he seems to mean moral weakness. But the weakness of a fictional character can be interesting, even attractive. The reason for the failure of the novel is Trollope's weakness as an artist. This writer who was capable of laboring like a navvy, turning out so many pages every day, even on board ship, was also capable of avoiding a serious treatment of the subject.

To understand Harry Clavering, one would have to share his life . . . even at the risk of tedium, as Flaubert shares the life of Frédéric Moreau. That is taking the thing one has created seriously . . . the life of imagination can take you into some dreary places.

But this is at the risk of putting off your reader. It is a risk Trollope is not willing to take. So he washes his hands of Harry Clavering and lets Victorian morality dictate the rest of the novel. In the light of that morality Harry is a "weakling"—the author has abandoned his task and taken a seat in the audience. "Look at what an ass Harry Clavering is making of himself, like the ass between two bundles of hay."

This reminds me of the inconsistency in *He Knew He Was Right*. At the outset Trollope makes Emily Trevelyan obstinate, even perverse, in refusing to accede to her husband's wish and continuing to receive the visits of Colonel Osborne. It is clear that she is engaged in a struggle with her husband for power. At the end of the novel, however, it appears that the fault is all on his side, and she is the loyal wife who has been unjustly accused—a figure in a painting by Augustus Egg.

In spite of his knowledge of men and women, Trollope is willing to settle for a conventional view. The perverseness of Emily Trevelyan is sacrificed to the cliché of the dutiful, long-suffering wife. Harry Clavering does not go to bed with Julia Ongar—instead he goes back to his fiancée. Then he comes into an inheritance, an ending with which no one can quarrel . . . the *deux ex machina* of the Victorian novel.

The truth about Trollope is that he was lazy—a more serious writer would have written less. As F. R. Leavis said, the novels do not say anything to justify their length; they merely serve to kill time, "which seems to be all that even some academic critics demand of a novel."

August

The same female protagonist, at different stages in her life, appears in Jean Rhys's novels, *Quartet, After Leaving Mr. Mackenzie, Voyage in the Dark,* and *Good Morning, Midnight.* She also appears in the short stories.

We can give her a composite history by rearranging the episodes. As she has several names, for the sake of consistency let us call her X.

She grows up on an island in the West Indies, before the Great War. Her father is an Englishman—her mother, West Indian.

Her mother dies and her father marries again. The stepmother is English, the worst sort of colonizing type—she despises the natives. When X's father dies, her stepmother sends her to England to finish her schooling, then swindles her out of her inheritance.

X finds work in the chorus of a road show that plays in the provinces. She becomes familiar with dreary streets and rooms. She takes a lover and loses her virginity. The lover abandons her. X is pregnant and has to have an abortion. The lover pays for this.

X has other relationships with men. At some point in this composite history one of the men settles an amount of money upon her, to be paid regularly through a lawyer. Then the payments stop.

X is in Paris, working as a fashion model. Then it is after the war, and she is married to a Dutchman who engages in shady speculations. X acquires a fur coat that represents a certain kind of success. Then her husband is wanted by the police, and suddenly X is poor. She has a child that dies because she can't afford to have it taken care of properly.

By the time she is thirty X has begun to deteriorate. She drinks too much. She isn't too proud to accept money from men who are practically strangers. She has been evicted from hotels. She is no longer young.

There is no sentimentality in Jean Rhys's perception of X. On the contrary, at moments she treats her with a kind of gallows humor. When things are as bad as they could be, X is sure to do something to make them worse.

The key to X's character and fate is in the following passage between her and her stepmother.

> "I hate dogs," I said.
> "Well, really!" she said.
> "Well, I do," I said.
> "I don't know what'll become of you if you go on like that," Hester said. "Let me tell you that you'll have a very unhappy life if you go on like that. People won't like you. People in England will dislike you very much if you say things like that."

X will not have a happy life, because she speaks her mind—it is as simple as that.

This reckless and admirable trait makes her an outsider. Respectable people dislike her instinctively and look for ways to humiliate her and beat her down.

They don't dislike her because she is a woman or because she is poor (Jean Rhys doesn't fall into the category of a feminist or a social reformer). They dislike X and seek to humiliate her because she speaks her mind and looks it, refusing to "knuckle under." As she is a woman alone, and has no money, they are able to treat her badly and get away with it.

In a confrontation with her sister who has done the "right thing" all her life, X says, "All the people who've knuckled under—you're jealous. D'you think I don't know? You're jealous of me, jealous, jealous. Eaten up with it."

She is right—they envy her freedom of spirit. And they will punish her continually for having it.

Jean Rhys drew on her life for this fiction—her autobiography makes this clear. But she is not sentimental; she stands away from X and lets you see her weaknesses. So we can believe her when she shows the others to be contemptible. The motif, man's inhumanity to man, that rises from this fiction rings true.

If instead of writing novels and short stories at intervals, Jean Rhys had written one big, continuous novel, she might be far better known. As it is, we have only these few short novels and short stories. As Ingres once remarked, "With talent, you do what you like. With genius, you do what you can."

August 25

Many years ago, having read *César Birotteau* and *Cousin Pons,* I decided I'd had enough of Balzac—it had been a painful experience. Now, with *Lost Illusions,* I am again puzzled by the pleasure he takes in showing the triumph of the strong over the weak.

Balzac is the novelist *par excellence.* If you had to choose one novelist to represent the genus, the energy a novelist needs to have, the curiosity about human behavior, the inventiveness, it would be Balzac. He was everything that the public believes an artist to be: romantic, extravagant, obsessed. Because he believed it himself.

Balzac is inexhaustibly creative. This one novel is a world in itself, full of living characters: Lucien Rubempré, the poet who longs to be admired and who betrays everyone; who becomes remorseful and, at the first breath of fame, recovers . . . Mme. de Bargeton, the romantic woman at thirty-six, sensitive, proud, verging on the ridiculous . . . Séchard, the old miser who is also a drunkard—masterly touch!—and who is willing to ruin his own son . . . Séchard is as comical a miser as Harpagon. In any other literature do misers loom so large?

The picture of manners among the provincial aristocracy seems to have been done from the inside. And Balzac's knowledge of the paper-manufacturing business is staggering—in fact, he knows too much. A young man, having proposed marriage to the woman he loves, and been accepted, sits with her in the moonlight and delivers a lecture on paper-making. "Labor is very cheap in China, where a workman earns three halfpence a day, and this cheapness enables the Chinese to manipulate each sheet of paper separately." Et cetera. This may very well be the most ridiculous love scene in literature.

This kind of extravagance, however, comes of superabundant energy—other novelists are not capable of rising to Balzac's faults. He cannot help plunging into the details of business and legal proceedings. When one of his characters draws up an "account of expenses," Balzac gives it to you, item by item. He invests facts with a vitality they have in no other novelist. In a novel by Balzac a debt of 6000 francs is alive—it breathes, pursues its prey and pounces.

In his passion for facts Balzac may, indeed, be closer to the urgent concerns of the nineteenth century than the innumerable novelists who wrote about love. He is the best historian of the rise of the bourgeoisie, and for this he has been praised by the Communists, from Lenin to Lukacs.

I concede that Balzac is writing history. Still, he strikes me as a kind of monster. To render the cruelties of life as energetically as Balzac does, and in such detail, is to take pleasure in them. He admires his human tigers of the counting house and Bourse.

A footnote . . . Henry James on Balzac. Speaking of Balzac's ambition, or compulsion, to write about everything, James says, "It amounts to a sort of suffered doom, since to be solicited by the world from all quarters at once, what is that for the spirit but a denial of escape? We feel his doom to be want of a private door, and that he felt it, though more obscurely, himself."

This is a profound observation. But then, so many of us have a "private door," and so few can create like Balzac.

August 28

His name was Benito Pérez Galdós. He was very famous in Spain before the Great War—his play, *Electra*, was a rallying point for liberals. His historical novels were read by everyone; his realistic fiction met with some resistance but came to be regarded highly. There was agitation to obtain the Nobel prize for Galdós—committees were formed, et cetera—but he didn't get it. He died in 1920.

And I had never heard of Galdós. There's no doubt that reputations in the arts follow the flag, and Spain is no longer a great empire. On the other hand, when I was growing up in the British West Indies we read Robert Louis Stevenson. There were hundreds of English classics, some French . . . and none in German, Spanish or Italian. I am exaggerating slightly—one had heard of *Don Quixote*.

As for the Russians . . . I suppose that one of the young men who were imported from Oxford and Cambridge to teach us might have heard of Tolstoy or Dostoyevski, but if so he never passed the word.

Now here is Galdós, and he can bear comparison with the novelists of England and France and Russia. I have only read *Miau*, his novel about an old civil servant who is out of work and seeking re-employment . . . but how many books does one have to read before one decides that a writer is "great"? One great book is enough to settle a man's claim, in my opinion.

Galdós has the quality all great novelists share—he is interested in everyone. A character has only to appear for a minute, and he's alive. There are no supernumerary characters—everyone has a life, and it's important. *Miau* gives off what Henry James described as "that vague hum, that indefinable echo of the whole multitudinous life of man, which is the real sign of a great work of fiction."

The novel centers on two people: the old man, Villaamil, who grows wilder and wilder as other, less deserving men are given positions or receive promotions while he, with all his years of loyal, honest service to the State, and his brilliant plan for instituting an income tax, is left out in the cold; and his grandchild, Luis, who is in the way of becoming a saint. Luis has visions of God and converses with him. It is very difficult to get his grandfather a job. God tells Luis. He tells people what to do, but they don't listen.

And if Luis doesn't do his homework, how can his grandfather find a position? Luis hasn't been studying; in his geography lesson he misplaced a town and a river. What's the use of making a world, if people are going to throw things around?

Besides Luis there are a family of "Miaus," his grandmother and his aunts, who have been given this nickname because they look like cats. There is Luis's father, who is wicked for the love of it. And a wonderful dog named Canelo.

The visions of Luis are not dreams or hallucinations—Galdós makes this quite clear, though you'd have to read the novel to see how. The realism of Galdós is "psychological"—everything is related to the workings of the minds of his characters, not conjured out of thin air. The God whom little Luis sees is as believable as the human characters, because Luis sees him.

By the end of the story the demarcation between "real life" and the life of ideas has vanished. Galdós shows that practically anything can be accomplished within the mode of realism—you can be as imaginative as you like, as well as "true to life."

Critics like to say that the term "realism" has no meaning. For what is the "real"? It is what you think—"thinking makes it so." They prefer to discuss realism as a literary movement, the leader of which was Champfleury, who may have been a realist but was certainly trivial.

But though you may not be able to define a thing exactly, it may exist nonetheless. Realism is a definite way of looking at things, and a way of writing, recognisably different from other kinds.

The realist aims to create an illusion of life. Fantastic images, supernatural events, and dogmatic ideas have no place in such writing unless they are presented as happening in the minds of the characters.

The realist attempts at all times to present a picture of life that is recognisably true.

Of course one can think of anything and assert it is true, but this is not useful. Truth is that which is true to our experience. In the words of William James, "True ideas are those that we can assimilate, validate, corroborate, and verify. False ideas are those we can not . . .

"The truth of an idea is not a stagnant property inherent in it. Truth *happens* to an idea. It *becomes* true, is *made* true by events . . .

". . . truth [is] something essentially bound up with the way in which one moment in our experience may lead us towards other moments which it will be worth while to have been led to."

Late Entries[1]

The Devil Makes a Wedding

Imagination . . . that's how the Devil makes a wedding.

One night on the way home I saw a dark mass moving erratically on the sidewalk in front of me, between the buildings and the curb. It was a man in a wheelchair. He swerved to the curb and fell over. He had no legs, only stumps. Strapped in the wheelchair he looked like a turtle.

Cars were coming off the bridge. I kneeled and lifted the chair. It wasn't easy . . . he was heavy and smelled of sweat and whiskey. I got the chair back on its wheels. He muttered, grasped the handles, and set off.

I might have followed and seen him across at the intersection. He probably lived nearby . . . a few blocks at most. I might have seen him safely home.

He lived with his daughter, a thin woman with yellow hair. She thanked me for bringing him home and I could see she was embarrassed. A few days later I went back to see how they were doing, and found her alone. She told me about her work at the laundry and how hard it was, taking care of her father.

Now we are living together. For some reason I've lost my job and

[1] Some "Late Entries" were published in *The Southern Review,* Vol. 24, No. 1. Winter 1988.

am unable to find another position. She says, "You must do something. You can if you try. You've got to face reality." We sit up late watching television and waiting for the old man to come home. He's out every night getting drunk.

Two Rebeccas

December 16, 1986

This morning's *Times* carried the obituary of Dr. Gordon Ray, Thackeray's biographer. I once had lunch with Gordon Ray to discuss some business of the Guggenheim Foundation, of which he was president. We talked about Thackeray and I remarked that Becky Sharp was Jewish. Gordon made no comment—he may have thought I was joking.

But I had come to that conclusion naturally. Becky is "sharp" and pushy . . . not above doing a little poisoning if necessary . . . a gentile's idea of a Jew.

Thackeray appears to have thought Jews fascinating. Two years after *Vanity Fair* he published a humorous sequel to Walter Scott's *Ivanhoe* in which he tells what happened to Ivanhoe and Rowena after their marriage. Rowena turns into a pious shrew and Ivanhoe yearns for the tender, heroic and beautiful Jewess, Rebecca.

Rebecca is the good witch—she practices healing as good witches do. Her counterpart, the bad witch, would be Becky Sharp. Put together they are the Jewish female as conceived by gentiles. She has magic for good or evil and is sexually alluring, especially when contrasted with the insipid heroines of Victorian fiction.

Stopping at Trasimeno

I seem to have always known the story. Hannibal is crossing the Alps: horsemen, spearmen, pack-mules, and elephants climbing the side of a mountain.

Hannibal defeats the Roman army. Then he stops at Trasimeno. That day and the next he goes no further.

When Sigmund Freud was a young man he set out on a train for Rome. At Trasimeno he had a fainting spell, got off the train, and went back to Vienna. Freudian psychology explains it: Rome is "the mother of cities." You wish to replace your father in your mother's affections. But if you do, your father will be very angry. So you faint and get off the train—it's better than facing annihilation.

That explains Freud, but what about Hannibal? Why did he halt at Trasimeno? The road to Rome was open, the city undefended.

It would have made a good silent movie ... "Epic sweep and adventure," *Daily News*. "An erotics of history," Susan Sontag. Hannibal is in his tent by the lake, ruminating. Enter Flavia, "a daughter of Rome." He doesn't know it, but she's the daughter of a Roman senator. She dances to the accompaniment of a lyre played by a slave. In the next scene Hannibal and Flavia are lying on a tiger skin. She feeds him grapes and passes a goblet of wine from her lips to his. So the nights go by. Meanwhile the Romans gather another army. Then a messenger arrives: the camp at Trasimeno is empty—Hannibal has marched away.

The war between Rome and Carthage drags on until, finally, "Carthago delenda est." Carthage has been destroyed. The closing caption reads, "Once again the world was lost for the love of a woman."

Are Hollywood versions of history so ridiculous? When I went to college we were taught that the causes of history were economic. Tell it to Hitler! Tell it to Stalin! It took being hit on the head to teach us that history is up for grabs. The leader of the people has an idea and they all act accordingly. "Let's cross the Alps." "Let's pull up stakes." And the circus sets off in another direction.

Unbalanced

Coleridge says that the poet "brings the whole soul of man into activity" ... fuses and unifies its faculties through the "synthetic and magical" power of imagination. This power is revealed "in the balance and reconciliation of opposite or discordant qualities."

If Coleridge is right we can understand why so much writing, though filled with passion, fails to move us. It shows no awareness of other ideas ... does not bring the whole soul of man into activity, only the prejudices of the author.

The World as Text

"Whatever the subject under discussion—be it philosophy, litera-ture, art, or even history itself—it must be viewed 'synchronically' (that is, ahistorically, as a system of essentially self-contained, inter-related signs; the world is recast as 'text' to be interpreted)." (Roger Kimball in *The American Scholar,* Winter 1987)

Unless words have no meaning—in which case what Structural-ists, Post-Structuralists, *et al* say has no meaning either—the world is not a text, it is the world, inescapably and at every moment itself.

No Access to Reality

"She concludes that, since neither poetry nor thought itself can come to terms with realities in a direct, explicit way, the pattern of thought, or 'inner dialectic,' becomes the whole point." (*The New York Times Book Review,* February 1, 1987)

Yes, no doubt there are minds that cannot come to terms with realities in a direct, explicit way, and many of them write literary criticism.

The Dining Car[2]

He was late getting home from school. The path went by the railroad and for some distance along an embankment. It had recently snowed. He saw a red glow and heard what sounded like an animal panting . . . a train had been delayed. Standing on the embankment he looked down at the dining car.

Waiters were hurrying to and fro, carrying covered dishes. The tablecloths were of the freshest, most shining whiteness, and each place was set with silver and crystal. The people were well dressed, especially the women. They wore colorful dresses, and brooches, bracelets, and rings.

Directly below him a young girl, no more than a child, was sitting with a man and woman he took to be her parents. She put a fork to her mouth. Then she made a face and pushed her plate away. She looked up and saw him. He saw her lips move as she pointed. Her parents looked up and he fled.

[2] I wrote this into the poem, "The Magic Carpet," 1987.

Now he was a famous director. He married an actress noted for her impersonations of women in society. The studio turned out to see them off on the "Honeymoon Express," and at every station people gathered to wave as the train went by.

By arrangement they had a dining car to themselves. "Please," he said, "push your plate away. And make a face. Like this."

Proustifying

Beginning *A La Recherche du Temps Perdu* again . . . opening Pandora's box, the life in a book, humming with energy. Unlocked, it produces streets, meadows, forests, and villages. There are crowds of people . . . among them faces you have to look at, voices with which you will become familiar, lives you must follow, step by step, to the end.

It doesn't get any easier to read as you get older. To the contrary, you hesitate to release those scenes that demand your attention, encounters that call upon your heart and lungs to participate. Reading can be a vigorous activity—to read well you have to be in good physical condition. Certain authors—Proust, Henry James—demand an inordinate amount of time besides. They write for young people who have all the time in the world and can spend hours listening to a voice without caring too much what it says.

I was sixteen when I first read *Swann's Way,* frequently losing my own way in the long sentences and digressions. Proust's sad idea of love appealed to me: to love is to be deceived. To read him again is to reconstruct my own past: the bedroom I shared with my brother; the bookcase with his law books and the books of "self-improvement" he preferred; my shelf of novels, beginning with *Pride and Prejudice* and ending with *The Rainbow.*

I was hospitalized after the war. When I got out a friend who knew of my interest in Proust made me a present of the Random House edition in two big volumes. I read or dipped into them continually, but after a while it occurred to me that Proust was contributing to the condition a doctor had described as "neurasthenic," so I carried the books down the hall and dropped them down the chute to the incinerator. I was foolish enough to tell the friend what I had done. I don't think he ever forgave me—the books must have cost him quite a bit, not to mention his thoughtfulness.

Once, in Paris, I met Proust's chauffeur, Odilon Albaret. I was walking by the Seine when I was spoken to by a stranger, a man between fifty and sixty. He was wearing a cap, the kind worn by middleaged men in Europe. I seem to remember a moustache and that he had a delicate, pink complexion. He appeared to be slightly drunk. He remarked that I was American and therefore wouldn't have heard of "Monsieur Proust." Monsieur Proust was a genius. Once he, the speaker, placed a hand on the wallpaper—for days after Monsieur Proust would go over to the wall and stare at it to see if the hand had left a mark. He seemed to think this was evidence of Proust's genius . . . and maybe it was. He told me he owned a hotel and that I was welcome to come around and talk some more. But I didn't take him up on the offer. I could see where it would lead: I'd feel obliged to write an article. But Proust was part of my life . . . I didn't want to spoil it by writing about it.

Many years later I was driving in Normandy and came to Cabourg. The name struck a bell: wasn't this the Balbec of *La Recherche?* I turned north and drove to the beach and, by sheer luck, arrived at the very place where young Marcel first saw Albertine. I sat on the beach in front of a hotel, and a girl came along who looked, I imagined, just like her. She was pretty, tanned by the sun, nubile . . . in the little scraps of cloth Albertine would have worn if she'd been a *jeune fille* in the 1980s. Around me other specimens of young womanhood were sunning themselves, having removed their tops to expose their breasts. *En fleurs* indeed!

Walking back to the car I saw that the houses had roofs of a peculiar shape. Another chime . . . I recalled Proust's saying something about these Norman roofs; he compared them to the bonnet Françoise wore when she was all dressed up.

It's true, books give you another life . . . hundreds of lives. Without them the world would be a desert. Or just a hotel on the beach, with the usual tourists.

Poetry and Facts

What's wrong with these lines?

> the terrible
> voice of the submachine guns . . .

Sharon Olds, "Nevsky Prospekt (July 1917)"

I'll be the first
to chase the white hope . . .

George Barlow, "A Dream of the
Ring: The Great Jack Johnson"

You have set yourself a task like a train
lugging its hard body from Chicago to
Montauk . . .

Lynn Emanuel, "Getting Born"

Answers:

1. They didn't have submachine guns in Russia in 1917.

2. Jack Johnson, who was black, held the heavyweight title—he didn't have to chase anyone. A white contender ("white hope") would have to chase him.

3. Have you tried taking a train from Chicago to Montauk? Or looked at the map?

Frost on Facts

. . . people say to me: "The facts themselves aren't enough. You've got to do something to them, haven't you? They can't be poetical unless a poet handles them."

To that I have a very simple answer. It's this: Anything you do to the facts falsifies them, but anything the facts do to you—yes, even against your will; yes, resist them with all your strength—transforms them into poetry.

Robert Frost

American Influence (and British Envy)

. . . the music-hall comedy which the British had loved for a century . . . was essentially class comedy, anti-aristocratic, often refreshingly vulgar. Regrettably the American influence drove it out.

Dilys Powell in *The Listener* (London) 5 February 1987

Regrettably? By whom is it regretted? It couldn't be the audience. Though the writer approves of "anti-aristocratic" comedy she doesn't think that the people know what is good for them—an aristocratic attitude if ever there was one.

> American capitalism might be hideous, brutal and politically corrupt, but it worked.
>
> Alan Ryan in the same issue

What does it mean to say that capitalism worked if not that the majority found it to their liking? So how "hideous" could it have been?

The British have never forgiven the States for kicking them out and making democracy work.

One Way or The Other

This is one of the terrible places of the world. Here thousands were killed or wounded, and more kept coming onto the field. What drove them to it?

Every configuration of the ground has its name and story. This is the Wheatfield where they charged. The ground kept changing hands; after each charge it was littered with more bodies.

This is Little Round Top where they scraped together piles of stones to shield them from the leaden rain. Facing it across a shallow depression are the rocks made famous in a daguerreotype, "Confederate sniper in Devil's Den."

The picture was posed. After the battle photographers carried the body from where it had fallen and placed it here, arranging its arms and legs.

Listen and you can hear shouting, the thunder and crack of artillery. A humming in the air and patter in the leaves. The whine of a bullet ricocheting.

They lay down and made piles of stones. At the shout of command they stood and went forward, hunched over, into the smoke. Regiments were swallowed and disappeared. A regiment from Minnesota had a casualty list of 80%.

It seems incredible. What made them do it? This battle wasn't fought by the generals, by Lee and Meade—the infantry took matters into their own hands. They had often been hungry, wet, and cold. They made long marches, faced death and, by terrible exertions, managed to stay alive. But all this went for nothing—all had to be done again.

They wanted to get it over and to sleep, one way or the other.

A Saying to be Kept in Reserve and Used when the Occasion Presents Itself, i.e., when a Friend Lets You Down

"Hang yourself, brave Crillon: we have fought at Arques and you were not there. (Pends-toi, brave Crillon, nous avons vaincu à Arques, et tu n'y étais pas.)"

Henry IV of France, *Letter to Louis de Balbes Crillon*, "the Ney of the 16th century." This is the version given by Voltaire. But he changed facts to suit his version of history: the letter was written in 1597 before Amiens, not in 1589 after Arques.

The sentence was later engraved on a plaque in the lobby of the Hôtel de Crillon at Paris.[3]

Writers and Poets

The phrase "writers and poets" implies there's a difference. I once had a letter from a publisher saying that he'd read one of my poems. Had I ever thought of writing?

Idiot! But still, there's a difference. Today, for example, February 25th . . . some snow remaining on the ground, the sun shining in a blue sky . . . Spring's just around the corner and I feel like writing.

But I couldn't write a poem. When I write poetry I'm unconscious of my surroundings, absorbed by an idea, rhythm, image or phrase.

Against Barthes

Man does not exist prior to language, either as a species or as an individual. We never find a state where man is separated from language, which he then creates in order to "express" what is taking place within him: it is language which teaches the definition of man, not the reverse.

Roland Barthes, "To Write: An Intransitive Verb"

[3] Adapted from an entry in *The Macmillan Book of Proverbs, Maxims and Famous Phrases*.

What Barthes says does not happen is exactly what happens. There are times when man is separated from language: Dante in his vision of Eros, Wordsworth experiencing a "spot of time," Proust tasting the madeleine. At such moments the writer has an experience or vision that is indescribable, and that is why he writes: to describe it.

Why do these theorists make these statements? Derrida also . . . According to Derrida, texts refer to nothing but other texts. Authors do not think so: they know that art originates in experience; that, to use Conrad's words, it appeals to temperament, and that for such an appeal to be effective it must be "an impression conveyed through the senses."

The statements of Barthes and Derrida are in direct contradiction to what has been said by authors about the art they practice. And here we come to the reason for these theories: envy of the author. These theorists are like the historians in Orwell's *1984*. In the totalitarian state, history is what the state says it is, and the experience and memory of the individual have to be destroyed.

For such theorists to prevail they would have to destroy all the books or substitute reading literary theory for the reading of poems. As long as people are able to read for themselves it will be evident that literature refers to experience. The more intense the experience of reading, the more intense the experience of the author.

Against Barthes there are these words of Proust. The task of the critic, Proust says, is "to reconstitute what could have been the singular spiritual life of a writer haunted by realities of . . . a special kind, his inspiration being the measure in which he had the vision of these realities, his talent the measure in which he could recreate them in his work." (Preface to *La Bible d'Amiens*)

Juan Ramón Jiménez

Working on the last volume of the writings of Juan Ramón Jiménez . . . Antonio de Nicolas's translation, which I'm editing to make the English idiomatic . . .

I cannot imagine a poet who appears on the surface further removed from my subjects and style. Yet how well I understand Juan Ramón, especially the logic of his ideas about God!

His poems are lyric and meditative. Mine are narrative with lyric passages. He writes about landscape, I write about people. Yet our aims are the same: to show that everything is infused with meaning.

Moreover, we have the same idea of form: it is shaped by the feeling one has as one writes, not fixed by tradition.

Naked Prose

I love words, but not when they draw attention to themselves like children called upon to perform in front of visitors.

I love writing that is transparent, where the things words mean shine through, like the pebbles in the Irati River where Jake and Bill went fishing.

I have just looked again at the passage, and there is no mention of pebbles. Yet I thought I had seen them. This is what "naked prose" can do.

Sacred Text

To be known is not my first business. That can be completely satisfying only to vain mediocrities. Besides, in regard to this matter, can you ever know where you are? The greatest celebrity does not quench your thirst and you almost always die uncertain of your reputation, unless you're a fool. Therefore being famous doesn't place you in your own view of things any more than being obscure.

I aim at something better: to please myself. . . .

I have in mind a way of writing and grace of language to which I want to attend. When I think I have picked the apricot I shall not refuse to sell it, nor reject the applause if it is good.— Pending that, I don't want to swindle the public. That is all.
Flaubert to Maxime Du Camp, 26 June 1852

Hurstwood

September 6, 1987

The partnership in the saloon on Warren Street has been dissolved. I read help-wanted ads and go from place to place looking for work. I warm a chair in a hotel lobby.

I stay at home reading the newspaper. I watch Carrie come in and go out again, and am helpless to speak. I go over to Brooklyn and scab in the streetcar strike.

I approach a well-dressed man and ask for ten cents. I see, through lighted windows, people dining. I stand with the other men in the snow.

September 10

Hurstwood is not likable. He is "l'homme moyen sensuel" and worse—he is selfish and deceitful. His suffering does not seem to have taught him anything. He is, in fact, a "publican and sinner," and this brings us to the point: this is the kind of person Jesus consorted with—not just likable people or intelligent people, but the unfortunate, among whom must be included those who have no sympathy for others. To be unaware of one's obligations to one's fellow creatures is as great a misfortune as being poor.

There is a light in the grim story of Hurstwood: the figure of the Captain who solicits alms for men who have no bed for the night. Hurstwood thinks that a world that has such a good man in it cannot be so bad after all.

I dreamed I was lying on my back and being moved about . . . dimly conscious I was being operated on, so these must be doctors. I felt I was leaving my body, then saw myself as a shadow leaving the body, being drawn upward. It was a delightful feeling. I said to those around me, "I am dying." There was no fear, but pleasure and a sense of freedom. Then I thought, "I have died."

But through their handling and moving the limbs about I was drawn back to life and reentered the body. The men around me would not believe it . . . all but one, the chief surgeon. I spoke to him and he understood what an extraordinary thing it was. Now I understood how Jesus had left his body and come back in—the process was delightful.

The dream ended and I woke and lay thinking about it.

"Ho Hai!"

A Mohammedan tells the following story. He was strolling at night in a group when a tiger rushed out of the jungle and seized one of the men. As it carried him off he uttered a cry, "Ho hai!" The terror of the moment, says the narrator, was indescribable. "Our limbs stiffened, and our hearts beat violently, and only a whisper of the same 'Ho hai' was heard from us."[4]

One morning in Paris I was walking to the Métro. I had turned a corner and gone a few steps when there was a crash behind me. A car came drifting backward with its door caved in. The driver was slumped behind the wheel. The car came to a stop with its rear wheels against the curb. The driver's eyes were not quite closed, a line of white shining beneath the lid.

I walked back to the intersection. A man was lying face down in the gutter, groaning and saying that it hurt. A motorcycle stood upright in the intersection with its handlebars twisted around. A few feet away, what looked like a doll in a helmet was lying face down as though it had been placed there. The big helmet made its trunk and limbs look small.

A waiter came from the café on the corner and went over to the man-doll. He lifted one of its arms, felt for a pulse, and put it down.

On an ordinary morning when everyone is going to work and your thoughts are somewhere else . . . "Ho hai!"

Envious Silence

The most passive and cautious technique is silence: the envious [person] pretends to ignore the goods, the position or the qualities of the envied person. If confronted with them he pretends ignorance, surprise or lack of interest. It is not true that he may erase the envied person from his mind by an energetic act of the will, rather, while having him present, he pretends not to know of his existence. In the womb of minorities the shared envy is usually translated into conspiracies of silence: *nec nominetur in vobis*. There are a large number of thinkers and artists to whom their contemporaries have denied not only their recognition but even their disagreements. It is an attempt at elimination by spiritual ostracism, a persecution by

---

[4] The incident is cited by William James in *The Varieties of Religious Experience,* as a footnote to the chapter, "The Sick Soul."

omission, the most hypocritical of all; it is envy disguised as contempt. Envious silence is the art of destroying the [individual].

Gonzalo Fernández de la Mora, *Egalitarian Envy*

Some Observations of Theory

. . . no communicable thought is possible independently of language.

John Sturrock, *Structuralism* (1986)

Structuralism was founded on this assertion. The key word is "communicable"—one can hardly quarrel with the proposition that no language, "communicable thought," is possible without language. But structuralists proceed from this to assert that there is no thought without language, and no thought beyond language.

> The formulations we were earlier used to, which implied that thought is "conveyed" by language, are misleading if they cause us to assume the existence of some "beyond" of language to which it gives us access.

They deal with the possibility of a thought beyond language as the Church dealt with Galileo: "We do not think so, therefore it cannot be."

Writers believe they are finding meaning in experience and expressing new ideas. Structuralists deny this. Experience is meaningless; all meaning comes out of language, which is given by society. Society owns all possible ideas and, in fact, owns the individual.

> Psychologically, setting aside its expression in words, our thought is simply a vague, shapeless mass.

Not for them the hour when the hairs stand on end, the limbs tremble, and the tongue cleaves to the roof of the mouth.

> Faun's flesh is not to us,
> Nor the saint's vision.

... spontaneity and originality ... are ... but *effects* of specific *formal* procedures.

Clifford Siskin, The Historicity of Romantic Discourse

... there is absolutely no correlation between life lived and literature written, and only the most imponderable causal relationship between experience and art.

Tony Tanner in The Listener, 22 October 1987

The fools are becoming desperate.

The Professor

Looking down I saw a professor.
He said, "Since no one leaves this place
to tell the truth, I'll tell you.

I taught there is no truth,
that words mean what we want them
to mean, and nothing else.

For which I am here with Pilate
and these others." Looking around
I saw there were many heads

like his, at the same level
in the substance they were increasing
continually out of themselves.

More Buzzwords

January, 1988

M. tells me that "words and phrases in vogue" are called buzz-words.

"counterproductive" ... as in, "Eating potato chips while on a diet is counterproductive."

"vulnerable." A rock singer being interviewed on television speaks of the "vulnerability" of her style. Pauline Kael writes in *The New Yorker,* "His new picture, 'Good Morning, Vietnam,' makes him out to be a vulnerable, compassionate, respectful-of-the-Vietnamese, wonderful guy . . . ."

The New York Times quotes a woman named Linda Grant DePauw on "the new history." " 'It doesn't disturb me at all,' she said when asked whether the new history had not all but knocked out conventional history. 'If you want to play Trivial Pursuit and get the dates right, that's one thing. If you want to be on the cutting edge, you've got to start with something quirky.' "

She might also have said "state of the art."

Who is He?

I am in a waiting room at the airport. On the sidewalk a taxi driver is arguing with a policeman. The driver, a middle-aged white man, seems to be pleading—he strikes his breast with his fists. The policeman walks behind the taxi to take down the plate number. The driver follows. The policeman says something and he goes to the glove compartment to fetch his papers.

"He's not just giving him a ticket, he's taking away his license." The speaker is a black man, perhaps in his sixties, with gray hair. He leans forward to see and continues to express pity for the driver. "It wouldn't be so bad if he was a young man, but he's a family man, an honest man trying to make a living." He puts a hand to his heart. "It makes me feel bad here to see that."

He picks up his suitcase, wishes me a good day, and leaves. Who is he? What's his occupation? There are said to be thirty-six just men living among us for whose sake God will not destroy the world.

"Je est un autre"

"I did what I did all year. I played hard, played the best I could, and let my ability take over."

Kirby Puckett in TV interview after 1987 World Series

Jiménez

Thought, sweet magnet
that takes us away from everything . . .
moon in the dark evening, large and clear,
more our homeland than the world!

translated by Antonio T. de Nicolás

Juan Ramón says that the Good Thief was a poet. If so, he no longer is. There is no poetry in Heaven, only the performing arts.

Edmund Wilson

Night of Nov. 11–12, 1958. In the evening I made love to Elena on the blue divan in the middle room—delicious and wonderful. I find that it takes longer nowadays from the moment my orgasm is launched to the moment the emission begins. We loved each other afterwards.

Edmund Wilson, *The Fifties*

If ever a man lacked a soul it was Edmund Wilson. A man who would write about sexual intercourse with his wife, and in these terms, talking of his emissions!

A Storyteller

. . . Rip Hanson told me about the invasion of France. Crossing the Channel he saw infantry, falling past him from split open cargo planes, still clinging to tanks and bulldozers. Statistical losses figured in advance.

Ruth Stone, "Translations"

Where were those cargo planes intending to land? On what airfields? That Rip Hanson was some storyteller.

Rewriting

Rewriting all day . . . words and sentences that aren't exactly what you mean. Dull ideas, exaggerations, complaints.

As I sit writing here, sick and grown old,
Not my least burden is that dullness of the years,
   querilities,
Ungracious glooms, aches, lethargy, constipation,
   whimpering *ennui*,
May filter in my daily songs.

Walt Whitman

Writing and Teaching

> . . . teaching something and writing about it demand com-
> pletely different techniques, ways of living, habits of mind.
>
> Edmund Wilson, *The Fifties*

I have known very few writers who live by their writing. They make a living in other ways, and teaching isn't the worst: it gives you time in which to write. But it keeps you in the company of dull people.

Here and there you'll find an intelligent teacher, but most have slavish minds. In the university they pride themselves on their knowledge of a field, gained over a lifetime. A beetle could have done as much.

I have spent as little time at the university as I could, going there only to meet my classes and hold conference hours, and making myself unavailable for committees and faculty meetings.

My colleagues were only too happy that I did.

To See the Company

> How many times go we to Comedies, to Masques, to places of
> great and noble resort, nay even to Church onely to see the
> company.
>
> John Donne

Belle Elmore and Molly Bloom

The year was 1910. At 39 Hilldrop Crescent in Camden Town, London, Doctor Hawley Harvey Crippen killed his wife with poison. He cut up the body, removed the head and limbs, and buried the trunk in the cellar. He gave out the report that she had gone to the United States on business and died there of pneumonia. Then he appeared in public escorting his typist, Ethel Le Neve. She was wearing a sealskin coat and brooch remarkably like Cora Crippen's.

Friends of Mrs. Crippen were suspicious and alerted Scotland Yard. Enquiries were made, whereupon Crippen bolted for the

Continent, accompanied by Le Neve. She disguised herself as a boy, and "Mr. and Master Robinson" sailed for Quebec on the "Montrose."

The ship's captain saw through the disguise and notified Scotland Yard by wireless. Detective-Inspector Dew followed on a faster ship, and when the "Montrose" arrived at the port of entry Dew was there to meet her. Crippen and Le Neve were brought back to England to stand trial. Crippen was hanged, Le Neve found not guilty of being an accessory after the fact.

Crippen's wife was a singer—she sang in music halls using the stage name, Belle Elmore. She had little success but liked to associate with "theatricals" and to dress up and entertain. She received attentions from men, notably one Bruce Miller. Crippen looked on smiling while his wife held her soirées—he appeared to be a complacent husband. Sir Edward Marshall had a theory about the case: could it be that Crippen, who was not robust, administered the poison, hyoscin, in order to curb his wife's sexual appetite, and mistook the dose?

James Joyce knew the story—it was in all the newspapers: the finding of the remains in the cellar; the use of "wireless telegraphy"; the chase at sea; the characters of Crippen, Cora Crippen, and Ethel Le Neve. One aspect would have appealed to Joyce particularly: he knew the tribe of vaudeville "artistes"—he himself sang in public, though not as a professional. There is a story in *Dubliners* about a concert singer; in *Ulysses*, Molly Bloom is such another.

Molly's affair with Blazes Boylan is remarkably similar to Belle's affair with Bruce Miller.

And the names . . . Belle Elmore . . . Molly Bloom.

A Bough Heaped With Snow

I can't deny it, World War II marked me for life, and though I've struggled to forget, certain scenes are indelibly etched in memory: approaching the coast of France; walking at night across a field in Holland littered with corpses; the snow-covered trees and fields around Bastogne.

A man from Czechoslovakia is conducting interviews with writers who saw combat in the war. He tells me that Russian veterans have the same memories, but recently their memories have begun to fade. So have mine, and I think this may be due to my being happy, living in the present and no longer haunted by the past.

Still, it's there. In winter when Miriam and I go for a walk with the dogs, as we do almost every day, and go through the woods, I feel that I am in the Ardennes. I have only to reach out and touch a bough. I am cutting a bough to cover my foxhole, and snow is shaking down, just as it does there.

Another Occurrence at Owl Creek Bridge

He was on his way to Battalion when a voice shouted "Halt!" and three men came towards him. He said, "I don't know any baseball answers. Why don't you try me on movies?"

The men aiming their rifles at him were fair-minded—Americans usually are. "All right," one of them said. "What's the name of the picture in which the guy says, 'You're going out there a kid and coming back a star'?"

"Are you kidding? Everyone knows that one. Incidentally, you ought to get it right. It's 'You're going out a youngster but you've got to come back a star.' From *42nd Street,* of course."

"Hey guys, we got us another!"

"What do you mean? That's the right answer."

"It's too damn right, Kraut Face."

How Do You Know?

How do you know? You can't judge the worth of a book by its popularity.

> Fame is no plant that grows on mortal soil,
> Nor in the glistering foil
> Set off to the world, nor in broad rumor lies . . .

Nor can you go by what "people of taste" say is good. They have often changed their mind.

What then? Milton says that Fame

> . . . lives and spreads aloft by those pure eyes
> And perfect witness of all-judging Jove . . .

You meet the eyes when you read. That is how you know.

"What Is There Left To Do?"

Walter Jackson Bate in *The Burden of the Past,* Harold Bloom in *The Anxiety of Influence* and *A Map of Misreading,* and Paul de Man in *Blindness and Insight* broach the question: how are poets to deal with "the mental or psychological anguish which results from the mere accumulation of the past, of the 'traditional' in art and poetry"? In the words of Bate, "What is there left to do?"[5]

The ones who ask this question are critics. Criticism is part of what De Quincey called the "Literature of Knowledge"—poetry is the "Literature of Power." Criticism can only say what poetry has been—it cannot tell what it may be. Power is always original. "What is there left to do?" The answer is, everything. Poetry begins again with every poet.

Prefaces

May 31, 1988. 4:40 A.M.

The first bird sings. The second and third. I get up, dress quietly so as not to wake Miriam, and go downstairs. Custis and Veronica are up, and I let them out—Willa won't budge. I have breakfast and go to the cabin.

The book of new poems is finished, though I'm sure to change the order and add two or three. I'll be rewriting the preface, that is, if the book is to have a preface. Editors don't like prefaces—you can see their point of view: you may be giving the show away. A preface may dispel the mystery that is a necessary part of fictional creation.

But I like a preface to a book. It is common ground where reader and writer meet, out of sight of the critics, who appear like grown-ups at children's games and tell us to go in and wash our hands.

I admire Joseph Conrad's ability in a preface to tell . . . nothing. A preface by Conrad deepens the mystery. There are glimpses of a place he visited, someone he saw long ago who had an air of destiny about him. Then the door closes and you find yourself outside. You have been entertained . . . that is all.

---

[5] I have paraphrased from Paul A. Bové, *Destructive Poetics: Heidigger and Modern American Poetry.*

A preface by Thomas Hardy hints at subterranean grumblings, movements of earth. Voltaire, Darwin, and the Spirit of the Years seem to be pushing toward a catastrophe that will leave the world as it was before the Romans: naked moorland across which a bird goes winging.

Conrad and Hardy ... I think more about dead authors—the good ones, of course—than the ones who appear every week, being advertised by publishers and praised by reviewers.

"I think," the editor writes, "we will do without the preface."

Modern Taste

> my passionate taste for the obstacle (mon goût passionné de l'obstacle)
>
> Charles Baudelaire, "Préface des Fleurs"

How much of Modernism is explained by this phrase! The ancient poets took good and evil for a subject—the modern poet chooses banality. It allows you to show how clever you are, making poetry out of planks and bricks. Yours is all the credit if you succeed, and you can thumb your nose at a Creator who is so boring.

In The Cemetery

We walked back from the unveiling. One of her sons was saying that she had always been dissatisfied. There were gravestones on either side the path, with names chiselled in the stone, some in letters of gold: Kaplan, Voburg, Schlegel ...

We arrived at the car park, shook hands around, and drove away. It was a weekday and the road was full of traffic. "In the midst of life we are in death." Yes, but in the midst of death we are in life ... grinding its gears and emitting fumes from its exhaust.

Afterword

Trouble

I went to see my old friend
Greg.

    He was in the kitchen
slicing radishes.

       I explained
what had brought me. He said,
"Let me see if I understand.
You're worried because you're happy?"

I said, "It's not so absurd.
Take any writer, even Tolstoy . . .
he talks about happy families
being all the same. Misery,
that's all people care about.
They won't go to a concert
unless it's discordant, a ballet
unless it takes place in a hospital
and the dancers are wound in bandages."

"Enough," he said, "already.
What do you care about such people?"

Having made the salad, he decided
it was his to do with as he pleased . . .
put his fingers in and mucked it about,
picked out a mushroom.

"Stay for dinner," he said. I said no thanks.

*

I take my trouble to bed with me.
When I wake in the morning
it's there, refreshed by a good night's sleep.

Writing poetry used to be easy.
"The stag at eve had drunk his fill"
got you off to a running start.

"What are you thinking?"
says Miriam, who for some time
has been awake.

   "I ought to do something
post-structural. A monkey version
of *Hamlet*."

She says, "I don't follow."

"It's a theory. If you chain monkeys
to typewriters, one of them
sooner or later will write *Hamlet*.
I'll write it, changing a few words . . ."

"Shakespeare," she says.
"Shakespeare was the monkey,
the one who typed *Hamlet*
exactly, word for word."

I stare at her, stunned
and speechless with admiration.

*

I'm looking out the window
at a beagle, a beagle-terrier,

and a westie. Some trees.
A sky empty and void of ideas.

I think the powers that be
have decided, "That's enough,
no more poetry for this fellow,
just life, since he likes it so much.

From where we sit, on Olympus,
as far as we can see
it's dirt and weeds and bricks
with creatures crawling between.

What we like is a burnt offering . . .
not just cooked, scorched black,
a heart turning on a spit
over the fires of greed
and lust and self-loathing.

But a white birch by a door,
sunlight breaking from a cloud,
yellow and purple tips
pushing up from the ground,
and the woman he's so fond of . . .

if that's all he wants, let him have it,
there's nothing we can do for him."